*Literary Executions*

# Literary Executions

*Capital Punishment and American Culture,*
*1820–1925*

JOHN CYRIL BARTON

Johns Hopkins University Press

*Baltimore*

© 2014 Johns Hopkins University Press
All rights reserved. Published 2014
Printed in the United States of America on acid-free paper

2 4 6 8 9 7 5 3 1

Johns Hopkins University Press
2715 North Charles Street
Baltimore, Maryland 21218-4363
www.press.jhu.edu

*Library of Congress Cataloging-in-Publication Data*

Barton, John Cyril.
Literary executions : capital punishment & American culture, 1820–1925 /
John Cyril Barton.
    pages cm
Includes bibliographical references and index.
ISBN-13: 978-1-4214-1332-7 (hardcover : alk. paper)
ISBN-13: 978-1-4214-1333-4 (electronic)
ISBN-10: 1-4214-1332-9 (hardcover : alk. paper)
ISBN-10: 1-4214-1333-7 (electronic)
1. Capital punishment in literature.    2. Executions and executioners in
literature.    3. American literature—19th century—History and criticism.
    4. American literature—20th century—History and criticism.
    5. Capital punishment—United States—Public opinion.    6. Public
opinion—United States.    7. Capital punishment—Moral and ethical
aspects—United States—History.    I. Title.    II. Title: Capital
punishment and American culture, 1820–1925.    III. Title: Capital
punishment & American culture, 1820–1925.
            PS217.C35B37    2014
    810.9'3556—dc23                    2013033296

A catalog record for this book is available from the British Library.

*Special discounts are available for bulk purchases of this book. For more
information, please contact Special Sales at 410-516-6936 or
specialsales@press.jhu.edu.*

Johns Hopkins University Press uses environmentally friendly book
materials, including recycled text paper that is composed of at least
30 percent post-consumer waste, whenever possible.

Depend upon it Sir, when a man knows he is to be hanged in a fortnight, it concentrates his mind wonderfully.

*Samuel Johnson*

# Contents

# Acknowledgments

This book began as a seminar paper for a course on the death penalty with Jacques Derrida in spring 2000 at the University of California, Irvine. Over the next several years, that essay morphed into a dissertation project directed by Brook Thomas, with Steven Mailloux, J. Hillis Miller, and Dickson D. Bruce serving as committee members. I am grateful for the time and energy that the committee contributed to my work, and I owe a particular debt to Brook Thomas. I cannot imagine a more supportive adviser and mentor than Brook, who not only read multiple drafts of the dissertation but also commented generously on new material as the project again morphed when I began an assistant professorship in 2005 at the University of Missouri, Kansas City. Several other faculty members and friends at UC Irvine helped give shape to this book through coursework and conversations, including Jacques Derrida, Michael P. Clark, Victoria Silver, John Carlos Rowe, Robert Folkenflik, Wolfgang Iser, Susan Jarratt, John Hollowell, Doug Higbee, Katherine Voyles, Andrew Newman, Greg Kimball, Bruce Barnhart, James Ziegler, Dave Puentes, and Rodney Rodriguez. I am also grateful for the financial support I received as a doctoral student at UC Irvine, especially a California Regents scholarship to begin my studies and the Dorothy and Donald Strauss Endowed Dissertation Fellowship to complete them.

I appreciate the guidance and advice of numerous colleagues from other institutions, especially Carolyn L. Karcher, Kristin Boudreau, Lillian S. Robinson, Gregg D. Crane, Larry J. Reynolds, Jerome Loving, Robert Milder, Austin Sarat, David Papke, and Wayne Franklin, each of whom read drafts of chapters or conference presentations based on material from the book. Participants of the Midwest Nineteenth-Century Americanist Group (John Evelev, Stephanie Fitzgerald, Susan Harris, Melissa Homestead, Laura Mielke, Patricia Okker, Francesca Sawaya, and Alexandra Socarides were present at my workshop) gave helpful advice for revising chapter 3. My colleagues in the English Department at the University of Missouri, Kansas City, have also been incredibly supportive. I am especially grateful to Tom Stroik and Anthony Shiu for reading and commenting on material from the manuscript, to Virginia Blanton and Jennifer Phegley for help in securing university funding, and to Sherry Neuerburg for always being so helpful in the office. Thanks, too, to dozens of students in my courses on "Nineteenth-Century Crime Fiction" and "American Culture and Capital Punishment" for challenging my ideas and forging discoveries in our exploration of print culture and the cultural rhetoric of capital punishment. I owe a particular debt to Ryan Davidson and Katherine Tirado and, especially, to Jarrod Roark, Desiree Long, and Megan Cross, for their copious and conscientious research assistance. Additionally, I am indebted to the University of Missouri for providing a semester's leave and a summer Faculty Research Grant that afforded me the time necessary for research and writing. Members of the university's library staff, especially those in the Interlibrary Loan division at Miller Nichols Library, were exceptionally helpful. A special thanks to both Diane Hunter and Amy Fortner and to David Bauer, who procured for me (among other things) three oversized volumes of the complete *New York Tribune* (1842–45) from the University of Chicago.

It has been a pleasure working with Matt McAdam, Melissa Solarz, Sara J. Cleary, and Brian MacDonald in preparing this manuscript for publication at Johns Hopkins University Press. I also wish to acknowledge the Press's anonymous reader, whose recommendations helped sharpen the book's focus and clarify its arguments.

I am truly grateful to my parents, Pansy and Cyril Barton, for their love, support, and guidance for so many years. Thanks for always believing in me. I also thank my father-in-law, Frank Friedman, for his crucial help as I worked to complete this project. Indeed, I would not have been able to finish this book without Gpa's special services in kid care and for timely sessions at "Frank's Think Tank." Thanks as well to big Allan Finamore for last-minute assistance with illustrations and to Matthew Danda for the photo shoot.

Most of all I thank my wife, Carrie, for her love and uncompromising support, good humor and sharp wit, and devotion to our family, and for helping me keep things in perspective.

This book is dedicated to my children—Frankie, Lottie, and Lainie—who have been a constant source of inspiration and motivation.

‧⁓

Chapter 1 first appeared, in a somewhat different form, as "The Anti-gallows Movement in Antebellum America," in *REAL: Research in English and American Literature*, vol. 22, ed. Brook Thomas (Tübingen: Gunter Narr Verlag, 2006):

145–78. That article was revised and reprinted in *The Demands of the Dead: Executions, Storytelling, and Activism in the United States,* ed. Katherine Ryan (Iowa City: University of Iowa Press, 2012), 139–61. Chapter 6 was revised and expanded from "An American Travesty: Capital Punishment & the Criminal Justice System in Dreiser's *An American Tragedy,*" in *REAL: Research in English and American Literature,* vol. 18, ed. Brook Thomas (Tübingen: Gunter Narr Verlag: 2002): 357–84. I thank both Gunter Narr Verlag and the University of Iowa for permission to reprint material from these essays. Several paragraphs from the epilogue first appeared in "Cooper, Livingston, and Death-Penalty Reform," in *James Fenimore Cooper Society: Miscellaneous Papers,* vol. 27, ed. Steven Harthorn and Shalicia Wilson (2010): 1–6. Roughly the first half of chapter 2 was published as "William Gilmore Simms & the Literary Aesthetics of Crime and Capital Punishment," *Law & Literature* 22:2 (2010): 220–43. I thank the University of California Press for permission to reprint material from *Law & Literature.*

*Literary Executions*

# The Cultural Rhetoric of Capital Punishment

> In hopes that these remarks may meet the attention of many who
> have hitherto considered it an innocent gratification to witness the
> death of a fellow being by hanging, they are respectfully offered to
> the public. They are the result of considerable reflection and
> careful observation during the scene of a late execution. It must be
> some uncommon and powerful motive which can impel multi-
> tudes to come from great distances, in a stormy season, and on a
> stormy day, avowedly for no other purpose than to witness such a
> scene.
>
> The Record of Crimes in the United States (1834)

So begins "Observations on the Curiosity of Those Who Go to Witness Public Executions," the 1833 preface to *The Record of Crimes in the United States*, a
collection of biographical essays on America's most notorious criminals that
was one of Nathaniel Hawthorne's favorite books.[1] Published anonymously but
signed "Humanity," the preface attempts to explain not only why people attend
public executions but why some commit murder in the first place. For Humanity, both killing and watching lawful killing are interrelated phenomena; what
compels people to do both stems from "the organ of destruction" in the human
brain.[2] Linked to hunting and self-defense, this propensity for violence is a necessary evil. More pronounced in some individuals than in others, it is manifestly
present at any execution scene, not only in the condemned but in the spectators
attracted to the scene of lawful death.

Humanity's phrenology-inspired "Observations," written the same year Rhode
Island became the second state to abolish the practice of public executions
(Connecticut was the first in 1830), is one of hundreds of works that participated
in a larger debate over "criminal jurisprudence"—what we would today call
criminology—in the decades preceding the Civil War. Like much of that discourse,

these observations lent support to the campaign to abolish the death penalty: "I perhaps need not add," Humanity later declares, as if it went without saying, "that I am opposed to all executions, for crime, and especially to those which are made public" (xi). Such a statement was far from radical for the period. Influential legislators and politicians, as well as prominent reformers, ministers, and writers, made such declarations in their published work. Once a cultural given, capital punishment thus became a major point of contention. For many, in fact, the practice was condemned rather than condoned by scripture, and it promoted rather than discouraged violent crime. Indeed, Humanity had precisely the latter argument in mind when he addressed his "Observations" to those who considered witnessing executions "an innocent gratification" and when he later objected to the death penalty "because," he affirmed, "crime is increased by such spectacles" (v, xi).

If earlier opponents like Humanity in the 1830s implicated spectators in the *in*humanity of the public execution, later ones around midcentury often stressed the individual responsibility that citizens bore each time an execution, although now largely removed from the public eye, was carried out. Walt Whitman drew from this argument in "Capital Punishment and Social Responsibility" (1842), one of his earliest anti-gallows writings published in New York's *The Sun*. "In a democratic republican form of government like our own," Whitman's article began, "the people, all the people, all cliques, all classes, all professions, all religious sects are immediately and directly responsible for wrong, oppressive, inhuman, cruel and tyrannical laws."[3] Universalist minister George Washington Quinby developed such an argument at length in *The Gallows, the Prison, and the Poor House* (1856). Subtitled a *Plea for Humanity*, Quinby's book provided an impassioned call for the abolition of capital punishment, a subject briefly touched upon in the preface to *The Record of Crimes*. In a chapter titled "Individual Responsibility" (and subtitled "Each Citizen's Responsibility"), Quinby reminded readers that every so-called private execution was nonetheless a public act for which a given state's citizens were collectively and individually responsible. He, in fact, began the chapter by foregrounding his own sense of responsibility as rationale for a principled stance against capital punishment: "Another reason why I labor for the abolishment of the gallows, is, that so long as men are executed in the State of which I am a citizen, *I feel that as a citizen, I with others, am responsible for the act; a sort of particips criminis—'accessory before the fact.'*" Appropriating the language of criminal law, Quinby defined the death penalty as murder and charged himself and others as accessories to a crime they commit not "as individuals" but "as citizens of the State." Citizens, he went on, committed these crimes not "with their own hands, but through the *instrumentality of the hangman*." For his own part, Quinby concluded, "I desire not to participate in any such responsibility."[4]

⁓

Today, the United States stands alone as the only so-called First World nation that still imposes the death penalty. During the first half of the nineteenth century, however, America was a worldwide leader in the campaign to abolish capital punishment. A perennial topic in the fields of law and sociology, the death penalty has attracted the attention of historians in recent years. Important studies such as Louis P. Masur's *Rites of Execution* (1989), Daniel A. Cohen's *Pillars of Salt, Monuments of Grace* (1993), and Karen Halttunen's *Murder Most Foul* (1998) have used capital crimes and punishment as touchstones for evaluating U.S. intellectual and cultural history from the colonial period to the Civil War, whereas Stuart Banner's *The Death Penalty* (2002) provides the first comprehensive legal history of the subject. Two literary studies, Ann Algeo's *The Courtroom as Forum* (1996) and David Guest's *Sentenced to Death* (1998), look at the twentieth-century American novel (primarily after 1925) in conjunction with capital punishment, and Kristin Boudreau's *The Spectacle of Death* (2006) explores literary and populist responses to well-known capital trials in U.S. history from the infamous 1833 "Haystack murder" (the subject of Catherine Williams's 1833 "docudrama" *Fall River*, an early nineteenth-century analogue to Capote's and Mailer's nonfiction novels, *In Cold Blood* and *The Executioner's Song*) to the 1998 execution of Karla Faye Tucker (whose story served as the basis for the 1996 film *Last Dance*, starring Sharon Stone).[5] In addition to these studies in American literature, Mark Canuel's *The Shadow of Death* (2006) examines British romanticism in light of capital punishment specifically and "the subject of punishment" more generally. Most recently, Paul Christian Jones has examined a range of antebellum writers in relation to the reformation of capital punishment in *Against the Gallows* (2011).[6]

Building on this work, *Literary Executions* analyzes representations of, responses to, and arguments for and against the death penalty in the United States over the long nineteenth century. It puts novels, short stories, poems, and creative nonfiction in dialogue with legislative reports, trial transcripts, and legal documents pertaining to criminal law, as well as newspaper and journal articles, treatises, and popular books (like *The Record of Crimes* and *The Gallows, the Prison, and the Poor House*) that participated in debates over capital punishment. The book focuses on several canonical figures—James Fenimore Cooper, Nathaniel Hawthorne, Lydia Maria Child, Walt Whitman, Herman Melville, and

Theodore Dreiser—generating new readings of their work in light of the controversy surrounding the punishment of death. It also gives close attention to a host of then-popular-but-now-forgotten writers—particularly John Neal, Slidell MacKenzie, William Gilmore Simms, Sylvester Judd, and George Lippard—whose work helped shape or was shaped by the influential anti-gallows movement. In this respect, I extend the project of David S. Reynolds and others in looking "beneath the American Renaissance" and bringing to light neglected or forgotten texts in order to read them alongside canonical or well-known works from the period.[7] Whereas Reynolds, however, surveys such literature in terms of various reform movements and cultural trends of the day, I offer sustained readings of literary works in relation to a single reform movement that, until recently, has been largely neglected by literary critics and historians of American literature.[8] Drawing from legal and extralegal discourse but focusing on imaginative literature, my study shows not only how novels, stories, poems, and creative nonfiction participated in debates over capital punishment but how this literature was often structured around the drama of the death penalty and the scene of execution.

I complement my analysis of how capital punishment influences the form and context of works of literature by giving sustained attention to the language and rhetorical form of important legal documents from the period. For example, I look closely at courtroom arguments and summations in famous capital cases delivered by Daniel Webster, Clarence Darrow, and others, as well as widely circulating legislative reports written by prominent lawyers and politicians, such as Edward Livingston, Robert Rantoul Jr., and John L. O'Sullivan. In this respect, I read law *as* literature as well as law *in* literature. If "Literary Executions" in my book's title most obviously refers to dramatic renderings of or responses to the death penalty in imaginative literature, it also calls attention to the care with which many of the works I examine are themselves rhetorically executed—*literary executions,* if you will. Reading literature against law (and law against literature), my study raises larger questions about sovereign authority and responsibility—two interrelated concepts, I argue, that cut to the quick of any discussion concerning the (il)legitimacy of the death penalty in liberal democracies in which "the people" lawfully put to death a person. Still resonant today, these questions enlivened political debate and animated a surprising number of literary works over the long nineteenth century. An object of analysis in and of itself, capital punishment was also a crucial site or scene in larger cultural narratives about universal human rights as well as the civil rights and liberties of U.S. citizens. I argue, in fact, that the death penalty for many of my writers dramatized the confrontation between the citizen-subject and sovereign authority in its starkest terms.

Formulating the conflict in these terms enables me to highlight what was for many a hypocrisy of American democracy: the execution of a citizen under a system of government in which citizens themselves are sovereign. In exploring this conflict, I give special attention to the subject position(s) occupied by what I call the "citizen-subject."[9] By compounding these terms—two discrete but by no means oppositional categories—I consider the individual before the law as both *citizen*, with certain protected civil rights and liberties, and *subject*, subjected not only to positive law and its ideological state apparatuses but to a psychological subject formation beyond an individual's control. By the same token, I use *citizen-subject* to register the productive tension between the two terms in question, since for many of my writers the concept of U.S. citizenship was defined against an understanding of the European subject and traditional modes of political subjection under monarchical forms of government.

A prime example of this tension can be found in James Fenimore Cooper's *The American Democrat* (1838), a political primer that presented a systematic review and defense of the republican institutions on which the United States was founded. In part a response to Whig critics and Cooper's own fears of democracy run amok, *The American Democrat* begins by differentiating a true republic from false ones then existing in Europe which in practice were "aristocracies," "limited monarchies," or even outright "despotisms."[10] In chapter 2, titled "On Republicks," Cooper identifies "direct representation" (15) as the fundamental basis for any republican form of rule, and in chapter 3, "On the Republick of the United States of America," he finds that element only (albeit imperfectly) guiding the political structures of U.S. government. In a later chapter, "On the Duties of Publick or Political Station," Cooper links "the private citizen" to the political processes carried out in his or her name, thus proclaiming that "American citizens are possessed of the highest political privileges that can fall to the lot of the body of any community; that of self-government" (84). Self-governance, made possible through direct representation in a true republic, is what "distinguishes the citizen from the subject" (85). Elaborating the differences between the two, Cooper continues: "The one rules, the other is ruled; one has a voice in framing the ordinances, and can be heard in his efforts to repeal them; the other has no choice but submission" (85). Such a definition of the *citizen* contra the *subject* raises important implications for any theory of popular sovereignty that necessarily underlies a *republic*—a term derived from the Latin, *res publica*, which, as Cooper reminds us, literally "means the public things or the common weal" (11). Since private citizens are linked to "the public things" that their representatives authorize and execute, the people of a republic bear responsibility each and every time the state kills in their names. It is for this reason that Whitman begins his anti-gallows *Sun* editorial by emphasizing how "the people, all the people" are responsible for executing laws in "a democratic republican form of government like our own," and why Quinby in his anti-gallows treatise feels that he participates in "murder" each time an execution takes place in the state wherein he is a citizen.

◡

If questions concerning sovereignty and responsibility drive my investigation, novels provide a major focal point for several reasons. To begin with, the novel as a literary form would become the dominant genre of the nineteenth century, as critics from Ian Watt and Georg Lukács to Frederic Jameson and Michael McKeon have shown.[11] The novel is also the century's literary genre most closely connected to popular discourse and public opinion, a traditional view given new life in U.S. literary studies by way of Jürgen Habermas's influential theory of the public sphere exemplified, for him, in the role the eighteenth-century English novel played in shaping British culture. Kristin Boudreau, for instance, has recently drawn from Habermas to articulate what she calls "execution literature," an understanding of crime literature and the discourse of capital punishment close in some respects to what I am calling *literary executions*. Likening "early American execution literature to the eighteenth-century novel," Boudreau argues that such literature was a primary means by which private citizens were moved to public action. Founding Fathers such as Thomas Jefferson and Benjamin Rush, she demonstrates, recognized the "grave power of literature" in shaping popular ideas and public attitudes. Both Jefferson and Rush (the latter of whom is an important figure in my study) saw the virtues and dangers to which popular fiction could be put, and novels in particular created what Boudreau calls "a literary realm, where individuals could be drawn toward or repelled from particular conduct depending on their private responses to strong characters and narrators."[12]

In addition to fomenting public sentiment, novels are unique among forms of crime literature in that they, as Lisa Rodensky contends, grant readers direct access to their characters' minds. In this way, they enable an examination of motive, intention, and responsibility unavailable through the law, a disciplinary mode that necessarily presumes certain facts about its subject and must approach such an examination from outside a criminal's head. As Rodenksy explains in

*The Crime in Mind,* a study of criminal responsibility and the Victorian novel, "Novels invite readers to imagine that they are in the mind of the criminal. This access to the mind distinguishes fiction—and the novel in particular—from law, from history, from psychology, and even from other literary genre, like biography and drama."[13] My work extends Rodensky's insight but shifts its focal point. Rather than emphasizing the interiority of a criminal's mind and the privileged perspective granted through the novel's "third person narrator,"[14] I stress the novel's free indirect discourse as well as its narratological and rhetorical strategies in representing or responding to the death penalty, an event whose complex structure and dramatic unfolding demand an analysis from the plurality of voices and perspectives that novelistic discourse puts into play.

*Literary Executions* thus relies on the socio-rhetorical theory of Mikhail Bakhtin, whose concept of *dialogism* (i.e., every word repeats or reenacts its previous uses and is saturated with prior dialogues) informs my thinking on a fundamental level. Drawing particularly from Bakhtin's notion of the "dialogized image" (e.g., the image-as-trope), I examine both fiction and nonfiction in relation to what I call the *cultural rhetoric of capital punishment*: that is, the tropes, arguments, and narratives that animated death penalty debates in the nineteenth and early twentieth centuries. In this way, I combine a Bakhtinian theory of language with a literary practice that Steven Mailloux describes as "rhetorical hermeneutics," explained in his most recent book as "a tracing of the rhetorical paths of thought in various cultural spheres."[15] Rhetoric, in these terms, refers not only to persuasive language but to what Mailloux calls "the political effectivity of trope and argument in culture,"[16] and the rhetorical paths I follow transverse various spheres—not only literature and law but politics and religion—in which debate over the death penalty has left a demonstrable trace.

Recent historians of U.S. culture, some of them writing on the death penalty, others on crime and murder more generally, have traced different contours of such thought from America's colonial origins through the antebellum period. Whereas Masur provides an astute intellectual history of death penalty debates from the American Revolution to the Civil War, emphasizing political assumptions in the formation of a republican ideology that opposed capital punishment,[17] Halttunen and Cohen have assessed crime and print culture from the Puritan execution sermon to popular literature (broadly construed) of the 1830s and 1840s. Halttunen, for instance, examines the paradigm shift in the interpretation of murder from the seventeenth- and eighteenth-century execution sermons, in which Puritan ministers and magistrates controlled the interpretation of crime and promoted a view of the criminal as "common sinner," to the diffuse body of secular authority that portrayed the murderer as monster or moral aberration. This shift in the cultural construction of crime and the criminal in the late eighteenth and nineteenth centuries gave rise to what Halttunen calls the "gothic imagination" and the "new murder narrative," which, in contrast to the execution sermon, focused on the details of crime as well as the mental and environmental factors that contributed to it.[18]

Cohen traces a similar shift from the New England execution sermon and early forms of crime literature—such as criminal conversation narratives, execution reports, crime ballads, and broadsides—to popular literature and print culture in the decades before the Civil War. Situating "romantic fiction" alongside trial reports and journalism, Cohen explains:

> The emergence of the trial report, the development of popular journalism, and the rise of romantic fiction were related cultural developments. Each was associated with the transition from a literary culture of piety, scarcity, and intensive reading to one of variety, abundance, and, at times, casual consumption. Each form was committed to an essentially modern epistemology that conceived social reality not primarily in transcendent, universal, or typological terms (as in early execution sermons) but as an aggregate of individual worldly events or experiences, each firmly if elusively embedded in its own particular spatial and temporal setting. Each also implied a conception of collaborative product of a multiplicity of independent speakers and viewpoints.[19]

Of the various forms that contributed to these cultural developments, nothing captured the "multiplicity" of voices and viewpoints quite like the novel. Whether or not the individual novels I examine directly take up the subject of capital punishment, each helps us see multiple positions within legal discourse—a discourse that is too often dismissed as simply monological. Trials, after all, have both a prosecution and a defense, while judicial opinions may contain a dissent that directly challenges the court's opinion. My work thus complements Cohen's and Halttunen's historical treatments of crime and popular culture through a Bakhtinian approach to the novel, short fiction, and popular discourse concerning capital punishment that strives to show the polyphony in what is frequently considered the monologic authority of (the) law.

If my methodology owes a general debt to Bakhtin, it owes a particular one to Brook Thomas, whose method of "cross-examinations" provides a model for my investigation of literature and law in each of the book's chapters. Such an approach, as Thomas has shown, helps to expose underlying cultural logics at play in a given historical moment.[20] It also affords a perspective in the disciplines that is unavailable when one studies each independently, thus enabling one to tell a story that otherwise might not be told. The story I tell stretches back to the late eighteenth century, when the Enlightenment critique of capital punishment first acquired popular currency in Europe and America, and projects into the decades surrounding the turn of the twentieth, but it concentrates on works from the American Renaissance, a literary period that roughly coincides with what one death penalty historian has called "the first great reform era" (1833–53) in the history of U.S. capital punishment.[21]

If the death penalty had its first great era of reform in the decades preceding the Civil War, my primary focus, the second great reform era began in the late 1880s in New York with debates over the electric chair and *electrocution*, a neologism for lawful death by electricity (the term " *electrocide*, constructed from the Latin root *cida*, "to cut or kill," as in homicide, was also introduced but did not stick). That debate reached a national level when the Supreme Court approved New York's use of the electric chair in *In re Kemmler* (1890) and later that decade, in 1897, when the federal government drastically reduced its number of capital offenses. It was also during this year that Massachusetts prison reformer Florence G. Spooner founded the Anti-Death Penalty League and that Colorado, following Iowa in 1872 and Maine in 1876, became the sixth state to abolish capital punishment (Colorado, however, reinstated the death penalty in 1900 when retentionists successfully argued that several recent lynchings resulted in part because official capital punishment was no longer a legal option). Thanks to the efforts of Spooner and others, Massachusetts came closer than it ever had to abolishing capital punishment in 1900, and during the 1910s there were more organizations advocating the abolition of capital punishment than at any time since the 1840s.

By 1917, nine more states had stricken the death penalty from their statutes, while several others since the turn of the twentieth century—Illinois, Ohio, and New Jersey among them—had come close to passing legislation entirely banning the practice. A crime wave following the aftermath of World War I led several states to reinstate the death penalty (e.g., Missouri, Washington, and Arizona re-enacted capital statutes in 1919), and in the early 1920s the reform movement began to slacken. But by the mid-1920s reformers regrouped and intensified their efforts. In 1925, prominent activists from different parts of the country joined forces to establish the American League to Abolish Capital Punishment, a national organization (with central offices in New York City) that "sought to organize and coordinate abolition attempts in state legislatures" across the country.[22]

Cross-examining literary and legal discourse on the death penalty enables me to give an account of the changing assumptions and evolving conceptions of sovereignty and (social) responsibility in terms of the state's—or, under our complex federal system, a plurality of states'—ultimate sanction against its citizens. My story begins in the early 1820s, when influential lawyer and politician Edward Livingston presented landmark arguments for the abolition of the death penalty and when early popular novels, such as James Fenimore Cooper's *The Spy* (1821) and John Neal's *Logan* (1822), directly responded to capital punishment or used its drama as an aesthetic principle. It concludes a century later with an examination of capital punishment and the criminal justice system represented in Dreiser's *An American Tragedy* (1925), the first major U.S. novel to attack the death penalty directly. Covering this hundred-year period helps me highlight changes in social attitudes toward crime and capital punishment as well as important shifts in the administration of lawful death. For instance, whereas religious arguments in the first half of the nineteenth century strongly influenced popular opinion about the death penalty and were a requisite for anyone who wanted to be taken seriously in debates for or against the practice, toward the end of century such arguments were deemed antiquated and passé. Thus, when Samuel Hand argued for capital punishment in an 1881 *North American Review* article, he consciously avoided standard appeals to Genesis 9:6 ("Whoso sheddeth the blood of man, by man his blood shall be shed") and God's covenant with Noah, assuming his readers would be "inclined to look with scant credulity upon the book of Genesis, its deluge, its ark, and its Noah."[23] Likewise, by the turn of the century, those who argued for abolition ceased to cite the Sixth Commandment ("Thou shall not kill") and God's prohibition against Cain's execution for fratricide to support their position. Instead, they often drew from theories of biological and environmental determinism informed by new scientific and sociological approaches to criminal behavior. And in the early twentieth century, proponents and opponents of capital punishment alike marshaled forth sophisticated statistical analyses of recidivism rates among murderers and murder rates in states or other nations with and without the death penalty.

Changes in the administration of capital punishment were just as significant. Following the Civil War, for instance, some states moved away from mandatory death sentences, thus allowing juries to find a verdict short of death for cases of first-degree murder.[24] In 1867, Illinois became the first state to adopt this procedure; it was followed by Minnesota and Nebraska in 1868 and 1869. Nine more states or territories would ratify such laws in the 1870s and 1880s—including California in 1874, whose distinguished Judge Robert Y. Hayne would indirectly take up the issue a decade later in the *North American Review.* "Men are no longer of that stern stuff which exacted an eye for an eye and a tooth for a tooth," Hayne mildly complained in an essay provocatively titled "Shall the Jury System Be Abolished?" (1884). "Sentiment, benevolence, and philanthropy have become potent forces," he continued. "Conscientious scruples against capital punishment are common, and numbers of men shrink from the idea of having blood on their hands, even in a legal way; some would no more condemn a man to death than they would carry the sentence into execution."[25] Hayne's remarks not only suggest the necessity of allowing for life sentences, so that jurors with such "scruples" would vote to convict rather than acquit if the only punishment were death; they also point to a deeper tension: the guilt jurors may feel when directly participating in a procedure that authorizes lawful death. Whereas Whitman and Quinby, as we have seen, appealed to that logic in arguing against capital punishment, Hayne, from the other side of the argument, ridicules the idea here of jurors "shrink[ing] from the idea of having blood on their hands, even in a legal way," in an effort to get not only jurors but private citizens to acknowledge and accept the role they play in legitimizing the lethal violence of law.

Besides the major move from private to public executions in the mid-nineteenth century, the most obvious administrative change in the death penalty over the long nineteenth century occurred in the mode of executions. Between 1888 and 1913, as Banner notes, fifteen states switched from hanging to electricity as the means by which death was legally administered. The change was directly related to new concerns about the physical suffering of those executed and the unnecessary pain inflicted through hanging in particular. Thus, when Texas became the sixteenth state to adopt the electric chair in 1923, it did so because the gallows, the state legislature declared, "is antiquated and has been supplanted in many states by the more modern and humane system of electrocution."[26] With this change in mode came a change in the spectatorship (or aesthetics) of executions, as much fewer witnesses could fit within the electrocution room as could stand within a prison yard to see a hanging. A shift in this "aesthetics" again occurred when some western and southern states, beginning with Nevada in 1921, turned to lethal gas as a more "humane" and cost-effective way (compared to the electric chair) to end life lawfully. By confining the condemned to a chamber, even fewer people could witness an execution, and this so-called advance in the technology of lawful death brought to mind horrors of its own. For instance, when in 1924 Chinese immigrant Gee Jon became the Nevada gas chamber's first victim, the *Philadelphia Public Ledger* invoked the gothic horrors imagined by Poe in "The Pit and the Pendulum," a story told from the perspective of a man sentenced to death by the Spanish Inquisition during the Napoleonic Wars: "There is a terror in this thing that Edgar Allan Poe could not equal," the *Ledger* observed. "There is a hissing from the walls, like Satan's hiss of the hooded cobra . . . The Invisible Thing strikes."[27]

In addition to these administrative changes, a subtler and perhaps more significant trend developed over the period I examine. Whereas the 1830s and 1840s witnessed a dramatic change from public to private executions, the decades surrounding the turn of the twentieth century saw a shift from locally to state administered executions. In fact, the first state-sanctioned execution (as we now think of it) did not take place until 1864, and executions were carried out by local officials and in county (as opposed to state) facilities well into the twentieth century.[28] As criminologist Raymond Paternoster explains, "Local authorities maintained control over the executions of condemned offenders until the early part of the twentieth century . . . Although the centralization of capital punishment under state control came slowly, it had (except in the South) replaced local authority by the 1920s. In the 1890s, 86 percent of all executions were performed under local authority, but by the 1920s almost eight out of every ten executions were conducted under state authority."[29] It was not, then, until the publication of *An American Tragedy* (1925), the end point of my study, that almost every state had centralized the administration of capital punishment under state authority. If earlier works I analyze illustrate a conceptual tension between sovereignty and responsibility in the republican procedures by which citizen-subjects were put to death, Dreiser's novel exposes a disjunction between these two concepts in the modern criminal justice system—a system that claims absolute authority over those it executes while endlessly deferring responsibility for those acts through the system itself.

◦～

Literary executions—like representations of or responses to the death penalty in newspapers, magazines, and other print media—provide crucial insight into this modernization process insofar as they dramatize, as my central thesis holds, the confrontation between the citizen-subject and sovereign authority in its starkest terms. By rendering the spectacle of lawful death both visible and public as it became increasingly less visible and moved behind closed doors, literary accounts of capital punishment play an important role in a complex network of discursive practices that raise challenging questions about state sovereignty and social responsibility. Central among such questions, as I suggested earlier, was the presumed right of the state (or again states, in the U.S. federal system) to take the lives of its citizens under a republican form of government. For many Americans in the early republic and later, that so-called right contradicted a fundamental principle of American democracy, because the lawful authority to execute properly belonged to a monarchy, in which a king wielded ultimate authority over the people (his subjects) but not in a republic wherein the people themselves are "kings." Masur, writing about the postrevolutionary era, notes that "if severe and excessive punishments marked monarchies, mild and benevolent ones would have to characterize republics. The logic of republicanism forced some Americans to reconsider the problem of deviance and to oppose capital punishment as unrepublican."[30]

Building on what Masur elsewhere describes as a "republican ideal" and "republican ideology" in death penalty debates, I give specific attention to what we might call *the republican argument against the death penalty*—a key component in capital punishment's broader cultural rhetoric. That argument had deep roots in the Democratic Party in the first half of the nineteenth century and strong advocates among prominent party members. Thomas Jefferson himself opposed the death penalty in principle, and later Jeffersonians and Jacksonians alike drew upon his theory of government in drafting influential proposals for abolishing capital punishment that were presented in state legislatures across the country. Originally delivered in legislative halls and courtrooms, these writings found their way to the court of public opinion and influenced an extralegal argument for abolition that made the death penalty an anathema to republican institutions and values.

One influential reformer from midcentury who embraced this argument and denigrated the gallows as "anti-republican" was William Lloyd Garrison.[31] Best known of course for his leadership in the campaign to end slavery, Garrison was also an active participant in the movement to abolish capital punishment. His participation in the anti-gallows campaign suggests the close affinities between what Mark Canuel, in writing about British romanticism, has recently called "the two abolitions" of the late eighteenth and nineteenth centuries.[32] In addition to Garrison, many other U.S. leaders in the campaign to end slavery, particularly in Massachusetts and New York, were staunch opponents of the death penalty. Lydia Maria Child, a Garrisonian and native Bostonian, passed out anti-gallows material at antislavery rallies, assuming shared interests and beliefs among those who supported each campaign.[33] She also wrote powerfully against capital punishment in several of her wildly popular "Letters from New York," a subject I take up at length in this book. The prominent Boston minister Theodore Parker preached against the death penalty in some of his sermons, denouncing it as "backwards law-making,"[34] while Wendell Phillips, one of Massachusetts's most celebrated slavery abolitionists, was an officer in Massachusetts's Society for the Abolition of Capital Punishment and one of the few important antebellum writers to take up the cause when the movement resurged in the 1880s.

Important Boston-based poets who opposed slavery also wrote against the gallows. John Greenleaf Whittier, for instance, published poems against the death penalty alongside ones against slavery in *Songs of Labor and Reform* (1848). In fact, his "Human Sacrifice" and "Lines, Written on Reading Several Pamphlets Published by Clergymen against the Abolition of the Gallows," as the latter's title suggests, were both written expressly to support the anti-gallows cause. Similarly, Henry Wadsworth Longfellow, who wrote his *Poems of Slavery* in the early 1840s, later wrote a letter for Marvin H. Bovee's *Christ and the Gallows* (1869), an anti-gallows book that included numerous statements against capital punishment by famous Americans. Longfellow began his contribution by declaring, "I am, and have been for many years, an opponent of capital punishment." He concluded it by wishing Bovee, a Democrat and tireless anti-gallows reformer who had successfully led Wisconsin's campaign to abolish the death penalty in 1853, "complete success in effacing the death penalty from all the statute books of our country."[35]

A decade earlier, Longfellow had expressed such sentiments poetically in "Ropewalk" (1859), a work tracing the cultural life of rope in a representative New England community. In one of the poem's meandering stanzas, Longfellow's speaker takes readers behind prison walls where he is horrified to find "the gallows-tree!," thus commanding: "Breath of Christian charity, / Blow, and sweep it from the earth!" In linking the rope of the gallows to that from which "fair maidens" swing and church bells ring (uses mentioned earlier in the poem),[36] Longfellow weaves the thread of capital punishment into the daily fabric of American life, thereby making it a vital (if hidden) part of a broader cultural narrative. Though not present in Longfellow's poem, the specific rhetorical threads of capital punishment and slavery were interwoven every time an antislavery newspaper or periodical reported on an execution when race was a factor. Ironically, by far the most famous of such executions concerned not one of the hundreds of slaves or free persons of color lawfully put to death but that of the famous white abolitionist, John Brown, whose impending hanging or "martyrdom," as Ralph Waldo Emerson infamously put it, "will make the gallows as glorious as the Cross."[37]

Not only individuals but antislavery periodicals frequently spoke out against the death penalty. For example, Child's widely reprinted New York letters were first published in the *National Anti-Slavery Standard*, whereas Garrison's *Liberator* chronicled the anti-gallows activism in the Massachusetts state legislature. In fact, a May 1844 article from the *Liberator* reported the role its editor played in

supporting an anti-gallows bill that challenged a countermovement among conservative Congregationalists and Presbyterian ministers to retain the death penalty: "A number of individuals, with Mr. Garrison at their head," the article began, "have been petitioning the Massachusetts Legislature to abolish capital
punishment, and, in case their prayer should be denied, they ask that the gallows
be erected near a meeting house, that the execution take place on the Sabbath
day, and that the minister be the executioner."[38] By suggesting that pro-gallows
ministers *ad*minister executions, Garrison put into practice the kind of argument
Whitman had made some two years earlier in his *Sun* editorial, "Capital Punishment and Social Responsibility." Garrison's "prayer" was not answered, for the
House of Representatives fell just short that year of passing a bill that would have
abolished the death penalty in Massachusetts.[39] Even so, all was not lost. Anti-
gallows activism in Boston helped to spark an interstate movement for abolition
in other cities across the North and Midwest, particularly in New York and
Philadelphia.

Evidence for that alliance can be found in the widely circulating *New York
Tribune*, which covered progress of Massachusetts's abolition bill, reporting that

> the awfully solemn duty of hanging the convicted criminal . . . instead of being
> longer imposed upon the sheriffs, whose humane feelings are often shocked by
> such brutality, may hereafter by assigned to *hangman*, such as your wisdom
> may enable you to select out of that numerous portion of the *clergy*, who are the
> most zealous advocates of *judicial murder*, and through whose influence the
> inhuman practice has been so long continued. (emphasis in original)[40]

In a dialogized discourse characteristic of a novel, this newspaper report mocks
and debases traditional religious authority cloaked in the minister, making him a
barbarous "*hangman*" and ridiculing his sanctioning of capital punishment as
"*judicial murder.*" In the *Tribune's* frequent coverage of anti-gallows activism,
which included a recurrent column headed "The Punishment of Death," we
also see the emergence of the "National Society for the Abolition of the Punishment of Death" (as the organization was called), with central offices and annual
meetings in Philadelphia. The goal of the society was, as a May 17, 1845, *Tribune*
article reported, to promote "this reform in all of the States of this Union." Horace
Greeley, the *Tribune's* influential editor, was himself a major player in the national
campaign to end slavery, but he also assumed a leadership role in New York's own
Society for the Abolition of Capital Punishment, an organization for which he
served as treasurer. Other members included the poet William Cullen Bryant, as
president, and William H. Channing, Josiah Hopper, and John L. O'Sullivan as

officers. With the exception of O'Sullivan, each of these committee members was a staunch opponent of slavery, and both Bryant and O'Sullivan were important literary figures and newspaper men.

Besides the *Tribune*, numerous New York papers endorsed the abolition of lawful death, including New York's *World*, *Herald*, *Evening Post* (which Bryant edited), *Evening Star*, *Commercial Advocate*, *News* (which O'Sullivan edited), *Mirror*, and *True Son*, as well as Albany's *Citizen and Daily Advertiser*, and Brooklyn's *Daily Eagle* (for which a young Walt Whitman wrote anti-gallows articles).[41] In addition to editing the *News*, O'Sullivan was founder and editor in chief of the *United States Magazine and the Democratic Review*, one of the nation's premier literary journals and a principal organ for promoting the anti-gallows cause. Another venue for reform was Boston's *The Hangman*, founded in 1845 and later titled the *Prisoner's Friend*, which was exclusively devoted to anti-gallows activism.[42] In fact, the magazine was designated by the National Society for the Abolition of the Punishment of Death as its official publication.[43] The founder and editor of *The Hangman* was Charles Spear, an influential Boston Unitarian minister who also opposed slavery but for whom death penalty abolitionism was a cause célèbre. Spear, in 1844, authored *Essays on the Punishment of Death*, what would become a key monograph in the movement. By May 1845, Spear's *Essays* had sold more than five thousand copies, and by 1846 it had gone through seven editions.[44] A dedicated anti-gallows reformer, Spear served in 1845 as the first president of Massachusetts's Society for the Abolition of Capital Punishment.

Yet not every influential reformer who opposed slavery also opposed capital punishment, and vice versa. Crucial exceptions were O'Sullivan, the influential politician and editor who led the anti-gallows campaign in the 1840s, and George B. Cheever, a prominent Presbyterian minister and the period's foremost spokesperson for the gallows who wrote two books in the name of its defense: *Punishment by Death: Its Authority and Expediency* (1842) and *A Defence of Capital Punishment* (1846). While O'Sullivan, in the years leading up to the Civil War, sympathized with slaveholders and would become a supporter of the Confederacy, Cheever during this time became a leader in the antislavery cause and joined forces with many of those with whom he formerly disagreed on the subject of capital punishment. Exceptional though they were, both O'Sullivan and Cheever serve as touchstones in my study, not only because of the leadership positions they occupied on opposing sides of the death penalty debates but because of the influential role they played in literary politics of the day. O'Sullivan, along with Evert Duyckinck (who incidentally also wrote against capital punishment, calling it in one article a "remnant of barbarity"),[45] helped to

orchestrate the "Young America" movement in literature.[46] In fact, he recruited
members of that group—notably Hawthorne, Whittier, William Starbuck Mayo,
and a young Whitman—to publish anti-gallows work in the *Democratic Review*,
while William Gilmore Simms, the only Young-America southerner, had proposed, through his agent Duyckinck, to write "a series of Sonnets agt. the punishment for death" for O'Sullivan's magazine.[47] Cheever, a college chum of Hawthorne's and Longfellow's at Bowdoin College, edited *Poets of America* (1847), the
first anthology of American poets, and wrote literary criticism and fiction himself,
including a temperance tale, "Deacon Giles' Distillery" (1835), for which he received minor celebrity and Hawthorne's sympathy when the story's representation
of a particular distillery landed him in a Salem prison for libel.[48]

Cheever—like Garrison, Child, Greeley, Parker, and countless other reformers—
saw in slavery a demonstrable conflict of laws: between positive laws, on the one
hand, that legitimated slavery and a higher moral law, on the other, that condemned it.[49] The scene of enslavement or "subjection," as Saidiya V. Hartman
would have it, dramatized this conflict in the same stark terms with which I have
characterized the scene of capital punishment—a scene pitting the subjected
subject (but not a citizen) against the tyranny of the state government.[50] Just as
some antislavery activists like Cheever failed to see the slave's plight as analogous to that of the condemned citizen or alien, some anti-gallows reformers like
O'Sullivan failed to see the significance of the analogy from the other end. For
the latter group, capital punishment was particularly horrifying in that it could
take the life of *any* person, regardless of race or class—although proportion-
ately the greatest number of the gallows' victims came from the working classes,
while the most draconian of capital statutes applied only to slaves in the South.
Spear pointed to the double standard in crimes with a racial component in cata-
loging capital offenses in the appendix to *Essays on the Punishment of Death*
(1844). Whereas northern states in the 1840s had capital statutes usually only for
murder and treason (but sometimes for arson and rape as well), southern states
often had capital penalties for those offenses and additional ones, "if a slave."
Georgia, for example, had several: "Rape on a free white female, if a slave. As-
saulting a free white female with intent to murder, if a slave. Burglary or arson of
any description contained in penal code of state, if a slave. Murder of a slave or
free person of color, if a slave."[51]

Hence, despite some differences among reformers epitomized in O'Sullivan
and Cheever, it would be difficult to overestimate the intimate connections
between these two antebellum abolition movements. As Masur puts it, "In the
minds of abolitionists such as William Lloyd Garrison and Wendell Phillips,

one campaign, against slavery or the gallows, was inseparable from the other. Both slavery and capital punishment, they argued, represented systems of brutality that coerced individuals, and both institutions merited attack."[52] While Masur does not mention it, it is important to note that besides liberal white reformers none other than Frederick Douglass, the preeminent black abolitionist of the day, spoke out against the death penalty on the eve of the Civil War. Joining Susan B. Anthony, a leader in the Women's Rights campaign, Douglass co-organized a meeting against the death penalty in Rochester, New York, in 1858, where he delivered his essay, "Capital Punishment Is a Mockery of Justice."

That Douglass was joined by Anthony in organizing this meeting suggests important affiliations between the anti-gallows and another major reform movement of the nineteenth century: the campaign for women's rights. In addition to Anthony and Child, other leaders in this reform vocally supported the abolition of capital punishment. Margaret Fuller, for instance, wrote anti-gallows articles for Greeley's *Tribune* while writing *Woman in the Nineteenth Century* (1845), arguably the most important U.S. work on the "woman question" before the Civil War.[53] After the war, Elizabeth Cady Stanton, a collaborator of Anthony's who headed the National Woman Suffrage Association from 1869 to 1890, lent her voice to the anti-gallows cause in Bovee's *Christ and the Gallows*, which included the Longfellow letter I cited earlier. In her letter, Stanton identified herself as a longtime opponent of capital punishment and told the story of an execution that took place in her hometown in upstate New York when she was twelve years old. Like the heroine of Sylvester Judd's *Margaret* (1845; revised 1851) who visits and brings flowers to a condemned man before his execution, a young Stanton frequently visited a condemned murderer in the weeks leading up to his execution. Recognizing this man's humanity and the inhumanity of the death penalty, she even tried to stop the execution by attempting to sabotage its proceedings the day the hanging took place. When it occurred anyway, the event left her traumatized. In the letter written some forty years later, a mature Stanton reflected that "every execution I now read of in our public journals brings back that terrible memory."[54]

While this anecdote concludes the letter, Stanton begins it by declaring her general opposition to the death penalty and expressing her disgust at how the criminal justice system is currently administrated: "It makes me shudder to think of the cruelties that are inflicted on criminals in the name of justice, and of the awful waste of life and force—of the crushing out of hundreds and thousands of nimble men and promising boys in these abominable bastilles of the nineteenth century."[55] Drawing on the idea of capital punishment as a "relic of barbarism"—a commonplace in the rhetoric of anti-gallows abolitionism used by Duyckinck, Whittier, William Cullen Bryant, Charles Sumner, and others[56]—Stanton emphasizes the cruelty and inutility of the criminal justice system while eliciting the sympathy of her readers. She continues in affective language to attack the practice of lawful death itself: "As to the gallows, it is the torture of my life. Every sentence and every execution I hear of, is a break in the current of my life and thought for days."[57] If, as Halttunen argues, the murderer was often constructed as a monster in the nineteenth century, Stanton, in the spirit of the Puritan execution sermon, saw the murderer as a "common sinner," a member of a compassionate community to be brought back into the fold rather than made alien to it. Whereas variations on the republican argument against the death penalty constitute the primary focus of my study, sentimental salvos like the one Stanton levies here account for an important subsidiary line of argument I explore in several chapters.[58] In chapter 2, for instance, I analyze a similar strategy in Lydia Maria Child's New York letters, wherein Child's contemplation of the beautiful, like the life current of Stanton's thought, is marred by the jarring reports of executions and the presence of capital punishment and the criminal justice system.

Stanton is best known for her leadership in the women's suffrage movement, but she began her career in reform with the campaign for temperance, the last of the major nineteenth-century reform movements with ties to anti-gallows activism. Of course, not all temperance reformers protested capital punishment— Cheever, again, marks a notable exception—but many did. And some temperance magazines, such as the *Journal of the American Temperance Union* and the *American Temperance Magazine and Sons of Temperance Offering*, made anti-gallows statements, just as Spear's *The Hangman* and *The Prisoner's Friend* frequently preached the virtues of temperance and linked murder to the consumption of spirits. The July 30, 1845, edition of *The Hangman* serves as a case in point. Among its many contributions, including one by Child, were two articles about one Henry G. Green, an intemperate man who murdered his wife, a temperance performer; a report titled "Another Capital Case in Massachusetts," in which a fight between two drunk brothers resulted in the murder of one of them; an article, "A Man Killed in Broadstreet, Boston," that tells how a man who was "intoxicated, for he vomited freely at the time the deed was done," was murdered for insulting a woman; and a temperance poem titled "The Drunkard's Home and Furniture." This edition of *The Hangman* also included humorous anecdotes of a popular street temperance performer, "Henry Smith, the Razor Strop Man," and a lead article, "Reasons Why Capital Punishment Should Be Abolished," by Unitarian minister Samuel J. May. The third of May's six reasons for abolition dealt with grog shops and liquor dispensation. "How large a proportion of criminals are," May asked rhetorically, "made insane by intemperance?" Blaming society in part for such inebriated insanity, he concluded that "so long as the Commonwealth licenses the sale of intoxicating drinks, and men of the highest respectability countenance the use of them by their example, so long no one should be held to pay the forfeit of his life for any crime, he may commit under their maddening influence."[59]

In a later edition of *The Prisoner's Friend*, Spear himself lent support to the idea that intemperance was a leading cause of crime. In his article, "Statistics: Temperance" (1849), Spear estimated that the approximate 10,500 distilleries in the United States would yield 41,502,707 gallons of liquor, "which, if sold at 20 cents per gallon, would produce 80,000,000,000 of quarrels, half a million of assaults and batteries, 100,000 thefts, 800 suicides, and about 100 murders."[60] Such "statistics" brought together an argument for prohibition with an argument for *abolition*—a term I use in this book, unless otherwise specified, for death penalty abolitionism rather than its more common usage for antislavery activism. Similarly, popular fiction that criticized capital punishment or at least analyzed the circumstances surrounding a homicide often linked alcohol consumption and murder. Poe, for instance, demonized the gin bottle as "that fiend Intemperance"— a primary factor, the confessed murderer of "The Black Cat" tells us, that led him to kill his wife and his pet cat. In linking the bottle to murder in "The Black Cat," a tale David S. Reynolds has classified in the "dark-temperance tradition,"[61] Poe was not making an anti-gallows argument; many writers, however, did precisely that when they drew such a connection. For instance, Whitman's passionate Phillip March in "Revenge and Requital" commits murder shortly after, we are told, "he drank not one glass, but three or four, and strong glasses they were to him, for he was habitually abstemious"; Sylvester Judd's sympathetic Chilion in *Margaret* angrily flings a file while drunk at a community husking bee that kills a man attempting to seduce his sister; E. D. E. N. Southworth's jilted lover in "Thunderbolt to the Hearth" commits an impassioned murder not long after his wife poured him a portentous draft—"I would she had not given him that brandy!" Southworth's narrator exclaims, foreshadowing the murder to come; and Clarence Darrow's representative murderer Hank in his novel *An Eye for an Eye* (1905) is drunk on whisky the night he kills his wife.[62]

Temperance, in contrast to capital punishment, has generated quite a bit of literary scholarship in recent years.[63] Women's rights, for all the right reasons, has produced even more interest. More work still has been done—and rightly so— relating American literature to the campaign to end slavery, certainly the most

important reform movement of the nineteenth century.[64] If our critical appreciation of the nineteenth century has been enriched in recent years by our understanding of how the antislavery, the women's rights, and the temperance
movements have influenced American literature and how particular literary
works have influenced these movements in turn, it is equally important to recognize how American literature and culture was affected by the campaign to end
capital punishment—a major culture movement that, as I suggested earlier, has
been largely neglected by literary historians until recently. To put matters in perspective, temperance and women's rights did not attain their major victories until Prohibition and the ratification of the Eighteenth and Nineteenth Amend-
ments in the early 1920s. Before the Civil War, however, three states had entirely
abolished the death penalty, and by the time the federal suffrage bill passed and
national prohibition went into effect, ten more states had stricken the death penalty from their statutes (although four of them, by 1921, had reinstated it).

Yet the campaign against capital punishment, unlike these other movements,
is not only important to American literature for its content and context of reform.
It is equally important in terms of how death penalty *re*form *in*formed literary
*forms*, particularly the novel. Cohen, as noted earlier, has persuasively shown
how social and legal practices built up around the administration of capital punishment in colonial and revolutionary America gave rise to several popular genres
of early gallows literature, most notably the execution sermon—an indigenous
art form that, like the captivity and slave narratives, is a uniquely American contribution to world literature. In contrast to Cohen, I show how the forms and
procedures of criminal law—particularly the capital trial and the enactment or
prevention of an execution—significantly impacted novels and works of short
fiction, providing writers with a dramatic structuring device that helped them
initiate or resolve conflict, or bring the central drama of a narrative to a climax.
For if, as more than one critic has suggested, the criminal and especially the capital trial—with its investigation, testimony, courtroom drama, verdict, and execution (or prevention of one) operates according to dramatic structures and principles, then an execution makes for the ultimate dénouement in the dispensation of
justice.[65] The finality of such an outcome, with its elaborate review process, last-
minute appeals, and so on, enacts the two counterpoints of Aristotelian poetics:
plot and spectacle, the high and low respectively in classic literary aesthetics.[66]

Attending to questions of aesthetic form—a "cultural poetics," if you will—
the chapters that follow examine mainstays within the cultural rhetoric of capital
punishment, such as republican arguments against the death penalty or appeals
to biblical dictates for or against its practices; tropes or diologized images of the

sympathetic prisoner or "great criminal," the Hangman, and the gallows itself; and narratives about actual innocence, deterrence, and justice, along with biblical parables like Cain's fratricide and Genesis 9:6 ("Whoso sheddeth the blood of man, by man his blood shall be shed"), which themselves became thematics that sounded keynotes in arguments both for and against the death penalty. Thus engaging the politics and poetics of capital punishment, this volume explores three central interrelated aims: how literature could and did influence death penalty reform; how legal forms *in*formed literary forms; and how the figure of capital punishment was configured into a broader metaphor for the confrontation between the citizen-subject and sovereign authority.

ᴄᴗ

A recent essay on "Capital Punishment" in *American Literature through History* has discounted the impact of the death penalty in American literature before the 1920s. "Although the debate about capital punishment was quite ardent," Nancy Morrow claims, "it served relatively infrequently as the source of inspiration for imaginative literature before the 1920s, especially in comparison with its widespread use in novels, plays, and films since then."[67] *Literary Executions* dispels this misconception, arguing that imaginative literature before 1920 was significantly influenced and shaped by the great debates surrounding capital punishment in the middle of the nineteenth century and again in the decades surrounding the turn of the twentieth century.

Chapter 1 presents an overview of the anti-gallows movement in antebellum America by cross-examining a range of legal and literary works participating in death penalty debates. Laying the foundation for the chapters to follow, it traces the development of several prominent arguments against capital punishment—especially the republican argument—in legislative reports and proposals written by Benjamin Rush, Edward Livingston, Robert Rantoul Jr., and John L. O'Sullivan, as well as fiction and poetry by John Neal, Hawthorne, Whitman, Whittier, and Melville. A principled objection to capital punishment—and the pet cause of O'Sullivan, who spearheaded the Young America movement in literature—was a key ideological issue of the Democratic Party of the 1830s and 1840s and one that runs through the works of many now-famous or then-popular writers from the period. The campaign to abolish the death penalty, I argue, should thus be seen as providing an essential part of the context that cultivated the flowering of the American Renaissance. In some ways, in fact, that campaign reveals more about the democratic assumptions informing the work of American Renaissance writers than the campaign to end slavery.

Chapter 2 goes "beneath" the American Renaissance to develop an aesthetic theory of crime and punishment that informs each of the book's remaining chapters. It focuses on Simms and Child, two of the period's most popular writers whose work has been largely neglected by critics of the period. By reading several of Simms's Border Romances in conjunction with Child's innovative journalism and fiction, I show how a common interest in anti-gallows reform similarly influenced two writers from opposite ends of the political spectrum and in opposing camps on the issue of slavery. Yet this shared interest in crime reform gives way to a sharp difference in each author's representations of crime and capital punishment. Simms, on one hand, obsesses over the details of murder and explores the psychological states of criminals; Child, on the other, ignores criminal acts themselves and turns our attention instead to environmental factors that produced crime. What I call Simms's psychological realism and Child's literary sociology provides me with two aesthetic models for literary interventions into death penalty debates that I draw upon and complicate in ensuing chapters.

Building on these aesthetics but emphasizing their cultural rhetoric, Chapter 3 broadens the scope by examining capital punishment as both topic and trope in a diverse range of antebellum novels, stories, and literary sketches. Whereas chapter 2 juxtaposed Simms and Child in an improbable pairing, this one focuses on a disparate trio—James Fenimore Cooper, George Lippard, and Sylvester Judd—in whose work executions (or near executions) figure prominently. Examining dialogues, exchanges, arguments, and particularly the scene of lawful death itself, I show how rhetorical performances within specific works not only engaged in cultural debates about the death penalty but used capital punishment as a metaphor or figural site to address broader questions about sovereign authority and social responsibility in a democratic republic. In doing so, the chapter goes beyond the question of anti-gallows reform per se to show how capital punishment (as trope and figure) was configured in larger cultural narratives or national mythologies dramatizing the confrontation between the citizen-subject and sovereign authority.

Chapter 4 signals a shift in focus. It not only turns to questions of evidentiary value in death penalty debates but looks at courtroom discourse and concentrates on the work of a single author. Hawthorne, I argue, presents a particularly interesting case study; for while he makes explicit statements against the gallows in several early tales, he draws upon the logic of capital punishment in complicated (at times, contradictory) ways in each of his major romances. In particular, the chapter explores the complex plotting of death sentences and figural executions

through a cross-examination of *The House of the Seven Gables* (1851) and two famous capital trials that likely influenced its composition: the infamous 1830
"Salem murder," which took place in Hawthorne's hometown; and the even
more infamous 1850 "Boston tragedy," which transpired in Cambridge, Massachusetts, while Hawthorne was writing *The House of the Seven Gables*. Through
his cross-examination, I show how Hawthorne, on the one hand, constructs a
literary counterargument to such legal narratives of guilt based on probability
and circumstantial evidence, while, on the other, he resolves the crime romance
by approximating the violence of capital punishment through what I call the
literary execution of Judge Pyncheon.

Whereas chapter 4 examines Hawthorne's work in terms of two notorious
criminal trials as they played out in legal courtrooms, chapter 5 revisits Melville's
in light of the 1842 *Somers* affair—a notorious military case involving a triple execution at sea—as it dramatically unfolded in the court of public opinion. One of
two famous cases that promoted death penalty debate in New York in the early
1840s, the *Somers* affair again attracted public interest in the late 1880s, when the
controversy in a postbellum context resurged in New York (and across the nation)
as Melville wrote *Billy Budd* between 1886 and 1891. My examination of Melville's
work is further complicated by reading it against that of Slidell MacKenzie, the
commander who authorized the *Somers* executions and who had written extensively about two executions he witnessed in two popular travel narratives published in the 1830s. This chapter differs from earlier ones in its attention to relations of authority *behind* the law rather than primarily considering the citizen
and criminal subject *before* it. Moreover, the chapter attends to a Civil War and
postwar context of military executions and examines what I call the Republican
justification for capital punishment, a political argument to be associated with
the (emerging) Republican Party and the widespread use of military executions
carried out by the Lincoln administration during the Civil War. Moving as it
does from *White-Jacket*, a Democratic reform novel of the 1850s, to *Billy Budd*, a
work produced in post-Reconstruction America, the chapter provides a brief cultural history of capital punishment from the Civil War to the end of the nineteenth century, thus paving the way for my concluding chapter.

If chapter 1 surveys the controversy over capital punishment in antebellum
literature and law broadly defined, chapter 6 concludes this volume by examining the complexities of that controversy almost a century later in a single work,
*An American Tragedy*. It begins, however, with an analysis of sovereign authority
and social responsibility in Dreiser's "Nigger Jeff" (first written in 1895), whose
extralegal execution scene provides a foil against which I read Dreiser's represen-

tation of the criminal justice system and the modern institution of capital punishment in *An American Tragedy*. In doing so, I show how the novel dramatizes a fundamental disjunction between sovereignty and responsibility in the modern administration of lawful death, one that assumes absolute sovereignty over its condemned citizens while endlessly deferring responsibility for those supreme acts of authority. The chapter develops this argument by cross-examining *An American Tragedy* with Clarence Darrow's famous summation in the 1924 Leopold and Loeb case and his arguments against the death penalty later that year in a widely publicized debate, "Is Capital Punishment a Wise Policy?" It concludes by reading the novel against a law professor's 1927 prize-winning essay on the novel for a contest sponsored by Dreiser's publishers and in light of Darrow's long-forgotten *An Eye for an Eye* (1905), the first American novel written solely for the purpose of protesting capital punishment.

Ending with Dreiser (and Darrow), my book concludes where two earlier studies on capital punishment and the twentieth-century American novel essentially begin: a reading of *An American Tragedy* in terms of what David Guest, in *Sentenced to Death*, calls the "execution novel," a novel that tells "the story of a life that leads to the gallows (or to the electric chair, the gas chamber, the firing squad, or the injection table)" and participates in a "discourse that enables both capital punishment and the criminal justice system."[68] While sharing some of Guest's concerns and strategies in my study of American literature over the long nineteenth century, I go beyond telling "the story of a life that leads to the gallows" to show how the works I examine were shaped by or helped shape the (extra) legal movement to abolish capital punishment during this transformative period in American history. In an epilogue that brings the book to a close, I reflect on nineteenth-century literature and the death penalty in an early twentieth-century transatlantic context and in terms of the contemporary situation in which the United States, once a leader in the fight to end capital punishment, is now among the very last Western nations still to impose it. But it is with America's progressive anti-gallows politics in the early nineteenth century that *Literary Executions* begins.

# Anti-gallows Activism in Antebellum Law and Literature

Put the scaffold on the Common,
Where the multitude can meet;
All the schools and ladies summon,
Let them all enjoy the treat.
What's the use of being "private"?
Hanging is a righteous cause;
Men should witness what you drive at,
When you execute the laws.

> *Anti-gallows poem (1849), in Louis Masur,* Rites of Execution

Capital punishment has played an important role in American cultural and political life ever since the inception of the United States. During the colonial period and in the early years of the Republic, "Hanging Day" and its concomitant practices—the execution sermon, the condemned's last words or dying confession, the public spectacle of the execution itself, and official narratives or popular broadsides documenting the event—served to promote religious order and good citizenship. However, the role and place of the death penalty changed dramatically in the decades following the Revolutionary War. In the late eighteenth and early nineteenth centuries, the Enlightenment ideal of a less severe, more proportional government and the belief in the benevolence of human beings, coupled with a republican disdain for the so-called "right" of a state to take its citizens' lives, led many prominent thinkers (as discussed in the introduction) to challenge the scope and legitimacy of capital punishment.

The reformation of penal codes and capital statutes had long been a concern in both New York and Pennsylvania (in 1794, for instance, Pennsylvania abolished the death penalty for all offenses except first-degree murder),[1] but the reform movement became a topic of national interest in the nineteenth century. In the 1820s, influential lawyer and politician Edward Livingston presented

landmark arguments for the abolition of capital punishment before the Louisiana state legislature, and the spirit of reform later peaked in the 1830s, 1840s,
and early 1850s when social organizations such as the Societies for the Abolition
of Capital Punishment of New York and Massachusetts were formed and debates
about the death penalty spread across the nation. During this time, many northern and some southern states began revising capital statutes and moving executions from the public square to the enclosed, "private" space of the prison-yard.
Moreover, New York, Massachusetts, and New Hampshire came close to abolishing capital punishment in the 1830s and 1840s,[2] while bills calling for abolition
passed or nearly passed during this time in one of the legislative houses in New
Jersey, Vermont, Ohio, and Connecticut.[3] In 1837, Maine passed a bill that sentenced those convicted of capital crimes to solitary confinement and made executions require an executive warrant issued by the governor one year after the
pronouncement of a death sentence. The "Maine Law," as it came to be known,
helped prevent any death sentence in the state from being carried out for twenty-
seven years.

By 1853, three states—Michigan in 1847, Rhode Island in 1851, and Wisconsin
in 1853—abolished the death penalty; and it was largely due to the impending
Civil War and the inevitable violence associated with the effort to abolish slavery,
a movement with which the campaign against capital punishment was intimately
connected, that death penalty abolitionism lost its momentum, not fully to return to the public spotlight until populist and progressive ideas at the turn of
the twentieth century prompted a more scientific attitude toward crime and
criminal behavior.

This chapter examines the anti-gallows movement in antebellum America. It
analyzes legislative reports, political writings, and imaginative journalism concerning the death penalty as well as poetry and especially fiction from the period
that overtly represented or responded to capital punishment. The death penalty
has a discourse as rich and contentious as any in the history of the United States,
and the legal, political, and literary texts I investigate were written at a time when
the question of capital punishment was hotly debated and the movement for
abolition was advancing its cause on many fronts. Abolitionists during this time
drew on religious and political arguments to claim that capital punishment violated both human and civil rights. They also challenged arguments about deterrence, while insisting that the death penalty made juries reluctant to convict
criminals of capital crimes. Among important legal and political reformers of the
era were Robert Rantoul Jr., who made innovative arguments about the inappropriateness of capital punishment in a republic, and John L. O'Sullivan, a prominent

New York Democrat and editor of the influential *United States Magazine and Democratic Review*.

Famous literary figures who contributed to the debate by publishing in O'Sullivan's journal include Nathaniel Hawthorne, John Greenleaf Whittier, and Walt Whitman. Others, such as Henry Wadsworth Longfellow and Herman Melville, criticized the death penalty in their work, while some popular writers—notably James Fenimore Cooper, Lydia Maria Child, George Lippard, Sylvester Judd, and William Gilmore Simms (each of whose work I take up in later chapters)—interrogated the use and purpose of the gallows in their fiction. The campaign to abolish capital punishment, I conclude, should be seen as an important part of the context that helped bring about the American Renaissance. In fact, in some ways that campaign reveals as much about the democratic assumptions informing the invigoration of American literature at midcentury as the campaign to abolish slavery. I begin, however, by looking closely at an early popular American novel that portrays an execution scene and, in presenting elaborate commentary on it, sets the stage for arguments to follow. Doing so will help illustrate the first of my central aims by showing how literature could and did influence law and debates about the death penalty in the court of public opinion.

## "DRAMATICK EFFECT": *LOGAN* AND LIVINGSTON

The final chapter of David Brion Davis's classic study *Homicide in American Fiction* (1957) provides the starting point for any inquiry into American literature and the death penalty. As its title suggests, *Homicide in American Fiction* attends primarily to questions about murder; but in its final chapter, Davis turns to the subject of capital punishment, claiming that "American fiction in the second quarter of the nineteenth century reveals a curious synthesis of . . . two positions: reformers who emphasized the effect of environment on moral behavior, arguing that criminals should be cured instead of being punished, and traditionalists who finally abandoned the rationalistic theory of deterrence and fell back upon a doctrine of intrinsic and absolute justice."[4] As helpful as this formulation is, it needs to be complicated. More than a "curious synthesis," U.S. fiction written during this time responded to and participated in cultural debates over capital punishment. A case in point can be found in John Neal's *Logan: A Family* (1822), a popular novel that dramatizes, with extended discussion, a public execution.

Early in volume 2 of *Logan*, Neal's protagonist, Harold, witnesses the hanging of several men convicted of piracy. The executions take place on board a commercial ship as Harold travels to England. The narrator vividly portrays the hangings, describing how the condemned were "successively drawn up . . . and then let down part way, with a sudden jerk, which caused the dislocation of their necks, like the report of a pistol."[5] At the sight and sound of these acts, Harold's "blood curdled" and his "heart turned sick, cold, cold as ice" (8). After the last of the men is hanged (one is pardoned at the last moment), Harold tells a stranger near him that he feels as if he "were a witness against these men" (9). In response, the stranger asks, "And what think you of the reprieve?" to which Harold replies: "I like that. I love mercy. I could kneel down and thank them for sparing one life. And the very sailors—see how they are affected by it! The populace too, in the boats—they are crying" (9). The sentiment of Harold's answer prompts a firm re-joinder from the stranger: "No. You are deceived . . . That reprieve was injudicious. Punishment should be *certain*. *Certainty* does more than quantity, in penal codes, to counterbalance temptation. Were there but one man in a million pardoned, every criminal would hope that himself would be that man. Each expects the prize in a lottery. No! these people are not weeping . . . They love sensation— they love spectacles" (9, emphasis in original).

As Harold persists in his objections, the dialogue takes shape as an object lesson in Enlightenment attitudes toward hanging and the deleterious psychological effects of public executions. In the exchange, Harold represents the young romantic subject (Byron's Childe Harold serves as a model), while the older stranger plays the role of a wise and skeptical philosopher who has thought much about the institution and practice of capital punishment. When Harold insists that the sympathy of the spectators for the condemned at an execution reflects society's innate love of humanity and abhorrence of a justice system that inflicts death for crime, the stranger again corrects him: "The populace," he tells Harold, "will assemble to execute a felon to day, with their own hands, and to mor-row beset the throne of justice for his pardon. I have seen this, again and again. I have seen ten thousand people in tears because a handsome boy was to be ex-ecuted; and I have seen the officer who brought his pardon, hooted and pelted from the ground, by a part of the same mob" (9). The stranger's remarks on the psychology of the death penalty's spectacle of violence occasions further com-mentary about its harmful effects: "There are several things to condemn in this affair," he later says. "In the first place, all the pirates are represented as penitent, and *assured* of heaven. In the next place, he who is pardoned is kept in ignorance of it, till the last moment" (10, emphasis in original).

The dramatic effect of the pardon prompts Harold to interrupt the stranger to comment on the spectacle they just witnessed: "Not the criminal only," he says, "but the populace [will] remember it, with greater seriousness," since the par-doned convict "has suffered all but death: —the ignominy, the anticipation, the horrour, and the pain of such a death is nothing, absolutely nothing" (11). In fact, Harold adds, the act of hanging itself was relatively uneventful and even merciful when compared to the dreadful anticipation of each execution: "I felt relieved when their necks were snapped. I expected something a thousand times more horrible—but how instantly they were motionless! Oh, there is no death so easy!" (11). Yet Harold's sentiment perfectly illustrates the stranger's argument against both the mode in which capital punishment is presently administered and the popular practice of issuing last-minute pardons: "Right, young man," the stranger replies,

> hence the glaring impolicy of such executions; hence too the frequency of suicide by hanging. Poor wretches! they see that the pain is momentary; all feel as you did, at the sight of the first execution. They expect to fall down, when the signal is given, and yet they find that the reality is nothing to the terrours of their own imaginations. But let me proceed. By delaying the reprieve until the last moment, for a presumptuous and idle piece of dramatick effect— *they teach every man, at the gallows, to expect, even to the last moment, the very last, a reprieve.* (11, emphasis in original)

The exchange between Harold and the stranger highlights some of the concerns that would come to preoccupy the anti-gallows movement in the decades preceding the Civil War: (1) the horrors and deleterious effects of public executions and staged reprieves; (2) the implication of spectators as witnesses complicitous in the act of lawful hangings; (3) the Enlightenment principle of *certainty* over severity (or "quantity," as the stranger says) in punishment as a useful deterrent; (4) the base desires for violence to which public executions cater; and (5) the false pretense of forgiveness and salvation that the ritual of lethal, legal violence instills upon the criminal mind. As the dialogue in *Logan* continues, Harold's response to the stranger's argument helps to bring out this fifth and final point: "Gracious God," he exclaims, "Hence, every man goes out of the world unprepared, in reality!" to which the stranger replies: "Yes—and hence too, the hardihood and carelessness, with which the most detestable ruffians go out of it; depriving the scene of all its terrours, making it a brutal farce, a trial of insensibility" (11). When Harold goes on to ask why the stranger should condemn the condemned's repentance, the stranger replies that he does so not in principle but in practice, because such "penitence" is likely to be affected and insincere. "Listen to me," he urges Harold:

> Our system of punishment, reprieve, and penitence produces in every villain's heart just this process of reasoning: —

I will indulge my mortal appetite for blood—because at the *worst*, if I cannot escape suspicion—*cannot* bribe the witnesses, nor the jury—and if my lawyer *cannot* get me clear by his wicked eloquence, by some flaw in the proceedings—and if I *cannot* get a new trial—nor escape by subornation—nor break prison—nor bribe the gaoler—nor get a pardon—nor a reprieve—nor a commutation of punishment—nor get clear by some revolution, political or moral, why, at the worst I can *repent, and go to heaven, at any rate*, with the whole publick opinion in my favour, and the passport of many a pious clergyman in my behalf; nay, who knows? I may have a procession, a monument, an epitaph, be interred in consecrated ground, and pass for a martyr, a martyr to what! to the inexorable cruelty of my country's laws. —A pretty way to have those laws respected! a most effectual antidote to temptation, and profligacy, indeed!" (11–12, emphasis in original)

*Logan* was published in 1822, the same year Edward Livingston presented the first of his influential arguments against capital punishment before the Louisiana state legislature. A former congressman and mayor of New York forced to Louisiana by financial scandal, Livingston was elected a member of the state assembly in 1820. In 1821, he drafted a revision of the state's criminal statutes. A year later he delivered his *Report on the Plan of a Penal Code*, a lengthy section of which called for the abolition of the death penalty.

Eloquently written and powerfully argued, Livingston's *Report* centered on the psychological effect of public executions—like the one discussed at length in *Logan*. And like Neal's stranger, Livingston found the current administration of capital punishment to be barbarous and ineffective. Livingston, however, attended to the criminal passions (notably ambition and avarice) aroused in the spectators of executions. When the "inflection of death" becomes frequent "it loses its effect," Livingston claimed; "the people become too much familiarized with it to consider it as an example; it is changed into a spectacle, which must frequently be repeated to satisfy the ferocious taste it has formed."[6] At the same time, when executions are infrequent and "kept for great occasions, and the people are seldom treated with the gratification of seeing one of their fellow-creatures expire by the sentence of the law; a most singular effect is produced; the sufferer, whatever be his crime, becomes a hero or a saint; he is the object of public attention, curiosity, admiration, and pity."[7] In either case, Livingston argued against public hangings; and in this respect, he echoed the general arguments against such punishment in Neal's novel, especially the claim that the condemned becomes an object of sympathy—a hero or martyr, even—in the eyes of the populace.[8] "Thus the end of the law is defeated," Livingston concluded; "the force of the example is totally lost, and the place of execution is converted into a scene of triumph for the sufferer, whose crime is wholly forgotten, while his courage, resignation, or piety, mark him as the martyr, not the guilty victim, of the laws."[9]

Livingston and Neal, one from law and the other from literature, speak out against the death penalty near the beginning of a reform movement that would come to occupy a prominent place in the cultural politics of the 1830s, 1840s, and early 1850s. Indeed, as a Pennsylvania paper declared in 1844: "The subject of capital punishment is claiming much and increasing attention, not only in our own State, but in many other parts of the country."[10] Drawing on such statements, historian Louis P. Masur writes: "During the 1840s, books, pamphlets, and reports by scores of writers flooded the public with arguments against capital punishment. Ministers, editors, and lecturers better known for their devotion to other moral and social causes adopted the anti-gallows movement as their own."[11] If the anti-gallows reform movement came to fruition in the 1840s, it had its origins before then. Reflecting upon his life in an 1866 autobiography, Neal credited *Logan* with prompting a particular development within that reform: the movement of executions from the public square to the enclosed space of the prison yard. "I believe that the changes which have followed," Neal wrote, "year after year, both abroad and at home, in the mode of execution, originated with my 'Logan.'"[12]

In his autobiography, Neal also identified himself as a longtime opponent of lawful death: "Upon the *death-penalty*, or what is called 'capital punishment,'" he wrote, "I have . . . written much, and not a little to the purpose; having no belief in the wisdom of strangulation, for men, women, and children, however much they might seem to deserve it, and being fully persuaded that the worst men have most need of repentance, and that they who are unfit to live, are still more unfit to die."[13] Neal, moreover, described in that work the experience that inspired both his anti–death penalty politics and the gallows scene in *Logan*:

When I wrote "Logan," after having seen two pirates, and two young men strangled by law, in the midst of a noisy, riotous crowd in Baltimore, at noonday, with the blue heavens, the green earth, and the golden sunshine testifying against their dread "taking off," I urged our lawgivers, if they would still insist upon strangling men, women, and children, to do it within the walls of a prison, at midnight, and with the tolling of a large, ponderous bell, or the sound of cannon, like minute-guns at sea; that murderers, and ravishers, and house breakers, and thieves, and highwayman, might be startled from their sleep, and set a-thinking; or be disturbed in their midnight revels, or their unaccomplished depredations, as by a voice from the other world, filling them with dismay, or with a mysterious unutterable horror, according to their guilt, in their dread loneliness and desolation.[14]

Neal's suggestion here echoes an idea for a more effective means of administering capital punishment hinted at by the stranger in *Logan*: "Another defect," the stranger tells Harold, "is this; men are executed in daylight, and the mob go home, about their usual occupations . . . But let executions be conducted at night, by torch light, with tolling bells, at midnight, and what would be their sensations then!" (*Logan* 13). This idea, of course, was never implemented, although the argument for prohibiting public executions in *Logan* preceded the first actual state law of that kind by eight years.[15] Even so, the anti-gallows movement in the United States has a richer, more complex history than Neal suggests—one steeped in Enlightenment philosophy and with Italian origins.

## "A WAR OF THE NATION AGAINST A CITIZEN": THE REPUBLICAN ARGUMENT AGAINST THE DEATH PENALTY

The origins of the movement to abolish capital punishment in America can be found in Cesare Beccaria's *On Crimes and Punishment*, a short treatise on the reformation of criminal law first published in 1764. Upon its publication in Italy and translation throughout Europe, Beccaria's book attracted much attention and sparked heated debates about criminal law reform and the death penalty on the European continent. Interest in Beccaria was every bit as keen in England and colonial America. The first English edition of Beccaria's treatise was published in London in 1767 and advertised in New York in 1773. The first American editions were published in Charleston in 1777 and in Philadelphia in 1778. What is more, *On Crimes and Punishment* was widely cataloged by American booksellers in the 1780s, "and newspapers such as the *New Haven Gazette and Connecticut Magazine* serialized Beccaria for their readers."[16]

Drawing upon Montesquieu's *The Spirit of Laws* (1748), Beccaria argued for less severe, more proportionate punishments in criminal law and reasoned that the death penalty was neither necessary nor useful. Capital punishment was not necessary, he claimed, because in times of peace life imprisonment would sufficiently protect society from any of its dangerous members.[17] Likewise, it was not useful because, while harsh, the penalty did not leave a *lasting* impression upon those whom it intended to deter. In Beccaria's words, "It is not the severity of punishment that has the greatest impact on the human mind, but rather its duration, for our sensibility is more easily and surely stimulated by tiny repeated impressions than by a strong but temporary movement" (49). Thus, according to Beccaria, life imprisonment provided a more effective deterrent to crime because the punishment would be "spread out over a lifetime," whereas "capital punishment exercises all its powers in an instant" (50). If, as Montesquieu repeatedly stated in *Spirit of Laws* and Beccaria reiterated in *On Crimes and Punishment*, any punishment that was unnecessary was "tyrannical," then the death penalty epitomized that tyranny.[18]

Beccaria's utilitarian attack on the death penalty challenged the social contract theories of Montesquieu and Rousseau. Like Rousseau, he subscribed to a theory of government in which citizens renounced part of their individual liberty in order to form a social compact. According to Beccaria, however, members of a social contract never gave the state the right to take their lives. To do so would be to contradict the underlying principle of the contract itself. "By what alleged right can men slaughter their fellows?" Beccaria asked in criticizing the all-but-universal practice of capital punishment. "Certainly not by the authority from which sovereignty and law derive. That authority is nothing but the sum of tiny portions of the individual liberty of each person; it represents the general will, which is the aggregate of private wills. Who on earth has ever willed that other men should have the liberty to kill him? How could this minimal sacrifice of the liberty of each individual ever include the sacrifice of the greatest good of all, life itself?" (48). As the repeated emphasis upon "liberty" suggests, Beccaria's argument hinged upon the rights and individual liberties the social contract was initially created to protect. First and foremost was the right to life, "the greatest good of all." From this line of reasoning, Beccaria concluded: "The death penalty, then, is not a *right* . . . but rather a war of the nation against a citizen, a campaign waged on the ground that the nation has judged the destruction of his being to be useful or necessary" (48).

Beccaria's politically charged language, his description of capital punishment as a civil war between a nation and its citizens, must have caught the attention of his many liberal-minded American readers, for whom the state's ultimate sanction against its people was anathema to a republican ideal of government. As Masur notes, "No less a figure than Thomas Jefferson credited Beccaria with awakening the world to the unnecessary severity of capital punishment."[19] Such an ideal was fundamental to the Founding Father's vision of an American Republic, and Beccaria is more important to this republican ideal than he is usually credited. For instance, when once asked as president in 1806 for a list of authors whose works were essential to understanding the proper "organization of society in civil government," Jefferson responded with only five names: Locke, Sidney, Chipman, the Federalist Papers, and Beccaria.[20]

Benjamin Rush was another influenced by Beccaria's utilitarian arguments against the death penalty. The foremost physician in America during the late eighteenth century and, like Jefferson, a signer of the Declaration of Independence, Rush emerged as the first great spokesperson for the anti-gallows movement in the newly formed United States. He first aired his views on the death penalty in an essay (later published as *An Enquiry into the Effects of Public Punishments upon Criminals and upon Society*) he delivered on March 9, 1787, at the home of Benjamin Franklin, himself an opponent of its practice. However, it was not until 1792, a year after the Bill of Rights was ratified, that Rush published *Considerations on the Injustice and Impolicy of Punishing Murder by Death*, his definitive statement for the abolition of capital punishment. Clearly influenced by Beccaria (who is referenced twice in the essay), Rush contributed to the Enlightenment argument by adding that mandatory death sentences for capital convictions made juries less willing to reach guilty verdicts. He also articulated a provocative claim that the death penalty encouraged murder by those who, believing suicide a graver offense than murder, took a life in order that the state might take theirs in turn. Rush's attack, however, centered on moral and religious objections to punishment by death—a predominant line of reasoning on both sides of the debate from the late eighteenth to the mid-nineteenth century to which we shall return. With the question of capital punishment and civil liberties before us, however, I want to consider first only the conclusion of Rush's *Considerations*.

In that conclusion, Rush draws an extended comparison between monarchical and republican forms of government:

> Capital punishments are the natural offsprings of monarchical governments. Kings believe that they possess their crowns by *divine* right; no wonder, therefore they assume the divine power of taking away human life. Kings consider their subjects as their property; no wonder, therefore, they shed their blood with as little emotion as men shed the blood of their sheep or cattle. But the principles of republican governments speak a very different language. They teach us the absurdity of the divine origin of kingly power. They approximate the extreme ranks of men to each other. They restore man to his God—to society—and to himself. They appreciate human life, and increase public and private obligations to preserve it. They consider human sacrifices as no less offensive to the sovereignty of the people, than they are to the majesty of

heaven. They view the attributes of government, like the attributes of the deity, as infinitely more honoured by destroying evil by means of *merciful* than by exterminating punishments. The united states have adopted these peaceful and benevolent forms of government. It becomes them therefore to adopt their mild and benevolent principles.[21]

Associating the death penalty with monarchical rule and the right to execute with a king's prerogative, Rush makes capital punishment antithetical to a republican government of, by, and for the people. Indeed, it would not be overstating the case to say that the birth of U.S. citizenship, for Rush, is predicated on the death of the death penalty and a repudiation of a state's ultimate authority over the lives of its citizenry. To highlight the disparity between monarchies and republics in these terms, Rush closes his essay with a striking analogy: "An execution in a republic is like a human sacrifice in religion. It is an offering to monarchy, and to that malignant being, who has been stiled a murderer from the beginning, and who delights equally in murder, whether it be perpetrated by the cold, but vindictive arm of the law, or by the angry hand of private revenge."[22] Likening an execution in a republic to a "human sacrifice in religion," Rush calls attention not only to the moral horror of capital punishment but also to its logic of give-and-take—a logic that, for him, is deeply problematic, since only God has legitimate power over life and death. Rush thus imagines the king, from a republican perspective, as a "malignant being" whose "delight" in murder—be it "perpetrated by the cold, but vindictive arm of the law, or by the angry hand of private revenge." Such a contrast conflates licit and illicit forms of capital punishment, thus suggesting an inherent similarity between these two forms of homicide: a likeness the state tries to mask by building elaborate rituals and formal procedures around lawful capital punishment to distinguish it from unlawful forms of murder.

Rush's Beccarian-based attack on capital punishment laid the foundation for what we can call the republican argument against the death penalty. Many antebellum reformers, including Livingston, would draw upon this argument. But it reached its fullest expression in the legal and political writings of Robert Rantoul Jr., a prominent lawyer and leading Democrat in Massachusetts who was the foremost opponent of the gallows in the 1830s. Rantoul grew up in a home committed to the reformation of capital punishment. Both his parents supported abolition, and his father publicly expressed his views in 1809, his first year as a member of the House of Representatives. His father represented Massachusetts in the House or the Senate for the next twenty-four years, and in 1829 he was appointed to a House judiciary committee to consider revising Massachusetts's penal code, particularly its capital statutes. Six years later, Rantoul followed in his father's footsteps. In 1834 he was elected to the House as a representative for Massachusetts, and the following year he chaired a committee to consider the "expediency of repealing all . . . laws" that "provide for the inflection of the punishment of death."[23] From 1835 to 1838, Rantoul delivered annual reports in favor of the abolition of capital punishment. The most famous was his 1836 *Report on the Abolition of Capital Punishment*. It was printed several times and "obtained a high reputation in Europe," writes Rantoul's nineteenth-century biographer, "being considered standard authority, and quoted as such in France, Belgium, Germany, and Italy" (429).

Rantoul begins his 1836 *Report* by identifying the question of capital punishment "as one of momentous importance, —deeply concerning the general welfare of society by its connection with, and influence upon the prevailing standard of moral rectitude" (436–37). This question, for Rantoul, is paramount because it involves "not only each legislator, but every member of the community [who] ought to feel a solemn interest and an individual responsibility" when weighing the "ultimate decision" over life or death (437). By emphasizing "individual responsibility" in this way, Rantoul puts the sovereign's ultimate power in the hands of the people in whose names executions are carried out. From this position he explores the contradictions underlying a system in which a republican people put to death its people in the name of the people. To this end, he draws heavily from utilitarian and social contract theorists, defining government as "nothing but a partnership"—"a limited partnership"—created and maintained for "benevolent and philanthropic" purposes; and the United States, he contends, has accomplished these goals "more uniformly and completely, and with less unnecessary suffering or avoidable injustice, than any association of men that has ever preceded us" (439). Nonetheless, as "the work of finite human faculties," the laws and administration of any government bear room for improvement, and Rantoul aligns his committee's report with a "class of reasoners" who "hold the infliction of capital punishment to be one of the most obvious vices in our present mode of administering the common concerns" (439).

This preamble on the role and place of government sets up the central question that Rantoul's *Report* seeks to address: "We are all of us members, they say," Rantoul notes, "of the great partnership. Each one of us has not only an interest, but an influence, also, in its proceedings. Shall the partnership, under certain circumstances which will probably happen now and then, proceed deliberately, with much ceremony, and in cold blood, to strangle one of its partners? Has society the right to take away life?" (439). The terms in which Rantoul poses the question provides its own answer: society's deliberate, cold-blooded act of "strangl[ing] one of its partners" reproduces the very act it often seeks to condemn. Rantoul supports this answer by elaborating two propositions of Jeffersonian democracy, the first being: "*The whole object of government is negative*" (439). The purpose of government, he explains, "is for the protection of property, life, and liberty. It is not for the destruction of any of them. It is not to prescribe how any one may obtain property, how long one may enjoy life, under what conditions he may remain at liberty. It was precisely to prevent the strong from controlling the weak in all these particulars, that government was instituted. It is to take care that no man . . . shall injure the person, or shorten the life of another" (439). This description of what government is and is not culminates with an image of the potential danger to which any government that encroaches upon civil liberties is susceptible: "It is not to become itself the most terrible invader of the interests it was created to protect, acting the part which the lion acted when he was made king of the beasts; nor, except where men are sunk in beastly degradation, will they permit it to usurp and monopolize all the prerogatives which elevate man above the brutes, and make him lord of the lower world" (439). By describing a government that sanctions capital punishment in terms of a "most terrible invader" of the people's interests, a "lion" that lords over the animal kingdom, Rantoul, speaking the "language" of Rush's republicanism, drives home the antidemocratic assumptions informing a government whose authority is founded on the death penalty.

Rantoul's emphasis on the negative objective of government and its potential for despotism brings him to his second proposition of Jeffersonian democracy: "*Government is a necessary evil*" (439). In elaborating this tenet, Rantoul identifies "protection" as "the only object of society" and claims that we, as citizens, surrender "only so much liberty as it is necessary" in order to preserve "our natural rights" (440). Rantoul, in this respect, follows Montesquieu and Beccaria in invoking a social contract model of government; and, like Beccaria, he rejects the notion that "any people has entered into a compact giving unlimited powers for all possible purposes to its government" (440). Rantoul associates this particular position with Rousseau, who "supposes that in consequence of the social contract between the citizens and society, life becomes 'a conditional grant of the State,' to be given up whenever the State shall call for it" (440). He belittles this idea as "an obvious absurdity" and denounces Rousseau's theory as "anti-republican and slavish" (440).

The death penalty, for Rantoul, epitomizes this "obvious absurdity," given that it destroys rather than punishes, thereby depriving a citizen of that essential liberty the social contract was designed to protect. Because the social contract makes sense only insofar as it protects the lives of its members, Rantoul claims that the burden of "positive proof" (443) lies with those who support capital punishment by virtue of a social contract theory. In his words, "Let there . . . be shown some reason for supposing that any sane man has of his accord bartered away his original right in his own existence" (442). According to Rantoul, such an argument presupposes a "preposterous sacrifice," and he takes this point a step further by examining the question of society's right to execute its condemned citizens from the perspective of Christian morality: "Not only has no man actually given up to society the right to put an end to his life, not only is no surrender of this right under a social compact ever to be implied, but no man can, under a social contract, or any other contract, give up this right to society, or to any constituent part of society, for this conclusive reason, that the right is not his to be conveyed" (443). That right, Rantoul claims, belongs only to God, the absolute sovereign who alone can take life, since he gave it. Thus, by situating an analysis of the death penalty via the social contract within a Christian paradigm, Rantoul redefines the subject positions of individuals and society as a whole. If, on the one hand, no individual has the right to relinquish life and, on the other, society has no right to take it, then any social contract under which a death sentence is enacted "would involve the one party in the guilt of suicide, and the other in the guilt of murder" (433).[24]

To bring the argument back round to republican politics, Rantoul later cites the opening sentence of the Massachusetts State Constitution, emphasizing its declared protections of *"natural rights, and the blessings of life"* (450, emphasis in original). He then shows, on the one hand, that the "celebrated instrument" in no way implies that individuals "surrender" this right and, on the other, that the state possesses no right "to take away any natural right of an individual, much less the last and dearest, or to debar him . . . from life itself." Rantoul supports this point by referencing federal law and citing the "first article of the declaration of rights," which protects a citizen's "liberties" and "those natural, essential, and unalienable rights which are common to all mankind" (450). This reference to the Declaration of Rights is followed in turn by a direct invocation of the U.S. Constitution and its protections of civil liberties. The Bill of Rights, Rantoul argues, is constructed around protecting a citizen's "unalienable right of enjoying and defending life." That "right," he acknowledges, "may be abridged, by the iron rule of stern necessity, when it comes in direct conflict with the same right in another, but, according to our Constitution, it can never be alienated. Let it not be said our Constitution does not forbid capital punishment; for neither does it, by that name, forbid slavery, or the whipping-post, or the pillory, or mutilation, or torture, yet all these are confessedly contrary to the spirit of the Constitution" (450).

Claims of capital punishment as barbaric and as a remnant of despotic regimes of bygone eras were common enough in the nineteenth century; but, as death penalty scholar and critic Hugo Adam Bedau suggests, Rantoul was perhaps the only abolitionist before the mid-twentieth century to argue against capital punishment on the grounds that it was inconsistent with the Constitution's Bill of Rights.[25] In his *Report*, this argument becomes overt when Rantoul associates the death penalty with the Eighth Amendment and its prohibition of cruel and unusual punishment: "The whipping-post and the pillory survived, for a period, the constitutional prohibition of cruel and unusual punishments. They have disappeared, and the gallows, which is more unusual than either of those barbarities had been, and infinitely more cruel and revolting, must soon follow in their train" (451). In turning from Rantoul and the 1830s to the proliferation of anti-gallows arguments in the 1840s, one finds a range of attacks deployed by political reformers and literary figures alike, for many of whom the gallows itself serves as a symbolic expression of outmoded cruelty. Rantoul, however, was the only activist from the nineteenth century who explicitly invoked an Eight Amendment argument. As the debate over capital punishment moved from the 1830s to the 1840s, it shifted from assembly halls and courtrooms to the court of public opinion. That shift was primarily orchestrated by John L. O'Sullivan, and it unfolded in the pages of his influential journal, the *United States Magazine and Democratic Review*.

## O'SULLIVAN AND THE LITERARY POLITICS
## OF ABOLITIONISM

If Robert Rantoul Jr. was the leading opponent of the gallows in the 1830s, John L. O'Sullivan was the foremost advocate in the 1840s. Like Rantoul, O'Sullivan was trained as a lawyer and deeply committed to the Democratic Party; however, he came to politics as a young newspaper and periodical editor. In 1840, O'Sullivan ran for a seat in the New York State Assembly. He won, and the campaign that secured him the election was largely based on the reformation of capital punishment.

During his two years in office, O'Sullivan dedicated much of his time to enacting that reform. In 1841, he was appointed chair of a special committee to consider the expediency of abolishing the death penalty in New York. That committee exhaustively researched the subject and presented an abolition bill that, after considerable delay in the House and negative publicity by opponents, was defeated by a slim margin. O'Sullivan was convinced that the measure would pass the following year, but it failed by the same margin. O'Sullivan's labor, however, was not wasted. It resulted in the production of his *Report in Favor of the Abolition of the Punishment of Death by Law*, an eloquent compendium of "the leading arguments and evidences, derived from revelation, reason, and experience, which are necessarily involved in the general discussion of the subject of Capital Punishment."[26] First published in great number for presentation before the New York state legislature on April 14, 1841, O'Sullivan's *Report* was reprinted as a book for popular consumption later that year. By October, "being called for by public demand" (4), a second edition of O'Sullivan's book was printed, and for the next twenty years it served as the standard reference in debates about the death penalty in the United States.[27]

The strength of O'Sullivan's *Report* lies in its popular appeal as well as its reformulation and polishing of powerful arguments developed earlier by Beccaria, Rush, Livingston, and Rantoul, to name the major influences. For instance, O'Sullivan closely attends to "scriptural evidence," first analyzed by Rush and others, to argue that the Bible condemns rather than supports capital punishment. He also points to historical precedent, showing not only that ancient Rome and Egypt experimented with periods of abolition but that abolition in contemporary Tuscany, Belgium, and even so-called despotic Russia (under Elizabeth and the Catherine II) had led to decreased rates in crime and murder. Turning to the United States, O'Sullivan claims that the drastic reduction in the number of capital statutes over recent years and the increasing reluctance of juries to convict in capital cases reflect evolving standards of morality. Such evidence, he reasons, suggests that changing the maximum punishment from death to life imprisonment would result in lower crime rates and higher rates of conviction. In addition to these arguments, O'Sullivan calls attention to the horrors of executing the innocent, emphasizing the fact that, once a death sentence is carried out, there is no way to undo it in the event of error. In this way, he synthesizes disparate arguments in favor of abolition—and he does so through a range of approaches. Partly statistical analysis and use of utilitarian and republican arguments against the death penalty, and partly moral anecdote and exegesis of biblical authority on capital punishment, the *Report* makes appeals to sympathy, reason, and historical example in its broad-scale assault on the gallows in America.

While deploying a range of arguments and rhetorical strategies, the *Report* is centered around the question of deterrence and the psychological impact of executions, a mainstay in debates about the death penalty and an argument developed at length by Livingston, from whose work O'Sullivan draws heavily. The punishment by death for murder, Livingston had argued in his introduction to the *Codes of Crimes and Punishment*, not only "fails in any repressive effect, but . . . promotes the crime."[28] Livingston made this point after citing a recent incident published in a Pennsylvania newspaper in which a man committed murder on the way back from witnessing a public execution. Through this example Livingston illustrates the proclivity of the human mind "to imitate that which has been strongly impressed on the senses" and warns the "lawgiver" to "mark this . . . propensity of human nature; and beware how he repeats, in his punishments, the very acts he wishes to repress, and makes them examples to follow rather than to avoid."[29]

Reformulating and quoting Livingston at length (he even cites Livingston's example from the Pennsylvania paper), O'Sullivan lays out his argument about the death penalty's failure as a deterrent and its adverse psychological affects roughly halfway through his *Report*. In doing so, one gets the sense that O'Sullivan has built his book around this argument, especially as he singles it out as the "strongest objection against the punishment of death" (84) and spends considerable time working through all its implications. In fact, he condenses the multiple dimensions of the argument into a pithy statement italicized and repeated verbatim some fifteen pages later, noting that "*the executioner is the indirect cause of more murders and more deaths than he ever punishes or avenges*" (85, 98, emphasis in original). This statement sums up a central objection to the gallows in a memorable trope. It turns the very instrument intended to deter capital crimes into an "indirect cause" of them. Yet, as the language of the trope indicates, O'Sullivan is more interested in the *executioner* than the gallows itself. Highlighting the role of the executioner (instead of the gallows) calls attention to human agency, thus placing responsibility for executions not only on those who perform them but also on those who support them—especially those who defended the gallows in the face of the surging reform movement.

At the center of this reform was the *United States Magazine and Democratic Review*, a leading antebellum journal founded and edited by O'Sullivan. In the 1840s, the *Democratic Review* published dozens of articles advocating the abolition of the death penalty, including feature essays devoted to the subject, reviews of important books on the topic, proceedings from anti-gallows conventions, and reports from legislative committees. O'Sullivan wrote some of these articles himself, such as "Capital Punishment" (April 1843), an extended reflection upon the cultural wars surrounding the death penalty, and "The Anti-gallows Movement"

(April 1844). The latter took shape as an "Address to the Public" (430), which called citizens to action through the announcement of *Anti-Draco,* a new "monthly" to be published by the American Society for the Collection and Diffusion of Information in Relation to the Punishment of Death.[30] O'Sullivan was the corresponding secretary of the society; its president was the famous poet William Cullen Bryant; and other committee members included Horace Greely, a well-known lecturer and the founding editor of the *New York Tribune,* and William H. Channing, a Unitarian clergyman with strong ties to Emerson and the transcendental movement.

O'Sullivan's journalism in the *Democratic Review* did much to galvanize public opinion about the death penalty. Perhaps nothing was more stimulating than "The Gallows and the Gospel: An Appeal to Clergymen Opposing Themselves to the Abolition of the One, in the Name of the Other," the lead article in the journal's March 1843 issue. Aimed at a conservative Presbyterian ministry, O'Sullivan's article attacked the opposition on its own grounds, elaborating his arguments based on "scriptural evidence" that he sketched to open his 1841 legislative *Report.* Religious concerns were not part of O'Sullivan's core argument—the republican argument against the death penalty was—but a closer examination of them in the *Report* and "The Gallows and the Gospel" provides insight into popular concerns about the reform movement and helps to set the stage for imaginative literature that engaged the debate.

Framed as "An Appeal," O'Sullivan's "The Gallows and the Gospel" begins by attacking the position of clergymen who, in the name of their faith, had recently come out in defense of the death penalty. "Some of you," O'Sullivan writes, "appear to have felt especially called upon to cast yourselves in the path of this advancing movement of opinion; to have taken the institution in question under your particular professional patronage and protection, and marshalling yourselves in organized array, as it were, around the foot of the Scaffold, have seemed ambitious to assume the function of the very Body-Guard of the Hangman."[31] Parodying a pro-gallows clergy, O'Sullivan envisions the debates surrounding capital punishment as a virtual war: on one side, reformers such as himself firing salvos at the gallows; on the other, retentionist clergymen "marshalling" themselves around the scaffold to serve as the hangman's "Body-Guard." With the battle lines drawn, O'Sullivan brings lay readers into the field, inviting "the large number of the undecided and indifferent, who may never have had a combined opportunity and disposition" to interrogate the death penalty through "Biblical criticism" and applied Christian ethics (228). O'Sullivan, on behalf of the abolitionists, affords readers that opportunity by presenting "an outline of the Scriptural Argument by which we refute the common objections opposed to us from the Bible" (228).

The argument O'Sullivan outlines here is essentially an elaboration of the position he asserts at the outset of his *Report*. That position holds that, contrary to popular opinion, the Bible condemns rather than sanctions the death penalty. O'Sullivan claims, for instance, that "the Bible contains no injunction nor sanction of the practice of capital punishment; but . . . the very reverse is most unequivocally impressed upon its pages, in their outset as in their close" (29). Rehearsing a familiar argument of Benjamin Rush and others, he reads Genesis 9:6 ("Whoso sheddeth the blood of man, by man his blood shall be shed") as prophecy rather than command. The verse serves as a prediction or a denunciatory warning of what ultimately becomes of violent behavior, much like the proverb derived from Matthew 26:52, "He who lives by the sword dies by the sword," or the one from Revelations 13:10, "He that leadeth into captivity shall go into captivity." It does not, for O'Sullivan, function as a universal commandment, such as "Thou Shall Not Kill" (Exodus 20:13).

As one might expect, the sixth commandment plays a crucial role in O'Sullivan's scriptural argument. That commandment stands "naked and sacred" in its "simplicity" and is "absolute, unequivocal, universal" (*Report* 22). It cannot be transformed into "Thou shall not commit murder—but mayest kill him who has committed murder" (22). To be sure, it contains "no proviso—no exception—no qualification" (22). O'Sullivan also finds evidence against capital punishment in the story of Cain and Abel, which he identifies in "The Gallows and the Gospel" as the "lesson set by the example of God himself in the case of the first murder" (233). In the *Report*, O'Sullivan had pushed this reading further: "Yet was death the sentence of Cain?" he asks rhetorically. "On the contrary, his doom is written that he should be 'a fugitive and a vagabond in the earth,' the earth ceasing to yield her strength to his tillage and a mark being set on him, '*lest any finding him should kill him*'" (28, emphasis in original). The proscription on taking Cain's life, for O'Sullivan, is reinforced through God's pronouncement: "*Whoso slayeth Cain, vengeance shall be taken on him sevenfold*" (28, emphasis in original).

In "The Gallows and the Gospel," O'Sullivan adds to and complicates his biblical criticism contra time-honored traditions through a linguistic analysis of Genesis 9:6. He begins by situating the verse within its supportive context, reminding readers that it should *not* be interpreted "in the absolute imperative sense for which our opponents contend—and made universal and perpetual, as they interpret its intended application" ("Gallows" 299). He then attends to the linguistic construction of the verse in its original Hebrew and provides a literal translation: "*Shedding blood of man in man his* (or *its*) *blood will be shed*" (299). To produce the common English translation of the verse, O'Sullivan argues, three assumptions must be made—none of them "necessarily resid[ing] any-where in the terms of the Hebrew itself" (299). Those assumptions are:

> 1. The participle *shedding* is not only made personal and masculine, but it is confined to the personal and masculine sense, in the words, "*whoso sheddeth*";
> 2. The verb which in the original is the simple future tense, so as to be ren-dered in Latin *effundetur* and in English *will be shed*, must receive an impera-tive sense so as to be read, *shall be shed*; and 3. The expression which is literally *in man* in the original, must be made to denote agency, by selecting and assign-ing to the preposition employed one only of its numerous meanings, so as to be converted into "*by man.*" It is only after the performance of this triple process that the original Hebrew . . . becomes translated, or rather transformed, into the common English reading of our Bibles. (229)

Of these three assumptions, O'Sullivan focuses on the second. The third is important because it denotes human agency and limits the traditional applica-tion of the verse, for in the original Hebrew the object pronoun (him or its) could be granting permission to put to death beasts—*not* men—who kill men. But the second assumption goes to the heart of the matter: should Genesis 9:6 be read as an injunction and thereby given "imperative force" (299); or should it be inter-preted as simply declarative of some "denunciatory future"? (230). Through this rigorous analysis of the mode and mood of the Hebrew verb *shophaich* (i.e., shed-ding/will shed/may shed), O'Sullivan examines what today we would call the performative force of the biblical verse in question. To do so, however, is not merely to engage in an academic exercise in splitting theoretical hairs; rather, it cuts to the quick of the issue by questioning the biblical authority upon which many prominent defenders of the gallows had staked their claims.

For O'Sullivan, as for his opposition, much hinged upon how Genesis 9:6 (and its operative verb) was interpreted, and O'Sullivan linked his interpretation to what I have called the republican argument against the death penalty. In a pow-erful analogy challenging the performative force often granted to Genesis 9:6, O'Sullivan links his biblical criticism to this political argument: "To give it [*shophaich*] the imperative sense," he argues, "and then to claim our obedience as a command is not only to beg the whole question, but even impiously to clothe in the garb of a divine authority that which is the mere imposture of human as-sumption. In the present application of it, it may not unfairly be compared to an act of forging a sovereign's signet to a death warrant" (230). Likening traditional interpretations of Genesis 9:6 as divine injunction to "the forging of a sovereign's signet to the death warrant," O'Sullivan brings the question of politics into his scriptural analysis, charging his opponents with "impiously" dressing up a mere "human assumption" in the garb of "divine authority" to serve their own position.

In his spirited assault on traditional interpretations of Genesis 9:6, O'Sullivan certainly had in mind Reverend George Barrell Cheever, a prominent Presbyterian minister and the foremost defender of the gallows who had recently authored *Punishment by Death: Its Authority and Expediency* (1842). In that book—what one death penalty historian has called "the most famous and influential defense of the gallows in American history"[32]—Cheever unequivocally champions capital punishment, building his argument primarily around an appeal to divine authority invested Genesis 9:6. Cheever devoted several chapters to interpreting the biblical passage, what he calls in the introduction to *Punishment by Death* "the Divine Statute" and elsewhere the "citadel of the argument, commanding and sweeping the whole subject."[33] Echoing the language O'Sullivan used to denounce such interpretations of Genesis 9:6 as "impiously . . . cloth[ing] in the garb of a divine authority that which is the mere imposture of human assumption," Cheever saw the biblical verse as an "ordinance confer[red] directly from God upon the civil majesty the power of the sword, the power of life and death," thus "cloth[ing] the administration of righteous law with a divine authority."[34] But it was not just the recent publication of *Punishment by Death* that would have prompted O'Sullivan to think of Cheever in writing "The Gallows and the Gospel" (an alliterative phrasing that Cheever denounced as "miserable slang").[35] A month before "The Gallows and the Gospel" was published, O'Sullivan had publicly debated Cheever in New York City on the question, "Ought Capital Punishment to Be Abolished?"[36] The debates, which were held at the Broadway Tabernacle on January 27, February 3, and February 17, were well attended and generated much press and further coverage for some time to come.

In fact, we get a literary rendition of the O'Sullivan-Cheever debate from the pen of Nathaniel Hawthorne—a former classmate of Cheever's at Bowdoin College and a close friend of O'Sullivan, as well as a contributor of more than twenty works to the *Democratic Review*, including "Egotism, or the Bosom Serpent," which was published alongside of "The Gallows and the Gospel" in the March 1843 issue of the magazine.[37] The allusion to the O'Sullivan–Cheever debate occurs in a pivotal moment in "Earth's Holocaust," Hawthorne's 1844 tale that recounts its narrator's journey to the American Midwest to witness the immolation of all the world's "worn-out trumpery," its "condemned rubbish."[38] Midway through the tale, following the successive destruction of signs of rank and social prestige, liquors and tea, articles of high fashions, and instruments of war, the body of reformers responsible for maintaining the great bonfire—this "Earth's Holocaust"—turns its attention to instruments of capital punishment: "old implements of cruelty—those horrible monsters of mechanism—those inventions which it seemed to demand something worse than man's natural heart to contrive, and which had lurked in the dusky nooks of ancient prisons, the subject of terror-stricken legends" (392).

Halters, headsmen's axes, and the guillotine are among the instruments of death thrown into the fire, but the imminent destruction of the gallows generates the most interest from the crowd, even sparking a debate between two men likely drawn from Cheever and O'Sullivan respectively: "Stay, my brethren!" cries a defender of capital punishment as the gallows is about to be thrust into the fire. "You are misled by a false philanthropy!—you know not what you do. The gallows is a heaven-oriented instrument! Bear it back, then, reverently, and set it up in its old place; else the world will fall to speedy ruin and desolation!" (393). In response to these assertions, "a leader in the reform" commands his brethren: "Onward, onward! . . . Into the flames with the accursed instrument of man's bloody policy! How can human law inculcate benevolence and love, while it persists in setting up the gallows as its chief symbol! One heave more, good friends, and the world will be redeemed from its greatest error!" (393). The gallows is finally pushed into the fire, and this act appears to be a good thing, as Hawthorne's narrator had moments earlier applauded the destruction of halters, axes, and the guillotine, commenting that their immolation "was sufficient to convince mankind of the long and deadly error of human law" (392). Yet one cannot say for certain that this radical reform will benefit society, since the tale slips unmistakably into parody as marriage certificates, written constitutions of all kinds, works of literature, and even the Bible later become fuel to feed the reformers' fire.

While it might be a stretch to call "Earth's Holocaust" abolitionist in orientation, one could say that about Hawthorne's "The New Adam and Eve," a story first published just one month before O'Sullivan's "The Gallows and the Gospel" in the February 1843 issue of the *Democratic Review*. In that story, Hawthorne imagines the return of the world's primogenitors after the "Day of Doom has burst upon the globe, and swept away the whole race of men."[39] Roughly midway through the tale, the "New" Adam and Eve are depicted as they enter a prison and wander through its bleak corridors and narrow cells. The novelty of Adam and Eve's experience provides Hawthorne's narrator with the opportunity to comment generally on the sad state of crime and punishment with which the recently deceased world was plagued, but nothing within the prison provokes strong reaction from either Adam and Eve or the narrator. All of that changes, however, when, "passing from the interior of the prison into the space within its outward wall, Adam pauses beneath a structure of the simplest contrivance, yet altogether unaccountable to him" (255). This structure, we are told, "consists merely of two upright posts, supporting a transverse beam, from which dangles a cord" (255). The menacing object that Adam finds "altogether unaccountable" is, of course, the gallows, and its foreboding presence elicits the following exchange between Adam and Eve:

> "Eve, Eve!" cries Adam, shuddering with a nameless horror. "What can this thing be?"
>
> "I know not," answers Eve; "but, Adam, my heart is sick! There seems to be no more sky,—no more sunshine!" (255)

Without knowledge of the world of sin to which the gallows belongs, neither Adam nor Eve can place "this thing" within an interpretive frame. Nonetheless, intuition into the instrument's cruel design sends a "nameless horror" through Adam and affects Eve with heartache and a momentary sense of despair.

Adam and Eve's response prompts the narrator to justify the couple's reaction:

> Well might Adam shudder and poor Eve be sick at heart; for this mysterious object was the type of mankind's whole system, in regard to the great diffi-culties which God had given to be solved—a system of fear and vengeance, never successful, yet followed to the last. Here, on the morning when the final summons came, a criminal—one criminal, where none were guiltless—had died upon the gallows. (255)

This authorial intrusion serves not only to endorse Adam and Eve's moral re-sponse but to raise questions about the institution of capital punishment, "a sys-tem," the narrator asserts, "of fear and vengeance, never successful, yet followed to the last." Such a description calls attention to negative effects of the death penalty (i.e., "fear" and "vengeance"), and these attributes are given dramatic expression through the example of that "final summons" when "a criminal—one criminal, where none were guiltless—had died upon the gallows." By shifting midsentence from the indefinite "a criminal" to the definite "one criminal," the narrator at once suggests the finality of all executions and the singularity of this one, while the emphasis upon the universal guilt of humanity undercuts the position of moral superiority from which a society typically justifies the death penalty. Yet this tale, like "Earth's Holocaust," presents a complicated stance toward capital punishment, and one not wholly consistent with the politics of abolition, as I argue in chapter 4.

In addition to Hawthorne, other prominent literary figures of the day wrote anti-gallows work for the *Democratic Review*. Four months before the publication of "The New Adam and Eve," John Greenleaf Whittier published "Lines, Written on Reading Several Pamphlets Published by Clergymen against the Abolition of the Gallows" in the October 1842 issue of the journal. Through an appeal to sympathy and compassion, and by situating the gallows at the tail end of a history of torture and cruelty inflicted by men in the name of God, Whittier indicts the practice of capital punishment in contemporary America, asking those of "milder faith" near the poem's end: "Will ye become the Druids of our time? / Set up your scaffold-alters in our land, / And, consecrators of Law's darkest crime, / Urge to its loathsome work the Hangman's hand?"[40] By linking the current administration of the death penalty to an ancient, barbaric past, Whittier strove to show that capital punishment was incompatible with democratic principles and civil liberties. He extended this line of argument in a second anti-gallows poem, "The Human Sacrifice," published seven months later in the May 1843 issue of the *Democratic Review*. The poem was written expressly for the anti-gallows cause and specifically, as its introductory headnote explains, in response to a clergyman's "warm eulogy upon the gallows" recently published in some of the nation's "leading sectarian papers."[41]

The writer of that letter was almost certainly Reverend Jared Bell Waterbury, author of numerous hymns and poems who also was an active participant in an *anti*-anti-gallows movement led by orthodox Protestant ministers such as Cheever, Albert Baldwin Dod, Leonard Bacon, and Waterbury himself.[42] Signed "W," the open letter to editors of periodicals such as the *New York Evangelist* described the minister's conversation with the condemned before his execution as well as his witnessing of the hanging itself; it concluded with a political message, warning that "the effort made by many to do away capital punishment, if successful, would prove disastrous in the extreme."[43] A decade later, Waterbury took his pro-gallows campaign to the Massachusetts legislature, where he joined other ministers—including a somewhat reluctant Lyman Beecher (father of Harriet Beecher Stowe)—in defending capital punishment in a debate with anti-gallows activists, including Mrs. Catherine S. Brown (a Garrisonian), Reverend Charles Spear, Reverend Theodore Parker, Wendell Phillips, and William Lloyd Garrison.

Arguing against the "radicalism" of his opponents, Waterbury began by grounding his conservative position in American Puritan origins: "I belong to the conservative class, and am supposed to fear changes. It is dangerous to uproot an
institution that was planted by our Puritan fathers. Yet I find you solicited to uproot a long-existing law."[44] Taking a page from Cheever's famous defense, Waterbury underscored the centrality of Genesis 9:6 as the framework for any civil
government and defended his position from challenges raised by Parker, Spear,
and Phillips. Beecher hesitantly joined forces with Waterbury, approving the
conservative wisdom of his colleague's argument and questioning the "*facts* to
warrant such a change," although acknowledging his willingness to experiment
with abolition if—and only if—the reformers' "facts" prove true. "If not," Beecher
added, "I will thank God that we get rid of their views."[45]

Anticipating the terms of this debate yet responding directly to W's letter in
the *New York Evangelist* and elsewhere, Whittier's "Human Sacrifice" sought to
humanize the condemned murderer against the cold and cruel process of capital
punishment. Sentimental and symbolic, the poem revolves around the central
figure of the gallows and explores the thoughts of two individuals intimately connected to it: the condemned, confined to his cell, waiting death in an hour's
time; and the minister who presides over the ceremony, "Blessing with solemn
text and word / The gallows-drop and strangling cord" (62–63). The minister's
blessing here sanctions what Whittier's speaker on two occasions calls "the crime
of Law" (65, 105), a denigrating description of capital punishment that resonates
with the central image figured in the poem's title—"Human Sacrifice"—which
itself calls to mind a key component in the republican argument against the death
penalty articulated fifty years earlier in Benjamin Rush's provocative claim, "An
execution in a republic is like a human sacrifice in religion."

While Whittier's anti-gallows poems may have been occasioned by remarks
from pro-gallows clergymen, their publication in the *Democratic Review* served
another end. To the disappointment of O'Sullivan and the delight of Cheever,
the great British poet William Wordsworth had recently published a series of
sonnets in support of the death penalty.[46] In the March 1842 *Democratic Review*,
O'Sullivan laid the groundwork for a counterattack in a featured essay titled
"Wordsworth's Sonnets on the Punishment of Death." He began the essay by
expressing sad regret that the "great English master" had written "in justification
and support of the practice of Capital Punishment," which O'Sullivan described
as "one of the most hideous and horrible barbarisms yet lingering to disgrace the
statute-books of modern civilization."[47] O'Sullivan acknowledged that, because
of "the strongly conservative cast of his mind and political opinions," one could

not expect Wordsworth to come out in favor of abolition. "Yet," he continued, "to behold him take to the sacred lyre, and attune its chords to the harsh creaking of the scaffold and the clanking of the victim's chains, seems almost a profanation and a sacrilege—as though a harp of heaven were transported from its proper sphere and its congenial themes, to be struck by some impious hand to the foul and hideous harmonies of hell."[48]

Following these introductory remarks, O'Sullivan cites in full Wordsworth's fourteen "Sonnets on the Punishment of Death" and offers a stanza-by-stanza critique of them. In doing so, he does not focus on the tone and meter of Wordsworth's verse, as one might expect given his metaphor of the "sacred lyre" and his description of the "harsh creaking of the scaffold and the clanking of the victim's chains" to which the sonnets are tuned. Rather, he attends primarily to the political assumptions informing Wordsworth's position, exposing the false premises he finds in the sonnets and providing counterarguments to them. For instance, when Wordsworth's speaker celebrates the gallows as an instrument of deterrence, O'Sullivan references empirical evidence suggesting the contrary and, again, evokes the executioner as *the indirect cause of a far greater number [of murders] than he has ever punished or avenged.*"[49] Near the end of the essay, O'Sullivan employs a different strategy by citing in full an anti-gallows poem by Lydia Huntley Sigourney. By quoting Sigourney's "The Execution," O'Sullivan attempts to displace Wordsworth's "Sonnets" with imagery and poetic language that argue for abolition—an act realized, for O'Sullivan, in Whittier's poems subsequently published in the *Democratic Review*.

In November 1845, Walt Whitman joined the conversation in the *Democratic Review* with "A Dialogue," an imaginative essay that stages a debate between a condemned murderer and society on the eve of scheduled execution. Like Hawthorne's "The New Adam and Eve," Whitman's "A Dialogue" is framed as a parable, thus giving literary form to the many anti-gallows editorials and reports he had published elsewhere.[50] It begins by posing the following question: "What would be thought of a man who, having an ill humor in his blood, should strive to cure himself by only cutting off the festers, the outward signs of it, as they appeared upon the surface?"[51] Starting off in this way enables Whitman to foreground questions about social complicity and responsibility for criminal acts; the "man" represents society as a whole, whereas the "festers" signify criminals who are, in turn, "outward signs" of a diseased social body or body politic. As Whitman explains: "Put criminals for festers and society for the diseased man, and you may get the spirit of that part of our laws which expects to abolish wrong-doing by sheer terror—by cutting off the wicked, and taking no heed of the causes of the wickedness" (360). Following this short preamble, Whitman proceeds with the dialogue, which adopts and revises the criminal conversation narrative—a popular form of crime literature since the seventeenth century—by staging an exchange between "the imposing majesty of the people speaking on the one side, a pallid, shivering convict on the other" (360).

The convict initiates the discussion by admitting to have committed a "wrong . . . in an evil hour" when "a kind of frenzy came over me, and I struck my neighbor a heavy blow, which killed him" (360). Summarizing the convict's crime in this manner emphasizes murder as an act typically perpetrated in a heat of passion and committed by a person much different in mind and disposition from the one now awaiting execution. To the convict's admission of guilt, society flatly responds that "you must be killed in return" (361). When the convict then asks, "Is there no plan by which I can benefit my fellow-creatures, even at the risk of my own life?" society again replies tersely in the negative: "None . . . you must be strangled—choked to death. If your passions are so ungovernable that people are in danger from them, we shall hang you" (361). To this response the condemned asks "Why?" suggesting that incarceration in a strong prison would protect society from him and that he would gladly work while in prison to defray the expense of housing him there. Once again, society gives its blunt response of "No," adding this time that "we shall strangle you; your crime deserves it" (361), to which the "murderer" (as Whitman now refers to him) asks: "Have you, then, committed no crimes?" (361)

Putting society on the defensive enables Whitman's murderer to implicate "the people" in the production of crime. The dialogue now shifts to a discussion of a variety of crimes that, in society's words, have not "come within the clutches of any statute," but nonetheless lead daily to the ruination and even death of many (361). This inadvertent admission of guilt provides the convict the opportunity not only to comment generally on social responsibility, thereby implicating society in the cause of crimes, such as the one for which he himself is to be executed, but also to expose a double standard in a theory of justice, which holds that an individual, when sinned against, should forgive, while society ought to withhold forgiveness and exact payment in kind for murder. When the convict argues this latter point and asks why should not the people, like the individual, be guided by the principle of forgiveness, society responds: "The case is different . . . We are a community—you are but a single individual. You should forgive your enemies" (361). The condemned then poses a rhetorical question, which he answers by way of analogy:

"And are you not ashamed," asks the culprit, "to forget that as a community which you expect me to remember as a man? When the town clock goes wrong, shall each little private watch be abased for failing to keep the true time? What are communities but congregated individuals? And if you, in the potential force of your high position, deliberatively set examples of retribution, how dare you look to me for self-denial, forgiveness, and the meekest and most difficult virtues?" (361)

The convict's comparison of the "town clock" to "each little private watch" is telling. It suggests that the internal watches (or alarm clocks) of each private citizen are set according to the town clock, which is held up as a model. Therefore, when society sets the example of retribution when a murder is committed, how can the people expect an individual, when provoked or enraged, to act according to a different and higher standard? The convict reinforces this point by saying that he killed simply because his "blood was up" (361), even though he knew the lawful penalty for such a crime would be death.

With society now squarely on the defensive, the convict mounts an assault upon the death penalty, deploying a series of questions that "the people" cannot answer satisfactorily. Through Whitman's Socratic dialogue (with the murderer playing Socrates' part), readers of the *Democratic Review* are thus left with a clear sense of the moral horrors and contradictions of a justice system that not only condemns lethal violence by using such violence itself but hypocritically demands forgiveness from its private citizens for acts it deems unforgivable. Near the end of "A Dialogue," the conversation takes a contentious turn when the issue of the death penalty's spectacle of violence is broached. Both the convict and society agree that the spectacle of an execution is "degrading and anti-humanizing" (362), and the people congratulate themselves on the passage of recent laws making executions in many states "private." The convict, however, points out that executions are still public in many states and, more importantly, that so-called private executions are by no means "private" when "everybody reads newspapers, and every newspaper seeks for graphic accounts of these executions," so that "such things can never be private" (362). Continuing in this vein, the convict accuses newspapers and various print media of carrying out, as it were, *literary executions*: pictorial depictions of lawful death that make the act present and palpable in the mind's eye. Thus, he disabuses the people of the notion that executions have become private and less visible in society. In fact, the convict argues precisely the opposite point, using press coverage of political acts in Congress as a heuristic analogue for executions dramatized literarily for the tens of thousands of newspaper readers:

> What a small portion of your citizens are eye-witnesses of things done in Congress; yet they are surely not private, for not a word officially spoken in the Halls of the Capitol, but is through the press made as public as if every American's ear were within hearing distance of the speaker's mouth. The whole spectacle of these . . . executions is more faithfully seen, and more deliberately dwelt upon, through the printed narratives, than if people beheld it with their bodily eyes, and then no more. Print preserves it. It passes from hand to hand, and even boys and girls are imbued with its spirit and horrid essence. Your legislators have forbidden public executions; they must go farther. They must forbid the relation of them by tongue, letter, or picture; for your physical sight is not the only avenue through which the subtle virus will reach you. Nor is the effect lessened because it is more covert and more widely diffused. Rather, indeed, the reverse. As things are, the masses take it for granted that the system and its results are right. (362–63)

By advocating restrictions upon the press and its coverage of executions, Whitman's convict pushes the argument forbidding the representation of lawful executions further than Whitman himself would take it.[52] After all, in publishing "A Dialogue" Whitman participates in the very discursive activity against which his convict speaks. And Whitman, the journalist, did go on to publish other such pieces, including a bitterly sarcastic article, "Hurrah for Hanging!," in the March 23 issue of the *Brooklyn Daily Eagle* (1846). That article, Whitman writes in the piece, was occasioned by "the butcher[ing] of five human beings last week in Cayuga co., in this state—as we have already published the dark and dreadful narrative." He went on to conclude the *Daily Eagle* report by ironically urging readers to "let the law keep up with the murderer, and see who will get the victory at last."[53] Yet Whitman's political agitation did not stop there. He also promoted the discussion of reports concerning capital punishment in the meetings and social activism of the Brooklyn Association for the Abolition of the Death Penalty, an organization Whitman cofounded in 1846.

Nonetheless, the point Whitman's sympathetic convict makes is an important one: the so-called privatization of lawful hangings in no way diminishes the psychological impact they may have upon society. Indeed, the proliferation of "printed narratives" ("A Dialogue" 362) of executions occurred in large part because the actual spectacle of lawful violence had moved behind prison walls and had therefore become much less visible. For this reason, and because of the unprecedented debates about capital punishment in the decades preceding the Civil War, one could follow the convict and say that executions in the 1840s and early 1850s had never before been so public.

## CAPITAL PUNISHMENT AND CLASSIC AMERICAN LITERATURE

More public than ever before, the great debates over the death penalty in the nineteenth century have, until recently, been largely forgotten by scholars of American literature. Yet a case can be made that the controversy surrounding capital punishment should be seen as a crucial part of the context for the flowering of the "American Renaissance" in the early 1850s. Whitman, of course, was a crucial figure in that movement, and if, as David S. Reynolds has suggested, Whitman's 1846 article "Hurrah for Hanging!" was likely influenced by "Hurrah for the Gallows!" (*Quaker* xxxi), a sardonic chapter lampooning capital punishment in George Lippard's *The Quaker City*[54] (1845), then the debates about capital punishment themselves lie "beneath" the American Renaissance and constitute some of the roots that led to the invigoration of American literature at midcentury.

In fact, these debates have left an indelible imprint on many works by classic American Renaissance writers. There is, for instance, the famous opening of Nathaniel Hawthorne's *The Scarlet Letter* (1850), which stages the scene of capital punishment even though an execution itself does not occur. Drawing upon the dramaturgy of the death penalty, the novel begins with the image of "The Prison Door," out of which Hester Prynne emerges like a "condemned criminal" coming "forth to his doom."[55] Readers are then told that the crowd gathered to witness Hester's punishment "betokened nothing short of the anticipated execution of some noted culprit, on whom the sentence of a legal tribunal had but confirmed the verdict of public sentiment."[56] And just before the punishment commences, some of the spectators push their way forward as if to be "nearest to the scaffold at an execution."[57] Even the dialogue among these spectators concerns the place and purpose of capital punishment: "This woman has brought shame upon us all and ought to die," a matronly woman declares. "Is there not law for it? Truly there is, both in the Scripture and the statute-book." In response, a man from the crowd asks, "is there no virtue in woman, save what springs from a wholesome fear of the gallows?"[58]

Hester, of course, is not executed; neither she nor the crowd expects such a punishment to occur. Nonetheless, her presence upon the scaffold around which the community gathers plays off and becomes part of the cultural ritual of capital punishment that is dramatized in many popular antebellum novels, stories, and works of creative nonfiction—the subject of my next two chapters. Such literature was influenced by, and likely influenced, the anti-gallows writings of reformers like Rantoul, O'Sullivan, and Charles Spear, the founding editor of Massachusetts's *The Hangman* and *The Prisoner's Friend*, periodicals dedicated to the abolition of capital punishment. Hawthorne, for one, probably knew the writings of Spear, a tireless prison reformer who may have inspired the character of Hollingsworth in Hawthorne's *The Blithedale Romance*,[59] and he certainly knew those of O'Sullivan and Rantoul. O'Sullivan, of course, was a close friend of Hawthorne's (whose children knew him as "Uncle John," their godfather), whereas Rantoul served as an attorney for the defense in Salem's famous 1830 Joseph Knapp murder trial, an important source Hawthorne drew upon when writing *The House of the Seven Gables* (1851). What is more, Hawthorne himself was an voracious reader of gallows literature and criminal reports like the *Record of Crimes in the United States*, and while an undergraduate at Bowdoin College he devoured novels by John Neal, the author of *Logan* whose execution scene and dialogue I began this chapter by analyzing.[60]

Published the same year as Hawthorne's *The Scarlet Letter*, Herman Melville's *White Jacket; or, the World in a Man-of-War* (1850) contains one of the most overtly dramatic enactments of a death "sentence" *as such* in antebellum literature. The scene takes place in chapter 70, "Monthly Muster Round the Capstan," and offers an intersubjective response to the death sentence as a linguistic act. In it White Jacket, Melville's principled yet good-natured narrator, describes an event singular but hardly exceptional in the world of a man-of-war: the reading of the Articles of War, the U.S. Navy's code of prohibitions and punishments. Melville stages the gravity of the monthly muster, "rendered even terrible," White-Jacket says, "by the reading of the Articles of War by the captain's clerk before the assembled ship's company, who, in testimony of their enforced reverence for the code, stand bareheaded till the last sentence is pronounced."[61] White-Jacket continues:

> To a mere amateur reader the quiet perusal of these Articles of War would be attended with some nervous emotions. Imagine, then, what *my* feelings must have been, when, with my hat deferentially in my hand, I stood before my lord and master, Captain Claret, and heard these Articles read as the law and gospel, the infallible, unappealable, dispensation and code, whereby I lived, and moved, and had my being on board of the United States Ship *Neversink*.
>
> Of some twenty offences—made penal—that a seaman may commit, and which are specified in this code, thirteen are punishable by death.

"*Shall suffer death!*" This was the burden of nearly every Article read by the captain's clerk; for he seemed to have been instructed to omit the longer Articles, and only present those which were brief and to the point.

"*Shall suffer death!*" The repeated announcement falls on your ear like the intermitting discharge of artillery. After it has been repeated again and again, you listen to the reader as he deliberately begins a new paragraph; you hear him reciting the involved, but comprehensive and clear arrangement of the sentence, detailing all possible particulars of the offence described, and you breathlessly await, whether that clause also is going to be concluded by the discharge of the terrible minute-gun. When, lo! it again booms on your ear— *shall suffer death!* No reservations, no contingencies; not the remotest promise of pardon or reprieve; not a glimpse of commutation of the sentence; all hope and consolation is shut out—*shall suffer death!* (292–93, emphasis in original)

The passage begins with marked solemnity, as White Jacket notes how each sailor's subjectivity is constituted through the Articles of War, a document "read as the law and gospel, the infallible, unappealable, dispensation and code, whereby I lived, and moved, and had my being on board of the United States Ship *Neversink.*" The passage also starts off matter-of-factly, stating the number of penal offenses under military law and specifying that thirteen of the twenty are "punishable by death." It then shifts dramatically in tone and perspective as White Jacket cites the operative phrase of these thirteen statutes, "*Shall suffer death!*," and provides his subjective response to it. Moving from the first-person, past tense to the second-person, present tense, Melville puts readers in the position of the sailors (the potentially condemned) upon whose ears the death sentence falls "like the intermitting discharge of artillery," and to whom they ("you") "listen to the reader as he deliberately begins a new paragraph," which ends with the same terrible injunction, "*shall suffer death!*" Within the scene, the "reader" (i.e., captain's clerk) plays the role of executioner, his reading taking shape as a carefully delivered performance to maximize fear and promote terror. Indeed, White-Jacket tells us the reader seems even "to have been instructed to omit the longer Articles, and only present those which were brief and to the point." Again, particularly to the point is the Articles' operative phrase. Exclamatory and italicized throughout, the repeated "*shall suffer death!*" embodies the letter of the law and, within the context of the chapter, functions as a leitmotif or poetic refrain pronounced eight times over the course of three pages. To each iteration, White-Jacket responds with ironic commentary that dialogizes the monologic letter of the law, exposing its tyranny and opening it up to criticism and ridicule.

In addition to influencing the work of Melville, Hawthorne, Whitman, and Whittier, the debate over capital punishment affected both Emerson and Thoreau. Holding a theory of individual rights and the state very close to Rantoul's and using the motto of O'Sullivan's *Democratic Review* to start his famous essay on civil disobedience, Thoreau made his own argument against hanging as a deterrent to crime in "A Plea for John Brown" (1859). In that speech, which was delivered on several occasions in the weeks following the raid upon Harper's Ferry, Thoreau turned the imminent execution of John Brown into a call for continued and even violent disobedience to laws supporting slavery. He also deified Brown, transforming him into a martyr as well as an executioner of a higher law. Near the end of the plea, Thoreau went so far as to say, "Some eighteen hundred years ago Christ was crucified; this morning, perchance, Captain Brown was hung. These are two ends of a chain which is not without its links."[62]

As Paul Jones has recently shown, the anti-gallows movement was an important cause for Emerson. In articulating his notion of the "believer," Emerson defined such an individual as "poet, saint, democrat, theocrat, free-trader, no-church, no capital punishment, idealist."[63] In the 1850s, as the crises over slavery came to a head, Emerson pronounced the "abolition of capital punishment," along with "emancipation" and efforts "to abolish kingcraft, feudalism, black-letter monopoly" as essential to what he called the "marked ethical quality" of the "American idea."[64] Like Thoreau, he saw this idealism personified in the (misguided) heroism of John Brown, whose impending death sentence would, Emerson infamously declared in a widely quoted speech, make "the gallows as glorious as the Cross."[65] Connecting the evils of slavery and capital punishment in public speech, Emerson would privately explore their interconnections in an unsent letter he wrote to Governor Wise protesting Brown's execution and defending the condemned as a mad idealist.[66]

Considerable energy has been devoted—and rightly so, as I suggested in my introduction—to revising our understanding of the American Renaissance in terms of race and the campaign to abolish slavery. In this opening chapter, I have laid the groundwork for understanding the American Renaissance in terms of that "other" antebellum abolition movement, a movement still unfulfilled in a country that once was a worldwide leader in a campaign to keep the state from exercising the power to curtail the most important civil liberty of all—life.[67] In the chapters that follow, I build upon this foundation through close attention to literature in relation to the death penalty and the national campaign for its abolition from the 1830s through the first quarter of the twentieth century.

# CHAPTER 2

# Simms, Child, and the Aesthetics of Crime and Punishment

A Murder in a novel, though a very common occurrence, is usually a matter of a thousand very thrilling minutiae. In the hands of a score of our modern romancers, it is surprising what capital they make of it! How it runs through a score of chapters!—admits of a variety of details, descriptions, commentaries, and conjectures! Take any of the great raconteurs of the European world—not forgetting Dumas and Reynolds—and see what they will do with it! How they turn it over, and twist it about, as a sweet morsel under the tongue! In either of these hands, it becomes one of the most prolific sources of interest; which does not end with the knife or bludgeon stroke, or bullet-shot, but multiplies its relations the more it is conned, and will swallow up half the pages of an ordinary duodecimo.

*Simms*, Beauchampe; or, The Kentucky Tragedy (1842; *rev. 1856*)

In editing his popular novel *Beauchampe* for a "New & Revised" edition in 1856, William Gilmore Simms thought anew about "A Murder in a novel."[1] Since *Beauchampe* was first published in 1842, the literary marketplace had become glutted with fictive accounts and explorations of crime, capital trials, and criminal justice following the revolution in print technology in the early 1830s.[2] Not that the market had not been saturated with such work before then. To be sure, part of the reason Simms wrote *Beauchampe* in the first place was to capitalize on the public's interest in and demand for crime fiction, a genre in which he had begun writing in 1829 with the publication of "The Story of a Criminal," which became the basis of his first short novel, *Martin Faber* (1833). In revising *Beauchampe*, Simms made few substantive changes to the narrative proper,[3] but those he did make usually occurred in passages dealing with murder or with the legal response of capital punishment.

Simms's meditation on "A Murder in a novel," significantly elaborated in the 1856 revision of *Beauchampe*, begins a long, intrusive chapter immediately following the novel's central event: murder. In it, Simms's narrator reflects on the thematic as both topic and trope in popular literature, noting how, in the hands of "our modern romancers," it not only prompts endless speculation but helps give dramatic shape to novels that involve or revolve around murder—many of them, like *Beauchampe*, culminating with execution scenes or offering explicit commentary about the lawful administration of death. Simms's reflections, as we shall see, provide a kind of metacommentary on a dominant literary aesthetic of the age, an aesthetics of crime and punishment that has important political ramifications when read in light of the national anti-gallows movement and against the influential countermovement, led by a conservative Presbyterian ministry, to defend the place and purpose of the gallows.[4]

That aesthetic, of course, was nothing new. As Daniel A. Cohen has convincingly shown, American popular culture had its origins in the execution sermon and related gallows literature, such as criminal (auto)biographies, criminal conversation narratives, and trial reports.[5] Popular since the late seventeenth century, these forms of early crime literature would later compete in the literary marketplace with novels and short fiction—from Charles Brockden Brown's *Wieland* (1798), which culminates with murder and a capital trial based, like Simms's *Beauchampe*, on an actual case—to Edgar Allan Poe's classic murder tales, including "The Black Cat" (1843) and "The Imp of the Perverse" (1845), which were written from the perspective of killers awaiting the gallows. Countless other writers from "beneath" the American Renaissance (Ned Buntline, Osgood Bradbury, George Lippard, William Starbuck Mayo, George Thompson, Elizabeth Oakes Smith, E. D. E. N. Southworth, Day Kellogg Lee, and Ben Boaz, to name a few) would plot their work around murder, and many of them would also explicitly comment on the lawful practice of capital punishment. One canonical writer to do so was James Fenimore Cooper, whose final work, *The Ways of the Hour* (1850), is perhaps the first novel entirely structured around a murder case and its concomitant courtroom drama—a point used to advertise a recent reprint of Cooper's now-forgotten novel.[6] Cooper's midcentury novel, like the many that Simms wrote, overtly responded to an interstate campaign to abolish the gallows, but so did many other novels that drew upon the drama of the death penalty. One such work was lawyer-novelist John Ludlum McConnel's *The Glenns: A Family History* (1851), which provided a case study in the hereditary traits and environmental circumstances that made one a criminal.[7]

Centered around a murder for which an innocent man is arrested and tried, *The Glenns* calls attention to the inherent drama of the death penalty while noting the presence of the anti-gallows movement. "Independently of any speculations about the propriety or expediency of capital punishment," begins a chapter midway through the narrative, "a trial at bar, where the issue is life or death to the accused, is one of the most astounding spectacles to be seen in a civilized land. It may be an arrogant assumption in society to claim the right to take human life; but if it be so, it is equally so to pretend that an individual may do so without blame in self-defence; for it is only this which justifies capital punishment."[8] In another novel, published the same year as *The Glenns*, Daniel Thompson similarly foregrounds the drama of a capital trial when his protagonist is arrested midway through volume 1 of *The Rangers; or, The Tory's Daughter* (1851). "Whatever may be the result of the present public movement for the abolition of capital punishment," chapter 6 begins,

> and however far future experiments may go towards establishing the expediency and safety of such a change in criminal jurisprudence, the history of every nation and people will show, we believe, the remarkable fact, that ever since Cain stood before his Maker with his hands reeking with the blood of his murdered brother, and his heart so deeply smitten with the consciousness of having justly forfeited his own life by taking the life of another, that he could not divest himself of the belief that all men would seek to slay him, no one principle has been found to be more deeply implanted in the human breast than the desire to see the wilful shedding of blood atoned for by the blood of the perpetrator. So strong, so active, and so impelling, indeed, seems this principle, that no sooner goes forth the dread tale of homicide, than all community rise up, as one man, instinctively impressed with the duty of hunting down the guilty and bringing them to justice; while the guilty themselves seem no less instinctively impressed with the abiding consciousness that the doom, which heaven and earth has decreed to their crimes, must inevitably overtake them.[9]

Whereas McConnel in *The Glenns* questions capital punishment, justifying it only in cases of self-defense, Thompson makes a case for the practice by drawing on the universal principle of guilt embodied in Cain and "the desire to see the wilful shedding of blood atoned for by the blood of the perpetrator," a principle "deeply implanted in the human breast." This pair of 1851 novels, with the question of the gallows at their structural centers, illustrates an obvious point that perhaps ought to be explicitly stated: an author, of course, need not be *against* capital punishment to use an execution or the drama of a capital trial as a structuring principle. Novelists trained in law from Charles Brockden Brown and his turn-of-the-nineteenth-century gothic tales to Thomas Dixon and his turn-of-the-twentieth-century racist thrillers capitalized on the scene of capital punishment without objecting to the lawful punishment of death. Many writers, however, did. Published at midcentury, along with Cooper's *The Ways of the Hour*, Thompson's and McConnel's novels are thus representative of a broader cultural aesthetic of crime and capital punishment that had moved into the specific literary form of the novel. Again, that aesthetic has a long history in popular American print culture, but novels did not become a dominant form through which crime and criminal behavior were critically explored in the United States until Simms began writing them in the early 1830s.

Focusing on plot construction and character development, this chapter introduces a view on the aesthetics of crime and capital punishment that informs each of the chapters to follow.[10] In it, I concentrate on two of the period's most popular and well-respected writers who, on almost all political issues, took diametrically opposed positions but nonetheless found a common cause in opposing the death penalty. The first is Simms. While largely forgotten today, Simms was a major figure in American literature from the early 1830s until the Civil War. Dubbed "the Cooper of the South" and the only novelist of the period to rival that author in terms of both critical and popular success, Simms did more than any other antebellum literary figure to shape southern culture as it was then known. He edited three prominent southern magazines during his life and published more than eighty books (including poetry, geography, history, biography, and literary criticism, in addition to the two dozen novels he wrote).[11] Among Simms's most popular work were his "Border Romances," a series of novels, spanning two decades, that were structured around a central crime (usually murder) and unfolded in southern borderlands and featured murderers, outlaws, organized crime gangs, lynch mobs, and private citizens who took the law into their own hands. Edgar Allan Poe, who criticized Simms's more sensational work, thought well enough of the author to champion him in 1845 as "the best novelist which this country has, on the whole, produced."[12]

Yet Simms offers an important perspective on the aesthetics of crime and punishment not only because of his popularity and critical success but because, unlike Poe and many other writers of popular crime fiction, he was trained in the law. In 1826, at the age of twenty-one, Simms was admitted to the bar in Charleston, South Carolina; he practiced law there until 1833, when he gave up being a lawyer to pursue a career in literature. Although Simms would end up leaving his legal practice, he stayed with law in theory. Much of his fiction dealt in some way with criminal law (a good deal of it with capital punishment), and in 1842, in part because of his treatment of legal themes in his fiction, he was awarded an L.L.D. from the University of Alabama. Simms's career in law and literature led to a brief one in politics. Always outspoken on political matters, he served in the House of Representatives for South Carolina from 1844 to 1846, leaving his seat the end of his second term to run as a last-minute candidate for the state's lieutenant governorship—a campaign he lost by a very slim margin.[13]

My second writer is Lydia Maria Child, a radical northerner who was a leader in the movement to abolish slavery and a noted women's rights advocate. Christened in 1829 by William Lloyd Garrison as "the first woman of the republic," Child was a major voice in antebellum culture as well as an important novelist, essayist, polemicist, and short-story writer. Today her life and work are much better known than Simms's, but what remains relatively unknown about Child is her fierce commitment to the campaign to abolish capital punishment.[14] Little more than a footnote in standard biographies of her life, Child's anti-gallows writing profoundly shaped the cause for abolition and influenced some of its key advocates, such as Universalist minister Charles Spear, who published Child's work in his anti-gallows journals and quoted authoritatively from her *Letters from New York* in his popular book, *Essays on the Abolition of Capital Punishment* (1844).[15] Though she never officially joined an anti-gallows organization, Child's influence on the movement is incalculable. As one historian of the death penalty has speculated in passing, "It is likely that one of her published letters, read by the thousands, had a greater effect on public sentiment than the numerous resolutions passed by all the anti-gallows societies combined."[16]

If Child's New York letters, "read by the thousands," shaped public sentiment against capital punishment in significant ways, Simms's Border Romances, commanding a comparable audience, must have affected something similar in the minds of his wide readership. However, while united in their shared interest in crime and the anti-gallows movement, Simms and Child were otherwise opposite numbers. It would indeed be difficult to find an odder pair of bedfellows in American literature than the liberal New Englander, a leader in the movement to abolish slavery, and the conservative Southron, who would become a vigorous defender of slavery and a spokesperson for southern culture and succession, and whose historical romance *Woodcraft* (1852; rev. 1854) has been read as the South's response to Stowe's *Uncle Tom's Cabin*.[17] That two figures, from opposing ends of the political spectrum, could find common ground in attacking the institution

of capital punishment says a great deal about the power of the anti-gallows movement in shaping the development of antebellum literature, in addition to how
that reform movement was, in turn, shaped by this literature.

This shared interest, however, gives rise to a crucial difference in terms of
what I am calling each author's aesthetics of crime and punishment. While both
structure much of their gallows writing around execution scenes as travesties of
justice rather than just punishments, they differ significantly in their representations of crime. Child, on the one hand, shies away from dramatizing criminal
acts themselves and accounts for them by sociological and environmental factors; society, for her, is not only largely responsible for creating criminals but
furthers its encouragement of crime by setting the bad example of lawful violence. Simms, on the other hand, obsesses over the details of criminal acts and
focuses on the criminal mind as a complicated paradox of human nature itself.
While sharing some of Child's concern in upbringing and environment in the
social construction of the criminal subject, Simms's primary interest lies in the
irrational passions and desires that compel criminal behavior. In this respect,
Simms is closer to a writer like Dostoevsky in that his novels evoke a psychological realism that emphasizes the principle of atonement and that forces us to
stretch our understanding of what it means to be human. Albeit sentimental in
style and subject, Child's work, in contrast to Simms's, tends toward a literary
realism influenced by principles we would now associate with sociology and exemplified in a writer like Dreiser, whose great crime novel provides the focus of
my final chapter. I begin this one, however, with the construction of the criminal
and the aesthetics of capital punishment in Simms's *Guy Rivers* (1834), the first of
his popular Border Romances.

### "GREAT CRIMINALS"

Writing what he later called his first "regular novel,"[18] Simms turned to a tried-
and-true formula: a murder novel—the kind of work he would come to celebrate
in *Beauchampe*. Revolving around a murder for which the novel's protagonist is
wrongfully convicted and sentenced to death, *Guy Rivers* chronicles the adventures of Ralph Colleton, a young South Carolinian aristocratic-farmer who, frus-
trated in love, has left home to try his luck in the border region of Georgia. That
murder is actually committed by Guy Rivers, Colleton's nemesis and the novel's
namesake. Colleton, as Simms's critics have noted, is little more than a stereo-
typical southern gentleman; Rivers, on the other hand, commands attention.[19] A
crafty, unscrupulous lawyer-turned-criminal, Rivers leads a gang of outlaws on
the Georgia frontier, as does the gang leader Clement Foster in Alabama terri-

tory in Simms's later Border Romance, *Richard Hurdis* (1838). Early in *Guy Rivers*, Simms sets the stage for the landscape of crime, violence, and desperadoes that makes up the terrain in many of his subsequent Border Romances: "The wild condition of the country—the absence of all civil authority, and almost of laws," he writes of Georgia's borderlands, "certainly of officers sufficiently daring to undertake their honest administration, and shrinking from the risk of incurring, in the performance of their duties, the vengeance of those, who, though disagreeing among themselves, at all time made common cause against the ministers of justice as against a common enemy—may readily account for the frequency and impunity with which these desperate men committed crime and defied its consequences."[20] Bereft of "all civil authority, and almost of laws," the social environment about which Simms writes is one in which the criminal justice system is not only slow in action and weak in administration but manipulated by banditti who have influence over state officials and judges.

As the first of the Border Romances, *Guy Rivers* also lays the ground for Simms's inquiry into criminal behavior and capital punishment, a recurrent topic in much of his later fiction. Significantly, that inquiry is first broached in terms of a literary aesthetics and articulated by Rivers—the novel's titular hero, or rather antihero—in an extended speech he delivers shortly before committing the murder for which young Colleton is framed. Speaking to Wat Munro, his confidant and cohort in crime, Rivers rhapsodizes about "great criminals," a category within which he classifies "the best heroes of the best poets" (244). Without such criminals in both life and literature, Rivers asks, "from what would the interest be drawn?—where would be the incident, if all men, pursuing the quiet paths of noninterference with the rights, the lives, or the liberties of one another, spilt no blood, invaded no territory, robbed no lord of his lady, enslaved and made no captives in war? A virtuous hero would be a useless personage both in play and poem—and the spectator or reader would fall asleep over the utterance of stale apothegms" (244). To underscore this point about the aesthetic value of crime, Rivers cites—of all things—an execution scene, a familiar example with which, he explains to Munro, "the million" would agree: "Look, for instance, at the execution of a criminal. See the thousands that will assemble, day after day, after traveling miles for that single object, to gape and gaze upon the last agonizing pangs and paroxysms of a fellow-creature—not regarding for an instant the fatigue of their position, the press of the crowd, or the loss of a dinner—totally insusceptible, it would seem, of the several influences of heat and cold, wind and rain, which at any other time would drive them to their beds or firesides" (244). Rivers's rhapsody continues in this vein for several pages. With only a few interruptions and interjections from Munro, he goes on to speak about criminal propensities and the motives that drive great men (such as himself) to commit crime, as well as social pressures and environmental circumstances that encourage criminal behavior, but he ends by returning to the execution example: "Think you, Munro, that the thousands who assemble at the execution of a criminal trouble themselves to inquire into the merits of his case—into the justice of his death and punishment? Ask they whether he is the victim of justice or of tyranny? No! they go to see a show—they love blood, and in this way have they enjoyment furnished to their hands, without the risk which must follow the shedding of it for themselves" (247).

In his analysis of public executions, Rivers develops an attack on the spectacle of lawful violence that one finds in early anti-gallows law and literature, such as John Neal's *Logan* (1822) and Edward Livingston's *Report* (1822), both examined in chapter 1. While sharing Neal's and Livingston's concern for the psychology of spectatorship, Rivers's argument differs in at least one crucial respect: it stresses the aesthetic dimension of an execution, calling attention to the subjective "interest" viewers derive from its dramatic unfolding. Rivers's argument also calls to mind a classic example from Edmund Burke's aesthetic theory in which the sensation of a public execution is compared to the high drama of "the most sublime and affecting" theatrical performance. "Chuse a day," Burke writes,

> on which to represent the most sublime and affecting tragedy we have; appoint the most favourite actors; spare no cost upon the scenes and decorations; unite the greatest efforts of poetry, painting and music; and when you have collected your audience, just at the moment when their minds are erect with expectation, let it be reported that a state criminal of high rank is on the point of being executed in the adjoining square; in a moment the emptiness of the theater would demonstrate the comparative weakness of the imitative arts, and proclaim the triumph of real sympathy.[21]

Simms's execution example, like Burke's, emphasizes the theatricality of state violence and conveys a derisive attitude toward popular interest in a criminal's public death. It ends, however, on a different note: "The same motive which provokes this desire in the spectator," Rivers concludes after citing the first of his execution examples, "is the parent, to a certain extent, of the very crime which has lead to the exhibition" (280). Linking the spectator's desire to witness law's violence to the illicit violence it seeks to condemn rehearses a familiar argument about the psychology of violence and spectatorship, one that would become a mainstay in the anti-gallows movement in the decades preceding the Civil War.

John L. O'Sullivan, we have seen, made particular use of that argument in his widely read *Report in Favor of the Abolition of the Punishment of Death by Law* (1841). For O'Sullivan, as for Benjamin Rush and Edward Livingston before him, the spectacle of law's violence produced more murders than it ever deterred. If for O'Sullivan capital punishment encouraged extralegal violence, for Rivers the desire to see that violence stemmed from the impulse to commit murder. In this respect, Rivers, a great criminal in the tradition of Jonathan Wilde or John A. Murrell (the infamous land pirate after whom Rivers was likely, in part, modeled),[22] sounds very much like a reformer, an abolitionist such as O'Sullivan, in his denunciation of executions as a blood sport rather than an effective means of deterrence. Rivers thus serves as a means through which Simms expresses anti-gallows sentiment, but this perspective is obviously problematic, given that it comes from a character who soon commits murder and who is himself "outlawed and under sentence" for an undisclosed crime committed before the action of the narrative begins (242). Rivers's ethos as a spokesperson is therefore compromised, but he is not the only character in the novel to speak out against the death penalty. Others make similar, if less pronounced, remarks in opposition to the gallows. For instance, Lucy Munro, the admirable niece and stepdaughter of Wat Munro, imagines the horrible details of Ralph Colleton's impending execution in a scene that echoes Rivers's criticism of the spectacle of lawful violence. Edith Colleton, Ralph's cousin and love interest, reacts similarly when she realizes that her lover's execution is all but certain. It is, however, from Simms's narrator that we get an anti-gallows statement to match the intensity of Rivers's. That statement unfolds in the novel's concluding pages, comprising what may be the novel's central statement; but before turning to it, we must first gauge the novel's participation in the movement to reform capital statutes.

As a popular and critical success, *Guy Rivers* can be seen not only as reflecting anti-gallows sentiment but as participating in the campaign to move executions behind prison walls—a campaign that was a significant component of the broader movement to abolish capital punishment, although not everyone who opposed public executions also opposed the death penalty itself. When the novel was published in 1834, two states (Connecticut in 1830 and Rhode Island 1833) had recently abolished public executions. Over the next two years, however, five others—including New York, where Simms's novel was first published—would ban the practice from public view.[23] *Guy Rivers* may not have directly impacted this shift in the lawful administration of death, but it would be a mistake to underestimate the role Simms's novel and like-minded work played in effecting this change in public sentiment—a point to which I will return in the conclusion of this chapter. At the same time, though, it would be a mistake to identify *Guy Rivers* as abolitionist in orientation or to conclude that its primary purpose was to effect a change in the administration of capital laws. If Simms used the novel to criticize what he considered the shameful practice of capital punishment, at the same time he shamelessly drew upon the drama of the death penalty and the promise of an impending execution to generate the kind of sensation against which Rivers rails in "The Bloody Deed," the chapter that ends with the murder for which Colleton is framed. The novel then moves dramatically through the pursuit, capture, trial, and conviction of Colleton, a sequence of events Simms's training in law enables him to handle adroitly and with convincing detail. *Guy Rivers* ends with an execution, or near execution (a last-minute suicide is committed)—but not that of Colleton. Justice ultimately prevails, as it often does in popular novels, and it is Rivers, the real killer, who is convicted of the murder for which an innocent man was initially sentenced to die.

In the tradition of the Newgate novel and early American gallows literature, *Guy Rivers* concludes with a focused study of its notorious criminal subject.[24] Indeed, the narrator tells us a good deal about Rivers in the novel's final chapters. We learn, for instance, that Guy Rivers is really Edward Creighton, formerly an ambitious young lawyer and up-and-coming politician from Carolina who is wanted for the murder of one Judge Jessup (the undisclosed crime alluded to early in the narrative). The particulars of the Jessup murder are never divulged, thus making the killing of a judge symbolic of Rivers's attack upon the establishment and law and order itself, rather than a significant feature of the novel's subplot. We learn even more about Rivers in the last chapter, "Last Scene of All," which, as its title suggests, draws from the conventional ending of popular exeution sermons, criminal biographies, and court reports that often dramatized the "last scene" or final hours of the condemned's life.[25] While Rivers awaits the gallows, Simms's third-person narrator takes us into the mind of the criminal as, according to Lisa Rodensky, only a novel can. For unlike legal discourse, which necessarily draws conclusions about its criminal subjects from evidence outside an individual's mind, the novel grants direct access to the minds of its characters and thus enables an examination of criminal intent unavailable through law, biography, or even psychology.[26]

In a paragraph from *Guy Rivers* beginning "The mind of Guy Rivers had been one of the strongest make—one of large and leading tendencies," Simms's narrator opens up the mind of his criminal to get at the source of his behavior. That behavior, we learn, has resulted from three interrelated factors: first, a passionate and ambitious nature that is biologically inherited; second, the lack of a "governing principle," either absent from his genetic makeup or not provided by his parents or through schooling; and, finally, a related and crucial factor, a poor education and moral training, for which Rivers's overly indulgent mother is principally to blame (430). Because of the environmental and biological factors that have contributed to Rivers's criminal behavior, Simms's narrator sympathizes with Rivers instead of condemning him as innately depraved and worthy of death: "Unhappily," we are told, "[Rivers] had not been permitted a choice." Without a choice, without a say in the criminal propensities he inherited and "the [mis]education of his youth" (430), Rivers should *not*, Simms suggests, be held fully responsible for his crimes and hanged for them. He is not a "moral aberration" or "moral alien," as Karen Halttunen has characterized the murderer in popular American print culture from the mid-eighteenth century onward.[27] Instead, he is the product of "the contradictions of the strong mind," a "subject" that "we daily see" and at which we "wondering[ly] . . . gaze, with unreasonable and unthinking astonishment" (430).

From this prognosis, Simms moves outside the narrative proper of *Guy Rivers* to appeal directly to reformers and social thinkers in theorizing a way to understand crime and criminal behavior: "Our philosophers," his narrator says, speaking in the collective first person,

> are content with declaiming upon effects—they will not permit themselves or others to trace them up to their causes. To heal the wound, the physician may probe and find out its depth and extent; the same privilege is not often conceded to the physician of the mind or of the morals, else numberless diseases, now seemingly incurable, had been long since brought within the healing scope of philosophical analysis. The popular cant would have us forbear even to look at the history of the criminal. Hang the wretch, say they, but say nothing about him. (443)

With so much of the novel clearly written for popular entertainment, Simms foregrounds the novel's moral lesson in the key paragraph from which I have been quoting. But rather than justifying the condemned's execution as a cautionary tale to promote good behavior—a commonplace of conventional gallows literature—he offers up his criminal subject for psychological investigation, placing him within the novel's "healing scope of philosophical analysis." Drawing an analogy to the physician's work in medicine, he prompts "the physician of the mind or of the morals" to see crime as a social disease rather than the willful act of an innately depraved individual. Moreover, he challenges such moral or mental physicians to resist the knee-jerk reaction expressed in the "popular cant" of the day: "Hang the wretch, they say, but say nothing about him."

Simms provides a similar diagnosis of criminal behavior in *Martin Faber* (1833), a novella he wrote while working on *Guy Rivers*. Subtitled *The Story of a Criminal, Martin Faber* is considered one of the earliest explorations of criminal psychology in American fiction.[28] The tale itself is told from the perspective of a condemned murderer awaiting execution. Like *Guy Rivers*, the story's criminal-protagonist and namesake is a passionate individual whose criminal propensities largely stem from a poor education. Faber avails us of these facts, but so does Simms, the "author" (the story was published anonymously) in the work's preface: "When the author speaks of education," Simms explains when first introducing the term, "he does not so much refer to that received at the school and the academy. He would be understood to indicate that which the young acquire at home in the parental dwelling" and among "the play-mates" and while visiting "the play-places."[29]

Faber is sentenced to death for murdering Emily, a pretty young country girl whom he seduced. Later engaged to the beautiful and rich Constance, he kills Emily when she threatens to tell Constance of their affair. While morally reprehensible, Faber's crime is understandable and one for which, according to the social theory of crime provided at the story's outset (both by Simms in the preface and Faber in the novella's opening chapters), he does *not* bear full responsibility. Lacking "governing principles" (3), a term also used in the narrator's assessment of Guy Rivers's behavior, Faber responds to Emily's threat with violence and with utter disregard of others. Yet in doing so he merely reacts in the manner in which he has been taught to handle his problems. In his confession, for instance, Faber describes how he handled one particular problem during childhood that foreshadows the murder and helps to account for his violent disposition. The episode occurs in grade school. Left alone during detention in the schoolmaster's office, a young Faber maliciously destroys the schoolmaster's new world globes, a prized possession of considerable value. Losing his temper, the schoolmaster flogs the unruly student, a punishment the mature Faber confesses to have "richly deserved" (9). At the time, of course, Faber does not see the punishment in this light. Fabricating "a story of greater wrongs and injuries" (9), he shows his bruises to his wealthy and influential parents, who succeed in driving the schoolmaster from town and in ruining any future prospects he may have in his profession. That the schoolmaster also happens to be Emily's father clearly links this act of violence and deception to the later and more serious one he commits.

While indulgent parents and a bad education may be primarily to blame for the crime that brings Faber to the gallows, his execution is, nonetheless, staged as a just act. As such, it flies in the face of Simms's general opposition to capital punishment—a contradiction that needs some explaining. We can account for this tension by looking at the gendered nature of justice that unfolds in Simms's story. For although Simms ultimately condemns Faber, he does so *not* for the legal crime of murder, which can be explained (away) in terms of Faber's lack of moral training and a proper education; instead, Simms condemns Faber for his brutal treatment of women and for perpetrating the social crime of seduction. Nowhere in the novella does Simms explicitly make this point, but it can be inferred from the novella's "Dedication," which is addressed to "my daughter" and signed by "A father" (2). The dedication itself serves to warn young women of the wiles of man and of an unspeakable social crime for which there is no legal recourse. Although indirectly stated in the dedication, Simms's condemnation of Faber's crime of seduction and misogyny is worked out more explicitly in the novella's dénouement, which comes by way of an execution. Again, it is not through capital punishment per se that justice is administered. Rather, poetic justice is rendered through Faber's inability, due to cowardice, to commit suicide in prison when given a dagger for that purpose. Instead, he tries to use the knife to kill Constance, the beguiled wife, who, albeit repulsed and terrified, stands by her condemned husband during his final hours.

So appalling is this attempted murder that Simms, in dramatizing the scene, breaks from Faber's first-person perspective to condemn his protagonist's craven act. No longer the "I" telling the tale, Faber momentarily becomes "the criminal" whose desperate attempt to kill his wife elicits horror and disgust from a third-person speaker (54). Scholars have traditionally viewed this abrupt shift in person as a technical flaw of a young writer learning to master his craft (Simms reverted to the first person in a later revised version of the novella), but it also suggests Simms's inability or reluctance to sustain the perspective of a protagonist whom he ends up morally abhorring and condemning, despite maintaining a progressive understanding of the social and environmental factors that make Faber into the criminal he becomes.[30] Faber, in this respect, is a perfect foil to Guy Rivers, the "great criminal" who cheats the state by killing himself just hours before his execution is to take place. This tension in Simms's thinking—his progressive understanding of criminal behavior and disapprobation of the death penalty as lawful institution, on the one hand, and his belief in the extralegal penalty of death for the "crime" of seduction, on the other—anticipates a contradiction that runs through much of his later fiction.

## CAPITAL PUNISHMENTS, LEGAL AND EXTRALEGAL

Simms offers a more complex exploration of murder, seduction, and capital punishment in his later Border Romance, *Confession; or, the Blind Heart* (1841). Like *Martin Faber*, *Confession* is narrated in the first person and, as its title suggests, written in the confessional mode. This novel, however, examines seduction from a different angle, telling the story of Edward Clifford, a passionate young lawyer (with a traumatic childhood and poor education) who comes to believe his wife, Julia, is having an affair with his childhood friend and law partner, William Edgerton. Like Shakespeare's Othello, after whom Simms modeled his protagonist, Clifford is convinced of his wife's infidelity by a preponderance of circumstantial evidence. He obsesses over the evidence, certain that Edgerton had stolen his wife's affection by brute force or knavish trickery. Clifford's monomania, fueled by his ungovernable passions and impetuosity (what the novel figures as a "Blind Heart"), leads him gradually to the belief that Edgerton and Julia must die—and die by his hand.

Clifford is first preoccupied with the idea of killing Edgerton, whose impending death he imagines as a just execution. As circumstance after circumstance confirms his suspicion, he rationalizes his murder plot by appealing to a cultural logic that condones the extralegal execution of a seducer. Taken as a given, this logic is more or less assumed in the novel and prompts little explanation or defense on Clifford's part. Instead, what Clifford provides is a step-by-step account of his growing conviction that his wife and friend must die for their crime. As Clifford puts it midway through the narrative, "The vague, indistinct conviction had long floated before my mind, that I would be required to take his life."[31] This conviction quickly takes shape as a cultural imperative, a directive coming from outside Clifford and calling upon him to perform the blood work: "The blood of William Edgerton must be shed, and by these hands!" (197). Restating the injunction by way of a passive construction (i.e., "must be shed") shifts responsibility for the murder from Clifford (the "I," the agent performing the act) to the society that demands this punishment for a crime of this nature. Moreover, its wording closely echoes that of Genesis 9:6 ("Whoso sheddeth the blood of man, by man his blood shall be shed"), the cornerstone of arguments for the death penalty that relied upon biblical evidence.

To fulfill this command, Clifford determines first to try honorable means. Confronting Edgerton with evidence and openly accusing him of seduction, Clifford challenges him to a duel. Edgerton refuses to duel but does not deny the accusation. Incensed, Clifford is forced to adopt another tactic. But first he resolves to poison his wife, an act he carries out with éclat: "I never did anything more firmly," Clifford recollects, when discussing his preparations for the murder. "My nerve was that of the executioner who carries out a just judgment" (363). Returning to Edgerton's home with two daggers, Clifford plans to force Edgerton into a mortal fray. His plans, however, are foiled; or, rather, he is saved from executing them. Out of shame and the desire to prevent his friend from becoming a murderer, Edgerton has hanged himself and left a note admitting his guilt but exonerating Julia, thus leaving Clifford to contemplate his wife's innocence and his own guilt as her murderer.

This revelation marks the novel's climax and sets up the dénouement to follow quickly. Frank Kingsley, friend and confidant to Clifford earlier in the novel, reappears in the final scene, just after Clifford has finished reading the letter exonerating Julia. Taking the letter from Clifford's "unresisting hands," he reads it muttering, "Poor, poor girl," to which Clifford responds: "I must make atonement! . . . I must deliver myself up to justice!" (397). Kingsley in turn replies, "This is madness," and the following exchange ensues between Clifford and Kingsley:

> "No: retribution only! I have destroyed her. I must make the only atonement which is in my power. I must die!"
>
> "What you design is none," he said solemnly. "Your death will atone nothing. It is by living only that you can atone!"
>
> "How?"
>
> "By repentance! This is the grand—the only sovereign atonement which the spirit of man can ever make. There is no other mode provided in nature. The laws, which would take your life, would deprive you of the means of atonement. This is due to God; it can be performed only by living and suffering. Life is a duty because it is an ordeal. You must preserve life, as a sacred trust, for this reason. Even if you were a felon—one willfully resolving and coldly executing crime—you were yet bound to preserve life! Throw it away, and though you comply with the demand of social laws, you forfeit the only chance of making atonement to those which are far superior. Rather pray that life may be spared you. It was with this merciful purpose that God not only permitted Cain to live, but commanded that none should slay him. You must live for this!" (397–98)

Like the *deus ex machina* in Greek drama, Kingsley steps in to resolve the dilemma toward which the novel has been precipitously heading for some four hundred pages. He frames that dilemma as a conflict of laws: "social laws," on the one hand, which demand payment in kind, an eye for an eye, the positive laws to which Clifford is willingly prepared to offer his life; and, on the other, the law of spiritual life, a divine law, which holds that human life cannot be situated in a logic of give-and-take. Kingsley thus reasons that death in turn for murder prevents "sovereign atonement," a concept through which he locates agency in the repentant subject, not through state laws that demand life for life. Like Guy Rivers in his central statement on the aesthetics of crime and capital punishment, Kingsley drives home his point with reference to an illustrative example involving a condemned felon. Whereas Rivers attends to the dynamics of the spectacle of lawful violence, Kingsley focuses on the subject position of the felon who, "willfully resolving and coldly executing crime," is nonetheless bound to preserve life, if only that life be his own. Again, the central issue in *Confession* takes shape as a conflict between divine and positive law (Sophocles' *Antigone* is the classic model), with the former trumping the latter. In short, Kingsley— functioning here as Simms's spokesperson—argues that the legitimate authority to take life belongs not to the state but to God alone, whereas the capacity to re- pent and to assume responsibility rests with the criminal subject, whose life should be preserved (rather than destroyed) for the purpose of repentance.

Kingsley's advice to Clifford ends, appropriately, with an oblique allusion to the biblical story of Cain and Abel, one of the key narratives in antebellum de- bates over capital punishment.[32] If Genesis 9:6 provided supporters of the death penalty with a central piece of evidence, the biblical example of God's mercy toward the world's first murderer gave abolitionists a powerful counterexample. Placed at the end of *Confession*, the reference to Cain therefore serves to displace the allusion to Genesis 9:6 ("Whoso sheddeth the blood of man, by man his blood shall be shed"), embedded in the cultural imperative that structures Clif- ford's revenge plot ("The blood of William Edgerton must be shed, and by these hands!"). In this respect, Cain's exile literally becomes a model for Clifford's re- pentance. In the two brief paragraphs that conclude *Confession*, Clifford finds himself en route to the "unstalked and wild" plains of Texas where, like Cain in his biblical banishment, he will live out rest of his life in " ATONEMENT" (398), the single word (in all capitals) that ends the novel.

Simms's model of atonement in *Confession* stands in stark contrast to the one articulated a year later in Reverend George B. Cheever's *Punishment by Death: Its Authority and Expedience* (1842), the first of the two books the influential minister wrote in defense of the gallows. For Cheever, an impending execution prompted repentance in the criminal in a way that nothing else could. Capital punishment, in his view, served the interests not only of society (by enacting retri- bution) but also of the condemned by *compelling* repentance—an unlikely outcome from Kingsley's perspective in *Confession*. In his *Defence of Capital Punishment* (1846), Cheever wrote at length about "the higher idea of Retribution," to which "utilitarian views of reformation and prevention" were subordinate. "It is because there is something higher from which they are suspended," Cheever explained, "or to give our metaphor a more convenient shape, something deeper on which they may be grounded, that they themselves have any sanction or stability—any true power either to *reform* or *prevent*."[33] Retribution thus provided the practical bases for the criminal justice system as well as the moral ideal toward which it aspired. "Take away capital punishment," Cheever concluded in a later chapter, "and our whole system of criminal jurisprudence, and all its moral and reforming as well as preventative power, suffers a proportionate deterioration."[34]

Cheever's pro-gallows argument, as noted in chapter 1, was built around an interpretation of Genesis 9:6 as God's law on earth. Such a decree, however, obviously contradicted God's response of mercy to Cain and the proscription against Cain's murder as retaliation to his murderous act. Recognizing the problem the Cain-and-Abel parable posed to his biblical defense of the death penalty, Cheever interpreted Genesis 9:6 as God's recognition of and response to his failed policy of mercy to the world's first murderer. The "mildness of that legislation," Cheever reasoned, "only tended to fill society with violence and crime. God spared Cain, and the consequence was, since no murder could ever be committed under more aggravating circumstances than that of Abel, that every murderer felt secure." Whereas the "mildness" of God's antediluvian legislation unsettled the ground on which secure social relations could be constructed, God's "ordinance" to Noah, Cheever went on to argue, provided "the commencement and foundation of society" itself.[35]

By reinterpreting Genesis 9:6 over and against the Cain-and-Abel parable as *the* founding law for human society, Cheever placed retribution rather than mercy at the center of an effort to build a Godly community on earth. In doing so, he reinvigorated a traditional argument for capital punishment, one that reformers had discounted ever since Benjamin Rush had popularized the interpretation of Genesis 9:6 as prediction rather than prophecy, a proverb instead of a commandment that was akin to the verse, "He who lives by the sword shall die by the sword." In addition to its biblical foundation, retribution became for Cheever an underlying principle in the intersubjective relations between society and its citizen-subjects in part because, as Kingsley posits in Simms's *Confession*, life cannot be situated in a strict logic of give-and-take. Cheever, however, takes the argument in the opposite direction: "The common proverb, Hanging is too good for him," he claims at one point in *Punishment by Death*, "shows a deep under-current of conviction in some cases as to the nature of Justice. What a man deserves he never receives here; if he did, this would be the place of final judgment, this the scene of final retribution."[36] Whereas Cheever here turns to popular opinion to express a desire for retributive justice that exceeds what state law can do in taking a life for a life, Simms, as we saw earlier in *Guy Rivers*, denounces such "popular cant" in his causal analysis of crime and dismissal of society's curt response, "Hang the wretch . . . but say nothing about him." Cheever's "common proverb," like the popular cant rejected by Simms, demonizes the criminal subject and underscores the principle of retribution—a precept that forms the basis of Cheever's pro-gallows argument in *Punishment by Death*. In fact, the book concludes with a chapter championing "Retributive Justice" and the "Law of Retribution." As if in response to Simms's invocation of "ATONEMENT!" as the final word in *Confession*, Cheever twice refers to "RETRIBUTION" (all caps) in the penultimate paragraph of his book.[37]

A central topic in both *Confession* and *Punishment by Death*, retribution serves as the organizing principle of *Beauchampe; or, The Kentucky Tragedy* (1842; rev. 1856), one of Simms's most popular Border Romances. If *Confession* is Simms's *Othello*, then *Beauchampe* is his grand revenge tragedy, a work inspired by Elizabethan drama and containing overt allusions to *Hamlet*, *Othello*, and *Macbeth*.[38] First published a year after *Confession*, it retells the infamous "Kentucky Tragedy," a sensational 1826 murder case that captivated the imaginations of writers from Thomas Holley Chivers, Charles Fenno Hoffman, and Edgar Allan Poe (whose closet drama the *Politian* was based on the murder) to Robert Penn Warren, who used the antebellum case as the primary source for *World Enough and Time* (1950).[39] Poe can be seen as speaking for this group of writers when, in writing about the "Tragedy" in *Graham's Magazine*, he claimed: "No more thrilling, no more romantic tragedy did ever the brain of poet conceive than was the tragedy of Sharpe [*sic*] and Beauchampe."[40]

The first volume of Simms's *Beauchampe* is organized around the social crime of seduction; the second is structured around Beauchampe's eventual murder of Colonel Sharpe, a friend and mentor to Beauchampe who also turns out to have been his wife's seducer before the two were married. Like Simms's other murderer-protagonists, Edward Clifford and Guy Rivers, Beauchampe is trained in law; and like all of Simms's criminal-heroes, he is subject to unruly passions. Simms, in fact, wastes little time in establishing Beauchampe's propensity for violence. For instance, when Beauchampe is formally introduced to readers, the narrator says: "He was of excitable constitution, passionate, and full of enthusiasm; and, when aroused, not possessed of any powers of self-government or restraint."[41] Pages earlier, when Beauchampe's name first appears in conversation, fellow lawyers (Sharpe among them) note his passionate nature, describing him as "too serious" and twice referring to him as a "madman" when aroused (57). Yet, as an educated, principled southern gentlemen, whose crime primarily results from a sworn promise to avenge his wife' prior seduction, Beauchampe is, perhaps, Simms's greatest criminal. By today's standards a caricature of chivalry and manly honor, he is repeatedly held up as the epitome of virtue; he is a man who, succeeding where less courageous men would fail, carries out the principled act of killing the destroyer of feminine virtue, a crime condoned by society but condemned by law.

If in *Martin Faber* and *Confession* Simms takes for granted the popular notion that the seducer of feminine virtue must die, in *Beauchampe* he works through the logic of that position in the scenes depicting Beauchampe's dialogue with John Covington, his confidant and advocate, and in the sustained narrative intrusions that appear in the aftermath of the novel's climactic revenge murder. Beauchampe's first conversation with Covington unfolds in chapter 32, "The Progress of Passion," which illustrates the growing cowardice of Sharpe to accept Beauchampe's challenge of a duel and the increasing resolve of Beauchampe to have Sharpe's blood by whatever means. Covington, reporting on his visit to the colonel, explains to Beauchampe that, since Sharpe has refused his challenge, only two options remain: he can "post" Sharpe as a coward, thus "disgrac[ing] him forever"; or, he tells Beauchampe, "You can go further. Horsewhip him—cowskin him—cut his back to ribands, whenever you meet him in the open thoroughfare!" (317) When Beauchampe refuses both modes of punishment, insisting on Sharpe's "blood, his life!" Covington responds with disapproval: "I do not see that you can do more than I have told you. He is a coward: you must proclaim him as such. Your poster does that. He is a villain—has wronged you. You will punish him for the wrong. Your horsewhip does that! You can do no more, Beauchampe" (317). And when Beauchampe persists in having Sharpe's atonement in blood, Covington withdraws his support: "I can do no more that I have told you. I will back you to this extent—no further" (318).

The conversation resumes in the next chapter, "The Avenger." Again, Covington represents the voice of reason and once more counsels Beauchampe against a revenge killing. When he appeals to law and the certain punishment of death to follow from personal vengeance, Beauchampe declares: "Do you suppose I fear death? No! If the gallows were already raised—if the executioner stood by,—if I saw the felon cart, and the gloating throng around, gathered to behold my agonies, I would still strike, strike fatally, and without fear!" (322–23). Besides demonstrating his courage, Beauchampe's declaration undercuts the argument that the gallows effectively deters would-be killers who know the likely consequences of their action. It also foreshadows both the murder and gallows scenes to come. The murder occurs in Colonel Sharpe's home. Since Sharpe, like Edgerton in *Confession*, had earlier refused the challenge of a duel, Beauchampe breaks into Sharpe's house and presents him with the choice of two dirks for the purposes of mortal combat. Sharpe again refuses to fight, but when he attempts to exonerate himself by claiming that Beauchampe's wife, formerly Margaret Cooper (Anna Cooke, as Sharpe had known her), had given birth to a stillborn mulatto, Beauchampe promptly answers with the "sharp edge of the dagger" (333). The murder at last consummated, Simms's narrator intrudes upon the scene to foreground the question toward which the novel has been heading for two volumes:

> The wrongs of Margaret Cooper were at last avenged!
>
> But were her sorrows ended?
>
> How should they be? The hand that is stained with human blood, in whatever cause—the soul that has prompted the deed of blood—what waters shall make them clean?
>
> *"Vengeance is mine!" saith the Lord—meaning "mine only!" Wo, then, for the guilty soul that usurps this sublime privilege of Deity! It must bide a dreary destiny before the waters of heavenly mercy shall flow to cleanse and sweeten it. We may plead the madness of the criminals, and this alone may excuse what we are not permitted to justify. Certainly, they had been stung to madness. The very genius of Margaret Cooper made the transition to madness easy!* (333–34, emphasis added)

Riddled with interrogatives and exclamation marks, this passage concludes by answering the question it begins by posing. Far from ending Margaret Cooper's sorrows, the murder indelibly stains the hands of Beauchampe and his wife, much like the "damn spot" that Lady Macbeth cannot wash out. The kind of justice administered by Beauchampe, the narrator argues here, lies with God alone—a point established with the citation from scripture, "Vengeance is mine!" (Deuteronomy 32:35; Romans 12:19). But this invocation of God's sole prerogative speaks as much to state-enacted vengeance through capital punishment as it does to the extralegal capital punishment carried out by Beauchampe. For Simms's narrator, in an extended meditation on the problem of murder in society that develops from his response to Beauchampe's act, rejects the right of the state to take the life of a murderer under any circumstances: "We may not defend the taking of life, even by the laws," he asseverates, speaking in the collective first person. "We regard life as an express trust from Heaven . . . [of which] no act but that of Heaven should divest us" (343). Simms's evocation of "Vengeance is mine!" (and the paragraph that follows) is also significant in that it was *not* part of the novel's original murder scene. Rather, it was one of the few additions Simms made to the 1856 revised edition (the italicized portion of the passage just quoted indicates the added material). As such, the appeal registered an issue that became a point of contention in death penalty debates since the novel's initial publication in 1842. Whereas abolitionists located vengeance with God alone (thus arguing against all forms of state violence), retentionists claimed that God's vengeance in heaven served as a model for state-imposed violence on earth.

For obvious reasons, the biblical passage in question posed problems for retentionists, and we can again turn to Reverend Cheever for a representative response. Scarcely referenced in his *Punishment by Death* (1842), the scriptural verse plays an important role in A *Defence of Capital Punishment* (1846), the second book Cheever published on the subject. Quoting "Vengeance is mine" and noting its presence in both the Old and New Testaments, Cheever mounts a counterattack to those who advocated abolition on the basis of this passage. "How often," he asserted, "do we find this text perverted to a sense the very opposite of that which was intended, —a sense, which, if carried out, would sweep all law from the universe, except that which was exercised by a direct, miraculous, personal act of the Deity, without the intervention in any case of any intermediate agents. Vengeance belongs to God, say some of our modern theologues, therefore human laws should not exercise it."[42] Cheever's counterargument works by charging reformers with textual perversion and by positing a slippery slope from which all laws will slide if vengeance in criminal law is to rest with God alone. Cheever further develops his argument by equating the anti-gallows movement with a "no-government" position: "Some of our acute men of the east," he argues, undoubtedly thinking of his archrival, John O'Sullivan, whom, as we saw in chapter 1, he had debated in person and in print, "starting with the anti–capital punishment principle, or some similar dogma, have carried it out to this extent, and become consistent no-government men . . . They utterly deny the right of society to punish any offences against itself, because 'Vengeance belongs to the Lord.'"[43]

In adding the "Vengeance is Mine!" paragraph to the revised edition of *Beauchampe*, Simms was likely influenced by O'Sullivan, one of the "acute men of the east" to whom Cheever sarcastically refers. The leading death penalty reformer of the day, O'Sullivan was also a key figure in the "Young America" movement in literature and, of course, the influential editor of the *Democratic Review*, who published anti-gallows stories, poems, and sketches in his magazine by Hawthorne, Whittier, Whitman, and others.[44] Simms, like Hawthorne, Melville, and Whittier, was a prominent writer of that movement and the only one from the South. He was also well aware of the literary attack on capital punishment, especially following O'Sullivan's criticism of Wordsworth's pro-gallows sonnets, that had unfolded in *Democratic Review* in the early 1840s. Indeed, in 1846 Simms had even proposed to O'Sullivan, through his agent Evert Duyckinck, to write "a series of Sonnets agt. the punishment for death & in reply to Wordsworth" for publication in O'Sullivan's journal.[45] Simms, apparently, never got around to writing those sonnets, but we can gauge his response in the recurrent anti-gallows scenes and arguments found in his Border Romances and his historical fiction. Of the latter novels, two examples from *The Cassique of the Kiawah* (1859), a pre-Revolutionary romance, deserve special attention. The first occurs at the novel's outset when Harry Calvert, an alleged pirate and the novel's protagonist, sails into the harbor of Charleston, South Carolina, with his wife and crew under the cover of night. Calvert has already warned his naive and inexperienced Spanish wife, Zulieme, that the gallows likely awaits him in Charleston, and this scenario literally plays out when the ship enters the harbor and Calvert's wife points inquisitively to a reef on which "stood a heavy framework of timber, the uses of which Zulieme could not conjecture." The structure, we are told, "stood out clearly defined in the starlight . . . a well-known object to the eyes of our English—not so familiar to those of the Spaniard." To Zulieme's horror, Calvert identifies the object as "the gallows . . . where they hang the pirates!" an answer that elicits Zulieme's pronounced disgust: "Ah, Dios, Oh, horrid!" she exclaims. "And just at the entrance of the city! Oh, what a horrid people!"[46]

Placed at the city's entrance, the gallows looms over Simms's revolutionary Charleston as the symbolic embodiment of tyranny and oppression under British colonial rule. Viewing it from Zulieme's innocent perspective enables Simms to register a moral response to capital punishment similar to that of Hawthorne's 1843 *The Democratic Review* story, "The New Adam and Eve." For like Hawthorne, Simms at first describes the gallows without naming it, thus placing it outside Zulieme's frame of reference. Such a description marks the hateful object as unnatural and un-American, a peculiarly "English" instrument. While Simms's narrator goes on to note the sanguinary role the *garrote* has played in Spain's own history of capital punishment, he invokes the gallows here to challenge its place in American cultural and political life. He does so by intruding into the scene and adopting Zulieme's innocent perspective for his own:

> What Zulieme ascribed to the popular taste, was, in that day, supposed to be the public policy. They hung men then, *"pour les encourager les autres"*; and the more conspicuous the place, the greater the elevation—the larger the crowd of spectators—the more horrible the writhings of the victim—the more beneficial the example. Whether we are justified in hanging a man as a warning and example, is a question which we do not care to discuss. There are so many crimes which are justified by law and society, that one feels it mere waste of time, if not of temper, to endeavor to prove their absurdity."[47]

Reminding readers of a time in America's colonial past when executions were carried out openly as a matter of "public policy," Simms derides the so-called utilitarian function of the death penalty, suggesting here (as he had more directly argued twenty-five years earlier in *Guy Rivers*) that hanging men, far from making a "beneficial" example, amounted to a mockery of justice, a conspicuous display of wanton bloodshed. Simms's reference to a more barbaric past when men "in that day" were publicly hanged has an ironic ring to it, for, at the time Simms was writing, executions were still publicly administered in much of the South (including Simms's native South Carolina, which did not abolish the practice until 1877, seven years after the author's death). A page earlier Simms had distinguished the gallows as peculiarly "English," a sign of British tyranny; now he associates it with refined practices of European government, an act ironically justified *"pour les encourager les autres"* (the courtly language of French adds a class dimension to the argument, and the phrase itself is likely taken from Voltaire's satiric reference to Admiral Byng's 1757 execution in *Candide*)[48] and one that he refuses to dignify with a serious answer.

Simms may refuse here to elaborate discursively on the "question" of capital punishment, associating it with a host of "crimes" legitimated by "law and society." He does, however, provide an answer through dramatic action some 350 pages later when Calvert, again sailing into Charleston harbor to initiate the novel's conclusion, is once more confronted with the gallows. Reminding readers of Zulieme's "horror and disgust at the sight of the gallows . . . when she first approached the city" (425), Simms now describes the city's colonial figurehead from the perspective of Calvert, to whom it appears an "imposing structure, ominous of death in its most terrible aspect," a hateful instrument representative of "the brute ferocity of the English race" (425). This time, however, Calvert does not pass silently by.

Calling for an ax, he commands his crew to "cut down this gallows! Let it no more disgrace the approaches to a town which boasts of human ties and affections. If the law requires human blood, let it not gloat over mortal agonies; let it not ostentatiously mock humanity with the show of the cruel engine on which it stretches humanity for death!"[49] The gallows, in this and the earlier gallows scene that frames the novel's dramatic action, serves as a broader trope for political tyranny in a way that I shall describe in chapter 3. At this point, it is only important to note that the death penalty here is an object of analysis in its own right, the butt of a larger polemic directed against capital punishment that one can clearly see when these gallows scenes are read in light of the pervasive anti-gallows imagery in Simms's popular Border and Revolutionary romances. Of the novel's framing gallows scenes, the second occupies a curious place in *The Cassique of the Kiawah*, what many of Simms's critics consider the author's finest work.[50] Other than pointing back to the opening scene, it has little to do with the story's plot, since no one dies or comes close to dying on the gallows in this novel, as many characters do in Simms's Border Romances. Yet the sheer gratuity of the scene is telling. It suggests that Simms worked the episode into his novel for the sole purpose of making a statement against the death penalty.

Simms's critique of capital punishment, as well as his exploration of crime and criminal behavior in his Border Romances and elsewhere, points toward an emerging field of study that today we would call criminology—then it was known as "criminal jurisprudence." Although this field first came into being with seminal Enlightenment studies, such as Cesare Beccaria's *Essays on Crime and Punishment* (1764) and Jeremy Bentham's *Principles of Morals and Legislation* (1789), it blossomed in the mid-nineteenth century—precisely when the anti-gallows movement in the United States reached its peak—with the publication of such studies as M. B. Sampson's *Rationale of Crime, and Its Appropriate Treatment* (1846), Jelinger C. Symons's *Tactics for the Times: As Regards the Condition and Treatment of the Dangerous Classes* (1849), Frederic Hill's *Crime: Its Amount, Causes, and Remedies* (1853), James Gerard's *London and New York: Their Crime and Police* (1853), and Cyrus Pierce's *Crime: Its Cause and Cure* (1854). The mid-century also saw the publication of the first periodical devoted entirely to the reformation of criminals and the anti-gallows cause: *The Hangman* (later renamed *The Prisoner's Friend*), which ran from 1845 to 1857 and was edited by Charles Spear, a Universalist minister and one-time president of the Massachusetts Society for the Abolition of Capital Punishment, whose *Essays on Capital Punishment* (1844) became, along with Robert Rantoul's and John L. O'Sullivan's legislative reports, a key text in the abolitionist cause.

Like the emerging body of work on criminal jurisprudence, imaginative literature that challenged capital punishment contributed to an extralegal discourse that advocated for the reformation of criminal statutes and the abolition of the death penalty. A diverse group of writers from various ideological positions, as I noted in chapter 1, participated in the abolitionist cause by making anti-gallows statements in their work. Of them, none provides a stronger contrast to Simms than Lydia Maria Child—a New Englander, a leader in the campaign to abolish slavery, and a woman who voiced her opposition to capital punishment not only in fiction but through her innovative literary journalism.

## "THE GALLOWS GAME"

Whereas Simms's attack on capital punishment comes almost exclusively through his novels, Child's occurs primarily in short stories and in her innovative New York letters, an early example of investigative journalism, that were first published as featured correspondence in the *National Anti-Slavery Standard* and later collected in book form. A recurrent subject in her *Letters from New York*, crime and punishment first become a central issue in Letter 14, dated February 17, 1842. Like many of her dispatches on crime, this one begins with an intent to experience nature's beauty that is disrupted by a visceral city image. This disruption comes in the form of "a little ragged urchin, about four years old," selling newspapers in the streets.[51] The jarring image of a mere child in such a situation prompts a meditation on the circumstances in which he has lived thus far and will continue to grow up. "Imagination," she writes, "followed him to the miserable cellar where he probably slept on dirty straw; I saw him flogged, . . . because he had failed to bring home pence enough for his parents' grog; I saw wicked ones come muttering and beckoning between his young soul and heaven; they tempted him to steal, to avoid the dreaded beating." With a childhood of neglect and abuse, Child imagines the boy being bred for a life of crime: "I saw him, years after," she continues, "bewildered and frightened, in the police-office, surrounded by hard faces. Their law-jargon conveyed no meaning to his ear, awakened no slumbering moral sense, taught him no clear distinction between right and wrong; but from their cold, harsh tones, and heartless merriment, he drew the inference that they were enemies; and, as such, he hated them" (60). Imaginatively tracing this boy's life, Child holds him up as representative of a criminal-in-the-making. Growing up under such circumstances, in and out of prison, his education is a *miseducation*, a counterexample to the privileged but neglected childhood Simms imagines in his representative "Story of a Criminal," *Martin Faber.*

Thus, Child's child becomes a victim of the system, an unfortunate participant in what she calls "the gallows game," a vicious game of cat and mouse in which the cunning of the criminal is pitted against that of the detective and chronicled "with interludes of damnable merriment from the police reports, whereat the heedless multitude laugh" (60). The principle players in this game are, of course, the criminal and the police, but society at large plays an important role, not only through its representation in the criminal justice system but also in terms of the entertainment that we, "the heedless multitude," derive from popular police gazettes and crime fiction. For Child, as we shall see, the criminal is primarily a social construction, a subject nurtured on parental neglect and shaped by environmental and hereditary forces beyond his or her control. This theory of criminal subject formation emerges as a central thesis in *Letters from New York*, and nowhere is it more poignantly stated than at the conclusion of her imaginative sketch about the representative criminal this little street urchin becomes: "When O when," she laments, "will men learn that society makes and cherishes the very crimes it so fiercely punishes, and in punishing reproduces?" (60).

This question reverberates throughout Child's letters. It implicates society, along with the police, in the gallows game—a vicious game whose rules are set by the popular press and social institutions such as literature, school, the criminal justice system, and the prison. Understandably, Child finds her key example of this culture of violence in the prison and through the enactment of capital punishment. She writes extensively about the latter in Letter 31, dated November 19, 1842, which focuses entirely on the execution (or near execution) of John C. Colt, a convicted murderer who, like Guy Rivers, killed himself just hours before his scheduled hanging.[52] A sensational event that attracted national attention for some time to come (Melville, for instance, discusses the case in "Bartleby" and George B. Cheever alludes to it as late as 1881 in a pro-gallows *North American Review* essay),[53] the Colt execution serves as Child's representative illustration of how the spectacle of violence continues to exert a cultural influence even though the actual spectacle has been removed from public view. Like Letter 14, this one begins by noting how America's culture of crime and punishment has disrupted Child's contemplation of the beautiful: "Today, I cannot write of beauty," the letter opens. "Heart, head, and conscience, are all in battle-array against the savage customs of my time" (137). Prepared for battle, Child goes on to savage the "savage" custom of capital punishment through an anti-gallows attack that combines sentimental language with caustic irony. She does so by opposing capital laws of the state to the universal "law of love" that "enfolds even murderers with its blessings"; yet she continues by asking her readers, at least for a day, *not* to ask her "to love governor, sheriff or constable, or any man who defends capital punishment" (137).

Against this language of sentiment, Child in Letter 31 derides the practice of so-called private hangings, which continue to attract throngs of sensation seekers at the execution site, even though the hanging itself is conducted within a concealed prison yard. With the masses now excluded from viewing lawful death in just about every northern state, the opportunity to see them bestowed upon the lucky few, Child ridicules the custom of printing circulars "to summon the number of witnesses required by law." With an eye toward posterity, she wryly comments: "I trust some of them [the circulars] are preserved for museums. Specimens should be kept, as relics of a barbarous age, for succeeding generations to wonder at" (137). By reading Child's description of the atmosphere surrounding the Colt execution against the execution scenes Simms describes in *Guy Rivers*, we see that little has changed since the days of public hangings. Indeed, while encouraged by the presence of those in the crowd who, like herself, oppose what she calls "legalized murder," executed "in cold blood" (138), Child marvels at "the very spirit of murder" that "was rife among the dense crowd, which thronged the place of execution" (137).

In shifting attention from the execution itself to the displaced spectacle of its spectators, Child makes the crowd, "swelling with revenge, and eager for blood," the object of her critique. "One man," for instance, "came all the way from New Hampshire, on purpose to witness the entertainment; thereby showing himself a likely subject for the gallows, whoever he may be" (137). This anecdote is followed by another portraying disgruntled women who are miffed because they are denied admission to the show: "*Women* deemed themselves not treated with becoming gallantry, because tickets of admittances were denied *them*; and I think it showed injudicious partiality; for many of them can be taught murder by as short a lesson as any man . . ." (137, emphasis in original). By mocking this double standard, Child belittles a genteel argument that played an important role in the movement to abolish public executions: that the spectacle of lawful violence, with its accompanying carnivalesque atmosphere, was particularly harmful to women and children. The Colt execution, like the gallows scenes Simms imagines in *Guy Rivers* and elsewhere, is a scene of bloodlust, vengeance, and entertainment, whose murderous spirit derives from the same desire that has brought the condemned before the gallows. Just as Simms adds an aesthetic dimension to the scene, Child plays up the theatricality of a private execution—a kind of closet drama performed behind a drawn curtain and before an invitation-only audience, although carried out "publicly," that is, in the people's name and as an official act.

Whereas the private drama and displaced spectacle of an execution provides the focus of Letter 31, the prison and criminal subject formation are the focal points of Letter 29, dated October 6, 1842. In this dispatch, as in Letter 14, Child turns to social and environmental factors to explain crime and criminal behavior. Here she describes a trip she had taken with some friends to Blackwell Island, home to "a penitentiary, madhouse, and hospital" (125). As in the other letters I have examined, Child's contemplation of the city's natural beauty is marred by the presence of crime and punishment—this time through the figure of the prison compound that "profane[s]" the "charming retreat" of the island. But it is the prisoners, not the prison, that attract Child's primary attention. The sight of them prompts her sympathy for their condition and her disdain for society, "with its unequal distribution, its perverted education, its manifold injustice, its cold neglect, its biting mockery," which has largely made the convicts what they are (320). Such an opinion, of course, runs counter to conventional attitudes toward criminals at the time—a point Child registers by positioning her expressed sympathy for criminals against the contempt of a companion, who, in response to Child, asks, "Would you have them prey on society?" Child replies by inverting the relationship between the prey and the predator: "I am troubled that society has preyed on *them*. I will not enter into an argument about the right of society to punish these sinners, but I say she [society] *made* them sinners" (320, emphasis in original). Making society responsible for crime, Child complicates her point by acknowledging her own complicity in criminal subject formation: "How much I have done toward it, by yielding to popular prejudices, obeying false customs, and suppressing vital truths, I know not; but doubtless I have done, and am doing, my share."

The rest of Letter 29 proceeds from these assumptions and works to develop a theory of social responsibility for criminal activity. Society, Child claims, is not governed by fair play; rather, it is a "game of chance, where the cunning slip through, and the strong leap over. The criminal feels this, even when incapable of reasoning upon it" (321). Like "the gallows game," this "game of chance" is predicated on inequality and ensnares participants (on the losing side) who are ill-equipped to play by the rules of the game. In her attempt to articulate what criminals know but cannot express, Child points to an ideology of manly honor and vengeance that permeates every aspect of American culture. According to her, "everything in school-books, social remarks, domestic conversation, literature, public festivals, legislative proceedings, and popular honours, all teach the young soul that it is noble to retaliate, mean to forgive an insult, and unmanly not to resent a wrong" (321). If Child herself, as she had earlier acknowledged, has done and *is doing* (albeit unintentionally) her own share to promote social conditions that foster crime, and if popular "literature" (Simms's Border Romances would be a prime example) is a particular means by which the young absorb these values, then she uses her later crime fiction as a way of changing that culture of violence and vengeance. The kind of crimes and criminals she realistically documents but creatively imagines in the letters—exemplified in her method of imaginatively following the "ragged little street urchin, about four years old" back to the conditions in which he currently lives and forward to the "criminal" he will certainly become—provides the basis for Child's contribution to crime fiction, which often explores factual or realistic circumstances set against the framework of sentimental fiction. We can see how this process works by looking closely at how Child plots executions and characterizes criminal subject formation in three representative tales.

### CRIME IN FACT AND FICTION

Four years after first writing the New York letters, and two after they were reissued in book form, Child returned to the problem of crime and criminal injustice in several of her magazine stories collected in *Fact and Fiction* (1846). Published alongside her now-famous "The Quadroons" (1842), "The Irish Heart" (1846), "Elizabeth Wilson" (1845), "Hilda Silfverling" (1845), and "Rosenglory" (1846) focused on particular criminal acts or behavior and situated them in a broader social context—a context beyond law's purview and often ignored in early forms of American crime literature, such as the execution sermon which explained crime as a product of sin, without giving any attention to contributing social or environmental factors.[54] Although sentimental in its rhetorical appeals, each tale (save one) is presented as based on "facts" or factual circumstances and imagines the realistic circumstances that produced crime. Of these stories, "Elizabeth Wilson" merits special attention for its dramatic depiction of an execution and its analysis of the environmental circumstances that influenced the protagonist's criminal behavior.

A story *"founded upon facts,"*[55] as Child notes in the tale's headnote, "Elizabeth Wilson" chronicles the tragic history of Lizzy, a young woman with "a delicate nervous organization" who is convicted of infanticide and sentenced to death (127). As in many of Simms's works, the execution serves as the narrative's dramatic endpoint; however, the story principally evaluates Lizzy's development in childhood and adolescence, paying particular attention to the poverty in which she grew up and the early trauma that shaped her being. Culminating in tragedy, the tale opens on a happy note: Lizzy, while poor, begins life with a loving mother and beloved older brother, William. But in contrast to her loving and affectionate mother, she has an indifferent and uninvolved father, who "fed and clothed his children, and caused them to be taught to read and write," but to whom it never occurred "that anything more was included in parental duty." That a child's mind needed "clothing" and that the heart required "food" were responsibilities about which Lizzy's father "knew nothing; for his own had never been clothed and fed" (128). Through such metaphors (clothing the mind and feeding the heart) and tracing Lizzy's development into adolescence and young adulthood, Child drives home the importance of nurture and social environment in one's subject formation.

Misfortune soon befalls young Lizzy. Her mother dies; her father remarries; and the children are forced to take jobs that separate them. Whereas William joins the service and goes to sea, Lizzy becomes a domestic servant in the home of a well-to-do family. A deeply "sensitive child" whose development is blighted in childhood, Lizzy never recovers from her mother's death and becomes prone to fits that, as her stepmother explains to her prospective employers, "affected her mind" and suggested that "there was something strange about Lizzy" (132). In characterizing Lizzy from her stepmother's perspective, which represents that of the community, Child positions her narrator's understanding of the girl against that of popular opinion: "Being of coarser and stronger natures," Child writes of the townspeople, "they could none of them imagine that the slow stagnation of the heart might easily dim the light of intellect in a creature so keenly susceptible" (132). Lizzy eventually adjusts to her new home and job, but the peaceful monotony of her new life is disrupted when a young man from a neighboring town, captivated by Lizzy's beauty, woos her. The two become engaged, but when the young man leaves to establish himself in a distant city prior to their marriage, his passion for Lizzy cools, and he later breaks their engagement in order to marry another woman. Meanwhile, Lizzy gives birth to a dead infant.

Her reputation sullied, her beloved brother at sea, and her father and stepmother sternly "reprov[ing] her sin" (139), Lizzy withdraws from society, and her violent fits return. Some years later, at the age of twenty-three, she takes a job in Philadelphia and again becomes pregnant. This time she gives birth to twins, but the infants are soon discovered to have been strangled. When apprehended by authorities, Lizzy submits with the same indifference that has come to characterize all her actions. She denies having committed the murder, but during her fits she also claims that the twins are still alive. Later in prison she tells her lawyer and her brother, who has come to be with her since learning of the arrest, that the infants' father killed them when she had met with him seeking money for child support. But she provides them with no other information—not even the father's name. Inconsistencies in her story, coupled with the fits and ravings to which she has become increasingly prone, make a less than sympathetic defendant, and Lizzy is thus found guilty of murder.

Stunned by the verdict, William draws up a petition on Lizzy's behalf, "setting forth the alienation of mind to which she had been subject, in consequence of fits, and the extreme doubtfulness whether she committed the murder" (144). After filling the petition with signatures, William travels a good distance to the governor in hopes of securing a pardon for his sister. However, the "fatal day and hour soon arrive[s]," for in "those days," we are told, "there was briefer interval between sentence and execution, than at present" (146). The governor does grant Lizzy's pardon, but William is delayed in delivering it by circumstances beyond his control. He frantically arrives to the execution scene just as the hanging is occurring. With William in eyeshot of the gallows, Child dramatizes the event from his perspective:

> From the top of a hill, he saw a crowd assembled round the place of execution. He waved his handkerchief, he shouted, he screamed. But in the excitement of the moment he was not heard or noticed. All eyes were fastened on the gallows; and soon the awful object came within his own vision. Father of mercies! There *are* a woman's garments floating in the air. There *is* a struggling, a quivering—and all is still. (147, emphasis added)

The tragic irony of the scene speaks for itself as William, pardon in hand, witnesses the lawful death of his beloved sister. Child, however, dramatically heightens the event to make a strong statement against capital punishment. She conveys a sense of immediacy by moving from the past to present tense as the enactment of death transpires, describing the floating garments and struggling form of the condemned as she falls from the gallows. Moreover, Child emphasizes William's pathetic response, as he rolls "senseless on the ground," shouting "A Pardon! A Pardon!" (147). Yet she goes even further to make her point, as her narrator intrudes upon William's suffering to sympathize with Lizzy and to indict the practice of capital punishment, which she equates to murder: "The poor young creature, guilty of too much heart, and too little brain to guide it, had been murdered by law, and men called it justice" (147).

Associating the death penalty with "murder" (or words to that effect) was a common strategy among reformers and abolitionists—common enough to draw the ire of Leonard Bacon, a New England minister who, like Cheever, advocated the retention of capital punishment. In "Shall Punishment Be Abolished?" (1846), a pro-gallows essay published the same year as Child's *Fact and Fiction*, Bacon lamented the frequent association of murder with the lawful punishment of death: "How often do we hear," he complained, "the phrase 'judicial murder,' or some similar language, as the appropriate description of capital punishment inflicted on a murderer. That there is no argument in such a use of language, need not be said. Every man knows that such language is simply taking the whole thing for granted."[56] Elsewhere in the essay, Bacon attacked anti-gallows reformers whose "religion," he claimed, "is a mere sentimentalism." Among such reformers, he singled out novelists and fiction writers for particular criticism: "Much has been done of late, in various ways, to promote sympathy with criminals. No small part of the popular fictitious literature of the present century, and especially of the last five and twenty years, has had that tendency."[57]

In his assault on popular crime literature, Bacon takes aim at not only the kind of anti-gallows sentimentalism one finds in Child's work but also the "great criminals" romanticized in popular novels like those of Simms. Such literature, Bacon argues, perverts the mind of its reader,

> whose imagination has been stimulated and whose habits of thought and feeling have been formed by familiarity with this Newgate literature—to the sensibilities that have been trained by studying these fictitious representations of the morbid anatomy of human nature—to the moral sense that has been bewildered by these attempts to throw the charms of poetry and the colors of romance over robbery and murder and piracy—any man who has committed a particularly atrocious crime, becomes immediately an object of special sympathy.[58]

For Bacon, it is precisely the aesthetics of crime—"the charms of poetry and the colors of romance [thrown] over robbery and murder and piracy"—that makes readers sympathize with the criminal and call into question the penalty of death. "So many of the heroes of modern fiction are criminals of this precise grade," Bacon concludes his thoughts on literary criminals, "that to a mind imbued with the spirit of that literature every criminal seems like a hero, or is at least a most picturesque and interesting character. Seen through such a medium, the criminal is perhaps a man of genius, whose genius has unfortunately taken a wrong direction; or perhaps a man of high and strong impulses, whose virtues not being happily balanced and harmonized, bring him into trouble and conflict."[59]

If Bacon had Child in mind when earlier denouncing what he considered the mawkish sentimentalism of anti-gallows reformers, he seems to be thinking here of Simms's Border Romances—particularly of Guy Rivers, "a man of genius," of "high and strong impulses," whose passion and misguided intellect lead him astray. Incidentally, Child's anti-gallows criticism of popular literature and its celebration of violence (articulated in her New York letters) shares much with Bacon's pro-gallows argument against the sympathy generated by crime fiction like Simms's. For both Bacon and Child, such literature promotes a culture of crime and violence in its representation of it. In response to her own disgust with what Bacon denigrates as "Newgate literature," Child wrote crime fiction according to a different model. But rather than structuring her work around a capital crime or sensationalizing its details—key aspects of Simms's aesthetics of crime and punishment—she emphasized the social and hereditary factors that cause criminal behavior. Violent crimes such as murder are never explicitly described in her fiction, only the lethal violence of law. "Elizabeth Wilson" demonstrates both these principles: on the one hand, through its detailed description of the environmental and biological factors that triggered Lizzy's behavior; on the other, through its omission of the crime itself but depiction of the execution—an approach quite different from Simms, who obsesses over the details of a crime and its dramatic enactment but never dramatizes the criminal's execution itself. In retelling the tragic tale of Elizabeth Wilson, an actual event with its own literary history in early American crime literature,[60] Child thus manipulates plot and character to make a dramatic argument against capital punishment.

Whereas Child looks at criminal behavior in "Elizabeth Wilson" and other stories in *Fact and Fiction* from the criminal's or the accused's perspective, in her later story "The Juryman" she explores the issue from a perspective within the law: that of a juror, one of "the people" selected to help decide on a case involving life or death. Published in *Autumnal Leaves* (1857), the story foregrounds the theme of "education," which it explores through a character study of Peter Barker, a typical, hardworking farmer who was "neither better nor worse than other men."[61] Like Lizzy, Mr. Barker, the future juror and a common-man figure, was orphaned in early youth and lacked the parental nurturing so vital in a child's formative years. Mr. Barker's "rough and lonely" upbringing thus plays a critical role in his own moral education as well as the education he later provides his beloved son, Joe.

The process by which Mr. Barker "educates" his son becomes a central event of the story (as does the education or miseducation of the future criminal in

Simms's *Martin Faber*). A telling description of the process occurs early in the narrative when Child explicitly links Mr. Barker's education, which is founded on principles of vengeance and violence, to the education he gives his son:

> Mr. Barker had himself been educated under the dispensation of punishment, rather than attraction, and he believed in it most firmly. If his son committed a fault, he thought of no other cure than severity. If a neighbour did him an ill turn, he would observe, in presence of the boy, "I will watch my chance to pay him for it." If the dog stole their dinner, when they were at work in the woods, he would say, "Run after him, Joe, and give the rascal a sound beating." When he saw the child fighting with some larger lad, who had offended him, he would praise his strength and courage, and tell him never to put up with an insult. He was not aware that all these things were education, and doing far more to form his son's character than any thing he learned at school. (51)

Through a series of snapshots, we are given a picture of Joe's "education," which is based on retribution and violence and reinforced through physical punishment. Among the many incidents contributing to Joe's miseducation, Child singles out one for special attention. It occurs when Mr. Barker and Joe, who is now thirteen, are riding home after a day's work when their horse takes fright at a piece of paper blowing in the wind. Mr. Barker, already in a foul mood because an unexpected squall had ruined the hay they collected, takes his frustration out on the horse. The incident provides Child with another opportunity to comment on both father's and son's educations: "Pursuing the system on which he had himself been educated, [Barker] sprang to the ground and cudgeled the poor beast unmercifully." The beating is witnessed not only by Joe but by one of their neighbors, a Mr. Goodwin, who remonstrates against the spectacle of violence. Goodwin, a "humane neighbour," mildly instructs Barker "that a horse was never cured of bad habits by violence." He also tells Barker that such violence "is a bad lesson for your son" (51), a remonstrance to which Barker, in front of his son, replies with the threat of more violence: "If you say much more, I will flog you, instead of the horse" (52).

With the education of father and son clearly established, the story flashes forward to the day, some years hence, when Barker is summoned to jury duty "in a case involving life of death." Always preoccupied with his own affairs, Barker, we are told, "had never reflected at all upon the fearful responsibility of a juryman." The case on which he serves is based on circumstantial evidence and involves a drunken youth who had, in a heated brawl, apparently killed another young man with whom he had previously quarreled. While several of the jurymen are reluctant to convict, others, with Barker leading the way, "talked sternly of justice, and urged that the Scripture demanded blood for blood" (54). During the jury's deliberations, arguments about the defendant's youth, his honest countenance, and his intoxicated state, coupled with misgivings about the dreadful penalty of death, are put forth by some jury members; but Barker's appeal to retribution, the principle of a life for a life, carries the day. "If anybody killed my Joe, drunk or not drunk," he declares, "I should want him to swing for it" (56).

Barker's words later reverberate with tragic irony. On his twenty-fourth birthday, Joe, drunk and embroiled in a love triangle, kills his rival in a case with circumstances very similar to the one in which Barker served as a juror years earlier. Brought again "into a court of justice on an affair of life and death" (60), Barker sees the errors of his ways. He realizes for the first time that "every human being is, or has been, *somebody's* little Joe" (62). Racked with guilt, he reflects upon the education he had provided his son, who is now condemned like the other young man for whose guilt Barker vigorously argued. Visiting Joe in prison, Barker recalls the horse-beating incident and neighbor Goodwin's remarks about the "bad lesson" he had given. He asks Joe if things might have been otherwise, if he "had a less violent father" (63). Joe, whose time in prison had provided its own education, responds with Christian principles of love and forgiveness, realizing that vengeance in any form is a kind of murder: "I see now that retaliation and hatred are murder" (63).

The anti-gallows message of "The Juryman," like that of "Elizabeth Wilson," is carefully worked out through plot structure and chacterization, making it hard to miss for any reader. It is, however, important to note another obvious feature central to both these stories. As aesthetic works, both draw from the drama of a death sentence and its lawful enactment. Whereas "Elizabeth Wilson" builds up to a capital trial and stages a dramatic execution in its climax, "The Juryman" is organized around two trials and executions in order to demonstrate the tragic consequences of Mr. Barker's (and his son's) miseducation. In this way, Child's crime fiction relies on an aesthetics similar to Simms's, although the crimes around which her fiction revolves are seldom directly represented and briefly reported at that. We can get a better sense of how the death penalty operates as a structuring principle in Child's fiction by looking briefly at "Hilda Silfverling," a final story from *Fact and Fiction* that uses capital punishment to promote conflict and give rise to dramatic action. This tale begins where "Elizabeth Wilson" ends. Hilda, like Lizzy, is sentenced to death for the crime of infanticide, but there is no doubt of her innocence. Though a "train of circumstantial evidence" connects her to a murdered infant, about the same age as Hilda's own child, readers know that the mother, ashamed at having given birth out of wedlock, had given the infant to an older, childless friend to raise until the she could care for the child herself. The friend, as she and Hilda planned, leaves their mid-eighteenth-century Swedish village with the child; but when evidence points to Hilda's guilt, neither the friend nor child can be found to exonerate Hilda.

Subtitled "A Fantasy" (it is the one story in *Fact and Fiction* not based essentially on facts), the story takes an unusual turn when a "very learned chemist in Stockholm" discovers a process "by which he could suspend animation in living creatures" (208). The chemist, "whose ideas were all gas," petitions the state to stay the execution process. His intervention, however, is motivated by neither a belief in Hilda's innocence nor an objection to capital punishment. Rather, in the interests of science, he asks that "Hilda, instead of being beheaded, might be delivered to him, to be frozen for a century." The state grants the request, and Hilda, in the official language of her sentence, is "put to sleep for infanticide, Feb. 10, 1740, by order of the king. To be wakened Feb. 10, 1840" (211). An early example of science fiction, "Hilda Silfverling" offers a playful critique of the death penalty in the first half of the story. It ridicules the idea of finding a more humane form of execution rather than abolishing capital punishment itself and eerily anticipates the horrors of the gas chamber (a technology of lawful death later used, of course, in the United States) in its description of the vaporous procedure by which Hilda is euphemistically "put to sleep." The story, moreover, parodies the social rituals built up around state-sanctioned executions. For instance, the minister commissioned to preside over the punishment is confounded by its unusual circumstances and cannot offer his customary words of consolation; instead he recites the old child's prayer, "Now I lay me down to sleep / I pray the Lord my soul to keep . . ." (211). The entire process ends up producing a fate worse than death, as Hilda eventually awakens to a world in which all of her friends and former associations are dead.

In its second half, the story takes another unusual turn—this time toward comedy—when Hilda leaves the village of her past and finds a place in this new world and eventually falls in love. But her newfound happiness is blighted when she realizes that her lover turns out to be the grandson of her own child, the infant daughter whom she was convicted of murdering a hundred years earlier! Read in the context of the anti-gallows movement, "Hilda Silfverling," at best, can be taken as a tale of condemned innocence, a veritable subgenre in antebellum crime fiction I take up in later chapters. That Hilda's life is spared, her death sentence commuted to one of a century of sleep, prevents the state from committing an irremediable wrong; but the state creates a state of affairs for Hilda that is unnatural and awkward, to say the least. The story ultimately ends on a comic (if not entirely happy) note when Hilda's lover convinces her to ignore her own tale of cryogenics and her preposterous belief that the two of them are related. A sort of anti-gallows comedy, "Hilda Silfverling" cannot be classified as an out-and-out anti-gallows story, as can "The Juryman" and "Elizabeth Wilson." But precisely for this reason, we get a clearer sense of how Child draws upon capital punishment as an aesthetic principle or structuring device, in addition to seeing how she used her fiction as a platform to attack the death penalty.

Simms, as we have seen, carried out a similar project, one thematized in his musings on "A Murder in a novel" and demonstrated through his principled assault on the gallows for more than twenty-five years in works from *Guy Rivers* (1834) to *The Cassique of Kiawa* (1859). Unlike Child, however, he never denounced the death penalty in print outside his fiction, perhaps because to do so would run counter to his pro-slavery ideology or, more likely, because he did not want to offend fellow conservative Southerners, for many of whom the abolition of capital punishment would be too radical a measure, too much in keeping with the politics of liberal northern reformers who often opposed both slavery and capital punishment—the period's two noted and often interlinked abolition movements. Taken together, then, Simms and Child make for two of the most unlikely partners in crime. Read alongside each other, their work not only demonstrates the reach of the anti-gallows cause but also encompasses many of the arguments, tropes, and narratives that would come to characterize a broader cultural rhetoric of capital punishment in popular literature of the period, one in which the symbolism of the death penalty set the stage for examining larger questions about individual rights and liberties vis-à-vis state authority.

# CHAPTER 3

# Literary Executions in Cooper, Lippard, and Judd

Ah, at the very moment the hangman speaks to his horse, the cart
moves on—look!
  There is a human being dangling at the end of the rope,
plunging and quivering in the air. Behold it, nor shudder at the
sight! That blackened face, livid, blue, purple at turns, those
starting eyes, —Oh, hide the horrid vision! What, hide the Poetry
of the Gallows?
Hide it you may, but still the thick gurgling groan of that dying
man breaks on your ear.
That is the Music of the Gallows.

> *George Lippard*, Legends of the Revolution; or, Washington and
> His Generals (1847)

First published at the height of the anti-gallows movement in antebellum
America, George Lippard's massively popular *Legends of the Revolution* dramatizes several enactments of lawful death. The scene depicts not just any execution but that of Major John André, the infamous British spy whose death George
Washington authorized during the Revolutionary War. In narrating the scene,
Lippard, like Lydia Maria Child in "Elizabeth Wilson," moves from the past to
the present tense, thereby giving the drama at hand a heightened sense of
immediacy. But whereas Child provides a distanced glance of the condemned's
"floating" (albeit "struggling" and "quivering") form, Lippard brings readers in for
a close look and lingers over the details. "Does this spectacle interest you?"[1] his
narrator pointedly asks in describing the elaborate procession bringing André to
the gallows. When the execution at last occurs, the narrator again intrudes, this
time commanding us to "look!" and ironically framing the hanging as an aesthetic
act to behold.

Attending to the execution's horrific details—the condemned's "blackened face," "starting eyes," and "thick, gurgling groan"—Lippard anticipates Austin Sarat's provocative and controversial argument for televising executions today in an effort to elicit broad-scale support for the abolitionist cause.[2] Lippard, however, was also participating in the debate over the gallows in his own day by responding to genteel reformers who objected to public executions but not to capital punishment per se. He was, moreover, responding to fellow novelists like William Gilmore Simms, who, for all his criticism of the death penalty in his fiction, never dramatized the spectacle of lawful death itself. Simms, in fact, went so far as to alter the historical circumstances of the infamous 1825 "Kentucky Tragedy" murder case on which *Beauchampe* was based, so that his hero died of self-inflicted wounds in route to the gallows rather than on the gallows itself, as the actual Beauchamp died.[3] Thus, to the genteel plea "Oh, hide the horrid vision!," Lippard offers a wry and incredulous rejoinder: "What, hide the Poetry of the Gallows?"

Lippard's question poses a key issue that writers, who were at all influenced by the anti-gallows movement, had to ask themselves when writing fiction that in some way involved an execution: whether to depict the enactment of lawful death. Reverend George B. Cheever, the nineteenth century's great defender of the gallows, took Charles Dickens to task on this issue, calling attention to what he considered the "shameful inconsistency" of the popular novelist's anti-gallows literary politics: "He seldom omits an opportunity to give a thrust at the 'barbarous and inhuman practice of punishment of death,'" Cheever complains, "and yet how he gloats over the luscious feast when he gets an occasion . . . of dwelling, in the most minute and soul-sickening detail, on all the mere animal horrors which his fertile imagination can present as belonging to a public execution."[4] On the one hand, as Cheever suggests, to dramatize the spectacle of lawful death could be seen as gratifying the perverse desires of potential readers, who, in much of the United States at least, could no longer witness legal hangings for themselves, thus making an author complicit with an act they might oppose. On the other, *not* to show the event could be taken as avoiding the real issue at stake: the killing of a person—a "human being," as Lippard humanizes the notorious British spy—in the name of the people. Lippard in *Legends* and elsewhere resolves the dilemma by forcing his readers to face the music, "The Music of the Gallows."

⁓

Whereas chapter 1 broadly surveyed the cultural rhetoric of capital punishment in terms of seminal legal and literary texts and contexts related to anti-gallows activism, and chapter 2 narrowly traced its rhetorical paths in works by two influential writers who opposed the death penalty but did so from opposing ideological perspectives, this chapter again broadens the scope to explore the literary politics of capital punishment through the work of three representative but radically different popular novelists from the period—two of them among the period's most popular writers and another who attained minor celebrity with a novel that staged the enactment of lawful death in its climactic scene. The first is James Fenimore Cooper, America's first recognized national novelist, whose *The Spy: A Tale of the Neutral Ground* (1821) hinges on a series of gallows scenes and curiously entertains the question of capital punishment in Revolutionary America. The second is Lippard, the period's most populist if not also most popular writer,[5] in whose work the death penalty functions as a master trope in a larger argument about class and state violence in contemporary America. And the third is Sylvester Judd, a prominent Unitarian minister and leader in Maine's influential anti-gallows campaign, whose revised execution scene in *Margaret* (1845; 1851) gets at the politics of dramatizing lawful death better than any literary work of the period. Taken together, Cooper, Lippard, and Judd (a Yankee, Mid-Atlantic, and New England writer respectively) make for a motley grouping whose stark differences—like those of Simms and Child in chapter 2—point to the broader significance of the death penalty as a crucial event and organizing principle in literary aesthetics and cultural politics. In this way, the chapter presents a case study that moves from a specific novel (Cooper's *The Spy*) to the work of an author (Lippard) and then to a particular scene (Judd's *Margaret*) to trace the capital punishment's cultural rhetoric in three distinct socioaesthetic visions of America and its republican values. Thus, it comes to center around Lippard, whose working-class literature provides an illuminating contrast to the more genteel anti-gallows writings of Simms and Child examined in chapter 2, and culminates with an analysis of the anti-gallows politics of Judd's literary execution scene in *Margaret*.

The chapter begins and ends, however, with Cooper's first popular novel and his last, which provide important bookends to my investigation for several reasons. Written thirty years apart by the same author, *The Spy* and *The Ways of the Hour* (1850) encompass the period under consideration and highlight two different ways in which the death penalty is artfully plotted without a lawful execution actually occurring. I focus on *The Spy* not only because it remained a popular and influential work over the rest of the long nineteenth century, but because it shows the significance of the death penalty as topic and trope in a work that has nothing ostensibly to do with the campaign for abolition just then accruing popular currency in the United States. Most importantly, I begin with Cooper because—unlike every literary figure examined in this study (with the possible exception of Melville)[6]—he did not use his work in part to make anti-gallows statements. In fact, Cooper can be seen, as we shall see, as making an explicit *anti*-anti-gallows statement in *The Ways of the Hour*, although his position on capital punishment in that novel and in his work as a whole is not that simple. It is precisely because Cooper did not overtly oppose the death penalty that we can begin to see how the figure of capital punishment was configured in a broader cultural rhetoric about the citizen-subject vis-à-vis sovereign authority—in Cooper's case, a probing questioning of the legitimacy of United States authority during its war for independence.

## COOPER'S "HANG-GALLOWS SPY"

Published a year before Neal's *Logan* (1822), the first American novel to make an out-and-out anti-gallows statement, Cooper's *The Spy* tells the story of Harvey Birch, an alleged British spy who is actually a double agent serving Washington during the American Revolutionary War. Birch is thrice sentenced to death: twice before the novel begins and once during the course of it. Reviled as "a hang-gallows spy"[7] when captured and condemned for a third time, Birch again escapes the gallows through trickery and dissimulation, skills that enable him to help Captain Henry Wharton, another alleged British spy, elude the same fate in the novel's dramatic conclusion. While Wharton's near execution marks the novel's climax and Birch's unfolds at its structural center, debate over the historical execution of Major John André initiates the novel's central conflict, which turns on the question of the legitimacy of the American Revolution and the nation formed in its name.

That conflict largely takes shape around legal questions. Charles Hansford Adams, in the most detailed study of Cooper's engagement with law in his Revolutionary romances, thus examines *The Spy* as the author's attempt to depict "A Lawful Rebellion," a restructuring of political authority rather than a radical act of rebellion. As Adams puts it, "Cooper's War is always finally an act of law, and thus profoundly conservative. The Revolution is conceived not as a celebration of liberation *per se*, or the prerogatives of the private self, but as the creation of a structure of political authority whose legitimacy for the present day ought to be unquestioned."[8] If Cooper, in writing his "Tale of the Neutral Ground" some forty years after the United States gained independence, was indeed providing readers with a legitimation narrative—a story of the grounds on which U.S. political authority was established—that authority hardly goes unquestioned in the narrative itself. In fact, it is precisely this disputed authority as expressed through the sovereign violence of capital punishment that drives the novel's plot and shapes its aesthetic structure. We can begin to see how by reading the debate over André's execution in light of Revolutionary rhetoric within which it is set.

In an illuminating essay on *The Spy* and its Revolutionary War context, Dieter Schulz has illustrated the significance of the family—especially the "sentimental family"—in the cultural rhetoric of the period.[9] From John Locke's line-by-line critique of Robert Filmer's defense of monarchical governments by way of patriarchal analogy in *Two Treatises of Government* (1689) to Thomas Paine's use of it in *Common Sense* (1776) and its figuration in the letters of John Adams and Thomas Jefferson, the family served as a "key metaphor" for political disaffection and the right of an abused people to seek a political liberty that naturally belonged to them.[10] Such a rhetoric constitutes what Schulz calls "a language of feeling" in which fathers were tyrants, sons exploited, and daughters imperiled. Nowhere in *The Spy* is such a language more apparent than in the Wharton family debate over André's execution in one of the novel's opening chapters.

André first comes up when Henry Wharton, who has crossed enemy lines in disguise to visit his father and sisters, is asked by a guest in his father's home if he has "heard that Major André has been hanged?" Discomfited by the question, Henry feigns disinterest to maintain his cover, but his father responds by asking, "Does his execution make much noise?" (52) Within the novel, the execution indeed makes much noise. A point of reference throughout, it prompts a heated debate over the legitimacy of U.S. authority between Henry and his sisters. The conversation begins, innocently enough, when Henry's father jokingly compares his son's disguise and the likelihood of its success to "men like Major André [who] lend themselves to the purposes of fraud" (61). Henry takes umbrage at his father's remarks, and the following exchange ensues between Henry and his sister Frances:

> "Fraud!" cried his son quickly. "Surely, sir, you forget that Major André was serving his king, and that the usages of war justified the measure."
>
> "And did not the usages of war justify his death, Henry?" inquired Frances, speaking in a low voice, unwilling to abandon what she thought the cause of her country, and yet unable to suppress her feelings for the man.
>
> "Never!" exclaimed the young man, springing from his seat, and pacing the floor rapidly. "Frances, you shock me; suppose it should be my fate, even now, to fall into the power of the rebels; you would vindicate my execution— perhaps exult in the cruelty of Washington." (61–62)

The disagreement between Henry and Frances signifies internal strife and divided alliances among the sons and daughters of America, thus putting in play competing perspectives on André's execution and its (il)legality that resonate over the course of the novel. Here, Frances appropriates her brother's argument on behalf of André and justifies his death by appealing to "the usages of war," a position from which Captain Vere justifies the death penalty in Melville's *Billy Budd* (1891), some seventy years later. Henry responds to Frances not with a counterargument but an emotional outburst that emphasizes their own filial bonds and recasts himself as a condemned spy, thereby foreshadowing his own fate in the novel's dramatic climax. Mr. Wharton, who first broaches the subject of André, is more or less absent from the debate, but the figure of "the father" as despot is symbolically present in Washington, whose "cruelty" in authorizing André's death sentence (and later Henry's) makes him akin to the patriarchal authority of England against which the Continentals are rebelling.

The debate momentarily ends when Frances takes offense at Henry's insensitive comments about her vindication in his potential execution, and Henry apologizes for them. It begins again, however, when Henry excuses his conduct by insisting on André's gallantry, which elicits a wry smile and some head shaking from Frances. Henry once more is offended, and the debate happens all over:

> Her brother, observing the marks of incredulity in her countenance, continued, "You doubt it, and justify his death?"
>
> "I do not doubt his worth," replied the maid, mildly, "nor his being deserving of a more happy fate; but I cannot doubt the propriety of Washington's conduct. I know but little of the customs of war, and wish to know less; but with what hopes of success could the Americans contend, if they yielded all the principles which long usage had established, to the exclusive purposes of the British?"
>
> "Why contend at all?" cried Sarah, impatiently. "Besides, being rebels, all their acts are illegal." (62–63)

Frances here again voices support for the American cause, this time defending "the propriety of Washington's conduct"—namely the execution of André. Henry, again, fails to offer a counterargument; but this time his sister Sarah responds for him, characterizing all political acts by Continental forces as "illegal." Sarah's interjection brings the discussion back to the question of the legitimacy of André's execution—an illegitimate act, from her perspective, because it was carried out in the name of a people that did not yet exist as such.

The Wharton family debate is important because it frames the novel's central question: an inquiry into U.S. sovereignty that is exemplified (indeed, emblematized) in the figure of the condemned spy—whether it be André, Henry, or Harvey, the novel's putative and problematic hero. The controversy surrounding the execution recurs in different contexts and between different interlocutors in the novel. British and American soldiers alike, as well as Skinners and Cowboys fighting with loyalty to neither side, all refer to André's death as shorthand to challenge or to justify the American war for independence. A symbol for internal strife and divided alliances when discussed within the Wharton home, André's hanging is later referenced when Henry, following the first of his improbable escapes from a probable execution, explains to a British colonel how he was threatened with capital punishment. "The gallows, Captain Wharton!" the colonel exclaims; "surely those traitors to the king would never dare to commit another murder in cold blood; is it not enough that they took the life of André?" (102) The colonel's question is, of course, a rhetorical one—a trope that builds on Sarah's refusal to recognize U.S. sovereignty in the debate with her brother. In this example, André's death is seen as a "murder" committed in "cold blood" (102) rather than a legitimate act from within a recognized state and according to its laws and codes.

With debate over André's execution framing the narrative and serving as a touchstone throughout, and the near executions of Birch and Henry Wharton plotted at critical moments in the narrative (not to mention the graphic description of an extralegal hanging of a Skinner in what is certainly the novel's nastiest scene), the gallows can be seen as providing *The Spy* with its basic architecture— its narrative scaffolding, if you will—much like the three scaffold scenes that help structure Hawthorne's *The Scarlet Letter* (1850). By organizing his first popular novel around a series of gallows scenes, Cooper was participating in what I described in chapter 2 as the aesthetics of crime and capital punishment, a dominant aesthetics of the era exemplified in Simms's Border Romances. Published before any of Simms's novels, *The Spy* is an early example of this popular aesthetic, particularly with its climactic race against the clock to save Henry, who is again captured by American troops and this time formally sentenced to be hanged by a military tribunal. While Henry's sisters rush off to obtain a pardon from Washington, Birch deploys a covert rescue operation that involves the slave Caesar, serving as a double for Wharton, and Birch himself posing as a minister to conduct the condemned's last rites. With Wharton, in black face, and Caesar disguised in the garbs of the condemned, Birch pulls off another hairbreadth escape preventing the execution of an innocent man.

In staging the Henry–Caesar body swap, Cooper likely drew from the famous head-swapping scene that prevents Claudio's unjust execution in Shakespeare's *Measure for Measure*.[11] That Cooper had the play and head-swapping scene in mind is evident in that he quotes from the play's execution plot in an epigraph

that begins chapter 27, the first of several chapters describing the efforts to prevent Henry's execution. If Cooper drew from Shakespeare in framing the conclusion to his first successful novel, an international bestseller in his own day and
a respected work since then, it is likely that later novelists drew, in turn, from him
in staging execution plots that capitalized on the drama of capital punishment—
specifically the race against the clock to prevent an execution (a convention we
have already seen in Child's later story "Elizabeth Wilson"). In fact, some of the
nineteenth century's most popular novels follow the formula Cooper put in motion. For instance, a similar body swap is famously used to conclude the drama of
Charles Dickens's A Tale of Two Cities (1859), a historical novel obsessed with the
guillotine as much as Cooper's is with the gallows. A half century later, Thomas
Dixon would employ a similar strategy to conclude his hugely popular racist
thriller, The Clansman: An Historical Romance of the Ku Klux Klan (1905). Like
the political drama of Cooper's historical novel, the drama of Dixon's ends when
one of its protagonists, Phil Stoneman, son of the Republican leader who orders
the execution, penetrates the prison holding the condemned Ben Cameron and
trades places with him on the eve of his scheduled hanging.[12]

    Of these three popular novels stretching across much of the nineteenth cen-
tury, Cooper's is of particular importance, not only because it is the first to
employ of the body-swap plot device but because of its extensive use of capital
punishment as both trope and topic at a time when arguments for its abolition
first emerged in America as a national concern. The Spy is also of note for its attention to espionage during wartime, the one crime and set of circumstances for
which Cesare Beccaria, who wrote the blueprint for the Enlightenment critique
of capital punishment, justified the use of the death penalty.[13] Written in 1821,
when Edward Livingston, the influential Democrat and former mayor of New
York, was writing what would become his influential penal reports advocating
abolition, The Spy concerns a period in American history when the question of
capital punishment's legitimacy first attracted the attention of the country's leading thinkers. As noted in chapter 1, Thomas Jefferson, Benjamin Franklin, Benjamin Rush and other Founding Fathers were admirers of Beccaria's On Crimes
and Punishment and opponents of the death penalty, which they associated with
monarchical rule and a king's prerogative.[14] Dr. Rush, a signer of the Declaration
of Independence and America's most famous physician during the Revolutionary
War and in the early republic, can be seen as speaking for this group when he later
denounced "capital punishments" as "the natural offsprings of monarchical governments" and likened an "execution in a republic" to "a human sacrifice in religion."[15] Such language, I argued earlier, characterized the influential republican

argument against the death penalty that originated with Beccaria and was perfected by Rush and Cooper's contemporaries, Livingston and Robert Rantoul Jr. And such language, I want to suggest here, was an important part of a larger argument for the American Revolution and civil rights since then. It is evident, for instance, in the doctrine of the right to life, the first of the "inalienable rights" enumerated in the American Declaration of Independence.

Interestingly enough, Cooper broaches a similar argument about capital punishment in the context of the American Revolution that critics of *The Spy* have overlooked. The scene stages a dialogue between the courageous Captain Jack Lawton, the novel's symbolic agent of "Law" (as his name, *Law*ton, suggests), and Dr. Archibald Sitgreaves, a comical yet philosophical physician whose enlightened musings and academic training suggest Dr. Rush as a model. Their conversation follows a day's skirmish and concerns Birch, who has yet again eluded Lawton's (and the law's) grasp. A dialectic of sorts, the dialogue unfolds as Sitgreaves, attending to Lawton's wounds, casually states, "If I have any wish at all to destroy human life, it is to have the pleasure of seeing that traitor hanged," to which Lawton replies: "I thought your business was to cure, and not to slay" (160). When the surgeon concurs but confesses to feel "a very unsophistical temper towards that spy," the captain responds with a firm rejoinder: "You should not encourage such feelings of animosity to any of your fellow creatures." Surprised by the sentiment of the usually severe Lawton, Sitgreaves agrees in principle, calling the captain's "doctrine" a "just" one, but maintains that cases like Birch's mark an "exception" to the rule. Pondering the matter further, however, Sitgreaves comes around to Lawton's point of view: "It is not only cruel to the sufferer," the surgeon says to conclude the conversion, "but sometimes unjust to others, to take human life where a less punishment would answer the purpose" (160).

In a novel in which the gallows plays such a prominent role, the Sitgreaves-Lawton exchange has general application. It colors the gallows scenes to come with a bit of anti-gallows logic, inviting readers to question not only the near executions of Henry and Harvey, whom we know are innocent, but that of any person—even a hang-gallows spy. That we are encouraged to adopt such a perspective appears evident from the role Lawton plays in the dialogue, especially when we contrast him to Sitgreaves. While it is not surprising that Dr. Sitgreaves, the novel's representative Enlightenment figure, comes to see the death penalty as cruel and unjust to any person, it *is* surprising (and Cooper registers Sitgreaves's surprise in the dialogue) that this dialectic on the illegitimacy of lawful death is initiated and initially supported by Lawton, an adherent to Mosaic law in an oft-cited scene in which he justly punishes the Skinners for "burning, rob-bing, and murdering" right after he justly rewards them for Birch's capture (226), and the voice of law's vengeance in an earlier scene in which his character is first introduced. "If I catch [Birch]," Lawton declares with pronounced malice when we first meet him in the Whartons' home, "he will dangle from the limbs of one of his namesakes" (79). Such a thinly veiled allusion to summary hanging asso-ciates Birch here with André, whose execution had been intensely debated by the Wharton family just before Lawton's arrival.

Birch has often been taken by scholars as a "crass double" for André.[16] As the novel's chief "hang-gallows spy," however, he is more than André's double. He also doubles for Henry, as noted earlier, and is thus a figure configured in a trian-gular relationship involving espionage and capital punishment—a subject to which The Spy keeps circling back in its investigation of lawful authority in the neutral ground. Lawton's opposing attitudes toward Birch and the death penalty in two of the scenes I have cited further complicate this investigation in obvious ways. They are, to say the least, contradictory. But rather than trying to reconcile the two, or privileging one perspective over the other, I want to suggest that this contradiction is further evidence of the tension of the death penalty, as opposed to open warfare under republican principles of government, that helps to found the new republic of the United States. Nowhere is this tension or contradiction more apparent than in André's execution, an event the novel condemns as much as it condones.

Recognizing this tension, one critic has read The Spy as "the novelist's partial vindication of André."[17] If, or perhaps because, The Spy can be read this way, Cooper clarified his position on the famous Revolutionary execution some seven years later in The Notions of the Americans: Picked up by a Traveling Bachelor (1828). Writing from the perspective of an enlightened European visiting the United States, Cooper sympathizes with André the man but roundly condemns his crime of espionage.[18] Ruminating further on "the office of a spy" and the specifics of the André case, Cooper's Bachelor justifies the execution as a necessary expres-sion of U.S. sovereignty during this founding moment in the nation's history:

> The Americans were determined to assert the dignity of their Government. The question was not one of vengeance, or even one of mere protection from similar dangers in future. It involved the more lofty considerations of Sover-eignty. It was necessary to show the world that he who dared to assail the rights of the infant and struggling republics, incurred a penalty as fearful as he who worked his treason against the Majesty of a King.[19]

Couched in the rhetoric of the Revolution, Cooper draws implicitly upon the family metaphor (the leitmotif of *The Spy*), with the fledgling United States as the representative "infant and struggling" republic abused by a despotic father. Hardly the ambivalent and at times sentimental figure he is in *The Spy*, André is here portrayed as a brazen son serving a tyrannical father. His execution is a symbolic one, an example and declaration of U.S. sovereignty; it *dignifies* (to use the Bachelor's term) the newly constituted United States by legitimating its authority and making other European states, especially England, take notice of its power. Yet there is unresolved tension in this justification, as there is each time the figure of André crops up in *The Spy*. That tension is not as pronounced as it is in the novel, but it is registered in the Bachelor's rationale for the execution itself—a "fearful" penalty he associates with the "Majesty of a King." Such an association with monarchical authority is precisely why Rush, Livingston, and Rantoul strove to disassociate the death penalty from the ideal of an American republic in which the right to life would be inviolable.

Cooper himself may not have been so liberally inclined, but his Bachelor's justification at least bears the influence of this argument. For in framing his remarks, the Bachelor qualifies his support for André's execution by explaining that it resulted from neither "vengeance" nor the interests of "mere protection"— two traditional arguments for capital punishment challenged on utilitarian grounds—but instead for "the more lofty considerations of Sovereignty." Cooper's Bachelor may or may not have been a disciple of Beccaria or an acquaintance of Dr. Rush (whose son, Richard Rush, is mentioned at one point in *Notions*),[20] but Cooper himself wrote *Notions* at the request of Marquis de Lafayette, who became an intimate of Cooper's when the famous American was living abroad while writing the work. A hero of the American Revolution and an object of high praise through much of *Notions*, Lafayette himself was a noted opponent of capital punishment who famously declared to the French Chamber of Deputies: "I shall ask for the abolition of the punishment of death until I have the infallibility of human judgment demonstrated to me."[21] Lafayette's statement would later serve as the motto of Charles Spear's *The Hangman* and *The Prisoner's Friend*, printed along the heading of each edition of the anti-gallows magazines during the run from 1845 to 1853.

Critics in Cooper's day and our own have complained that the fictive framework of *Notions*—that is, the Bachelor's correspondents and the gentlemen's club that occasions his reflections—diminishes its import as a political document back then or primary source for historians today.[22] But the epistolary form is crucial to the work's political message in that it establishes a transatlantic dialogue between Europe, on the one hand, represented in the Bachelor and his European cronies, and America, on the other, personified in Cooper's ideal gentleman-democrat, John Cadwallader of Cadwallader, New York (an obvious stand-in for James Cooper of Cooperstown, New York), to whom the work is dedicated. Thus, the Bachelor's justification of André's execution, which occurs in an epistle written to a retired French colonel (a member of the fictitious gentlemen's club), suggests an acceptance among enlightened Europeans of a founding act of sovereign violence that had generated controversy ever since its execution. Yet the relative ease with which André's execution is legitimated in *Notions* highlights the productive tension embedded in the trope of André and the staging of capital punishment in *The Spy*. We can better understand how this tension works by briefly considering it through the Benjaminian distinction between founding and conserving violence from which my critique of violence has been implicitly drawing.

On the one hand, founding violence is law-making violence, the kind of violence marshaled forth by a state during war or a people or group through revolution or resistance. It is law directed from outside itself; such violence not only precedes or comes before established law but brings that law into existence. The American Revolution, Cooper's subject in both *The Spy* and *Notions*, is a prime example of this violence—a founding violence that brought into being a nation and people that did not before exist as such. Conserving violence, on the other hand, is directed from within the law and by way of established statutes, codes, and regulations to preserve laws or enforce state policy. Policing and punishment in general serve as primary albeit problematic examples of conserving violence— problematic because, as Walter Benjamin shows in his "Critique of Violence" (1921), such acts *make* or *found* the law each time they preserve it. To illustrate the slippage between founding and conserving violence, Benjamin turns to "the sphere of punishments" and specifically to capital punishment and the movement for its abolition at the time he was writing, one hundred years after the publication of *The Spy*. According to Benjamin, those who argued for the retention of the death penalty (what would seem to be an example of conserving violence) do so because they feel, "perhaps without knowing why and probably involuntarily, that an attack on capital punishment assails, not legal measure, not laws, but law itself in its origin."[23] For him, the purpose of such punishment "is not to punish the infringement of law but to establish new law. For in the exercise of violence over life and death more than in any other legal act, law reaffirms itself." In the case of the death penalty, in other words, the law affirms itself through conserving violence that, in its enactment, paradoxically becomes an act of founding violence—a muddled process through which, Benjamin notes, "something rot-ten in law is revealed, above all to a finer sensibility."[24] Benjamin, presumably, was among those of a "finer sensibility"; but so, too, I will suggest, is Cooper's refined Bachelor and the implied reader for whom Cooper was writing a century before Benjamin revealed this paradox.

The inherent instability between founding and conserving violence, exempli-fied in warfare and the death penalty respectively, informs Cooper's treatment of André's execution in both *The Spy* and *Notions*. Both forms of violence are also present in the first of the novel's two scenes staging near executions and play out in an exchange between Birch and an American dragoon guarding him on the eve before he is to be lawfully hanged. "As to killing a man in lawful battle," the dragoon reasons in a conversation with Birch about warfare and the death penalty, "that is no more than doing one's duty" (*The Spy* 217). The dialogue that follows echoes the Lawton–Sitgreaves exchange on the illegitimacy of capital punishment. Whereas Birch at one point confesses, "Thank God! . . . I have never yet taken the life of a fellow-creature," the dragoon who initially condemns treason (Birch's alleged offense) later reasons that even it "may be forgiven, if sincerely repented of" and ultimately declares that he, for one, "dislike[s] greatly to see a man hung up like a dog" (218). If Cooper, like the dragoon, more or less assumes the right of members of one army to kill those of another in open com-bat, he is more troubled by the presumed right of a state or people to take life from within the law and by means of its statutes. Cooper, in fact, says as much in his musings on André's execution in *Notions*. While justifying the Revolution's founding violence by way of natural law ("It was men battling for the known rights of human nature"), the Bachelor, like Benjamin, who senses something "rotten" revealed through the death penalty, identifies a "wayward feeling of man, that it is far less offensive to his power to kill a general in open conflict, than to lead a subordinate deliberately to an execution, which is sanctioned only by a disputed authority."[25] In *The Spy*, it is precisely this "disputed authority" that initiates conflict over André's execution and that permeates each of the novel's gallows scenes. Those scenarios include not just the near executions of Henry and Harvey—plotted at the novel's center and climax respectively—but the extra-legal execution of a Skinner by "Cow-boys," Tory partisans who opposed the American cause. That scene graphically unfolds in the novel's dénouement, almost as if to fulfill the promise of an execution that the novel twice stages but never performs. Coming as it does on the heels of Henry's narrow escape from the gallows, the Skinner's illicit hanging invites readers to associate it with the practice of capital punishment conducted within the law.

In fact, two of Cooper's best readers have made such a connection, although they surprisingly (at least by my account of the novel) find justice in the Skinner's brutal punishment. "Cooper does not explicitly connect the two cases or comment on the relative virtues of wild and formal justice," writes James Grossman in comparing the Skinner's execution to Wharton's condemnation; but "the reader feels" that the Cow-boys' deed "has its own rightness."[26] Similarly, Donald A. Ringe, in building on Grossman's point, sees Wharton's trial as "grossly unjust," but what he calls "the lynching of a Skinner by the Cowboys" as an essentially just act "in that it is so richly deserved."[27] Ringe and Grossman are certainly right to find in Wharton's legal conviction and near execution a criticism of martial law and summary justice; but they are wrong, I think, to find this legal injustice counterbalanced by unlawful justice in the Skinner's hanging. Rather than privileging one act at the expense of the other, it is more in keeping with *The Spy*'s republican ethos to see both in a negative light, both as fundamentally unjust in their disregard for human life. After all, that the Skinner's execution is carried out, as Grossman puts it, "so casually and callously that [the Cow-boys] do not even wait to see him die in screaming agony but ride away smug in the success of their joke,"[28] all the more condemns it and underscores its vicious inappropriateness. The Cow-boys may not stick around to watch the victim's agony, but Harvey, the novel's moral barometer, does. Taken into the Cow-boys' custody just before they capture the Skinner chief and "sentence" him to death, Birch is prevented from interfering with the summary but sadistic execution proceedings and thus made a reluctant witness to them.

In a work rife with tension over sovereign authority and the use of lethal violence, the illicit capital punishment of the Skinner is the novel's most problematic scene. Without the dramatic build up of the earlier staged but foiled hangings, this one delivers in terms of sheer spectacle. That the Skinner's execution in some way substitutes for Birch's is emphasized by the Cow-boy leader presiding over the affair (Cooper's narrator calls him "the executioner") who warns Birch, "offer to touch that dog, and you'll swing in his place" (400). Thus prevented from intervening but "yield[ing] to an unconquerable desire to witness the termination of this extraordinary scene" (400), Birch finds a bush from which to watch the proceedings unobserved. We see what Birch sees, and the grisly spectacle is brought to the fore as the disinterested Cow-boys begin to depart:

> But as [the Skinner] heard the tread of the horses moving on their course, and in vain looked around for human aid, violent trembling seized his limbs, and his eyes began to start from his head with terror. He made a desperate effort to

reach the beam; but, too much exhausted with his previous exertions, he caught the rope in his teeth, in a vain effort to sever the cord, and fell to the whole length of his arms. Here his cries were turned into shrieks.

"Help! cut the rope! captain!—Birch! good peddler! Down with the Congress!—sergeant! for God's sake, help! Hurrah for the king!—O God! O God!—mercy, mercy—mercy!"

As his voice became suppressed, one of his hands endeavored to make its way between the rope and his neck, and partially succeeded; but the other fell quivering by his side. A convulsive shuddering passed over his whole frame, and he hung a hideous corpse. (401)

Shame and embarrassment, not to mention horror and revulsion, explain the place of hiding from which Birch witnesses the event and we, as readers, are meant to experience it. Thus what Grossman describes as the scene's "rightness" is seen by Birch in all its wrongness, for Birch flees from the scene with "his hands to his ears," and, we are told, "it was many weeks before his memory ceased to dwell on the horrid event" (401).

It is precisely such violence that the Lawton-Sitgreaves exchange warns against in its disapprobation of capital punishment for any person—and not mere innocents like Henry and Harvey but guilty parties as well, such as the brutal Skinner chief and the genteel Major André. Indeed, read against that earlier exchange, the horror of what Birch sees disabuses the Dr. Sitgreaves of the world of the misguided desire of seeing a traitor or any so-called deserving person hanged. In tracing the rhetorical thread of Cooper's "hang-gallows" spies, I have uncovered an anti-gallows logic that informs the novel's republican politics and aesthetic design. I am not, however, suggesting The Spy be considered an anti-gallows novel or that Cooper was consciously making an argument against capital punishment. Instead, my point is to show the complex role the death penalty plays in a larger cultural narrative about the founding of the United States and the birth of U.S. citizenship—issues about sovereign authority, republican ideals, and the death penalty to which we shall return in chapter 5 in my discussion of Melville's work.

Those issues are also present in the work of George Lippard, a writer who differed from Cooper in so many ways—socially, politically, aesthetically—but who shared with him a concern about sovereign authority as well as an interest in the American Revolution and the use of capital punishment during the war for liberty. In fact, a quarter century after Cooper published The Spy, Lippard wrote his own legitimation narrative of the American Revolutionary War that obsessed

over execution scenes (including those of Americans Nathan Hale and Isaac
Hayne executed by the British) and raised the question of the legitimacy of
André's execution. If André's execution in *The Spy* serves as a touchstone for debates over sovereignty and founding authority, in Lippard's *The Legends from the
American Revolution* it occasions a bit of anti-gallows criticism in and of itself as
the gallows on which André is hanged is called a "hideous thing of evil,"[29] and
the execution itself depicted in gruesome terms to underscore its cruelty. In turning to Lippard, I make a case for the centrality of the death penalty and the cause
for its abolition in his politicoaesthetic vision. I also demonstrate how Lippard's
sardonic depictions of execution scenes and his pervasive use of gallows imagery
serve a broader narrative about class struggle and exploitation in America. We
can begin to see how by looking at the uniquely literary argument against capital
punishment that Lippard levies in his best-selling novel, *The Quaker City* (1845).

## LIPPARD'S "HURRAH FOR THE GALLOWS!"

Ironic and indirect, that argument is most fully developed in two scenes involving Devil-Bug, a grotesquely deformed murderer and the pimpish Doorman of
"Monk Hall," a secret den of debauchery patronized by Philadelphia's leading
citizens. The first of these scenes occurs in "Devil Bug's Dream," the dramatic
climax of book 3 of the novel. An apocalyptic, dystopian fantasy, the chapter
imagines life in Philadelphia one hundred years into the future when America's
dream of democracy has given way to the nightmare of despotism and monarchical rule. Devil-Bug's dream unfolds like a twisted version of Dickens's *A Christmas Carol* (1843), which was first published a year before Lippard began writing
his novel. The chapter begins as a "ghostly form" emerges from a group of "gay
wayfarers" and leads Devil Bug through a city he vaguely recognizes as Philadelphia but cannot quite place as such. Prominent buildings and landmarks remain,
but political life in the city has been radically restructured. Through the crowded
streets roll "proud chariots," Devil-Bug learns, carrying a "proud and insolent
nobility, who lord . . . over the poor people of the Quaker City!"[30] Once the
birthplace of American democracy and the city in which the Declaration of
Independence was signed, Philadelphia is now home to kingly palaces and man-
sions for the new nobility. "The spirit of the Old Republic is dethroned," the
Ghost tells Devil-Bug, "and they build a royal mansion over the ruins of Independence Hall!" (373)

Devil-Bug learns more about the fallen city and its future tyranny as he and
the Ghost (who serves as a tour guide) discuss what they see around them. Walking from Independence Hall and the Old State House, Devil-Bug observes that

Girard College and other civic institutions have been torn down, with marble palaces built in their ruins. When they reach Washington Square, Devil-Bug takes note of an enormous prison, wherein are confined "brave patriots," the Ghost tells him, "who struck the last blow for the liberty of the land, against the tyranny of this new-risen nobility" (374). Struck at first by this "great big jail of a building," Devil-Bug is soon distracted by a familiar sight, the gallows. The conversation between Devil-Bug and the Ghost that ensues affords readers an ironic lesson in the horrors and hypocrisies of capital punishment:

> "Hello! mister, isn't that a gallows I see yonder—opposite the jail? It's quite confortin' to see that old-fashioned thing alive yet!"
>
> "It is a gallows!" said the Ghost. "And thanks to the exertions of some of the Holy Ministers of God, it is never idle! Day after day its rope is distended by the wriggling body of some murderer, day after day these merciful preachers crowd around its blackened timbers, sending the felon into the presence of God, his ears deafened by their hallelujahs, while his stiffened hands grasp that Bible whose code is mercy to all men!"
>
> "Hurrah!" shouted Devil Bug. "The gallows is livin' yet! Hurrah!"
>
> "For some years it was utterly abolished," said the Ghost. —"Murders became few in number, convicts were restored to society, redeemed from their sins, and the gaols began to echo to the solitary footsteps of the gaoler. But these good Preachers arose in the Senate, and the Pulpit and plead [sic] beseechingly for blood!"
>
> "Hurrah for the Preachers! Them's the jockies!"
>
> "Give us but the gibbet," they shrieked. "Only give us the gibbet and we'll reform the world! Christ said mercy was his rule, we know more about his religion than he did himself, and we cry give us blood! In the name of Moses, in the name of Paul, and John, and Peter, in the name of the Church, in the name of Christ—give us the gibbet, only give us the gibbet!"
>
> "They said this? The jolly fellers!"
>
> "The gallows was given to them. The gibbet arose once more in the streets. Murder became a familiar thing. Crime dyed its hands in blood, and went laughing to the gibbet. The good Preachers plead [sic] for blood, and they had it!"
>
> "Hurrah!" screamed Devil-Bug. "The gallows is livin' yet! Hurrah!" He sprang from his feet in very glee, and clapped his hands and hurrahed again. (375)

The Ghost disappears at the end of this exchange, and the gallows is left with a poor spokesperson in Devil-Bug. Didactic in nature, the dialogue works through its comic juxtaposition of the Ghost's obvious sarcasm and ironic citation of these "good" Preachers' arguments and Devil-Bug's failure to interpret his re-marks as such. The dialogue thus speaks for itself—ironically illustrating how the institution of capital punishment oppresses liberty and supports the tyranny of the new state—exposing for readers the iniquities of capital punishment and whom we can blame for them, but it is worth commenting further on the history lesson it imagines. That lesson illustrates the gallows' failure as a deterrent by envisioning a time in Pennsylvania when the abolition of capital punishment had led to a drastic reduction in murder rates and the reintegration of convicts into society. Such a time, of course, is purely fictive; for while Pennsylvania (like Massachusetts and New York) came close, it would not abolish the death penalty before the Civil War, as Michigan, Rhode Island, and Wisconsin would do only a few years after *The Quaker City* was published.[31] Lippard's imaginary history lesson is significant in that it offers a literary counterpoint to support argu-ments for abolition by well-known reformers, such as Robert Rantoul Jr., John L. O'Sullivan, Charles C. Burleigh, and Charles Spear, that cited statistics in the reduction of crime that followed abolition in other states or foreign nations.[32] Unlike these reformers, Lippard, of course, can imagine whatever facts and sce-narios suit his purpose and shape material through graphic language certain to leave a lasting impression. It is also important to note that Lippard's imaginative counterhistory concerns Philadelphia, a city with a long and dynamic history in death penalty reform. Home to William Bradford and Benjamin Rush, early spokespersons for abolition, Philadelphia was the birthplace of anti-gallows activ-ism in America and the place where abolitionist discourse first flourished at the turn of the nineteenth century.[33] Philadelphia was, moreover, the city in which John Neal's *Logan* was published, and Pennsylvania was the first state to reduce drastically the number of capital statutes and to establish degrees of murder in 1794. Written in and about the "Quaker City" during the height of the anti-gallows movement, Lippard's novel draws upon the city's leading role in the ref-ormation of criminal law in the United States in its ironic critique of capital punishment.

If Lippard exposes the hypocrisies of the death penalty as a political institu-tion in "Devil-Bug's Dream," later in the novel he utterly savages the practice through a sardonic representation of a state-sponsored execution in a chapter ironically titled "Hurrah for the Gallows." The chapter provides a break in the novel's many overlapping plotlines as the police raid Monk Hall and round up and jail several of its criminals. Manacled and awaiting further police action, the criminals get to talking while Devil-Bug perversely sings the virtues of hanging.

One of the criminals, in response to Devil-Bug, asks him to "give us a leetle ser-man on that point" (*Quaker City* 504); Devil-Bug does not disappoint.

Appropriately titled "The Hangman's Glee," the sermon tells of a time when Devil-Bug served as the state's hangman and oversaw the execution of a sympa-thetic youth for a crime he probably did not commit. It begins with mock senti-mentality and a celebration of the gallows: "Hurray for hangin' say I!" says a jubilant Devil-Bug. "It's only a kick an' a jerk, and a feller goes like a shot, right slap into kingdom come. It does wons heart good to look upon them two pieces o' timber, with a beam fixed cross-wise, and a rope danglin' down—hurray for hangin'!" (504). The gallows' loathsome and austere framework—the mere sight of which intuits moral revulsion in works by Hawthorne and Simms examined in previous chapters—brings joy and elation to the morally bankrupt Devil-Bug. For him, it betokens a death that could not be easier ("only a kick an' a jerk") and that sends the criminal "right slap into kingdom come." Describing death by lawful hang-ing in this way echoes a literary argument against the practice we saw in chapter 1: namely, young Harold's relief in Neal's *Logan* at the snapping of the con-demned's neck ("Oh, there is no death so easy!" he says), and the Stranger's anal-ysis of the criminal's "process of reasoning," which holds that if one cannot es-cape the gallows, then at least the formal procedures surrounding the execution will inspire the public's and church's good opinion, thereby paving the way to heaven.[34]

Lippard, however, goes further than Neal by depicting in painstaking detail the last hour of a condemned's life from the perspective of Devil-Bug, an agent of the state and representative of the people. A far cry from a disinterested officer of the court, Devil-Bug (himself a murderer) is emblematic of the most de-bauched contingency of a mob gathered to witness an execution; in this respect, he is the worst sort of sensation seeker whom both Simms and Child chastise in their criticism of the spectacle of law's violence. To be sure, the bloodlust of Lippard's Devil-Bug exceeds anything described by these other authors, and the perverse pleasure he derives from hanging invites comparisons with Poe's de-praved narrator in "The Black Cat," himself a condemned murderer writing on the eve of his execution. For Devil-Bug graduates from hanging pets to hanging men: "It war'n't more nor five years since," he fondly remembers, "that I hung a man. Talk o' hangin' a dog or a cat, wot is it to hangin' a man? When I was quite a little shaver I used to hang a puppy or a pussy-cat, and I used to think it quite refreshin'. But hangin' a man? Ho-hoo ! That's the ticket!" (*The Quaker City* 505). The "man" Devil-Bug hangs is actually little more than a "boy," a nineteen-year-old English lad found guilty of killing the captain of a ship he served on while at sea.[35] Poor Charley, as we come to know the condemned, is a pathetic figure drawn from sentimental tradition of anti-gallows literature that Child helped to popularize in her New York letters and crime fiction. Sentenced to death in a case with "considerable doubt about it" by a judge and jury who "thought the best thing they could do for him wos to hang him" (505), Charley is condemned primarily because the court fears that, as a poor immigrant without stable work, he will become a burden on the state the coming winter.

Lippard's mock-sentimental tale of injustice gradually comes to a climax as Charley, proclaiming his innocence and worrying about the future of his indigent mother and sister back home in England, is escorted by an euphoric Devil-Bug to the gallows. Caught up with the day's excitement, the state's hangman joins the mob in hooting and jeering: "There's somethin' so jolly in seein' a live man, walking to a gallows," Devil-Bug recollects, "that I could'nt help joinin' in with' e'm; Hurray, ses I, Hurray for the gibbet! The good old gallows law for ever an' Amen!" (509). Devil-Bug's attention to the striking image of a "live man, walking to a gallows" anticipates the "Dead Man Walking" trope recently popularized in Sister Helen Prejean's 1993 book and Tim Robbins's later film by that name.[36] The power of such an image (both Lippard's and Prejean's) resides in the unnatural phenomenon brought about through a "death sentence," a peculiar performative that renders death and engenders nonbeing, though not at the moment of utterance.[37]

Charley's procession to the gallows is painfully protracted. In it, Lippard slows his narrative pace down to a crawl to emphasize the final hour of the condemned's life. When Charley and the hangman at last reach the scaffold, Lippard brings us in for a closer look, describing the event from Devil-Bug's perspective as the final minutes of Charley's life tick away:

"Charley didn't say a word arter that [his proclamations of innocence], but went up the gallows' steps without so much as a start. Wasn't it a grand sight for us fellers on the platform? There was the Marshall, a fine fat faced feller; there was the Parson, in his white cravat and black clothes, there was I, Devil-Bug, the Hangman, with the crape over my face, and there was the poor devil, as wos to be hung, standin' in the midst of us all, dressed in a white round about, with a face like a cloth, and curly hair, dark as jet."

"Hurray," ses I, "wot a sight ! Keep up yer spirits Charley. Jist look at the people, come to see yo' hung! Look at the Soldiers with their feathers and bagnets, jist look at the women, with babies in their arms, look at the gamblers, playin' thimble rig, look at the rum, my boy, in the tents yonder, and then, hurray! Look at the folks scattered all over Bush Hill, on the house tops away off yonder, and far down the streets! Hurray, my boy, there's a big crowd come to see you die, and so wot's the use o' grumblin' about yer mother and sister, and a cussed white pidgeon?"

"The mob giv' a howl! It was near twelve o'clock, and they wanted their show."

"It wants ten minnits o' th' time," ses the Marshall, an' the Parson, comes up to Charley, and taps him on the shoulder, and ses he, "Look up, my friend. God is merciful. Let us pray!"

"And then we all kneeled down, and the Parson made a short prayer about the Mercy o' God and the widders and orphans, and them deluded devils as hadn't sich a good Gospel an' sich a stout Gallows. While he was prayin' I saw two gentlemen, with knowin' faces, slyly creepin' up the ladder, and lookin' over the edge o' th' platform. I know'd 'em well. I'd stole dead bodies for 'em a hundred times. They were doctors, a-waitin' for the dead body o' Charley the English boy." (507–8)

The description continues in this way, with the mob eagerly awaiting "their show" and both state and church officials carrying out their duties. It lingers a bit over more details, such as the "delicate knot" that Devil-Bug conscientiously ties around Charley's "smooth neck" and a pathetic baptism administered with a glass of water that is abruptly ended by the Marshall's persistent "Time's up" (508–9). Mercifully, the chapter concludes with the execution itself. After Charley's final declaration of innocence, Devil-Bug disengages a trap door from which the condemned plunges down and, to the hangman's delight, "ho, hoo! There quiverin', strugglin', twistin', was the body of a dead man, plungin' at the end of a rope, with his tongue—black as a hat—stickin' out from under the edge o' th' white cap—hurray!" If the macabre humor of Devil-Bug's misplaced enthusiasm and exclamatory apostrophes isn't enough, the sermon comes to a close with a group of prating parsons sanctioning the event and enterprising doctors "huddling the carcase into a pine coffin" (509).

Brutal and excessively violent, the execution scene in The Quaker City makes a mockery of the criminal justice system—the site of policing violence par excellence in nineteenth-century America. From sanctimonious ministers and enterprising doctors to the gambling and liquor sales in the tents surrounding the site, the scene indicts society as a whole for its participation in the rituals and the business of state killing. While the people are implicated in the crime of capital punishment, the real villain is the state and the establishment, represented here

by the sheriff and hangman, on one hand, and doctors, lawyers, judges, and clergymen, on the other. Lippard, in short, presents a travesty of justice, and I have
dwelled on his sardonic object lessons in "Hurrah for the Gallows" for (at least)
two reasons: first, because they represent a distinctly literary form of anti-gallows
intervention into death penalty debates by imagining a scenario that calls attention to the horrors of capital punishment that cannot be reached through historical example or empirical evidence; second, because Lippard's use of fiction and
the fictive is designed to reach unconscious motives and irrational desires. In this
respect, his anti-gallows arguments creatively supplement the logical, rational,
religious, and sentimental arguments that were mainstays among those advocating abolition over the long nineteenth century. It is, then, no accident his
didactic lesson in the horrors and hypocrisies of capital punishment unfold in
Devil-Bug's unconscious dream state, or that his ironic representation of Charley's
execution finds expression through what David S. Reynolds would call the "shock-
gothic" rhetoric of Devil-Bug's sardonic sermon, "The Hangman's Glee."[38] Such
strategies, for example, utterly differ from the rational exchange between Lawton
and Sitgreaves on the illegitimacy of lawful death or the sentimental treatment
of André as a victim of an unjust or illegitimate law. Such arguments are more at
home in the work of Cooper's contemporaries, Simms and Neal (both of whom
also wrote Revolutionary War romances), but I focused earlier in this chapter on
Cooper's *The Spy* in part to show how such arguments can be found in unlikely
places and play an important role in larger cultural narratives.

Like Cooper's treatment of capital punishment, Lippard's argument against it
drew from the republican argument against the death penalty but in different
ways and toward different ends. Lippard too was concerned with the rhetoric of
the Revolution, surrealistically deployed in Devil-Bug's nightmarish vision of
an American future without democracy, but he made an altogether different
argument about class exploitation. More than any novelist of the period, Lippard linked capital punishment to capitalism, and he used the execution scene
symbolically to dramatize an epic class struggle between, on the one hand, exploited workers representing "the people" and, on the other, the rich and powerful, aided by a conservative ministry, who used the gallows as a central means
of political oppression. While this class struggle is implicit in the execution of
the exploited and innocent Charley, a victim of law's tyranny, it becomes pronounced in Lippard's overtly political *The White Banner* (1851), a collection of
fiction, sketches, and propaganda that Lippard self-published at the height
of his career to help finance his radical socialist enterprise, "The Brotherhood
of America."

## CAPITALISM AND CAPITAL PUNISHMENT

Much of *The White Banner* first appeared in Lippard's radical working-class penny press, the *Quaker City Weekly*.[39] We can get a sense of Lippard's radical Jacksonian politics by looking briefly at an editorial from the paper's first edition responding to the recent fall in France of Louis Philippe, the so-called Citizen-King (whose initial rise to power in the July Monarchy in 1828 in part occasioned Cooper's *Notions of the Americans*). Celebrating the fact that Philippe had been "tumbled from his Kingdom and his wealth," Lippard hoped the event would spur "the People of the World" to unite "in arms for their rights." He also wondered: "Will the Kings be able to manacle the People, and tread them into slavery once more?"[40] Turning from Europe to the United States, Lippard raised similar questions about his own country: "And our land—is there no cloud upon its horizon? Does not Black Slavery sit brooding in our very Capital—are not our Great Cities thronged with Armies of white slaves?"[41] As Shelley Streeby has pointed out, in the same issue of the *Quaker City Weekly* in which Lippard posed these questions, couched in a rhetoric of revolution, he began serializing *The Entranced*, a sensational story about the political future of America that linked it to the most oppressive period of rule in ancient Rome.

*The Entranced*, a novella that imagined a cosmic confrontation between the citizen-subject and sovereign authority mediated seemingly at every turn through the scene and tropes of capital punishment, would be revised and published as *Adonai: The Pilgrim of Eternity*, the lead and main work of *The White Banner*. But before turning to that work, it will be helpful first to trace Lippard's use of capital punishment as a trope and thematic for class exploitation in the other works collected in *The White Banner*. To begin with, in "The Dollar," an early sketch from "Legends of the Every Day" in the volume, Lippard describes the final hours of a terminally ill "rich man," who owned "hovels and courts" in Philadelphia and iron and copper mines elsewhere in the state. Sarcastically dubbed a "good" and "benevolent man" for his petty philanthropy,[42] the dying capitalist is also described ironically as "a just man" in whom "the Gallows and the Jail always found . . . a faithful and unswerving advocate" (105). In a later sketch from the collection, Lippard targets the pro-gallows ministry, the buttress of the establishment and the butt of his attack on capital punishment in "Devil Bug's Dream." While acknowledging the importance of sincere and virtuous ministers in effecting "political, moral, and religious purposes" (125), Lippard censures those whose message is centered around vengeance and intolerance— exemplified, for him, in anti-Catholic and pro-gallows rhetoric. "To visit the sick, to unfold clear views of a future state to the dying, to feed the hungry, to educate the orphan"—in short, the tenets of Christian charity—"are tasks far beneath them," Lippard writes of the conservative Protestant ministry. "They strike at nobler aims. To attack the Pope and hallow the Gallows, and to invest the Gallows with the sanctity of divine Revelation,—such is their highest task. 'Down with the Pope and up with the Gallows!'—you have their whole theology in these words" (126).

Lippard's sardonic attack on the clergy moves from the general to the particular as he holds up his contemporary, Reverend John Hughes of Philadelphia and New York, for special attention. Hughes's principle message, as Lippard characterizes it in *The White Banner*, is "to defend the Gallows and blackguard the Pope!" These causes

> are his pet subjects. To blaspheme the name of Christ by making him the prop of the Gallows, and turning his Gospel of Love into a Gospel of the Gibbet and the Hangman, —such is one of the great objects of this individual's ministry. Set a Gallows before him, and he is alive. A Gallows stirs him. It enlivens him. Give him a sight of a gallows, and he jumps into the controversial ring, with his comb up and his feathers spread—the very gamecock of the Gallows. (127)

The "gamecock of the Gallows," the Reverend Hughes whom Lippard lampoons here is not unlike Devil-Bug, who also becomes "enliven[ed]" at the sight of lawful death. While Lippard in this sketch focuses his assault on the historical John Hughes, a Catholic priest who emigrated from Ireland and who apparently became a figure of local interest in Philadelphia death penalty debates,[43] he undoubtedly also had in mind Reverend George B. Cheever, the nation's foremost proponent of capital punishment who is said to have "possessed a bookmark embroidered with the hanging scene."[44] Cheever, as we saw in chapter 1, famously entered the "controversial ring" when he sparred against John L. O'Sullivan in debates reported throughout northern presses, when Lippard himself was a newspaperman writing for Philadelphia's *Spirit of the Times* and *Citizen Soldier*. Although Lippard does not mention Cheever by name here or elsewhere in *The White Banner*, he does in "Jesus and the Poor" (1848), a nightmarish tale in which the death penalty serves as a central trope for tyranny and class oppression in Lippard's contemporary Philadelphia.[45] In it, Lippard invokes the famous progallows minister by name and reputation, linking "Dr. Cheever's last letter in favor of the Gallows" to a towering "Phantom Gallows" that casts a hideous shadow over the Quaker City. Given that Cheever, in his debates with O'Sullivan, had taken offense to O'Sullivan's alliterative association of "The Gallows and the Gospel" in O'Sullivan's essay by that name,[46] one can only imagine what Cheever would have said in response to Lippard's imaginative epithet—"the gamecock of the Gallows"—for clergy of his flock.

In addition to attacking the pro-gallows ministry and moneyed America for their support of capital punishment in *The White Banner*, Lippard adds a historical dimension to his class-based argument by dramatizing the 1414 execution of Martyr John Huss for insubordination. Huss's execution marks a dramatic highpoint in what Lippard calls the *"unwritten* history of the People" (128, emphasis in original), a history he opposes to the official record written by "Kings," "Popes," and "Rich Men"—a triumvirate representing monarchy, religion, and capitalism. Moreover, he uses Huss's historical execution to mark the symbolic birth of his Brotherhood and the universal struggle of "the People" against tyranny and oppression. Although Lippard identifies Huss by name in the sketch's title ("John Huss in 1414: The Martyr of Brotherhood"), he is known in the sketch itself as only "the CRIMINAL," a figure who is consistently opposed to "AUTHORITY," which is personified in the "iron types" of the pope and emperor. By capitalizing and opposing the CRIMINAL to AUTHORITY ("BROTHERHOOD" is the only other term consistently capitalized in the piece), Lippard creates an allegory in miniature for the people's confrontation with the tyranny of church and state, which anticipates what he sees as the despotism of capitalism and capital punishment of his own day. This tale of class oppression and injustice, like the one that Devil-Bug tells of Poor Charley in *The Quaker City*, culminates with the scene of execution itself. Shown, however, from a sympathetic perspective and from the vantage point of the spectators, it stands in stark contrast to Devil-Bug's viciously sardonic recounting of Charlie's hanging. The "silent spectators" in this sketch, unlike the boisterous mob led by Devil-Bug, identify with (rather than objectify) the condemned; they catch only a glimpse of the CRIMINAL's face through the flames and clouds of smoke that envelop him as he is burnt at the stake for the crime of suggesting that Christianity is a religion of and for the poor, since Christ himself had come "in the garb of a Poor Man." No longer merely witnesses to the event, the spectators become "THE PEOPLE" for whom the CRIMINAL dies, and their presence at the execution symbolizes the birth of the "BROTHERHOOD" for which Lippard is writing some four centuries later (134).

Lippard reworks the scene of execution from another perspective in *Adonai: The Pilgrim of Eternity*, a gothic, religious fantasy and counternarrative of sorts to the futuristic vision of "Devil-Bug's Dream." The novella is set in ancient Rome under the rule of Nero, the notorious tyrant famous in part for ordering the execution of his own mother, and begins in the catacombs, wherein a group of early Christians has been condemned to die by starvation. To escape death, they need only to renounce their faith and to *"deny the Felon who died upon the Cross"* (12, emphasis in original). Describing Christ as an executed felon is only one of the ways Lippard evokes the scene of capital punishment at the novella's outset. Like his other execution scenes, this one dramatizes a primal conflict between the oppressed and the oppressor. Whereas Lippard figured that confrontation symbolically between the CRIMINAL and AUTHORITY in the Martyr Hayne sketch, and ironically between a poor immigrant youth and society at large in *The Quaker City*, the confrontation in *Adonai* takes shape between the condemned Christians and those who work for Nero. In fact, a barrier between the two is literally erected, for between the condemned in the catacombs and those in the outside world of Roman luxury stands an "Iron Door," sometimes called "Law" or "Custom," Lippard's narrator tells us, but more often "Religion." This politicoreligious allegory is then completed with a Kafkaesque figure of a "solitary man" who guards the Iron Door (16).

The solitary man becomes the main character of *Adonai*. A doorman of sorts, this figure is an everyman type rather than an arch-criminal like Devil-Bug, the murderous doorman of Monk Hall, or the hideous "Doomsman," the mad executioner who presides over torture and execution scenes in Lippard's first extended work of fiction, *The Ladye Annabel; or, The Doom of the Poisoner* (1844). The guardian of the Iron Door begins the novella as Lucius, a Roman nobleman and friend of Nero, who is confounded but intrigued by the Christians' sacrifice for their faith. Curiosity turns to sympathy when Lucius discovers the dead Christians and, moved by their profound suffering, converts to Christianity himself. By doing so, he soon finds himself sentenced to death as well. Whereas the Christians were condemned to starvation, Lucius is to die by the headsman's sword. With his neck bared and the headsman's sword poised for the lethal blow, Lucius launches into a long, final speech that begins by criticizing the tyranny of the "Priest," "King," and "Rich Man" (precursors, for Lippard, of capitalism) and then looks forward to a new age, "sixteen hundred years hence . . ." when "every man will dwell on his own land; or else men, as brothers, will live in community, like the early followers of the Lord, for whom I am about to suffer" (22). Lucius is cut off in the middle of his speech, but not by the headsman's blow. Instead, he falls into what Lippard's narrator calls a "magnetic trance" induced by a hateful figure known only as "the Executioner."

In the narrative that follows the Executioner grants Lucius's dying wish, as Lucius is transformed into "Adonai" (which in Hebrew means "God, look!") and transported into the future to see if his prediction comes true. The Executioner accompanies the newly Christianized Adonai but not as a travel guide, the role the Ghost plays in the futuristic "Devil-Bug's Dream"; rather, he functions as a menacing entity that materializes at various moments and in a variety of guises: sometimes as the state's henchman; other times as a representative capitalist. On his pilgrimage through eternity, Adonai witnesses key moments in world history—founding, revolutionary moments like the one I explored at length in Cooper's *The Spy*. He first visits Germany during the Reformation and speaks with Martin Luther; later he travels to different locales in Europe and the United States during the eighteenth and nineteenth centuries, at one point conversing with the ghost of Robespierre (himself a notorious executioner *and* a victim of capital punishment) beneath the guillotine in some heavy-handed symbolism. Adonai's journey culminates in Washington, D.C., in the late 1840s, where he is joined by the spirit of George Washington. Like Devil-Bug and the Ghost who traverse the futuristic nightmare of monarchical rule in Philadelphia, Adonai and "Washington the Arisen" (as he is called) wander through the fallen present of the nation's capital and end up in the Senate Hall, where they listen to "the Great Men of the New World—gathered in solemn council." What they hear, however, does not impress them. One distinguished senator claims that the Constitution, while "a very fine piece of writing," contains "a great many errors," including the notion that "all men are born free and equal" (51–52). Highlighting the flaws of such a theory, the senator rationalizes a class system in which there must be "rich and poor, Masters and Slaves" (52), thus prompting the disbelief of both Adonai and Washington. Learning that the senator hails from Carolina, Washington vents his disappointment, alluding to a Revolutionary War execution to drive home the irony of the senator's speech: "The land of Martyr Hayne!" he laments of the senator's home state of Carolina. "And Hayne was hung, some seventy years ago, by the creatures of a Tyrant, in order that words like those uttered by the Senator, might be spoken to-day, in the Senate of a redeemed People!" (52)

The executed "Martyr" to whom Lippard's Washington refers is Colonel Isaac Hayne, who was captured and executed by the British forces during the American Revolutionary War, just as André was captured and executed by the Americans. Whereas Cooper, as we have seen, uses André's execution to explore the complexities of sovereign violence when used by "the people" in the name of liberty, Lippard here uses Hayne's hanging to symbolize a crime against the people by "creatures of a Tyrant." Washington's pronounced sarcasm is thus representative of what he and Adonai come to feel as they realize that neither Christianity nor U.S. democracy, with liberty and equality guaranteed by the Constitution, has prevailed over universal tyranny. Through the scene on the Senate floor, Lippard's religious allegory becomes decidedly political as it takes up the rights of citizens in this world. While the Carolina senator argues against the people's interest by promoting chattel slavery through a racially exclusionary interpretation of the Constitution, a "great senator from the North" defends wage slavery and the interests of industrial capitalists at the expense of "the People," whose interests the Constitution was designed to protect: "We must protect the man who builds a factory," the northern senator asserts; "we must protect the man who owns a ship! Commerce and Manufacturers—these are the great ideas of America! Unless you foster, and protect them—even at the expense of nine-tenths of the People, and by robbing nine-tenths of the fruits of their labor—your Constitution is in vain!" (52) Benefiting only moneyed America, the senators' arguments utterly disgust Adonai and Washington. Adonai, for instance, associates mid-nineteenth-century life in the United States with life behind the "Iron Door" under Nero's regime, where on "the one side the Senators wrangle for plunder," and "on the other, the People starve and die." Washington echoes Adonai's sentiments with typical Lippardian gallows imagery: "It was for this that we fought the battle and dared the winter's snow, and went to war with the gibbet's rope about our necks!" (54).

Gallows imagery indeed abounds in *Adonai*. It is ever present in both Washington's and Adonai's language and embodied in the absent presence of the hateful Executioner. Whereas Washington, for instance, frequently invokes the spirit of executed patriots and speaks of fighting for liberation with "the gibbet's rope about our necks!," Adonai comes to see that the world has not progressed much since the days of Nero's oppressive regime. He complains to Washington about the failed promise of American democracy: "Liberty! The Liberty to work, to starve, to die. This was the object of your Revolution—was it not? The Liberty to obey laws which were made for Capital and through Capital, drive Labor to the jail, the gibbet, or the grave" (71). The gibbet, coupled with laws made for "Capital and through Capital," is one of the many instances where Lippard links capitalism to capital punishment in his work. Another occurs in "Jesus and the Poor," the popular tale (to which I earlier alluded) in which an enormous "Phantom Gallows," propped up by ministers and supported by capitalists, casts an ominous shadow over the Quaker City.

That shadow, present in his early work, evolved and darkened into a master trope for class oppression as Lippard matured from an imitative writer of gothic fiction to an innovator of what David S. Reynolds has called "dark reform literature" lurking beneath the American Renaissance. Lippard's use of capital punishment—and especially the execution scene—to argue against class exploitation exemplifies what Michael Denning has aptly termed Lippard's "labor aesthetic": a "literature," as Lippard himself puts it, "that work[s] practically, for the advancement of social reform" and that "is not too dignified or too good to picture the wrongs of the great mass of humanity," for that kind of literature "is just good for nothing at all."[47] Lippard's *literary executions* best demonstrate this political aesthetic in that they flagrantly disregarded rules of decorum that many reform-minded novelists obeyed by criticizing capital punishment but *not* showing an execution itself. Lippard, as we have seen, flouts this etiquette by forcing readers to see "the poetry of the gallows" and to hear "the music of the Gallows"—central components in his case against capital punishment. A prime example of a literary execution scene that abides by the conventions of genteel reform can be found in Emily Catherine Pierson's *Jamie Parker; The Fugitive* (1851), a popular novel published the same year as Lippard's *The White Banner*. To elicit sympathy for enslaved Africans in her antislavery novel, Pierson borrows a page from conventional anti-gallows reform fiction by dramatizing the legal proceedings on the day a sympathetic slave is executed but stopping short of depicting lawful death itself: "We would turn from his scaffold and death," Pierson's narrator writes just before the hanging takes place, "and from the cruel, hard-hearted curiosity which led people who *thought they were civilized*, to look on and feast their eyes with seeing a fellow-being hung!"[48] By calling attention to the spectacle of lawful death but then forcing readers to look away, Pierson at once denounces the hypocrisy of so-called respectable spectators *"who thought they were civilized,"* while refusing to indulge the "hard-hearted curiosity" of sensation seekers.

Simms's Border Romances, as I suggested to begin this chapter, provide numerous instances of an author following a similar etiquette of aversion epitomized by Pierson, but there are important examples by other authors as well. To be sure, much of the period's fiction that both censured capital punishment and involved an execution either placed it (if there was one) offstage or resolved the conflict before it transpired by dramatizing a last-minute pardon or revelation of actual innocence. Two such novels were Elizabeth Oakes Smith's *The Newsboy* (1854) and Day Kellogg Lee's *Merrimack; or, Life at the Loom* (1854), both published the same year. While Smith's novel openly attacks the "shocking details" of capital punishment in an early scene that takes readers through New York City's infamous "Egyptian Tombs"—where the death penalty is likened to "the act of murder," its administration constituting "legal crimes," and its purpose designed to "harden and brutalize the mind"[49]—the novel ends by staging the

trial and execution of "Flashy Jack," a sympathetic criminal and central character who impulsively commits a murder to avenge a child abduction. Amid a flood
of tears and prayers, the execution is carried out but in no way dramatized; we
realize that the condemned has at last been killed through a glimpse of the
hearse carrying away his body.[50] We get an example of an eleventh-hour pardon
in Lee's *Merrimack* and, in an effort to set up my discussion in chapter 4, I would
like to look more closely at its strategies in criticizing capital punishment but
avoiding an execution, before turning to Sylvester Judd and returning to Cooper
to conclude this one.

Like Smith's *The Newsboy*, Lee's *Merrimick* culminates with a capital trial
and a scheduled execution that serves as the work's dénouement. It, too, foregrounds an anti-gallows message early in the narrative—but not through a direct
attack. Instead, it does so through the sympathetic figure of "the Crazy Juror," a
sensitive man whose guilt from serving on a jury in a capital case has literally
driven him mad. The old man was, when younger, we are told,

> one of the jurors who doomed that poor impulsive boy, [Stephen] Merrill
> Clark, to the gallows, for arson, which others induced him to commit: that he
> witnessed his execution, and saw his bright yellow hair float on the wind as he
> struggled with the pangs of death, and he was smitten with such horror for
> the heart-rending scene, and for his own action in the tragedy, he went home
> a maniac, and had continued a maniac to that day. This melancholy object
> was often before our eyes, smiling and weeping by turns; crying now, "Poor
> Merrill! it was my voice that killed thee!" then, starting up with a look of fran-
> tic joy, and saying, "Thank God! we saved Merrill—he was such a pretty, ten-
> der boy—we saved him from the gallows, and he is not dead!"[51]

Plagued by a guilty conscience for "his own action in the tragedy," the Crazy
Juror had participated in a process of lawful death when others, as Smith contends in her anti-gallows statement in *The Newsboy*, "refuse[d] to act as jurors
where the punishment is death."[52] While Lee's argument, unlike Smith's, is indirect in its criticism and conveyed through an unreliable character rather than
through authorial pronouncement, it is directly connected to the real world, for
Stephen Merrill Clark was an actual seventeen-year-old boy executed in Salem,
Massachusetts (the setting for part of Lee's novel). A young Nathaniel Hawthorne,
as we shall see in the next chapter, expressly refused to attend young Clark's
execution.

A deranged but sympathetic man, the Crazy Juror imagines scenarios in
which the dreadful punishment of death could be reversed, thereby psychically

atoning for his role in authorizing an irreversible penalty. Disguised as a woman at one point in the novel, he even disrupts a meeting on the subject of "Capital Punishment" to "bear *her* testimony against it!"[53] Such incidents pepper the novel with anti-gallows sentiment, but Lee returns to and drives home the novel's argument against the death penalty in its concluding action: a race against the clock to prevent the execution of a ne'er-do-well and petty criminal, the narrator's brother, who is sentenced to death (like the historical Merrill Clark) for the crime of arson. Debates between rival ministers in the novel's final scenes highlight the hypocrisy and inhumanity of capital punishment, as the narrator (like Lizzy's brother in Child's "Elizabeth Wilson") circulates a petition seeking a pardon for the condemned. The governor, despite sympathy for the condemned and his family, refuses to grant clemency because of his obligations to uphold the law. The execution, however, *is* ultimately prevented—thanks to a last-minute confession from the individual who actually committed the crime. This revelation presents its own argument against capital punishment by stressing the fallibility of circumstantial evidence and the irreversibility of an execution in cases of error—an argument I examine at length in my next chapter on Hawthorne and evidentiary value.

The important point here is that Lee's *Merrimack* and Smith's *The Newsboy* represent two ways novelists from the period argued against capital punishment without dramatizing death, thus providing both a context and a point of contrast for understanding Lippard's approach. Distinct and original in his literary representations of lawful death, Lippard of course was not the only writer to dramatize the enactment of a capital sentence as a form of anti-gallows protest. Indeed, he did not even pen the period's most controversial literary execution scene. That distinction belongs to Sylvester Judd, an unlikely candidate who was in many ways Lippard's opposite number. A prominent Unitarian minister from rural New England, Judd married a senator's daughter and into one of the wealthiest families in Maine, thus becoming part of the "establishment" against which Lippard vehemently rails in his work. He was, moreover, chaplain to the state legislature, but lost that position in 1842 because of his extreme pacifist views and because he preached sermons condemning any and every act of war, past and present, including the hallowed American Revolution, in whose violence Lippard at times revels in *Legends* and elsewhere and Cooper ultimately legitimates in *Notions* if not *The Spy*. Like both Lippard and Cooper, Judd wove the figure of capital punishment into a larger cultural narrative—in his case one that promoted Universalism, nonresistance, temperance, and fraternity. Indeed, the abolition of the gallows near the end of Judd's *Margaret: A Tale of the Real and Ideal*,

*Blight and Bloom* (1845) marks a key symbolic moment transforming Livingston, Judd's representative "real" New England community, into *Mons Christi*, an "ideal" community whose "bloom" in large part depends on a principled renunciation of the death penalty. In this respect, Judd's utopian vision of a future world without the gallows at once complements and sharply contrasts with Lippard's dystopian vision of an American future (and present) in which the gallows is used on a massive scale to oppress the masses and to protect the interests of capitalist elites.

But rather than focus on capital punishment in Judd's construction of a broader cultural narrative, as I have with Cooper and Lippard, in what follows I attend to *Margaret's* execution scene in the context of anti-gallows activism. Doing so will help me engage directly with the politics and poetics of dramatizing a literary execution.

## JUDD'S JUDGMENT

First published the same year as Lippard's *The Quaker City*, *Margaret* (1845) tells the story of a young woman's coming of age in rural New England at the end of the eighteenth century. While Judd's novel centers on its titular protagonist and her spiritual development, a capital crime and execution involving Margaret's beloved older stepbrother, Chilion, serves as the climactic event of part 2 of the novel. The murder for which Chilion is executed occurs when, during an evening Husking Bee, he notices that Solomon Smith, a local taverner, "had penned [Margaret] in the chimney-corner, where he seemed to be urging some point, with drunken and dogged pertinacity."[54] Drinking himself, and incited by Rose, a friend of Margaret convinced of Smith's dishonorable intentions and who says as much, Chilion "violently hurl[s]" a husking file across the room. The file strikes Solomon who is, Judd's narrator tells us, "then and there fell[ed], killed, murdered, under the agency of passions that from innocent pastime]had mounted to criminal excess."[55]

Despite mitigating circumstances and the narrator's questioning of "agency," Chilion is summarily charged, tried, and convicted of murder. Knowledge of prior "differences" between Chilion and Solomon, along with the respectable community's prejudice against Chilion and Margaret's family—poor, hard-drinking, but well-meaning farmers who live on the outskirts of town—play a key role in Chilion's conviction. The penalty of death for Chilion's crime is thus a foregone conclusion, and after a touching scene in which Chilion accepts guilt and assumes responsibility for his rash act, the execution approaches and Chilion—like Christ, himself a victim of capital punishment (as Lippard is fond of pointing out)—is transformed into a kind of martyr, a figure of condemned innocence that one finds in so much of the period's anti-gallows literature.

Judd takes great care in dramatizing "The Execution," the title of chapter 10 of part 2 of *Margaret*. The chapter begins:

> The morning of the Execution, like that of the resurrection, brought out "both small and great, a multitude which no man could number." They came "from the East and the West, the North and the South." Highways were glutted with wagons and horses, by-ways with foot-people. They came from distances of eight, twenty, and even forty miles. Booths, carts, wheel-barrows supplied a profusion of eatables and drinkables. A man with a hand-organ in cap and bells, hawkers of ballads, a "Lion from Barbary," . . . gaming tables, offered attractions to the crowd, and contributed to the variety of objects with which the Green brimmed and overflowed.[56]

Imitating the Puritan plain style and writing in biblical cadences, Judd imbues the execution scene with a sacred aura. He even quotes from the New Testament, giving the execution of Chilion an atmosphere similar to the crucifixion of Christ and likening the morning of Chilion's death to the morning of the Resurrection. At the same time, however, the grandeur of the scene is undercut by the profane activities of the crowd: an organ grinder preparing for a performance; hawkers selling ballads, presumably ones commemorating Chilion's crime and hanging in the tradition of early American gallows literature; and entrepreneurial townsfolk setting up gaming tables for profit and amusement. In addition to setting the stage for the main event, Judd's narrator chronicles the events that transpire on Hanging Day. For instance, he cites substantially from an execution sermon written and preached for the occasion. He also describes the event from the crowd's perspective: "Am I too late for the hanging?" a man asks as he arrives breathless to the execution site. "I haven't missed one of these for thirty year[s]," he goes on to say. Another spectator, looking to secure a good view for his family, prods his daughter to move forward: "Your mother, dear, is waiting for us; she says seeing a man hanged is the most interesting sight she ever beheld" (347).

With the crowd growing exponentially, Judd's narrator turns to "the current of general attraction," detailing the pomp and ceremony of the procession leading Chilion to his death. The event culminates with the execution itself, which Judd narrates from the perspective of both Chilion and the crowd gathered to witness it:

The drop fell, on the part of the spectators a gasp, a sudden blink of the eye, a suffocating sensation in the throat, a sicker *one* in the stomach, responded for a moment to the struggles of the dying man, and, on both sides, all was over. The body was decently laid in the coffin, . . . borne to its last resting-place, in the grave-yard. The crowd dispersed to drink, to game, to riot, to wrestle, to race horses, see the Lion, hear the hand-organ. (349, emphasis in original)

Like Lippard in *The Quaker City* and elsewhere, Judd brings readers up close to witness a hanging. But in Judd's account there is, of course, no gleeful Devil-Bug figure, no ironic "Hurrah for the Gallows!" cheer through which the institution of capital punishment is lampooned. Instead, he registers both the crowd's and Chilion's perspectives, emphasizing bodily sensations in a series of fragmentary images that drive home the physical disgust and moral revulsion to be experienced by men and women of proper moral feeling. Moreover, by shifting between these perspectives, Judd blurs the boundaries separating victim and spectators, thus calling attention to the common humanity of the condemned and the crowd—a common rhetorical ploy of the traditional execution sermon but used here toward different ends.[57] Yet this scene, like the stage he sets prior to the execution, is undercut by baser desires, as the crowd "disperses to drink, to game, to riot."

In dramatizing an execution, Judd, like Lippard, showed his readers a public act, carried out in the people's name, that they could no longer see for themselves. Public executions in Judd's Maine and Lippard's Pennsylvania, as well as through almost all the North by the mid-1840s, had been outlawed for some time, in large part because of genteel arguments which held that such acts were psychologically harmful to spectators. Such events created, so the argument went, a vulgar and lewd atmosphere particularly unsuited for women and children. Interestingly enough, genteel literary critics (who would not deign to criticize Lippard's work) levied a similar argument against Judd for the "vulgarity" in which his novel indulged through its representation of violence and intemperance as well as its use of course language and rural idioms drawn from backwoods culture.[58] Indeed, the murder and execution scenes can be seen as exemplifying what such critics found offensive and crude in a novel many of them otherwise praised. For instance, in a twenty-page review of *Margaret* in the *North American Review*, fellow Unitarian minister William B. O. Peabody cited the novel's drinking and murder scene as a prime example of such vulgarity, calling it "the greatest failure in all the work." Those remarks were written in a lengthy paragraph that began, "The subject of capital punishment . . . ," and went on to summarize the trial and execution scenes, before returning to the topic with which it began. "But the question of capital punishment is not reached by such an imaginary case as this," Peabody wrote, returning to the question and responding specifically to the trial's outcome. "Evidently nothing could be more absurd," he continued,

> than such a penalty inflicted on such a person, where it was obvious that he could not have intended to give a fatal wound. The question is, whether capital punishment can be dispensed with. It is not to the purpose to say, that "the worst use you can put a man to is to hang him"; for this, though doubtless a smart saying, would apply equally well to shutting him up in a jail. When the truth is made clear, that this fearful penalty does not answer its purpose, or that some others can be resorted to instead of it, the public mind will be ready to surrender it; but if this is not done, it must endure till it is displaced by the advance of civilization, which has many remains of barbarism yet hanging round it, but will sooner or later lose all its taste for blood."[59]

Peabody's review offers no new insight into the debate over the death penalty; its significance, however, lies in what it represents: a representative critic prompted by Judd's novel to write not only on the "subject" and "question" but on the "purpose" of capital punishment in an elite, widely circulating periodical. Such a rhetorical situation epitomizes what I have called the cultural rhetoric of capital punishment—a rhetoric in which popular fiction played an important role by imagining criminal cases and dramatizing or staging executions. In fact, in the criticism from Peabody's review cited earlier, we see commonplaces of the anti-gallows argument, such as "the worst use you can put a man to is to hang him," that are critically evaluated—an evaluation prompted by an engagement with Judd's novel. In rejecting this particular argument as a "smart saying," that is, an empty rhetorical flourish, Peabody quibbles with Judd's dramatization but more or less agrees in principle with Judd's judgment, seeing the death penalty as a "remains of barbarism" (another anti-gallows commonplace) to be abandoned with the advance of civilization. This opinion is echoed and developed at length in another long review essay published in the same volume of *North American Review* as Peabody's "Margaret" article. That article, "The Punishment of Death," discusses three works: O'Sullivan's *Report in Favor of the Abolition of the Punishment of Death by Law* (1842), Cheever's *Punishment by Death: Its Authority and Expediency* (1842), and Spear's *Essays on the Punishment of Death* (1844), the last of which included a testimonial from Judd. That Peabody's "Margaret" review was published alongside "The Punishment of Death" in the

January 1846 *North American Review* suggests the important role imaginative literature, especially novels, had in shaping debates about the death penalty—particularly the argument to abolish the death penalty. That argument, as I have shown in my previous chapters, was developed in significant ways by a diverse range of writers including Neal, Simms, Child, Hawthorne, Fuller, Whitman, Whittier, and Lippard.

Of the many writers whose poetry or fiction contributed to the anti-gallows cause, Judd deserves special attention for his direct participation in the influential anti-gallows movement in his home state of Maine. In the late 1830s, he had joined two of Maine's most prominent citizens in the campaign. One of them was Thomas C. Upham, a well-known Bowdoin professor whose influential *Manual of Peace* (1835) included an argument for the abolition of capital punishment; the other was Tobias Perrington, a state senator (and colleague of Judd's father-in-law) who authored an 1836 *Report of the Committee on Capital Punishment*, a legislative review (and later popular book) that unequivocally called for the repeal of capital statutes.[60] Given Judd's commitment to the anti-gallows cause, it is not surprising that he staged and dramatized a pivotal execution in his first novel. Judd himself, however, was surprised by how that scene was received by the literary establishment—evinced by a "Note," as we shall see, appended to a new and revised edition of *Margaret* published in 1851. In that edition, Judd heeded some of the criticism in Peabody's review and elsewhere. By and large, however, these revisions were light, the most substantial occurring in the execution scene. Yet rather than omitting the scene entirely or placing it off-stage, Judd blotted out the description but let it stand as such—producing, in effect, a black rectangular box, suggestive of a coffin or a dark abyss into which Chilion drops. The omission produced a textual elision that might best be described as a veiled window preventing one from seeing an act carried out by the government in semisecrecy. Thus, by blackening out the description, the execution scene remained in the book but was literally placed under erasure. Like the so-called private hangings of condemned criminals behind prison walls, the blackened-out passage served to remind Judd's readers not so much that executions occurred with regularity but that readers, as citizens, could no longer see for themselves these public acts—"public" insofar as they were carried out in the people's names.

Structurally, Chilion's execution plays a crucial role in both the original and revised editions of *Margaret*. It at once marks the climax of part 2 of the novel and sets up the elaborate dénouement that unfolds in part 3. As if in punishment for Chilion's death, a conflagration consumes the town of Livingston almost

The religious ceremonies being concluded, the procession was formed for the place for the end of Chilion — a sandy plain in the North part of the town. Bristling bayonets, funeral music, a dismal retinue of twenty thousand people, are some of the items of the showy route.

Margaret, unable to contain herself within doors, anxious, if possible, to find her own family, plunged again into the woods. She went by an obscure and devious way towards the Pond. Night was approaching ; but an untimely glare of light while it quickened her senses appalled her heart. Over Mons Christi rolled up dark, cold clouds, but in the North-east the heavens were distinctly illuminated. She saw smoke rising and occasional tongues of flame. Astounded and forlorn, as she came near her old home, a giant form stood before her. It was the Indian and his grand-daughter. Seizing her arm, this fearful patriarch of the forest, silently and unresistingly, led her forwards. He took her by an old and familiar path up the Head. What had been a streak of light in the horizon, they now beheld a boiling angry river of flame. The woods on the North of the village, an extensive range of old forests, were on fire. The Indian, without speaking, slowly raised his arm, and pointed steadily at the scene of the conflagration.

Each moment the effect increased, and the fire, driven by a brisk wind, seemed to be making rapid progress towards the Green. Sheets of sluggish smoke were pierced and dispersed by the nimble flames which leaped to the tops of the tallest trees, assaulted the clouds, and threw themselves upon the solid ranks of the forest as an exterminating battle. Beyond the fire, and up in the extreme heavens, was a pitchy, overshadowing blackness ; the faces of the three shone in a blood-red glare ; behind them gathered clouds and darkness ; below, the water, the house, the mowing, the road, were immersed in impenetrable shade. Margaret gazed with a mixed expression of anguish, surprise, and uncertainty. The Indian stood majestically erect, his mantle folded over his breast, his countenance glowing with other than the fire of the woods, his pursed and wrinkled features di-

Blotted-out execution scene from Sylvester Judd's 1851 revised edition of *Margaret.*

immediately after the execution. In the place of the old community, a new one, christened *Mons Christi*, emerges—an idealized township based on temperance, Universalism, and fraternity. With crime no longer a problem, the gallows is torn down; in its place is "erected a monumental piece, representing *Moses kneeling to Christ* and surrendering the Book of the Hebrew Code" (457). Like the town's consumption by fire, the symbolism here is clear: the statue of Moses relinquishing the "Hebrew Code" to Christ represents a paradigm shift in the administration of criminal justice as capital punishment in *Mons Christi* is stricken from the statute books.

The anti-gallows message of Judd's *Margaret* is hard to miss, even (or perhaps especially) in the revised edition with its blotted-out execution scene. But lest one does, Judd appends a "Note" to the end of the "Execution" chapter in the revised novel. That note responds directly to critics who charged him with vulgarity and sensationalism in depicting Chilion's death upon the gallows: "We have been chided," Judd writes,

> for carrying the story of Chilion to so sad a termination. "Shocking!" is the epithet applied to such management and such results. There is an illusion here. Nine tenths of executions are equally shocking. The mistake is this, our readers look at Chilion from the Margaret side, and his home side, and his own heart's side; as if every man that is hung had not a Margaret side, a home side, and his own heart side![61]

Chilion's execution, in short, is representative of "every man that is hung." It emphasizes the common humanity of the condemned by showing a "side" of the condemned's life often ignored in accounts of executions presented in the popular press. Responding to critics in this way enables Judd to *tell* readers of the revised 1851 edition what the original had *shown* through its dramatic representation of Chilion's hanging. In the "Note," Judd goes on to apply his moral lesson in *Margaret* explicitly to the current administration of the death penalty: "There would be no hangings if suspected individuals were to be regarded in the light in which some tenderhearted persons have allowed themselves to regard Chilion." Then, immediately following this comparison, Judd asks: "Would we create a prejudice against the law of capital punishment?"[62]

In writing *Margaret*, Judd certainly meant to stir prejudice against this law. Judd's judgment—his strong condemnation of capital punishment—rings out in this "Note" and in Chilion's unjust and unnecessary execution. John Evelev, one of *Margaret*'s few critics today, has examined the novel in terms of "Picturesque Reform" and what he calls a "picturesque sensibility," an aesthetic that incorporates the roughness and irregularity of nature but focuses on its beauty.[63] If Judd's novel fits within this tradition, as Evelev convincingly shows, it is easy to see why genteel critics like Peabody had a problem with the spectacle of execution, which was more at home in a *picaresque* (rather than a picturesque) narrative and the subversive, dark reform literature of Lippard than the more demure reform tradition to which Judd seemed to be contributing. That Judd included a decidedly unpicturesque scene in the first edition, and then blotted it out to make an ugly picture in the second, all the more shows his commitment to anti-gallows reform and the hope he had for *Margaret* to effect legal change. However, despite the efforts of Judd and others involved in the state's campaign, Maine—unlike Michigan, Rhode Island, and Wisconsin—would not officially abolish the death penalty before the Civil War. Even so, in 1837 the state legislature revised capital statutes and passed a new law, no doubt influenced by Judd and others, that led to de facto abolition for the next twenty-seven years. The "Maine law," as it would come to be called, required those convicted of capital crimes to be housed at the state prison for one year from the time of sentencing. At the end of that grace period, the governor would then have to sign a death warrant in order for an execution to be carried out. Thanks to this cooling off period, and because of the heightened sense of personal responsibility that any governor no doubt would experience in signing a death warrant, no one in the state was executed for almost three decades.

In writing and revising *Margaret* in the wake of the Maine Law, Judd extended his participation in the anti-gallows reform beyond the state level and into a national campaign for abolition. Read across the nation (albeit not to the extent of Lippard's *The Quaker City*), Judd's novel forced readers to confront the "heart side," the "Margaret side," of a representative murderer, much like the Maine Law forced governors to reconsider the life of a convicted murderer apart from the immediate circumstances of the crime. Such a law thus reinforced the sovereign agency invested in a governor as a state's chief representative and the responsibility any governors would have to face when they signed off on an execution. Likewise, Judd's readers were meant to feel the responsibility they bore when the state in which they were residents killed in their name. Lippard, in his literary executions, took a different approach by forcing readers to experience the irrational brutality of capital punishment and to see it as an abusive tool of the state. Different in many ways but unified in their shared opposition to capital punishment, Lippard and Judd make for a striking pair—almost as much as my coupling of Simms and Child in chapter 2. In this chapter, I have complicated such a comparative approach by looking at a third figure, one perhaps more influential than Lippard and Judd put together. That figure, of course, is Cooper, who wrote several novels in the 1840s, including *Afloat and Ashore* (1844), *The Chainbearer* (1845), and *The Redskins* (1846),[64] whose characters make pro-gallows statements—as a counterargument, no doubt, to popular novels like *The Quaker City* and *Margaret*.

Nowhere was Cooper's *anti*-anti-gallows attack more pointed than in two scenes from his final novel, *The Ways of the Hour* (1850), published one year after a revised edition of Lippard's *The Quaker City* (1849) and a year before Judd's revised edition of *Margaret*. The first of those scenes unfolds in a dialogue between Tom Dunscomb, an aristocratic gentleman-lawyer of the old school who is often taken as Cooper's spokesperson, and Squire Timms, an uncouth young lawyer with working-class roots who is one of many epitomes of "the ways of the hour"—in Timms's case, what Cooper sees wrong in contemporary legal practices. Worlds apart in their ideologies of law, the two lawyers are brought together as co-councils to defend Mary Monson, a beautiful, mysterious woman charged with a double murder and arson. Anti-gallows reform, as a faddish, misguided "way of the hour," comes up when the two lawyers are discussing the particular jury in the Monson case as well as the merits of the trial-by-jury system, the main target of the novel's attack.[65] When Dunscomb, unaccustomed to analyzing juries for their biases and prejudices, asks Timms what he makes of the jury in the Monson's trial, the following exchange ensues:

> "It's what I call reasonable, 'Squire [Dunscomb]. There are two men on it who would not hang Cain, were he indicted for the murder of Abel."
>
> "Quakers, of course?"
>
> "Not they. The time was when we were reduced to the 'thee's' and the 'thou's' for this sort of support; but philanthropy is abroad, sir, covering the land. Talk of the schoolmaster! Why, 'Squire, a new philanthropical idee will go two feet to the schoolmaster's one. Pro-nigger, anti-gallows, eternal peace, woman's rights, the people's power, and anything of that sort, sweeps like a tornado through the land. Get a juror who has just come into the anti-gallows notion, and I would defy the State to hang a body-snatcher who lived by murdering his subjects."[66]

As the conversation develops, Dunscomb upholds the integrity of law and its traditional practice, while Timms disabuses his senior's naivety and introduces a set of pragmatic strategies designed to manipulate jury sympathy and to speak to the jury's biases. One of these strategies involves playing up the "anti-gallows notion," which, along with other newfangled notions, have swept across the country "like a tornado through the land." Another strategy calls for the careful study of individual jurors. When Dunscomb reluctantly acknowledges the importance these days of scrutinizing jurors but then hopefully asks if that means "rely[ing] on one or two particularly intelligent and disinterested men,"[67] Timms

again corrects him in explaining his successful tactics: "I rely on five or six particularly ignorant and heated partisans, on the contrary; men who have been
reading about the abolishing of capital punishments, and who in gin'ral, because
they've got hold of some notions that have been worn out as far back as the times
of the Caesars, fancy themselves philosophers and the children of progress."[68]

Playfully ridiculing the anti-gallows movement here through Timms's superficial perspective, Cooper gives it more serious thought in a later exchange between Dunscomb and Mrs. Horton, one of the novel's misguided "children of
progress." Again, the conversation turns on the jury and speculations about its
opinions on the death penalty, and Mrs. Horton is quick to give hers: "For my
part, I wish all hanging was done away with. I can see no good that hanging can
do a man." Dunscomb politely concedes the point but claims that Mrs. Horton
has mistaken the purpose of punishment. She responds by rephrasing her argument by way of another anti-gallows cliché—that "the country hangs a body to
reform a body; and what good can that do when a body is dead?" Again, Dunscomb concedes the point but argues this time that "society does not punish for
the purposes of reformation; that is a very common blunder of superficial philanthropists." When Mrs. Horton goes on to ask "for what else should it punish?"
Cooper gives Dunscomb the final word on the subject: "For its own protection,"
the gentleman-lawyer declares. "To prevent others from committing murder."[69]
A far cry from the Lawton-Sitgreaves exchange in The Spy through which Cooper had entertained a general argument against the death penalty (and as he
does elsewhere in his fiction), these two scenes make unmistakable arguments
against the anti-gallows movement and for the place of capital punishment in
the criminal justice system.

⁓

If we take Dunscomb's opinions and arguments for those of the author's (a position I complicate in the epilogue), then the late Cooper was obviously skeptical
of reformers, such as the Mrs. Hortons of the world as well as the George Lip-
pards and Sylvester Judds. Another writer of the time who, upon closer inspec-
tion, shared Cooper's skepticism was Nathanial Hawthorne. Clearly concerned
with capital punishment but not a strict opponent, as were Lippard and Judd,
Hawthorne might have even considered Judd (a genteel reformer whose Margaret he greatly admired) somewhat misguided in thinking that the death penalty
would be abolished. Nonetheless, Hawthorne does share much with Judd and
even Lippard in the two reformers' misgivings about capital punishment. Like
Judd, on the one hand, he often sympathizes with criminals and the accused,
seeing in the gallows a useless and unwarranted destruction of life. Like Lippard,

on the other, he recognizes that state officials sometimes abuse authority and that the poor and friendless are most often the gallows' victims. But Hawthorne's gravest concerns, as we shall see, involved the fallibility of human laws and the finality of an execution. In this respect, he shares something with the late Cooper of *The Ways of the Hour*. For Cooper's final novel centers around a miscarriage of justice in which an innocent woman is tried, convicted, and sentenced to death. In fact, Monson's conviction is overturned only because one of her alleged murder victims is spotted in the courtroom aftermath following her death sentence. In the next chapter, we will explore similar issues—especially the complexities of legal evidence and the plotting of literary death sentences that inform Hawthorne's work, particularly *The House of the Seven Gables*.

# CHAPTER 4

# Hawthorne and the Evidentiary Value of Literature

The best of us being unfit to die, what an inexpressible absurdity
to put the worst to death!

*Hawthorne*, American Notebooks, *October 1851*

A loyal Democrat and major player in the "Young America" movement,
Nathaniel Hawthorne provides a unique perspective from which to explore the
relationship between antebellum literature and capital punishment. As we saw
in chapter 1, he made overt statements against the practice in two of his tales
from the mid-1840s. In another, "The Hall of Fantasy" (1843), he alluded to death
penalty reform and openly praised John L. O'Sullivan for his painstaking efforts
"to wash the bloodstain from the statute books."[1] Yet Hawthorne's interest in
capital punishment preceded the fervor of the anti-gallows movement of the
1840s. In "The Gentle Boy" (1832), for instance, he questioned the purpose of the
penalty from the perspective of a child who, in the story's opening, is found at
the foot of the gallows from which his father had recently been hanged. Like the
"heart's side" from which Sylvester Judd narrates Chilion's execution in *Margaret*
(a novel he greatly admired),[2] Hawthorne's sentimental perspective in this early
tale complements the moral revulsion toward the gallows he would express in
"The New Adam and Eve" and "Earth's Holocaust." And yet, despite such statements and strategies for criticizing the death penalty, Hawthorne's work as a
whole cannot be considered abolitionist in a strict sense. Instead, it offers a complex and not wholly consistent engagement with the politics of abolitionism. We
can begin to get a sense of those complexities by returning briefly to the mid-
1840s tales in which Hawthorne explicitly attacked the punishment of death.

"Earth's Holocaust" (1844), as we have seen, staged a debate between an
abolitionist and a retentionist, likely modeled after O'Sullivan and George B.
Cheever. Hawthorne knew both men well. O'Sullivan, of course, was a close

personal friend; Cheever—the man who would become the leading spokesperson for the gallows in the 1840s—had been a classmate of Hawthorne's when the two were at Bowdoin, and he was later an ordained minister at Howard Street Congregational Church, from 1833 to 1837, in Hawthorne's native Salem. Cheever had, moreover, published a temperance story, close in style and content to Hawthorne's "Young Goodman Brown" (1835), that stirred controversy in Salem when the former classmates were both living there. When Cheever was publicly cowhided and later imprisoned for libel for writing "Deacon Giles' Distillery" (1835), Hawthorne sympathized with the chastised author and visited him several times in jail.[3]

Despite that sympathy, Hawthorne (or rather his narrator) sides against the Cheever figure in "Earth's Holocaust." "That was well done!" the narrator exclaims when the gallows is at last thrust into the reformers' fire. But this approval is undercut by the remarks of a "thoughtful observer" who responds to the reformers' actions with "less enthusiasm" than the narrator had anticipated: "Yes, it was well done," the observer tepidly agrees, "well done, if the world be good enough for the measure."[4] This observer, who serves as the tale's voice of practical reason and wisdom, then qualifies his response, cryptically situating it in a broader spiritual context: "Death, however, is an idea that cannot easily be dispensed with, in any condition between the primal innocence and that other purity and perfection, which, perchance, we are destined to attain after travelling round the full circle" (393). Its deeper meaning lost upon the overzealous narrator, the observer's qualification looks beyond the mania for reform and speaks to the universal death to which we, as human beings, are all sentenced.

Hawthorne's attitude toward death and the death penalty is similarly complicated in "The New Adam and Eve." While the gallows elicits the horror and disgust of the New Adam and Eve, it also betokens the world of sin and mortality into which they have entered, thus reminding us (again) that each human being is sentenced to death. In this respect, "The New Adam and Eve" conveys a message similar to that of "Earth's Holocaust," only the latter pushes the point further by associating the death penalty with sin and death, themselves, rather than an outmoded institution in need of reform. In doing so the tale suggests that, despite all the reformers' efforts, eradicating capital punishment would be as likely as eliminating sin and death from the world. Hawthorne had sketched an idea along these lines in an 1842 fragment that was likely cut from the story: "When the reformation of the world is complete," he wrote, "a fire shall be made of the gallows; and the Hangman shall come and sit down by it, in solitude and despair. To him shall come the Last Thief, the Last Prostitute, the Last Drunkard, and other representatives of past crime and vice; and they shall hold a dismal merry-making, quaffing the contents of the Drunkard's last Brandy Bottle."[5] A figure of gloom and despair like Lippard's "Executioner" in *Adonai*, Hawthorne's hangman is less of a trope for abolition and more of a representative figure of past "crime and vice" that, like prostitution, thievery, and drunkenness, are ineradicable elements of human nature.

Thus, whereas Hawthorne joined O'Sullivan and others in recognizing the flaws of capital punishment as a social institution, and while he made statements against its practice, he, like the thoughtful observer in "Earth's Holocaust," maintained a skeptical perspective toward the cause for abolition. It is precisely at this point where Hawthorne differs from anti-gallows reformers and where we can begin to appreciate his complicated take on the death penalty. There is, in fact, evidence to suggest that Hawthorne approved of capital punishment in certain situations. Nonetheless, he also recognized that to convict someone of capital punishment requires *certain* proof of guilt. Because human beings are fallible, and because death is final, evidence used to convict one of death must, for Hawthorne, pass the bar of a higher standard than that used to sentence convicted criminals to lesser penalties.

If the reform-minded Hawthorne of the 1840s attacked the gallows, the early Hawthorne willingly accepted it as a necessary component of the criminal justice system. For instance, in a letter to an Ohio cousin in 1830, Hawthorne wrote with utter contempt about a dissolute young man who stabbed and (it was believed) fatally wounded another in a barroom fracas in Salem: "I do not know whether he is in custody," Hawthorne wrote of the alleged murderer, "but if the story is correct, he certainly deserves death, and will very probably be brought to the gallows."[6] In another letter to the same cousin a few months later, Hawthorne wrote at length about the Joseph and Frank Knapp murder trials, a sensational case that had engrossed him and much of the nation at the time. While expressing sympathy for one defendant, Hawthorne condemned the other: "For my part, I wish Joe to be punished, but I should not be very sorry if Frank were to escape."[7] As Hawthorne well knew, Joe's punishment, if convicted, would certainly be death. Joe was in fact executed, but so was Frank, despite the painstaking efforts of his lawyers—one of whom was Robert Rantoul Jr., the Massachusetts Democrat whose later *Report on the Abolition of Capital Punishment* (1836) would become a key document in the anti-gallows movement. Indeed, it was his defense work in Frank Knapp's 1830 trial that first inspired Rantoul's advocacy for abolition.

The Knapp murder trials must have struck a chord in Hawthorne's imagination. Twenty years later they served as source material for *The House of the Seven*

*Gables* (1851), his second romance and the primary focus of this chapter. That work, as we shall see, was plotted around two death sentences—one of them in a capital case with circumstances very similar to those of the Frank Knapp trial. While this chapter concludes with an analysis of capital punishment as a trope or setting in each of Hawthorne's major romances, it centers around a cross-examination of *The House of the Seven Gables* and two of the most famous murder trials of the antebellum period. The first is the aforementioned Knapp trial, which revolved around questions of circumstantial evidence and took place in Salem (the setting of Hawthorne's book and, of course, the author's hometown). The second is the 1850 John W. Webster trial, which also revolved around circumstantial evidence. Even more sensational than the Knapp trial, the Webster case would become *the* trial of the century and took place in Cambridge, Massachusetts, just as Hawthorne was beginning to write his crime romance.

I concentrate on the Knapp and Webster trials not only because they influenced Hawthorne but because they were major cultural events in their own right, each generating popular court reports that competed with fiction and poetry in the literary marketplace. Both cases also represent key developments in the history of U.S. criminal law insofar as they altered the evidentiary standards necessary to bring about a capital conviction. By writing a work of imaginative fiction that rigorously engaged questions of evidentiary value, Hawthorne offered readers a literary counterargument to legal narratives of guilt based upon circumstantial evidence and involving the ultimate penalty of death. *The House of the Seven Gables* offers an intriguing perspective on these issues precisely because, unlike much of the literature in preceding chapters, it does *not* present an overt argument for or against capital punishment. In this respect, we can link Hawthorne to Cooper (and Melville, as we shall see) as an important literary figure who engages questions about the death penalty without, in Hawthorne's case, fully supporting the abolitionist cause.

## "SUSPICIOUS CIRCUMSTANCES"

In *Strong Representations: Narrative and Circumstantial Evidence in England,* Alexander Welsh has convincingly shown that, following the Enlightenment, a new paradigm emerged for the persuasive presentation of facts in both law and literature of the mid-eighteenth and nineteenth centuries. During this time, circumstantial evidence and inferential reasoning derived from it displaced direct testimony, which could be mistaken or perjured, as the basis for "strong representations," Welsh's term for efficacious narrative or argumentation "built on carefully managed circumstantial evidence."[8] Thus, what went unseen but fit within a larger pattern of corroborating circumstances was often given more evidentiary value than what eyewitnesses claimed to have seen or heard. As Welsh points out, "Circumstantial cannot lie!" became a motto explicitly invoked in courtrooms as well as a guiding principle implicitly at work in the literature of the period.[9]

In *The House of the Seven Gables*, however, Hawthorne presents a challenge to Welsh's paradigm. Rather than reconciling an assortment of circumstances in order to make the facts of a case or a past event speak for themselves, Hawthorne constructs a narrative around circumstances that are not only misleading but manufactured. His romance revolves around two cases that involved "suspicious circumstances," a term found, as we shall see, in *The House of the Seven Gables* and in both the Knapp and the Webster murder trials. Hawthorne uses the phrase ironically to denote artifice and duplicity; prosecutors in the Knapp and Webster trials use it dramatically to put a particular construction upon the facts—a rhetorical strategy that shifted the burden of proof from the state and onto the defendant. A literary work that calls into question legal narratives of probability and circumstantial evidence, *The House of the Seven Gables* contests the privileged status granted to such arguments through its own careful management of evidence and plotting of death sentences.

The first of those death sentences takes place in colonial New England and is recounted in the romance's introductory frame. In it, we learn that a land dispute involving Matthew Maule and Colonel Pyncheon led the latter to accuse the former of witchcraft. After presentation of the colonel's testimony and corroborating circumstances, Maule is put to death by the community for his alleged crime. Although the "leaders of the people" supported the sentence and attended the execution, their actions are likened to those of the "maddest mob." The execution itself is described in decidedly negative terms: "Clergymen, judges, statesmen,— the wisest, calmest, holiest persons of their day,—" Hawthorne's narrator tells us, "stood in the inner circle round about the gallows, loudest to applaud the work of blood, latest to confess themselves miserably deceived."[10] A scene in which one individual manipulates the law for his own gain and to the detriment of another, Maule's execution frames the narrative proper and leaves readers with an important moral: that a community's leaders, those responsible for upholding the law and through whom its sovereign violence is exercised, are themselves fallible and at times susceptible to corruption.

The romance's second death sentence resonates with the first and puts in play the narrative's central drama. Unlike the first, however, it is not enacted, and the narrator initially provides little detail or commentary about it. Rather, it is shrouded in mystery as a complex part of the Pyncheon family history to be gradually re-vealed as the story unfolds. The narrator, in fact, tells us only that it involved "the violent death—for so it was adjudged—of one member of the family by the crimi-nal act of another." "Certain circumstances," he adds,

> attending this fatal occurrence had brought the deed irresistibly home to a nephew of the deceased Pyncheon. The young man was tried and convicted of the crime; but either the circumstantial nature of the evidence, and possibly some lurking doubt in the breast of the Executive, or, lastly—an argument of greater weight in a republic, than it could have been under a monarchy—the high respectability and political influence of the criminal's connections, had availed to mitigate his doom from death to perpetual imprisonment. (22)

Over the course of the narrative we learn that Clifford Pyncheon—the ghostly, skittish old man who returns to the House of the Seven Gables—was the "young man tried and convicted" for the murder of the wealthy uncle with whom he was then living. It is, however, not until the end of the narrative that we get a fuller picture of the circumstances surrounding the uncle's death. Returning to these circumstances, the narrator divulges the incriminating evidence that pointed to Clifford's guilt. What brings about this disclosure is the sudden death of Judge Pyncheon, the work's antagonist who almost certainly dies from natural causes, even though the circumstances surrounding his death indicated foul play.

The apparent fact of the judge's natural death, coupled with the recent dis-covery of a predisposition to apoplexy in the Pyncheon family, strongly suggests that Jaffrey Pyncheon, the wealthy uncle Clifford was convicted of murdering some thirty years earlier, also died from apoplexy. As the narrator explains,

> The medical opinion, with regard to [Judge Pyncheon's] recent and regretted death, had almost entirely obviated the idea that a murder was committed, in the former case. Yet, as the record showed, there were circumstances irrefra-gably indicating that some person had gained access to old Jaffrey Pyncheon's private apartments, at or near the moment of his death. His desk and private drawers, in a room contiguous to his bedchamber, had been ransacked; money and valuable articles were missing; there was a bloody hand-print on the old man's linen; and, by a powerfully welded chain of deductive evidence, the guilt of the robbery and apparent murder had been fixed on Clifford, then re-siding with his uncle in the House of the Seven Gables. (310)

The case against Clifford, "a powerfully welded chain of deductive evidence," fol-lows the logic of probability Welsh describes in his account of legal and literary narratives during this period. I will later return to this metaphor of the "chain" and to the accumulation of circumstantial evidence against Clifford;[11] but in the spirit of *The House of the Seven Gables* (or any good detective story), which delays the revelation of the truth in the interest of promoting mystery and suspense, I want to hold in abeyance further discussion of Clifford's legal predicament as I turn our attention to the sensational murder trial of Frank Knapp.

In April 1830 Captain Joseph White, an elderly and wealthy Salem merchant (on whose ship Hawthorne's father once worked), was found murdered in his bedroom. News of the murder spread quickly through Salem, and a vigilance committee was formed that pursued all leads with a zeal that, for some, called to mind the witch hunts of almost two centuries earlier. Suspicion eventually fell upon two sets of brothers, both from prominent Salem families: Frank and Joseph Knapp (the latter of whom was related to White through family marriage); and Richard and George Crowninshield. The state's theory of the crime held that Joseph had hired Richard to kill Captain White and that, while Richard was committing the murder, Joseph searched for and destroyed a recent will that had cut Joseph's mother-in-law out of the White inheritance. It was Joseph's belief, the state contended, that without this will the White estate would be divided equally among White's relations. Joseph, however, had destroyed the wrong will; the right one was safely locked up in the office of White's attorney. While neither Frank nor George directly participated in the crime, the prosecution argued that both were equally guilty because they served as accessories before the fact.

Similarities between the historic White murder and the (apparent) murder of old Jaffrey Pyncheon in *The House of the Seven Gables* are striking.[12] Both involve the death of an elderly rich bachelor, a stolen or destroyed will, and suspects related to the (alleged) victim who stood to inherit from the deceased. Both, moreover, include an aspect of judicial misconduct or abuse: whereas "the high respectability and political influence" of the Pyncheon family unduly influenced the commutation of Clifford's death sentence (in spite of Clifford's actual innocence) and ultimately led to his release from prison, the district attorney's office in the White murder hired, as lead council for the prosecution, Daniel Webster. Without question, Webster was the most famous lawyer and orator of the time, and many citizens of Salem were outraged that Webster, a hired gun, was brought in from outside the county to lead what they considered a modern-day witch hunt. In fact, one Salem resident went so far as to call the role Webster played for the prosecution "an example of judicial murder,"[13] a phrase that calls to mind Hawthorne's description of the Salem witch trials and Mathew Maule's execution as one of history's "judicial massacres" (8).

Webster's summation has long been considered as a classic in the literature of criminal law. Widely read in newspaper and pamphlet form in Hawthorne's day, the summation has been anthologized since then for its literary merits.[14] At least one legal historian has called Webster's summation the "greatest ever delivered to an American jury."[15] In fact, Webster himself thought enough of his closing argument to include it for publication in volume 6 of his *Collected Works* (1851), a popular book published the same year as *The House of the Seven Gables.* Hawthorne was certainly familiar with Webster's summation, and he likely heard it delivered in court, given that he was living in Salem at the time of the trial and, as one scholar has speculated, was probably covering aspects of the trial for the *Salem Gazette*.[16] Hawthorne's presence at Webster's summation seems even more likely considering that, shortly after the trial, he wrote a tale about a thwarted murder and "ambiguous circumstances" that ironically alluded to Webster's prowess as an orator.[17]

In the Knapp trial, it was Webster's job to transform the "ambiguous" circumstances in the White murder case into evidence that would convict Frank Knapp of first-degree murder. Webster accomplished this goal by constructing a dramatic narrative of guilt based entirely on circumstantial evidence. To this end, he began his summation by invoking the popular notion of "murder will out": that God's providence, along with the vigilance of a concerned community, had illuminated "every circumstance connected with the time and place" of the crime. The defendant was thus ensnared in a "net of circumstance" from which he could not extricate himself.[18] Such imagery and rhetorical strategies were characteristic of Webster's language during the trial. Earlier the defense had reduced the state's case to little more than "circumstantial stuff" (416), but in his summation Webster managed to turn the phrase to his advantage. Waiving before the jury an incriminating letter allegedly written by Frank, he declared, "Fix your eye steadily on this part of the 'circumstantial stuff' which is in the case, and see what can be made of it" (419). For his part, Webster made a great deal of this "circumstantial stuff"; from it, he inferred that Frank bore legal responsibility for White's murder, even though he neither planned the crime nor was present at its commission. According to the prosecution's theory, the actual killer was Richard Crowninshield, whom Knapp aided and abetted by meeting in Brown Street, a location clearly removed but not far from the murder scene.

At issue in the trial, then, were two technical aspects of law: the distinction between principal and accessory; and the legal definition of "constructive presence." To appreciate Webster's strong representation in the case against Frank, we can look first at his application of the principal-accessory distinction and then

at his legal definition of constructive presence, the keystone in Webster's archi-
tectonics of circumstantial evidence. At the time of the White murder, Massachusetts law stated that a principal must first be convicted in order for an accessory, such as Frank, to stand trial. Learning of this legal technicality, Richard
Crowninshield, an obvious principal (the other would have be Joseph, who had
initially turned state's evidence), promptly hanged himself in an apparent effort
to save the necks of his alleged coconspirators. In light of Richard's suicide, Webster and the prosecution team changed their theory of the crime and the strategies they would use in making their case. They now charged Frank as a "principal," on the assumption that he played a central role in the murder. Yet when it
came to his closing argument, the point Webster hammered home had little, if
anything, to do with Frank's role in orchestrating the crime. Instead, Webster
built his entire case around the legal theory of constructive presence, a concept
that allows for culpability to be defined *not* in terms of actual presence or participation but strictly in terms of whether a defendant knowingly aided and abetted
in a criminal act. For to aid or embolden a murderer in any way was, as Webster
dramatically put it, "the same as though the person stood at his elbow with his
sword drawn" (425).

According to Webster's loose interpretation of constructive presence, the only
issue in question was whether Frank was on Brown Street at the time of the murder and there by appointment with Richard Crowninshield. The defense offered
a different interpretation of the law, one that rejected a formal application of
constructive presence in favor of a consideration of the practical consequences
arising from Frank's so-called participatory presence. "Even if he was in Brown
street," the defense reasoned, "he was not present except by a mere fiction of law.
To make a man constructively present, he must be in a capacity to render assistance, and must be there for that purpose, and must actually assist."[19] Calling
attention in this way to "a fiction of law" raises a subtle point to which I will later
return: that legal narratives, like legal theories, necessarily incorporate and rely
on the fictive, since they cannot speak with certainty about how unseen events
actually transpired. But the important point here is that Webster did not so much
respond to the defense's position as he dismissed its claim as wholly irrelevant. As
Webster told the jury: "The question for you to consider is, did the defendant
go into Brown street in aid of this murder? Did he go there by agreement, —by
appointment with the perpetrator? If so, everything else follows. The main
thing—indeed the only thing—is to inquire whether he was in Brown street by
appointment with Richard Crowninshield" (423). By placing great weight on

Frank's constructive presence and ruling out the question of whether any actual assistance was given, Webster provides the key link in the chain of circumstances he assembles. With that link in place, Webster speaks with confidence about the "fearful concatenation of circumstances" that has put Frank "to an account" (429).

In *The House of the Seven Gables*, Hawthorne's attention to the instability of circumstances calls into question legal arguments like that of Webster's in the Knapp trial. In sharp contrast to the utter certitude with which Webster speaks of the circumstances indicating Frank's guilt, a deep skepticism and uncertainty punctuate Hawthorne's narrative as a whole and the case against Clifford Pyncheon in particular. Indeed, whereas Webster strives to reconcile various circumstances to establish an unbroken chain of evidence pointing to Frank's guilt, *The House of the Seven Gables* emphasizes, as its narrator at one point puts it, "the tendency of every strange circumstance to tell its own story" (144). Such a remark suggests that, while circumstances can be pieced together to tell a unified story (as in Webster's summation), a collection of seemingly related circumstances can just as easily pull a given story in different, even contradictory, directions.

Hawthorne's romance teaches this lesson by demystifying the circumstances that had, in a court of law, proved Clifford's guilt beyond a reasonable doubt. In the final analysis, it turns out those circumstances were not only misleading but manufactured. Holgrave, the boarder of the House of the Seven Gables who plays the role of detective, comes to this conclusion when he discovers the body of Judge Pyncheon. He explains the judge's death as an "idiosyncrasy" of the Pyncheon family (304), a death resulting from natural causes and *not* from foul play, as the circumstances of the bloodstained shirt and the sudden disappearance of Clifford and Hepzibah Pyncheon from the house suggest. In offering his explanation to Phoebe Pyncheon, who has just returned to the family mansion, Holgrave emphasizes "a minute and almost exact similarity in the appearances" (304) of Judge Jaffrey Pyncheon's death and the death of old uncle Jaffrey Pyncheon, the judge's namesake. Connecting these two deaths by way of a congenital heart defect peculiar to Pyncheon men, Holgrave concludes that Clifford was innocent of the murder for which he served a thirty-year sentence.

Despite or perhaps because of this discovery, Holgrave is quick to acknowledge the compelling evidence in the legal case against Clifford: "It is true," he tells Phoebe, "there was a certain arrangement of circumstances, which made it possible nay, as men look at these things, probable, or even certain—that old Jaffrey Pyncheon came to a violent death, and by Clifford's hands" (304). When Phoebe asks, "Whence came those circumstances?" Holgrave emphatically replies:

They were arranged . . . at least such has long been my conviction, —they were arranged after the uncle's death, and before it was made public, by the man [Judge Pyncheon] who sits in yonder parlor. His own death, so like that former one, yet attended by none of those suspicious circumstances, seems the stroke of God upon him, at once a punishment for his wickedness, and making plain the innocence of Clifford. But this flight,—it distorts everything! (304)

Read against Webster's argument in the Knapp case, Holgrave's explanation is instructive. It suggests that just because circumstances present a "probable" account of what happened, they do not provide a transparent reflection of the truth. Thus, Holgrave calls attention to the "arrangement of circumstances" that made it not only "possible" and "probable" but almost "certain," in the eyes of the law, that Clifford killed Jaffrey. Although circumstances cannot lie themselves, they can be manipulated or artfully "arranged" by criminals like Judge Pyncheon or even lawyers like Daniel Webster. They can also be misleading, as are the circumstances surrounding the recent death of the judge. While those circumstances may suggest that "the stroke of God" had descended to punish the judge and to make "plain the innocence of Clifford," they also present more problems for Clifford and Hepzibah, whose flight from the house make them potential murder suspects. As Holgrave puts it, "this flight, it—distorts everything!"

This potential for distortion—that is, the potential for circumstances to be twisted to fit probable narratives—is emblematic of the shifty, unstable social world of action and interpretation that drives the plot of The House of the Seven Gables. Nothing in this world can be taken for granted; facts are socially produced through interpretation rather than freestanding entities of a preexisting reality. Nowhere is this principle of uncertainty more apparent than in the narrator's concluding explanation of the events surrounding old Jaffrey's death, the ground on which the entire narrative is constructed. Unlike the conclusion to a conventional detective or crime novel, which stabilizes circumstances and clarifies motives to prove "whodunit," The House of the Seven Gables resists closure by offering a perspective on the circumstances of Jaffrey's death but self-consciously marking it as only a possible explanation or version of the "facts." As the narrator puts it in his final assessment of the circumstances surrounding young Jaffrey's involvement in his uncle's death, "Now it is averred,—but whether on authority available in a court of justice, we do not pretend to have investigated,—that the young man was tempted by the devil, one night, to search his uncle's private drawers, to which he had unsuspected means of access" (311). Hedging his claims, the narrator undercuts or at least qualifies his authority to speak definitively about how this death occurred. Instead, he offers his explanation as "a theory," one first proposed by Holgrave and later "affirmed" by many "that undertook so to account for these circumstances as to exclude the idea of Clifford's agency" in the death of old Jaffrey (310–11). "According to this version of the story," the narrator reports, "Judge Pyncheon, exemplary as we have portrayed him in our narrative, was, in his youth, an apparently irreclaimable scapegrace." Only after labeling it as a "theory" or "version" of the crime does the narrator proceed with a sketch of Judge Pyncheon's character in youth and an account of what he (the narrator) believed transpired when old Jaffrey caught his nephew late one night ransacking his private drawers. The shock of discovering young Jaffrey "thus criminally occupied" induced "the crisis of a disorder to which the old bachelor had an hereditary liability;—he seemed to choke with blood, and fell upon the floor, striking his temple a heavy blow against the corner of a table" (311). With the body of his dead uncle lying before him, young Jaffrey, the narrator speculates,

> continued his search of the drawers, and found a will, of recent date, in favor of Clifford,—which he destroyed,—and an older one, in his own favor, which he suffered to remain. But, before retiring, bethought himself of the evidence, in these ransacked drawers, that some one had visited the chamber with sinister purposes. Suspicion, unless averted, might fix upon the real offender. In the very presence of the dead man, therefore, he laid a scheme that should free himself at the expense of Clifford, his rival, for whose character he had at once a contempt and a repugnance. (312)

Inasmuch as it confirms Holgrave's theory, the narrator's account of Old Jaffrey's death and young Jaffrey's scheme constitutes a *strong representation*: a careful reckoning of circumstantial evidence to produce a probable narrative. But again, by self-consciously marking it as a speculation, an interpretation of the facts, Hawthorne allows for the possibility of Clifford's actual guilt and the accuracy of the legal verdict that condemned him. That verdict is no longer probable, given the new evidence brought to light, but it is still possible—a possibility Hawthorne underscores rather than rules out. The self-conscious, perspectival account of a probable murder scheme contrasts sharply with Daniel Webster's account in the Knapp trial of how the old Joseph White surely met his end. To begin with, Webster presents his narrative as certainty rather than probability. He describes the murder itself as if he had been an eyewitness to it. Speaking in the present tense, he puts the jurors (and future readers) in the room where the crime occurred, providing, like a good novelist, minute details and artistic touches for dramatic effect. There is nothing in Webster's account to mark it as a theory or interpretation of facts. In fact, the *facts* or "circumstances" are made to speak for themselves, with Webster merely serving as their medium: "The circumstances now clearly in evidence spread out the whole scene before us," Webster tells the jury. "A healthful old man," he goes on,

> to whom sleep was sweet, the first sound of slumbers of the night held him in their soft but strong embrace. The assassin enters, through the window already prepared, into an unoccupied apartment. With noiseless foot he paces the lonely hall, half lighted by the moon. He winds up the ascent of the stairs, and reaches the door of the chamber. Of this he moves the lock, by soft and continued pressure, till it turns on its hinges without noise, and he enters, and beholds his victim before him . . . The face of the innocent sleeper is turned from the murderer, and the beams of the moon, resting on the gray locks of his aged temple, show him where to strike. The fatal blow is given, and a victim passes, without a struggle or a motion, from the repose of sleep to the repose of death! It is the assassin's purpose to make sure work; and he plies the dagger, though it is obvious that life has been destroyed by the blow of the bludgeon. He even raises the aged arm, that he may not fail in his aim at the heart, and replaces it again over the wounds of the poniard! To finish the picture, he explores the wrist for the pulse! He feels for it, and ascertains that it beats no longer! It is accomplished. The deed is done. (409)

Like the narrator of a popular crime novel, Webster adds high drama and suspense to this climactic act of murder and all but enters into the mind of his criminal. His account, however, is presented as fact, not fiction—a re-presentation rather than a representation of what happened. It constructs a *presence* by putting jurors (and readers) in the room when the murder occurs. Such a picture is crucial to Webster's portrait of guilt but, strictly speaking, immaterial to it, since the defendant on trial was not there himself but only present through what the defense had dubbed "a fiction of law."[20] Webster does much to distinguish his narrative as a truthful account because the "truth," he later says, "always fits"; but the fictive, which properly belongs to the realm of literature, is there as well. We see this influence in Webster's subtle details ("mellow[ing] the lights," as Hawthorne says in *The House of the Seven Gables'* preface [1]) but also in the terms with which he introduces the account. The murder narrative is described as a "bloody drama"; those participating in it are "actors," and the murder itself is presented as a "new lesson for painters and poets" (408).

Insofar as it inspired Hawthorne, Webster's depiction of the White murder indeed proved to be a new lesson for poets. But in reimagining the circumstances of such a murder through the lens of his crime romance, Hawthorne provided his own lesson—one that spoke to the criminal law and its privileging of probable narratives constructed from circumstantial evidence. As we have seen, *The House of the Seven Gables* demonstrates that such circumstances could be manipulated to convict or condemn innocent persons, such as Clifford or Mathew Maule. However, for many at the time of the White murder, it was less the possibility of Frank Knapp's innocence and more the frightening display of abusive state authority—evident, for instance, in the hiring of Webster to ensure a conviction—that raised criticism of Frank's conviction and execution. The trial and its outcome, moreover, drew the attention of some, such as Robert Rantoul Jr., away from the verdict and toward the question of capital punishment itself, a penalty that could not be reversed or redressed in the event of error. Hawthorne himself had learned a lesson along these lines, one about the irreversibility of the death penalty, when little more than a boy. "I did not go to see Stephen [Merrill] Clark executed," a seventeen-year-old Hawthorne wrote to his mother about a Salem youth of his own age who was hanged for arson in 1821. "It is said that he could have been restored to life some time after his execution. I do not know why it was not done."[21]

Perhaps this memory came to mind when a still young Hawthorne realized that his "wish" (as he expressed it to his Ohio cousin) for Joseph Knapp's punishment came at Frank's expense. And perhaps it returned again to a mature Hawthorne when, in writing *The House of the Seven Gables*, he contemplated the irreversible punishment to which Maul was subjected or the eventual "restoration" of Clifford, made possible through his commuted death sentence. Whether or not the memory of Stephen Clark continued to haunt Hawthorne, it did affect another antebellum romancer—one familiar with Hawthorne's work who also set a novel in Salem that dealt with crime, capital punishment, and misleading circumstances. That writer was the Universalist minister Day Kellogg Lee, whose *Merrimack; or Life at the Loom* (1854) I touched on in chapter 3.[22] In fact, Lee's depiction of "the Crazy Juror," who participated in the case involving Stephen Clark (Lee writes the historical Clark into his fiction), can be seen as a mirror image of Hawthorne's Clifford; for, like Clifford, Lee's juror is an elderly "sensitive little man" but one who spends twenty-odd years in infantile lunacy not because of a crime he allegedly committed but for the role he played in sanctioning the penalty that claimed young Clark's life.

## BODIES OF EVIDENCE AND ACTUAL INNOCENCE

A lurid case of alleged murder and dismemberment, the 1850 John W. Webster trial captured the nation's attention at the time Hawthorne was writing his tale about crime, suspicious circumstances, and the irreversible penalty of death. In fact, Hawthorne's October 1851 notebook entry, "The best of us being unfit to die, what an inexpressible absurdity to put the worst to death!," may have been written in response to Webster's execution,[23] which occurred little more than a year before Hawthorne penned his remarks about the absurdity of executing even the worst criminals. Certainly one of the "worst" of us, if one believed the vampiric sketches of the disgraced professor that flooded the popular press, Webster was only the fourth person in Massachusetts executed since 1837 and by far the most famous and recent of the gallows' victims.

The Webster case involved two prominent members of Boston society: George Parkman, a professor at the Harvard medical school and member of one of Boston's richest and most distinguished families (his brother was Francis Parkman, a prominent minister and the author of The Oregon Trail); and John W. Webster, Erving Professor of Chemistry and Geology at Harvard and a colleague of Parkman's at the medical school. In an age of modern print technology, the Webster trial became a national and transatlantic sensation. Nearly every newspaper in Massachusetts, and papers in every major city across the United States, covered the trial proceedings, as did papers in London, Paris, and Berlin.[24] Interest in the trial continued long after 1850. When Charles Dickens came to Boston years later in 1867, one of his first requests was to see "the room where Dr. Parkman was murdered."[25] Webster may or may not have killed Parkman, but Parkman did mysteriously disappear on November 23, 1849, and Webster was the last person known to see him alive. A week later, Webster was arrested for Parkman's murder.

At trial, the state painted a gruesome picture of Webster as a calculated killer who dismembered his victim, thus providing a real-life analogue to the kind of murderer Poe portrays in his classic tales, "The Black Cat" and "The Tell-Tale Heart." Webster, the prosecution argued, killed Parkman because he owed him a considerable sum of money ($2,432) and because Parkman had recently threatened him with exposure. That Webster let it be known among friends and acquaintances that he had settled his account with Parkman when they last met became, in the state's eyes, evidence that he had premeditated the murder. Simple and sensational, the case against Webster had but one flaw: it was built entirely on circumstantial evidence. In fact, even the "fact" of Parkman's death was circumstantial. The (alleged) victim had disappeared without a trace, until human remains discovered in a furnace in Webster's laboratory suggested foul play. Yet those remains, which were incomplete and damaged by fire, could not be positively identified as belonging to Parkman; thus there was no way of knowing for sure if Parkman was dead, let alone murdered. Ironically, the key evidence used to identify Parkman's body at trial was not even an actual part of his body but a set of false teeth discovered, along with some bones, in Webster's furnace.[26]

There was, of course, other evidence linking Webster to the crime. In addition to motive and to the artificial teeth and bones found in the furnace, there were human remains discovered in other parts of Webster's laboratory. The discovered remains certainly did not help Webster, but circumstances could explain them. A medical professor who worked with cadavers, Webster suggested those bones and artificial teeth came from another body (or bodies). Furthermore, the discovered evidence had problems of its own. It was obtained not through an official police investigation but through a private search conducted by Ephraim Littlefield, the medical school's janitor who was not on good terms with Webster. Because of Parkman's disappearance and what he deemed Webster's odd behavior, Littlefield searched areas of Webster's laboratories overlooked by the police. At trial, Littlefield's testimony could not be sufficiently discredited by Webster's attorneys, but the defense did raise the possibility that Littlefield was engaged in the black market trade of cadavers. Motivated by a reward of three thousand dollars (close to the amount Webster owed Parkman), Littlefield could have framed Webster for the crime, just as a young Jaffrey Pyncheon likely manipulated circumstances in the case against Clifford in *The House of the Seven Gables*.

At the time of the Webster trial, evidentiary standards in capital cases held that *corpus delicti* (literally, "the body of the crime") had to be established through direct evidence. The law also held that only after the fundamental fact of the crime had been positively proved could the state present an argument to show a defendant's guilt beyond reasonable doubt. These standards were perceived as necessary safeguards so that the state could avoid, or at least reduce, the possibility of convicting and executing an innocent person. As legal historian Robert Sullivan, in writing about the Webster case, put it:

> Starkie, McNally, and Roscoe, the leading authorities upon the law of criminal evidence in 1850, made it quite clear that the fact of the *corpus delicti*, or the commission of the homicide, had to be proven by direct evidence to an absolute certainty, or beyond the least doubt. After this had been established

absolutely, then the burden of proof was on the prosecution to show that the defendant had committed the crime beyond a reasonable doubt. These legal authorities of the English-speaking world were firm on this point, and they advanced the explanation that this rule of certainty of the fact of the homicide was altogether warranted by the melancholy experience of the conviction and execution of supposed murderers of "victims" who had in fact survived their "murder."[27]

Such "melancholy experience[s]," as we shall see, were frequently recounted in anti-gallows literature and provided the basis for several works of antebellum fiction that questioned capital punishment. In fact, Hawthorne himself had drawn from such material by plotting *The House of the Seven Gables* around a central murder that, in the final analysis, most likely never was one.

In the Webster trial, the issue of *corpus delicti* took center stage because Parkman's death could not be established as a certainty. During the trial, however, that issue was more or less resolved in the presiding judge's "charge" to the jury before its deliberations commenced. The charge was delivered by Chief Justice Lemuel Shaw, a distinguished Massachusetts jurist who was also Herman Melville's father-in-law. As Sullivan has shown, Shaw's charge set a new evidentiary standard by reasoning that *corpus delicti* could be established through circumstantial evidence alone. Today Shaw's charge is considered an "all-time classic in the field of criminal law" and still cited in case law for its authoritative definitions of circumstantial and direct evidence, moral certainty, and the degrees of homicide.[28] When it was first delivered, however, Shaw's charge was hardly hailed a landmark in the literature of criminal law. On the contrary, a significant portion of the legal community deemed it a gross violation of judicial authority. For example, one pamphleteer, identifying himself as a "Member of the Legal Profession," denigrated Shaw's charge as "law manufactured for the occasion." "From beginning to end," he claimed, it was "an argument against the prisoner" and thus constituted "an extraordinary judicial usurpation" of established authority. This writer joined many others at the time in "affirm[ing] that the *corpus delicti* cannot be established by circumstantial evidence and that Shaw cannot find authority or precedence for his assertion—the well-settled law is precisely the reverse of that stated by the judge to the jury."[29] One lawyer in agreement was Stephen A. Phillips, editor of America's leading legal journal, the *Monthly Law Reporter.* "The Court," Phillips wrote of the Webster trial, "evidently thought it necessary to secure an unanimous verdict, and such a verdict as would correspond with public opinion. This is the only way we can account for the extremely ARGUMENTATIVE character of the charge of Chief Justice Shaw."[30]

What outraged Phillips and others was that Shaw's charge appeared to be an attempt to ensure a guilty verdict in a case where political influence and popular opinion were stacked against the defendant. Such concern, however, was motivated less by a belief in Webster's innocence and more by a commitment to upholding the integrity of the criminal justice system by providing an unpopular defendant the due protection of law. But again, there was the possibility that Webster was in fact actually innocent, that "The Pedestrian," as Parkman was known throughout the city for his distinctive gait, would be found someday soon walking the streets of Boston, as two witnesses had sworn in court to have seen him doing *after* Webster allegedly killed him.[31]

In the 1840s and 1850s, the issue of actual innocence had become a hot button in antebellum debates over the death penalty, especially in popular studies that advocated the abolition of capital punishment. In his widely read *Report in Favor of the Abolition of the Punishment of Death by Law* (1842), for instance, John L. O'Sullivan had written with grave apprehension about capital convictions in cases involving "suspicious circumstances," a term he used in discussing a handful of cases in which defendants were convicted and executed for crimes of which they were subsequently proven to be innocent.[32] O'Sullivan began that discussion with a claim about the imperfectability of legal evidence and the irreversibility of an enacted death sentence: "The imperfection inseparable from all human evidence, whether positive or presumptive, ought to make us shrink from the infliction of a doom thus forever *irremediable*."[33] Charles Spear, a Universalist minister and noted Massachusetts death penalty opponent, echoed O'Sullivan and employed a similar strategy of documenting cases of actual innocence in his popular book, *Essays on the Abolition of Capital Punishment* (1844). In a chapter titled "Irremediability," Spear examined nine cases of innocent persons who were executed for crimes they did not commit.[34] If capital punishment's failure as a deterrent was for O'Sullivan the main reason for abolition, for Spear the possibility of executing the innocent was his primary reason and cause alone for doing away with the practice. In fact, as a motto for his abolitionist magazine, Spear used Marquis de Lafayette's famous remark, "I shall ask for the abolition of the penalty of death until I have the infallibility of human judgment demonstrated to me," as the heading for each issue of *The Hangman* and *The Prisoner's Friend*.

Reverend George Washington Quinby takes a different approach in his book, *The Gallows, the Prison, and the Poor House: A Plea for Humanity* (1856). Citing the case of one Boyington, a young Louisianan recently hanged for a crime he did not commit, Quinby stages a dialogue with readers, forcing them to acknowledge their complicity in the execution of innocent victims:

> Now permit me to inquire of my reader: "*Who killed* that young man?" "Who killed him?" you respond: "Why the sheriff, the hangman." No, my friend, you mistake. The hangman acted simply as an instrument of the government. "Ah, yes," say you, "I see how it is, the *government* killed him. The government made the law declaring that he should be killed; described *how* he should be killed, and *who* should be used as an *instrument* in the work of death. Then the *government* strangled the man, simply using the hands of the sheriff to adjust the knot—place the rope—draw down the cap, and let him swing."[35]

Quinby continues in this vein for some time, providing readers with a civics lesson on republican politics to show from where the authority for such executions emanates. "Just so," he goes on. "But then there is another question behind all this, in which *you* and *I* should have been specially interested if we had been citizens of Louisiana at that time, viz: *Who, or what, constitutes the government of a State?*"[36] Through this dialogue and dialogic engagement with readers, Quinby traces responsibility back to readers (the emphatic "*you* and *I*" of the dialogue) when such miscarriages of justice occur in states in which they are residents.

While Quinby, Spear, and O'Sullivan drew on the execution of the wrongfully convicted in their studies, narratives of circumstantial evidence and actual innocence made for common plotlines in antebellum fiction that challenged capital punishment. Even Cooper's *The Ways of the Hour* (1850), which explicitly criticizes the anti-gallows campaign, turned on such a plot. The problematic, however, was overtly thematized in several short stories from the period that focused on the issue. One was John Quod's "Harry Blake, A Story of Circumstantial Evidence, Founded on Fact," published in the November 1842 issue of the *Democratic Review*, just three months before Hawthorne's "The New Adam and Eve" appeared in the journal.[37] Revolving entirely around a case in which an innocent man is suspected, convicted, and executed for a crime he did not commit, Quod's story concludes by underscoring its moral—"that Harry Blake was another of those who had gone to swell the list of victims to Circumstantial Evidence."[38] Four years later, William Starbuck Mayo published a similar tale about condemned innocence that also first appeared in the *Democratic Review* (and was reprinted in an 1851 collection of short works the same year as *The House of the Seven Gables*).[39]

Mayo's "The Captain's Story" (1846) starts *in medias res* with a heated debate over the death penalty already underway: "TALKING of circumstantial evidence,"[40] the voice of the captain declares to begin the tale itself and to initiate a new line of argument for his position against capital punishment. The captain, a moderate and reasonable man, is debating an overzealous pro-gallows clergyman whose argument for "the necessity and propriety of killing men as punishment for murder" belies, as Mayo's narrator tellingly puts it, a "nasty conservatism" that was prone to "wordy rhetoric," "false logic," and trite appeals to " 'God's immutable laws,' &" (34). Over the course of his story the captain tells how one Mr. Clark, a mate once on his ship, was tried, convicted, and executed because of suspicious circumstances and misleading testimony that condemned him. The captain, one of the witnesses at trial, learns of Clark's innocence and his own mistake five years later when he randomly encounters Clark's alleged victim, whose tale of what really happened the narrator holds up, in the story's conclusion, as "living proof of the fallibility of human testimony, and the danger of relying upon circumstantial evidence" (54).

Another example of such a tale is Alice Gray's "The Red Cloak; or, Murder at the Roadside Inn" (1855), whose narrator foregrounds the story's argument in the opening sentence: "THE strongest argument held by those persons who are opposed to capital punishment is that many persons innocent of crime are known to have suffered an ignominious death on the scaffold."[41] Gray's narrator goes on to pose an alternative to the death sentence that reads like a gloss on Clifford's circumstances in *The House of the Seven Gables*:

> If a convicted criminal were, instead of being doomed to death, made to suffer the living death of life-long imprisonment, should it ever be proved that he was innocent, while he still lived, although nothing could ever recompense him for the long and unmerited suffering he has endured, at least, he could have the satisfaction of knowing that at last his innocence was proved to the world; he would meet with the sympathy of all men, and his relatives and friends could again rally around him and receive him amongst them with a fondness and affection rendered stronger than ever on account of the undeserved calamity to which he had been subjected and the years of mental anguish and physical privation that had ensued.[42]

*The House of the Seven Gables* can easily be read in the context of this popular anti-gallows literature, especially with its plot revolving around the executed Matthew Maule (a figure like Harry Blake and Mr. Clark) and Clifford, who, in

the words of Gray's narrator, is "made to suffer the living death of life-long imprisonment," instead of death itself, but ultimately has "the satisfaction of knowing that at last his innocence was proved to the world." Thus, whereas Maule's
wrongful execution in Hawthorne's romance serves as a painful reminder of the
irreversibility of the death penalty, Clifford's spared life enables his grievous
wrong to be partly redressed through the general acceptance of his innocence
following the death of Judge Pyncheon. In this way, Hawthorne counterbalances
his tale of actual innocence with an enacted and a commuted death sentence,
just as he balances Hester's external shame against Dimmesdale's internal tor-
ment in plotting the two forms of punishment that structure *The Scarlet Letter.*

If cross-examining *The House of the Seven Gables* and the Knapp trial enabled us to see how Hawthorne drew from a legal source in his literary interrogation of evidentiary value, reading his romance against opening and closing arguments in the Webster murder case will help us see how Hawthorne was influenced
by and participated in a broader cultural debate not only about evidence but
about judgment and capital punishment as well. Like the Knapp trial, the Webster trial boiled down to, as Judge Shaw put it in his charge, "a question of evidence."[43] While the prosecution did all it could to present a highly probable
narrative in which the circumstances would speak for themselves, the defense
mustered all its rhetorical force to emphasize the possibility of Webster's innocence and the consequences of an unjust execution. To this end, the defense
opened its case by underlining the profound responsibility that comes with the
decision that each juror will have to make: "A duty devolve[s] upon you," defense
attorney Edward D. Sohier told the jury; "and if you err, you see the victim. He it
is, and his is the family, who must be offered up as an atoning sacrifice to that
error, unless indeed, you err on Mercy's side— . . . on a side where no woman's
groan, no widow's sob or orphan's tear, bears witness to it" (124). Although Sohier
here and elsewhere made sentimental appeals to the jury to drive home the consequence of its decision, his primary line of argument strove to break crucial
links in the prosecution's construction of the chain of evidence that pointed to
Webster's guilt. In this respect the defense, like Hawthorne in *The House of the
Seven Gables*, can be seen as critiquing Alexander Welsh's theory of "strong
representations" by demonstrating how a strict adherence to probability could
lead one astray from the truth. In fact, later in his opening statement, Sohier
cited the very phrase, "Circumstances cannot lie!" that Welsh identifies as a
"rallying-cry" in nineteenth-century courtrooms and novels.[44] That phrase, however, is used ironically when Sohier, after providing several examples of misleading or manufactured circumstances, warns against a "blind reliance upon

the dictum 'that circumstances cannot lie,'" since it "has occasionally exercised a mischievous effect in the administration of justice" (Stone 139).

Read against the 1830 Knapp case, Sohier's defense can be seen as a warning regarding the preponderance of circumstantial evidence by which Daniel Webster ensnared his defendant. Circumstantial evidence, Sohier explains, "requires substantial elucidation," whereas "direct evidence needs no explanation." Direct evidence is transparent and straightforward, consisting of "testimony derived from persons who have actual knowledge of the facts in dispute"; circumstantial evidence, on the contrary, is indirect and obfuscating, positing hypothetical scenarios in which "a fact is attempted to be proved, not by anybody who saw it, not by anyone who knows it, but by proving in advance certain other circumstances, and certain other facts, and then drawing a conclusion, from those facts and circumstances, that these particular facts which we are endeavoring to ascertain exist" (115). Sohier's language, in contrasting these forms of evidence, does much of the argument's work by showing how convoluted and intricately connected a case, such as the present one, relying exclusively on circumstantial evidence may become. Sohier thus develops this comparison as one of his chief strategies. Whereas earlier in his argument he works hard to contrast these two forms of evidence, later he claims that, in terms of evidentiary value, there is really no comparison: "Circumstantial evidence is weak," he says, "compared with direct; and for the reason that the opportunities for human error are multiplied. All we can do, in the investigation of facts—all we ever can do—is to approximate towards certainty" (137).

As *The House of the Seven Gables* demonstrates, an approximation of certainty may not be enough when the irreversible penalty of death is at stake. Webster's defense makes a similar point by arguing, "The proof sometimes consists, as in this case, of numerous facts—of scores of facts. Every single fact is a distinct issue. Every single fact must be proved, beyond a reasonable doubt . . . Here the chances of error accumulate" (Stone 137). Thus, the defense repeatedly argues, "Nothing human is infallible," which becomes a sort of mantra in Sohier's opening and closing arguments. Rhetorically, the claim works to challenge the "one great chain of circumstantial proof with which *they*," as Sohier at one point characterizes the state, "have endeavored to surround the defendant, and by the weight of which *they* have endeavored to crush him" (118, emphasis added). This us-versus-them rhetoric makes out the defendant as the victim and highlights the dangers of relying wholly upon circumstantial evidence. From this perspective, Sohier argues near the end of his opening statement that "if in a long train of circumstances upon which the case is hung up by the Government, there is any one single circumstance which fails, there is an end to the whole case at once. They undertake to anchor their case by a chain of circumstances. If one link breaks, by its own intrinsic weakness, or by any force which the opposite party brings against it, there is an end to the case" (139).

In its closing argument, the prosecution directly responds to the defense's attack on the evidentiary value of circumstantial evidence. But rather than insisting on the merits of such evidence (as Daniel Webster had explicitly done two decades earlier in the Knapp trial) and pointing to the liabilities of direct testimony, the prosecution argues instead that *all* evidence is more or less circumstantial: "Now, Gentlemen, what is the nature of the evidence upon which you are to arrive at your conclusion?" the prosecution asks the jury. "It is circumstantial. So, I think, it must be said, is almost all evidence. We are not here . . . dealing with or expecting to find absolute verities—pure, absolute truth. That, Gentlemen, belongs not to fallible man but to the omniscient and infallible God" (225). Like Sohier, the prosecution stresses the fallibility of human judgment. It does so, however, *not* to warn against the possibility of wrongful executions but to excuse such executions as unfortunate but necessary consequences of a robust criminal justice system: "Innocent men have doubtless been convicted and executed on circumstantial evidence, but, innocent men have sometimes been convicted and executed on what is called positive proof. What, then? Such convictions are accidents, which must be encountered; and the innocent victims of them have perished for the common good, as much as soldiers who have perished in battle" (227).

Appropriating the trope of "innocent victims," the prosecution lays claim to the wrongfully executed as martyrs of the state who, like soldiers in battle, "have perished for the common good." Such an argument, of course, draws from the age-old assumption of a government's right to the lives of its condemned citizens—a presumption of governmental authority repudiated by thinkers such as Benjamin Rush, Robert Rantoul Jr., and O'Sullivan, for each of whom capital punishment was anathema to a democratic government. But for the prosecution, wrongful executions could be shirked off as a necessary occurrence for which the state bears little responsibility: "All evidence," after all, "is more or less circumstantial" (227), a claim the prosecution reiterates immediately after acknowledging that the state has executed, and will continue to execute, innocent victims.

Hawthorne relies on a similar assumption about the complex nature of all evidence in *The House of the Seven Gables*. Up to this point, I have argued that the romance unsettles the privileged status granted to circumstantial evidence in nineteenth-century legal and literary narratives based on probability. But direct evidence in *The House of the Seven Gables* is equally problematic. A telling example occurs when Holgrave explains to Phoebe, upon her return to the House of the Seven Gables, that Judge Pyncheon has just died. He evinces the fact of the judge's death *not* by showing her the corpse, which lies within the house, but by presenting her with a daguerreotype of the recently deceased. This photograph prompts Phoebe to exclaim, "This is death! . . . Judge Pyncheon dead!" to which Holgrave responds: "Such as there *represented* . . . He sits in the next room. The Judge is dead, and Clifford and Hepzibah have vanished. I know no more. All beyond is conjecture" (302, emphasis added). Holgrave certainly knows more than he lets on (enough, in fact, to free Clifford and Hepzibah of suspicion and to exonerate Clifford of his murder conviction); but the important point here is that he provides evidence of the judge's death through a *representation*—a daguerreotype, to be more precise, which, by the legal standards of the time, constituted a form of indirect rather than direct evidence.[45] This appeal to indirect evidence when direct, incontrovertible proof of the judge's death—the corpse itself—lies in the very next room complicates rather than simplifies matters, presenting Hawthorne's readers with the mirror image of the problem of *corpus delicti* in the Webster trial. For in the Webster case there is a probable murder but no positively identifiable body, whereas in the case of Judge Pyncheon's death there is a positively identifiable body but an unlikely case of murder.

Just as characters within Hawthorne's romance have examined Uncle Jaffrey's death as a murder scene, critics of the work have done the same with the suspicious circumstances surrounding Judge Pyncheon's death—treating it as a "murder."[46] Yet Judge Pyncheon, as we have seen, most likely died from natural causes, as did old Jaffrey before him. Ending the judge's life through apparent natural causes allows Hawthorne to conclude his romance positively with Maule's curse being lifted from the Pyncheons and the house they inhabit. Thus, whereas the romance had begun with the cycle of revenge perpetuated by the Pyncheon-Maule feud of yore—a conflict initiated when Colonel Pyncheon manipulated circumstances and bore false witness to bring about the original Mathew Maul's execution—it ends with an uplifting tale of reconciliation and forgiveness. Holgrave plays a crucial role in this ending. Born into the feud as a Maul, Holgrave breaks the pattern by deciding not to participate in violence against the Pyncheons. Hawthorne illustrates this point by drawing a comparison between Holgrave and his ancestor Mathew Maule, the carpenter, in "Alice Pyncheon," the chapter in which Holgrave tells Phoebe the legend of her long deceased relative whose will (and life) were taken hold of by the carpenter Maule in retaliation for Colonel Pyncheon's original crime. When Holgrave realizes that his power as a storyteller and skills in mesmerism have enabled him inadvertently to hypnotize Phoebe, just as Maul in the story had intentionally mesmerized Alice in plotting his revenge, he breaks the spell and frees Phoebe—a symbolic act that marks the first step in breaking the cycle of retribution in which the Pyncheons and Maules had participated for generations. That cycle is finally broken when Holgrave, at the end of the narrative, confesses to be, "in this long drama of wrong and retribution," a representative of "the old wizard" and then asks for Phoebe's hand in marriage (316).

Through his positive action, Holgrave counteracts what Hawthorne had spelled out in the romance's preface as the moral "truth" it sought to amend: "that the wrong-doing of one generation lives into the successive ones, and, divesting itself of every temporary advantage, becomes a pure and uncontrollable mischief" (2). By providing in Holgrave a positive example of how to work against the romance's negative principle, Hawthorne structures his plot—with the death sentences of Mathew Maul and Clifford Pyncheon as its two major coordinates— according to the logic of forgiveness. To get a sense of how that logic works, we can turn briefly to Hannah Arendt's theory of action in which the faculty of forgiveness plays a fundamental role. For Arendt, human action is inherently boundless and unpredictable, since we never know in advance the consequences of our actions. At the same time, however, human action enables us to have new beginnings and to avoid being controlled or dominated by external forces, such as those perpetuating the Pyncheon-Maule feud. Yet the consequences of action, Arendt argues, are potentially endless; for while a single agent may initiate an action and therefore be held responsible for it, that action often gets caught up in a "web of human relations" from which new consequences, in turn, are generated.[47]

Action, for Arendt, is also irreversible in principle. But while deeds themselves cannot be undone, their consequences can be reversed through the faculty of forgiveness. Forgiveness thus "serves to undo the deeds of the past, whose 'sins' hang like Damocles' sword over every new generation"[48]—or, as readers of Hawthorne might say, hang like the body of the original Maule from the gallows, which prompts the retaliation of each new generation of Maules. Nonetheless, while Maule's execution cannot be undone, one of its consequences—the thirst for vengeance symbolized in Maule's curse—can, and Holgrave shows how through his model actions. It is, after all, by forgiving the Pyncheons of the wrongs committed against his ancestors that Holgrave brings into being the new beginning symbolized in his marriage with Phoebe, which unites the two families that had been in perpetual conflict. Without performing such an act,

Holgrave would be condemned to repeat the vengeance of his forefathers. As Arendt puts the problem in a statement that could have been spoken by the mesmeric, philosophical Holgrave, "Without being forgiven, released from the consequence of what we have done, our capacity to act would, as it were, be confined to one single deed from which we could never recover; we would remain the victims of its consequences forever, not unlike the sorcerer's apprentice who lacked the magic formula to break the spell."[49]

In breaking the spell of Maule's curse, *The House of the Seven Gables* is, by Hawthorne's own definition, a romance: a work concerned with the "possible" rather than the "probable." Even so, Hawthorne's tale of reconciliation and forgiveness is not quite as innocent as it seems, for it depends on a central act of violence: killing off the story's villain, Judge Pyncheon. There is, in other words, a counterlogic of vengeance and retribution that supplements (in a Derridean sense) Hawthorne's primary message of reconciliation.[50] That dangerous supplement occurs in one of the book's most famous chapters, "Governor Pyncheon," in which Hawthorne's narrator celebrates the death of a bad man. Whereas much of the romance up to and after this chapter focuses on questions of evidentiary value and condemns the practice of retribution epitomized in Maule's execution, "Governor Pyncheon" indulges in that vengeance and stages the judge's death as if it were an "execution," a concept that more than one critic has used to describe the scene.[51]

There are at least two ways of reading what I would like to call the literary execution of Judge Pyncheon. The first way is to interpret it biographically and to see the judge's death as enacting Hawthorne's own revenge on those in Salem who did him an injustice. That injustice is famously depicted in the introduction to *The Scarlet Letter*, wherein Hawthorne publicly portrays himself as the victim of a spoils system that took away his position as a Custom House surveyor. In fact, Hawthorne describes his loss of that position as an execution, a decapitation at the hands of his political foes. If "The Custom-House" introduction depicts Hawthorne's victimization, his deposed status as a "Decapitated Surveyor,"[52] *The House of the Seven Gables* marks his revenge—a vengeance that comes through the death of a character whom many of Hawthorne's contemporary readers and later critics have associated with Charles Upham, the local Whig responsible for Hawthorne's firing.[53] Maule's curse, in this biographical reading, stands in for Hawthorne's curse on his political enemies. That curse may be lifted from the world of the romance, so that the cycle of violence animating the Pyncheon-Maul feud can be broken, but only because it finds a new victim in Judge Pyncheon, whose vindictive death scene expresses Hawthorne's vengeance.

But instead of reading the judge's figurative execution as an act of personal revenge, we can see it as Hawthorne indulging an artistic freedom given to romancers—the liberty, as he puts it in *The House of the Seven Gables'* preface, to commit a "literary crime" (1). Hawthorne uses that term to describe a transgression, a breach, that would mar the fidelity of a realistic work but not a romance, which encompasses the "Marvelous" and bestows a certain "latitude" on the romancer (2). Hawthorne's "literary crime" is to resolve his drama by killing off the judge through an apparent act of divine judgment, a contrivance that allows him to indulge in the violent punishment of a wicked man but without taking responsibility for it. As such, the judge's death functions as a *deus ex machina* insofar as it resolves the work's central conflict through the blood work of vengeance but without bloodying anyone's hands. That the judge's wickedness is left for God alone to punish can be seen as an argument against capital punishment, since to kill him through lawful means would be, by the book's implicit logic, an usurpation of divine authority. We have seen that argument explicitly articulated at the end of Simms's *Confession*, which employs a similar *deus ex machina* to resolve that novel's conflict of laws: its condoning of extralegal capital punishment in cases of seduction but condemning of capital punishment as a lawful institution. *The House of the Seven Gables* is more complicated than Simms's *Confession*, but it abides by a similar logic—one that rejects the death penalty but endorses a kind of extralegal capital punishment exacted, in this case, on the wicked judge.

Thus, whether we read it biographically or as a *deus ex machina*, the literary execution of Judge Pyncheon weaves a powerful thread of vengeance into the romance's dominant narrative of reconciliation. *The House of the Seven Gables*, however, is not the only work in which Hawthorne draws upon the trope of capital punishment as an expression of figurative or poetic justice. In fact, each of his major romances is in some way structured by allusions to or parodies of executions in crucial punishment scenes. By looking first and briefly at execution scenes in these other romances, I hope to open up a third way of reading Hawthorne's execution of perhaps his greatest villain, Judge Pyncheon.

## LITERARY EXECUTIONS REDUX

We can begin by returning to the famous opening of *The Scarlet Letter*. As I argued in chapter 1, an execution all but occurs in the romance's first scene. Hawthorne draws an extended analogy between Hester's punishment and that of a "condemned criminal" coming "forth to his doom,"[54] and Hester is made to stand before a group of spectators on the "scaffold," a word commonly used to signify the gallows. Well schooled in New England history, Hawthorne likely modeled Hester's punishment after the Puritan practice of *simulated hangings* in which an individual convicted of a capital crime would spend an hour (or specified time) upon the gallows before the community as an alternative to capital punishment itself. Such a punishment for a crime like Hester's was regularly practiced during the period in which the romance is set. As legal historian Stuart Banner explains, "When the colony decapitalized adultery in 1695, the penalty substituted for death was an hour on the gallows with a rope around the neck, plus whipping, plus the wearing of the letter A forever." Banner goes on to note parenthetically that this "last punishment, of course, was the basis for Nathaniel Hawthorne's novel *The Scarlet Letter*,"[55] but we can in fact view the entire scene as a simulation of lawful death to be experienced as such by both the criminal subject and the spectators there to witness it. There is, obviously, no proverbial rope around Hester's neck, but everything else is staged as though an execution were going to take place.

Execution scenes also appear in *The Blithedale Romance* and *The Marble Faun*. Whereas a public hanging during the Salem witch trials literally foregrounds the dramatic action of *The House of the Seven Gables*, such an image occurs in the climactic scene of *The Blithedale Romance* when Miles Coverdale finds himself a reluctant witness to the final reckoning of Hollingsworth, Zenobia, and Priscilla. In the scene, Zenobia speaks of Hollingsworth's interrogation of her as a "trial for my life," and Coverdale extends the metaphor as his eyes wander "from one of the group to another," seeing

> in Hollingsworth all that an artist could desire for the grim portrait of a Puritan magistrate holding inquest of life and death in a case of witchcraft; in Zenobia, the sorceress herself, . . . and, in Priscilla, the pale victim, whose soul and body had been wasted by her spells. Had a pile of fagots been heaped against the rock, this hint of impending doom would have completed the suggestive picture.[56]

Here we have the primal scene of tyrannical authority in colonial New England—a scene similarly painted in the preface to *The House of the Seven Gables* and one that haunts the contemporary world of the romance, finding its fullest expression in Judge Pyncheon's abuse of authority and, particularly, in his persecution of Clifford. Zenobia, in the scene just cited, completes Coverdale's "grim portrait" by calling Hollingsworth a "judge, jury and accuser" tyrannically "comprehended in one man!"; she even pronounces his judgment of her "equivalent to a death sentence!"[57] Of course, Zenobia, like Coverdale, is speaking metaphorically in describing the recent events of her life in terms of a trial and death sentence; but the figure rings true in that Hollingsworth's judgment precipitates the romance's tragic ending: Zenobia's suicide, a sort of figurative death sentence for which Coverdale holds Hollingsworth indirectly responsible.

An execution scene factors more directly into the plot of *The Marble Faun*. If *The House of the Seven Gables*, as I have argued, is plotted around the death sentence, then so too is *The Marble Faun*—and in more obvious ways. For the plot of that romance is organized around a central murder that takes the form of an act of capital punishment. The murder is foreshadowed when Miriam and Donatello join Kenyon, Hilda, and a group of traveling artists on a moonlight ramble through Rome that brings them to the Tarpeian Rock, an execution site from which condemned political prisoners in ancient Rome were lawfully thrown to their deaths. Kenyon glosses the symbolism of the rock when he explains that its close proximity to the Capitol enabled government officials "to fling their political criminals down from the very summit on which stood the Senate-House and Jove's temple; emblems of the institutions which they sought to violate."[58] It is Miriam, however, who gives the famous execution site its thematic import when Donatello later asks her if what took place there was "well done." "It was well done," she answers. "Innocent persons were saved by the destruction of a guilty one, who deserved his doom."[59]

Miriam utters these words in a chapter titled "On the Edge of a Precipice." The chapter ends with Donatello, inspired by Miriam's remarks, killing a bad man (the model blackmailing Miriam) in the same manner in which ancient Rome executed its notorious political prisoners. Of course, in killing Miriam's persecutor (a kind of Judge Pyncheon figure) as he does, Donatello acts without the authority or sanction of the state. In doing so, he becomes himself a criminal, guilty of violating the very laws he seeks to uphold. Even so, Donatello's enactment of extralegal capital punishment calls into question the difference between killing inside and outside of the law, but it does so *without* absolving Donatello of responsibility for the deed, as Hawthorne absolves himself (or his narrator) in the execution of Judge Pyncheon.

Significantly, *The Marble Faun* does not end with an act of capital punishment, although it could be argued that it closes with Donatello awaiting execution in prison. Given Donatello's sincere repentance, it is more likely that, by submitting himself to justice, he has been sentenced to a long prison term, thus trading in his psychological imprisonment for a physical one. In this respect, the book's resolution differs pointedly from the conclusion Miriam had earlier reached when contemplating the good use to which ancient Rome put the

Tarpeian Rock. If Donatello is like a biblical Adam before his fall, then afterward he becomes a sort of Cain, who, like Simms's murderer in *Confession*, is driven from humanity but ultimately brought back into the fold rather than severed from it through lawful death.

Donatello's action, like Hollingsworth's and Chillingsworth's in their respective romances, demonstrates the dangers of individuals taking justice into their own hands—a prominent theme in Hawthorne's work. In *The House of the Seven Gables*, however, Hawthorne emphasizes the potential fallibility of the state in its attempts to achieve justice. But despite its potential to commit grave errors, state violence is ultimately, in Hawthorne's world, preferable to individual acts of revenge, which is why of all his villains Judge Pyncheon is, in many ways, the worst. He is the worst because he pretends to be, and is taken for, one of the best. For the judge, we are told, "beyond all question, was a man of eminent respectability. The church acknowledged it; the state acknowledged it. It was denied by nobody" (*The House of the Seven Gables* 228). But beneath the judge's immaculate public persona—symbolized in his impressive dress and superficial smile, akin to "the shine on his boots"—lies a perjurer, a false witness, a manipulator of evidence that led to the condemnation of his cousin, an innocent man.

We see through the judge's fake smile and fine clothes in the scenes depicting Hepzibah's private confrontation with the public judge. The key episode occurs when Judge Pyncheon pays his second and final visit to the House of the Seven Gables. He has come to interrogate Clifford, who he believes has secret knowledge of materials—"the schedule, the documents, the evidences" (235)—that would entitle him to the vast property and wealth Colonel Pyncheon was believed to have acquired before his untimely death. When Hepzibah denies him access to Clifford, the judge describes himself as Clifford's "only friend, and an all-powerful one" (233). When Hepzibah persists in her refusal, he boasts that Clifford was released from prison not in spite of his influence but because of it: "I set him free!" he declares repeatedly. "And I have come hither now to decide whether he shall retain his freedom" (233). Such a declaration, with its emphasis on his capacity "to decide" on Clifford's freedom, underscores the judge's authority and suggests the power he holds over the lives of Clifford and Hepzibah. Lest his threat be taken as idle words, Judge Pyncheon displays the evidence he has gathered against Clifford, giving Hepzibah a good idea how he would use it should she refuse to cooperate: "My dear cousin," he tells her,

> since your brother's return, I have taken the precaution . . . to have his deportment and habits constantly and carefully overlooked. Your neighbors have

been eye-witnesses to whatever has passed in the garden. The butcher, the baker, the fishmonger, some of the customers of your shop, and many a prying old woman, have told me several of the secrets of your interior. A still larger circle—I myself, among the rest—can testify to his extravagances at the arched window. Thousands beheld him, a week or two ago, on the point of flinging himself thence into the street. From all this testimony, I am led to apprehend—reluctantly, and with deep grief—that Clifford's misfortunes have so affected his intellect, never very strong, that he cannot safely remain at large. The alternative, you must be aware,—and its adoption will depend entirely on the decision which I am now about to make,—the alternative is his confinement, probably for the remainder of his life, in a public asylum, for persons in his unfortunate state of mind. (235–36)

The language of evidence (e.g., "eye-witnesses," "testimony") pervades the judge's threat. Through it, he constructs a compelling case against Clifford—one that, along with the judge's political influence, would surely prove effective in a court of law.

Thus, in his ability to keep Clifford and Hepzibah under constant surveillance and to marshal (false) evidence against them to meet his own ends, Judge Pyncheon is a symbolic embodiment of the despotism and corruption Hawthorne sees in his contemporary world. That abuse, as we have seen, is epitomized in the historical example of the Salem witch trials, to which the good judge is repeatedly linked through associations with his Puritan forebear, Colonel Pyncheon. If Judge Pyncheon is, as Robert A. Ferguson describes him, "Hawthorne's blackest villain,"[60] it is not only because—like Hollingsworth, Chillingsworth, and other antagonists associated with witchcraft or the witch trials—he wields sovereign authority over others. He is so because, in claiming to be an impartial administer of the law, a "judge," he uses the law for personal again. And it is such individual misuse of state power that elicits Hawthorne's sharpest attack.

The judge's supreme villainy is also marked by the fact that he is the only Hawthornian villain who is made to suffer a violent and disreputable death, the kind of death administered through capital punishment. This, of course, is not to say that Hawthorne does not punish his villains in other works but that the judge's punishment is given special treatment. Chillingsworth, for instance, merely withers away and dies, like a noxious weed, at the end of The Scarlet Letter. Hollingsworth, the bombastic prison reformer, is similarly deflated and demoralized at the end of The Blithedale Romance, but he is not killed off or put to death. Judge

Pyncheon, in contrast, is subjected to a grand, ignominious death, one that is carefully choreographed and plotted in "Governor Pyncheon," one of the most famous and celebrated chapters in all of Hawthorne's work.[61] To appreciate how that death is staged we need to look at Judge Pyncheon's literary execution in relation to a final Hawthornian villain who escapes punishment.

That villain is Professor Westervelt, whose beaming smile (of false teeth) and fine clothes make him akin to the judge. Although a minor character, Westervelt plays a major role in the conclusion of *The Blithedale Romance*. In offering his judgment of the events that have transpired, Coverdale has nothing but scorn for Westervelt, whom he holds (along with Hollingsworth) largely, if indirectly, responsible for Zenobia's suicide. This contempt culminates in Coverdale's plea for divine judgment to befall the vile professor: "Heaven deal with Westervelt according to his nature and deserts!—that is to say, annihilate him."[62] An appeal for a death sentence of sorts, Coverdale's proclamation calls for precisely the kind of vengeance exacted upon Judge Pyncheon: annihilation through divine judgment. Lacking, however, the authority of God (or that of a third-person omniscient narrator who lords over and controls events and characters), Coverdale's condemnation has little illocutionary force. Indeed, it lacks even the power of suggestion that animates Mathew Maule's curse, itself a kind of death sentence, on the Pyncheons with quasi-performative force.

As a quasi-omniscient agent, one with intimate knowledge of characters and events, the narrator of *The House of the Seven Gables* shapes events and characters of his tale in ways that Coverdale cannot—at least not without committing a "literary crime" by violating the plausibility of his first-person narrative. Like Coverdale, however, *The House of the Seven Gables'* narrator is limited to the evidence brought to light by his story. But this limited perspective does not prevent him from participating in the violence directed against the judge. While neither executioner nor the direct means through which the judge is killed, the narrator contributes to the execution scene by playing the role of the vindictive spectator to witness the death of a condemned subject. To this end, Hawthorne's narrator repeatedly taunts the dead judge, commanding him again and again to rise up from his chair, to consult his watch, and to join the dinner party in progress, where he will "virtually" become "governor of the glorious old State! Governor Pyncheon of Massachusetts!" (274). Yet time vindictively ticks away, marking the judge's untimely exit from this world and all the worldly engagements he will miss. Narrated in the present tense, the scene brings us in close to linger over the corporeal fact of the judge's death. The terms in which Hawthorne narrates the judge's death obviously differ from those in which Lippard describes poor Charley's execution in *The Quaker City*, but Hawthorne conveys the same mean-spirited jubilation that characterizes Devil-Bug's sardonic sermon, "Hurrah for the Gallows!"

If, as Garrett Stewart has argued, the death of a major character is always a pivotal moment in a work of fiction, then the literary execution of Judge Pyncheon is no exception. It marks the dramatic climax of the work and serves as the principle means through which punishment is administered, thereby satisfying what Stewart identifies as a "well-worn vernacular formula" for justice in popular culture that "is still very much with us": the death of "the villain who 'got his.'"[63] In "Governor Pyncheon," Hawthorne gives high form to the proverbial punishment of the villain, and nowhere is it more apparent than in the mock appeal with which the chapter ends: "Rise up, thou subtile, worldly, selfish, iron-hearted hypocrite," the narrator jeeringly commands the dead man, "and make thy choice whether still to be subtile, worldly, selfish, iron-hearted, and hypocritical, or to tear these sins out of thy nature, though they bring the life-blood with them! The Avenger is upon thee! Rise up, before it be too late!" (283). It is, of course, too late, as the narrator well knows; and his attitude toward the deceased smacks of one vindictively present to witness the execution of a great criminal. Indeed, Hawthorne's narrator gloats over and celebrates the death of the judge in a way similar to the mob gathered to witness Mathew Maule's execution in the romance's opening chapter and not unlike the hateful glee with which Devil-Bug celebrates poor Charley's execution in Lippard's *The Quaker City*. Lippard's language is sensational and extreme, whereas Hawthorne's here is elevated and subdued by comparison; but they both revel in the execution scene itself. As we saw in chapter 3, however, Lippard's ironic "Hurrah for the Gallows!" critiques the administration of capital punishment in its sardonic parody of the execution, whereas Hawthorne happily participates in the judge's righteous death. To be sure, the judge's justified death can be read only as payback for Maule's wrongful one—an act of retribution, as I have argued, that runs counter to the romance's dominant logic of forgiveness.

The ignominy of Judge Pyncheon's death is most fully expressed in the image that closes the chapter. While the judgment rendered in the narrator's final appeal to this "subtile, worldly, selfish, iron-hearted, and hypocritical" man is first registered in solemn and religious terms, it shifts near the end to the mundane and quotidian (anticipatory of Dickinson's great mock encounter with death in "I Heard a Fly Buzz When I Died") as the narrator delivers a parting blow to the would-be chief magistrate:

What! Thou art not stirred by this last appeal? No, not a jot! And there we see a fly, — one of your common house-flies, such as are always buzzing on the window-pane, — which has smelt out Governor Pyncheon, and alights, now on his forehead, now on his chin, and now, Heaven help us! is creeping over the bridge of his nose, towards the would-be chief-magistrate's wide-open eyes! Canst thou not brush the fly away? Art thou too sluggish? Thou man, that hadst so many busy projects yesterday! Art thou too weak, that wast so power- ful? Not brush away a fly! Nay, then, we give thee up! (283)

The elevated style in which the villainous judge *gets his*, replete with "thee's" and "thou's" and other formal markers betokening a judgment of biblical propor- tions, is at once sacred and profane. The punishment is designed to be cathartic, a purging of evil from the world; but again, as an act of retribution it undercuts the romance's expressed moral purpose enacted through Holgrave's gesture of forgiveness and reconciliation and the restoration of Clifford's innocence. If the judge's death is aesthetically (if not also morally) satisfying, it is so not just (or only) because the condemned is unquestionably wicked but because the punish- ment comes by way of law. Not, of course, through positive law; or even necessar- ily through divine law, as Holgrave (and perhaps Hawthorne himself) would have it. Rather, it comes through the literary law of poetic justice, a popular law in fiction, as in criminal law, that demands a criminal be punished, so long as the punishment is carried out in a prescribed manner and according to estab- lished rules. In fact, much of the popular literature examined in earlier chapters of my study abide by such a law, including Simms's Border Romances and Poe's classic murder tales in which, to quote the title of a Simms's tale, "Murder Will Out." Whereas in Hawthorne's classic tales such as "Young Goodman Brown" and "The Minister's Black Veil" secrets remain buried in the subjects who pos- sess them, in *The House of the Seven Gables* the secret crime eventually comes to the fore and the inglorious villain is gloriously punished. Of course, many crimi- nals in life and in literature are never brought to justice, but that does not mean the popular demand for justice does not persist.

For many of Hawthorne's time, this demand for justice assumed a logic of its own—a retributive logic that was to operate irrespective of one's feelings for or against the condemned. So far in this book I have focused on literature in relation to the death penalty and its reform in part because much of the nineteenth cen- tury's progressive fiction—notably the "Young America" movement of which Haw- thorne was a part—was significantly influenced by the anti-gallows movement.[64]

But it is important to note, as I have from time to time in preceding chapters, that there was an influential countermovement to retain capital punishment. One prominent argument among retentionists was that the death penalty was inherently just, that it was sanctioned by scripture and meted out the only appropriate punishment for some crimes or criminals.[65] Such an argument, in fact, was a mainstay of the pro-gallows books of Reverend George B. Cheever, Hawthorne's former classmate at Bowdoin whose relationship with Hawthorne I began this chapter by discussing. And such a logic, as I hope to have shown, runs through Hawthorne's "Governor Pyncheon" chapter but against *The House of the Seven Gables* as a whole.

In addition to the literary execution of Judge Pyncheon, traces of this logic can be found in Hawthorne's public endorsement of perhaps the most controversial execution of antebellum America: the hanging of John Brown, whose raid upon Harper's Fairy resulted in the death of more than twenty men. Whereas Brown's supporters condoned the violence as a necessary evil and saw those killed as casualties in an imminent war declared on a government that sanctioned slavery, Brown's detractors condemned the violence and argued that its participants merited death in kind for their acts. Counting himself among the latter, Hawthorne endorsed Brown's execution in "Chiefly about War Matters" (1862), an essay featured in the *Atlantic Monthly*:

> I shall not pretend to be an admirer of old John Brown, any farther than sympathy with Whittier's excellent ballad about him may go; nor did I expect ever to shrink so unutterably from any apophthegm of a sage, whose happy lips have uttered a hundred golden sentences, as from that saying, (perhaps falsely attributed to so honored a source,) that the death of this blood-stained fanatic has "made the Gallows as venerable as the Cross!" Nobody was ever more justly hanged.[66]

In defending Brown's execution, Hawthorne sympathized with Whittier but took exception to Emerson's apophthegm, through which Brown's death sentence was transformed, to appropriate Hawthorne's turn of phrase, into a "golden sentence." By taking the state's law into his own hands, Brown had, in Hawthorne's view, forfeited the right to his own life. Thus, to mitigate what he considered the pernicious effects of Emerson's claim that Brown "made the Gallows as venerable as the Cross!" Hawthorne offered the terse, prosaic rejoinder: "Nobody was ever more justly hanged." The rhetorical thrust of such a flat, matter-of-fact avowal served to deflate the poetry written into Brown's execution by Whittier, Emerson, Thoreau, and others.

Yet Hawthorne's take on Brown's execution is not that simple. He complicates his position by conceding Brown's bravery and rationalizing the punishment, first from the perspective of the condemned himself and then from that of "any common-sensible man": "He won his martyrdom fairly, and took it firmly," Hawthorne writes of Brown. "He himself, I am persuaded, (such was his natural integrity,) would have acknowledged that Virginia had a right to take the life which he had staked and lost; although it would have been better for her, in the hour that is fast coming, if she could generously have forgotten the criminality of his attempt in its enormous folly."[67] Playing off the logic of warfare with which Brown and his supporters had justified his act in the first place, Hawthorne upholds the state's right to Brown's life, which the militant slavery abolitionist had "staked and lost." Yet Hawthorne immediately qualifies this conclusion by noting the volatile politics surrounding Brown's act and the national *impolitics*, so to speak, of the execution. But this point, in turn, is further complicated when Hawthorne goes on to "look at the matter unsentimentally," through the eyes of "any common-sensible man." Such a man, he explains, "must have felt a certain intellectual satisfaction in seeing him hanged, if it were only in requital of his preposterous miscalculation of possibilities."[68]

Like Hawthorne the romancer, Brown the revolutionist was interested in "possibilities" rather than probabilities, of how the world might be rather than how it actually was. Brown's miscalculation was, from Hawthorne's perspective, the belief he could take justice into his own hands. In doing so, he emulates various Hawthorne's characters but none more than Donatello, whose innocent desire to rid the world of evil transforms him, like Melville's Billy Budd, from a figure of innocence into one of guilt.

# CHAPTER 5

# Melville, MacKenzie, and Military Executions

*Hanging from the beam,*
*Slowly swaying (such the law),*
*Gaunt the shadow on your green,*
*Shenandoah!*
*The cut is on the crown*
*(Lo, John Brown),*
*And the stabs shall heal no more.*

*Hidden in the cap*
*Is the anguish none can draw;*
*So your future veils its face,*
*Shenandoah!*
*But the streaming beard is shown*
*(Weird John Brown),*
*The meteor of the war.*

Herman Melville, "The Portent" (1859)

"*Hanging from the beam,*"[1] John Brown's body casts a foreboding shadow over Herman Melville's collection of Civil War poems, *Battle-Pieces and Aspects of War* (1866). "The Portent (1859)," the book's opening poem, is not about capital punishment per se; nor does it deify Brown (who remains "Weird") in a way that Hawthorne found regrettable, although its imagery of the "crown" and "stream-ing beard" connotes the passion and crucifixion of Christ, who also was put to death as an enemy of the state.[2] The poem instead matter-of-factly attends to the sovereign force of law, a force expressed parenthetically as a matter of course "*(such the law),*" and the gallows serves as its vehicle, the means through which Brown is transformed into a "*meteor*" (rather than a martyr), a prescience of things to come. For by the time *Battle-Pieces* was published, more than 260 Americans had been put to death under military law during the Civil War—a staggering number given that only 6 military executions of U.S. citizens occurred before 1861 and only 192 over the rest of U.S. history.[3]

Whereas Hawthorne, as we saw in chapter 4, explores questions of evidentiary value in the administration of capital punishment, Melville interrogates the sovereign force invested in a death sentence, the judicial performative par excellence. Up to this point, my study has principally examined literature in relation to the agency or means of lawful death—often personified in the hangman or embodied in the gallows itself—and particularly in terms of the representative condemned subject, frequently figured as a "Great" or sympathetic criminal (the product of social and hereditary forces beyond his or her control) or as an innocent victim of misleading or manufactured evidence. These issues remain concerns of Melville, most notably in the grandeur of John Brown's crime and the overt symbolism of Billy Budd as condemned innocence personified; but his work in many ways is less interested in the subject "before the law," to invoke Kafka's memorable parable, and more in the authority that lies *behind* it.

Melville's first literary musing on the death penalty occurs in a chapter contrasting "Civilized and Savage Life" in *Typee; or, a Peep at Polynesian Life* (1846), a work published at the height of the anti-gallows movement in antebellum America. With the history of capital punishment in mind, Melville's narrator Tommo sardonically asks "whether the mere eating of human flesh so very far exceeds in barbarity that custom which only a few years since was practised in enlightened England:—a convicted traitor, perhaps a man found guilty of honesty, patriotism, and suchlike heinous crimes, had his head lopped off with a huge axe, his bowels dragged out and thrown into a fire; while his body, carved into four quarters, was with his head exposed upon pikes, and permitted to rot and fester among the public haunts of men."[4] Comparing cannibalism to capital punishment in this way, Melville expresses one of *Typee's* central aims: the unsettling of the savage-civilized opposition that was often used to justify Western colonialization and imperialism in the South Seas and elsewhere. The comparison, one certain to evoke for today's readers Michel Foucault's famous opening to *Discipline and Punish*, not only questions but inverts the savage-civilized opposition, a point to which Tommo returns as he rounds off his thoughts about the death penalty and other savage practices of "civilized" nations: "The fiend-like skill we display in the invention of all manner of death-dealing engines," Melville writes in an oft-cited passage, "distinguish[es] the white civilized man as the most ferocious animal on the face of the earth."[5]

The ferocity of white civilization, in the context of Melville's work, is perhaps best illustrated in the execution and decapitation of the African slave Babo at the end of "Benito Cereno" (1856). That violence is enacted by the Spanish rather than the British crown, but it is clearly anticipated in Tommo's remarks on capital punishment as it had recently been "practised in enlightened England." But lest we take Melville's disdain for the death penalty here as unqualified support for the anti-gallows cause, it is necessary to return to the passage in *Typee* wherein Tommo contrasts savage and civilized life by way of capital punishment. Extending his thoughts on the savagery of "civilized man," Tommo scoffs at the "remorseless cruelty" one finds in "the institutions of our own favoured land."[6] As an example of that cruelty, he points to a criminal statute "lately adopted in one of the States of the Union, which purports to have been dictated by the most merciful considerations." That law proposed substituting the death sentence with life imprisonment:

> To destroy our malefactors piece-meal, drying up in their veins, drop by drop, the blood we are too chicken-hearted to shed by a single blow which would at once put a period to their sufferings, is deemed to be infinitely preferable to the old-fashioned punishment of gibbeting—much less annoying to the victim, and more in accordance with the refined spirit of the age; and yet how feeble is all language to describe the horrors we inflict upon these wretches, whom we mason up in the cells of our prisons, and condemn to perpetual solitude in the very heart of our population.[7]

Anticipating Bartleby's condemnation "to perpetual solitude in the very heart of our population," Melville's remarks here are more of an attack on prison reform and misguided reformers (like Hawthorne's Hollingsworth) than they are an endorsement of "the old-fashioned punishment of gibbeting." Even so, they are a far cry from the spirited assault he levies against the death penalty in *White Jacket*, a subject I touched on in chapter 1 and to which I will later return in this one. If capital punishment was little more than an idle curiosity, a sign of oxymoronic *civilized savagery* in Melville's first work, it would become a primary concern in his last, *Billy Budd*.

Focusing on *White-Jacket* and *Billy Budd*, two works separated by almost a half century, this chapter examines the death penalty in relation to the texts and contexts of Melville's work. More than Hawthorne, Melville provides a complicated perspective from which to explore literature and capital punishment in part because, unlike many writers associated with the Democratic Party and with the "Young America" movement in literature (including Hawthorne), he never explicitly came out against capital punishment. Moreover, of the many now-famous antebellum literary figures to write about the death penalty, Melville is virtually the only one (besides Wendell Phillips) to take up the subject when debates over the punishment—largely dormant in the public sphere since the outbreak of the Civil War—again became a national issue in the mid-1880s, when he began work on *Billy Budd*. My examination of Melville is further complicated through a close look at the work of Alexander Slidell MacKenzie, a U.S. naval commander and popular writer of some acclaim who stood at the center of the 1842 *Somers* mutiny affair, one of the most infamous capital cases of the antebellum period and source material for both *White-Jacket* and *Billy Budd*. The same age as Melville's beloved Hawthorne, to whom *Moby-Dick* is affectionately dedicated, and author of seven books (totaling over a dozen published volumes) and essays in Frances Lieber's *Encyclopedia Americana* and the prestigious journal *North American Review*, MacKenzie is a figure of interest in his own right for any study of American literature and the death penalty. Not only did he authorize a triple execution at sea, but he wrote vividly about two foreign executions he witnessed in his popular travel narratives, *A Year in Spain: By a Young American* (1829) and *Spain Revisited* (1836). Intriguing in himself, MacKenzie is even more interesting when considered in relation to Melville. Both writers were from upstate New York where their families belonged to the same social circles; both had influential brothers in politics; and both had gone to sea at an early age—MacKenzie into naval service and Melville, of course, into the whalery and then a brief stint in the navy himself.[8]

Much has been made of the *Somers* affair in Melville scholarship for important and obvious reasons, some of which I rehearse in what follows; but little work has been done connecting the writings of Melville and MacKenzie and none examining the two authors in relation to the death penalty.[9] No one, moreover, has studied the *Somers* mutiny case in light of the controversy over capital punishment, although one death penalty historian has identified the event in passing as one of two cases that fomented debates over the issue in the early 1840s in New York, an epicenter of the anti-gallows movement in antebellum America.[10] That Melville refers to the *Somers* affair and to MacKenzie's role in it in two works, separated by forty years, when interrogating the force behind the law, suggests the power it had in his imagination and the influence it exerted on the distinct contexts in which *White-Jacket* and *Billy Budd* were written.

Of course, the central event separating *White-Jacket* and *Billy Budd* is the Civil War, a period of profound national crisis when military and civilian law existed in close relation to each other, habeas corpus was suspended by presidential decree, and a new notion of "Nation" emerged with the rise of the Republican Party that challenged the predominantly Democratic Party perspective from which I have chiefly read nineteenth-century literature in connection to capital punishment. Recent cultural historians and literary critics who have examined the death penalty in a U.S. context have largely ignored the Civil War, using it for the most part as a convenient marker to end the anti-gallows movement in antebellum America.[11] It would, however, behoove us to examine capital punishment in the context of nineteenth-century America's great war when civil liberties were drastically curtailed and at least 267 U.S. citizens were executed under military law. Such an examination goes beyond the scope of this chapter. Instead, drawing from this context and building on the recent work of Brook Thomas, Stanton Garner, Deak Nabers, Gregory Jay, and Michael T. Gilmore, I conclude the chapter by arguing for the importance of reading *Billy Budd* in a (post) Civil War context.[12] I begin, however, with the *Somers* affair—a touchstone throughout the chapter that not only brings together *White-Jacket* and *Billy Budd*, Melville and MacKenzie, but ultimately helps me distinguish the death penalty politics of *White-Jacket* and *Billy Budd*, in addition to illustrating the changing sense of state authority behind the law that comes with the war and affects debates about capital punishment.

## "THIS FLOATING GALLOWS": THE *SOMERS* AFFAIR AND SUMMARY JUDGMENTS

On December 14, 1842, the USS *Somers* returned to New York City from its second voyage as a training ship for midshipman. Two weeks earlier, on the first of the month, Commander Slidell MacKenzie had sentenced to death and executed three men for plotting a mutiny. The condemned ringleader was Philip Spencer, a young midshipman whose father was the U.S. secretary of war in the Tyler administration; the other two were seaman Elisha Small and Boatswain's mate Samuel Cromwell, the latter of whom died protesting his innocence. MacKenzie's decision to execute the men at sea, rather than having them ironed and brought home to stand trial, sparked a national controversy that dominated headlines for some time to come.

At about the time of the *Somers* mutiny, Melville himself had participated in a mutinous act by jumping ship from the Whaler, *The Lucy Ann*, in September 1842.[13] That act led to his Polynesian adventures recorded in *Typee*, a novel of a young American's exotic experiences written in a spirit similar to MacKenzie's foreign travels recorded in *A Year in Spain: By a Young American* (1829). Melville would later learn of the *Somers* affair when in May he enlisted as an ordinary seaman on *The United States*, a war frigate like the *Somers*. The contrast between native life in the South Pacific Islands and naval life on a man-of-war, with its strict laws and military regiment, must have left a strong impression upon a young Melville. A young MacKenzie, writing a decade earlier in the *North American Review*, noted something similar when he described the stern governance of naval life from the perspective of a civilian: "One of the very first things which strike landsmen when they enter a man-of-war is the entire restraint, nay, absolute surrender of volition in all except one of those embarked; the stern superiority of him who orders, and the mechanical unqualified submission of those who obey."[14] The absolute authority of a naval captain, which MacKenzie marvels at and justifies in his essay, would become, as we shall see, a chief object of attack in Melville's critique of military provisions for corporal and capital punishment in *White-Jacket*. The *Somers* affair would have interested any enlisted man whose life was subject to military law and a captain's discretionary authority, but it must have been of special interest to Melville, whose first cousin, Guert Gansevoort, was second-in-command on the *Somers*, a ship dubbed a "floating gallows" in one of the many articles criticizing MacKenzie's actions.[15] In fact, it was Lieutenant Gansevoort who first relayed the alleged mutiny plot to the captain and who later gave the order to hang. If Melville's thoughts had first been with Gansevoort, the older cousin he idolized while growing up, they would have naturally settled on MacKenzie, whom Gansevoort in later court testimony would call "a man of so much decision."[16]

When news of the affair broke following the *Somers*'s return to New York, it created a national sensation. The *New York Tribune* reported on December 22 that the affair had become "the almost universal theme of conversation in this city."[17] A week later, lawyer and literary luminary Richard Henry Dana Jr., who would later write in defense of MacKenzie, was hardly exaggerating when he wrote in his journal: "All the world is talking about the Somers mutiny and the execution of Spencer" (29). A week after that, Washington's *National Intelligencer* echoed both the *Tribune*'s public and Dana's private remarks, noting that "the exciting subject of the Mutiny" was "the one table-talk—the theme of the boys at the corners, of the hackmen in the street, of servants and masters, of the grave and the gay, the busy and the idle. The case is every where argued and tried, and the precedent will at least be well understood hereafter" (70). Major papers in New York, Boston, and Washington all "argued and tried" the case (to use the *Intelligencer*'s courtroom metaphor), and Dana was certainly not the only celebrity of the legal and literary worlds to support MacKenzie publicly. Among others, Charles Sumner and Henry Wadsworth Longfellow—powerhouses in their respective spheres of law and literature—would come out in defense of the *Somers* executions. James Fenimore Cooper was virtually the only famous writer who censured MacKenzie in the immediate aftermath of the affair, although Melville would openly chastise the ship's captain some years later in his pointed allusions to the hangings in *White-Jacket*. MacKenzie's greatest detractor, however, was Secretary of War John Spencer, father of the executed ringleader; and the *Somers'* now-infamous captain became a target of reproach in the popular press, particularly in the *New York Herald*, which adopted an anti-MacKenzie position as the events of the affair came to light.

Debate about the executions in the popular press centered around questions of authority and responsibility. Both issues, in fact, animated the *Herald's* initial report of the affair, which approved of MacKenzie's action. "By this one act," the paper declared in its December 18, 1842, edition, MacKenzie had "done more to sustain the supremacy of naval authority and to vindicate outraged law, than anything which has ever occurred in our Navy." The article went on to acknowledge the good fortune "that on such a man as Slidell MacKenzie devolved the high responsibility of such a critical hour" (4). While other New York papers, such as the *Courier and Enquirer*, continued to champion MacKenzie, the *Herald* quickly changed its perspective. In a report the next day, it noted that a "great many members of the bar begin to object to the legality" of MacKenzie's action; the report also suggested that the "boldness and decision with which a United States officer acted" in this case was not unlike the action of a despot from "the early history of the Roman Republic" (5).

News stories and editorials like this one found support in Washington's *Madisonian*, the official organ of the Tyler administration, which also highlighted issues of authority and responsibility in the affair. In a notice later attributed to Secretary of War Spencer (it was cryptically signed "S") and written on behalf of "the friends of young Spencer, who was executed," the *Madisonian* challenged the legality of MacKenzie's actions, arguing that they constituted "the first instance in our history in which law has been violated—the first in which prisoners—not of the enemy, but our own citizens—have been put to death in cold blood" (9). By underscoring the condemned as "citizens," the *Madisonian* highlighted the bare rights of individuals in an unprecedented act of unwarranted authority. Calling attention to the "awful responsibility rest[ing] on those officers, and above all on their commander," the notice went on to question the integrity of the many published reports of the affair that relied on facts furnished by "officers who had a hand in the bloody deed" (8). Far from offering a fair assessment of the tragedy, these reports had, the notice claimed, "so perverted" and "so exaggerated" the facts, and "interspersed [them] with so much surmise, and so much downright falsehood, as to evince the deep anxiety felt to make sure of the first impression upon the public mind." The *Madisonian*, of course, strove to make its own impression by presenting an alternative account of the affair, one that portrayed Spencer's plot as a harmless fiction, "a mere romance of a heedless boy," and MacKenzie's actions as "the result of unmanly fear or of despotic temper, and wholly unnecessary at the time to repress or prevent a mutiny" (9).

Later, at the naval court of inquiry that officially investigated the alleged mutiny and the executions, the questions the *Madisonian* raised about MacKenzie's character were put directly to the brig's officers by MacKenzie himself. When asked in court if he observed in the captain "any signs of unmanly fear, or of a despotic temper, or of anything unbecoming the character of an officer and gentleman," First Lieutenant Gansevoort answered decidedly in the negative: "I saw nothing of the kind. The conduct of the commander throughout the whole was of the most unexceptional character, and I consider the country fortunate in having had such a commander, a man of so much decision, at such a time and under such circumstances of responsibility and danger as then existed" (75). Gansevoort's testimony echoed the many pro-MacKenzie accounts in the popular press that lionized the commander as a man of action, duty, and cool decision at a troubling hour. While the *Madisonian* notice had taken aim at those accounts, its chief target was a detailed, quasi-official "Report" of the affair written by MacKenzie himself and later used as evidence in the court of inquiry and at MacKenzie's subsequent court-martial. The report, a document of some thirteen thousand words written with an eye to its literary merits, created its own sensation when printed in full, along with accompanying court transcripts, in the *New York Tribune* and elsewhere. Evert Duyckinck, Melville's onetime confidante and the editor of the *Literary World,* called it a "thrilling narrative full of character and a paper that will not be forgotten in the history of the country" (68). When MacKenzie's report—a romance of the real culminating with three real-life executions—was later published in both pamphlet and book form for popular consumption, it joined countless other court reports and transcripts, like those of the 1830 Francis Knapp and 1850 John W. Webster trials examined in chapter 4, that competed with novels and short stories in the popular literary marketplace.[18]

Yet MacKenzie's report differed in crucial ways from most popular antebellum court reports and trial transcripts. For one thing, it was told from a perspective *within* or *behind* the law, offering a naval captain's "inside narrative" (to borrow Melville's term in *Billy Budd*) of a case in which a captain served not only as witness but as a judge and jury in a summary case involving life and death. For another, it dealt with *military*—not criminal—law and concerned a case in which a single individual (in consultation with subordinate officers), rather than multiple agents within the criminal justice system, reached a decision in which the ultimate penalty of death was at stake. Nonetheless, while the *Somers* affair was a case of military law, it had important implications for criminal law and debates over the administration of lethal authority in a republic. The case, moreover, played an instrumental role in shaping debates about the death penalty in the civilian realm. Unfolding as it did when the anti-gallows cause was rapidly gaining momentum in the early 1840s, the affair moved some of its critics to protest capital punishment itself.

One such account can be found in William Lloyd Garrison's *The Liberator*, which published numerous articles advocating the abolition of capital punishment from the mid-1840s through the 1850s. In fact, *The Liberator's* earliest statement against the death penalty appeared in an article titled "The Case of the *Somers*": "Was it justifiable for Mackenzie to kill Spencer and his associates?" the article asked. Its author responded by appealing to the tenets of Christianity, arguing that "the execution of Spencer was," according to those principles, "therefore unjustifiable, and, being the deliberate, unauthorized destruction of human life, it was MURDER." This conclusion prompted the writer to raise another question, to which an immediate answer was given: "Will it be said that [Spencer's] death is justified by the laws and customs of the navy? Then those laws, being anti-christian, should be abolished."[19] Published in Boston, *The Liberator's* response suggests the influence the *Somers* case had on anti-gallows politics outside New York. Within the state, the event was one of two major cases in the early 1840s primarily responsible for fomenting debate over capital punishment in New York.[20] The other was the 1842 John C. Colt trial, which occasioned Lydia Maria Child's most sustained criticism of the death penalty in her popular New York letters, and about which Melville later mused from the perspective of his lawyer-narrator in "Bartleby."[21]

The impact of the *Somers* affair in the context of death penalty debates is most clearly seen in the editorial columns of the *New York Tribune*, the state's leading daily paper, which from December 31, 1842, to March 31, 1843, had printed all documents and transcripts related to the case, including MacKenzie's report and his court-martial proceedings. Edited by influential reformer Horace Greeley, the *Tribune* frequently reported on the controversy surrounding capital punishment and often lent its support to the anti-gallows cause in a recurrent column headed, "The Punishment of Death."[22] Some of those columns were published alongside articles on the *Somers* case. One of them printed "Private correspondence of the Editor," which consisted of an excerpted letter sent to Greeley supporting a recent editorial in which Greeley had debated another correspondent who argued for retaining the death penalty: "You are right, too, on the subject of Capital Punishment," the excerpt began. "Your correspondent who undertook to read you a lecture for taking ground in favor of abolishing that barbarous law, had better read his Bible entirely through." Beginning with a brief discussion of scriptural evidence, the letter rehearsed some familiar arguments in opposition to capital punishment; it went so far as to "deny the right of the government, in any case, to take human life."[23]

A week later, the debate over the death penalty and the controversy surrounding the *Somers* affair literally crossed rhetorical paths. In spite of Greeley's well-known opposition to capital punishment, the *Tribune* had published several articles sympathetic toward MacKenzie and supporting his use of lethal force. Those articles elicited a personal response from Greeley himself, who clarified the circumstances of their publication in an editorial headed "The Punishment of Death":

> The Responsible Editor of The Tribune was absent at the East during the week that the tragedy of the Somers was developed and made the paramount topic of newspaper discussion. Some of the comments indulged in the columns of this paper (Editorial and otherwise) were so adverse in spirit as well as in bearing to the views I am known to entertain in relation to Punishment generally, and especially the Punishment of Death, that they may well have occasioned surprise among that large class of readers who do not know or consider that no one person ever does or can write all the Editorial matter which appears in a Daily journal of the present time, and that the views of those associated with the responsible Editor of a journal in preparing matter for its columns may vary materially differ, on the questions aside from its main purpose which are continually arising, from those he is known to entertain.[24]

Dropping the veil of "Responsible Editor" and adopting "the first person singular," Greeley went on to speak directly to readers, offering them "a few explanatory remarks in regard to the Punishment of Death." Those remarks constituted Greeley's (and the *Tribune's*) fullest statement to date in support of abolishing capital punishment. They had, however, little ostensibly to do with the particulars of the *Somers* case and instead considered the general question of the practice of lawful death. Equating "retributive justice" with "vengeance" and describing "the most flagrant criminals" as "victims of unfortunate circumstances and of defective or vicious Education," Greeley concluded the column by outlining five specific reasons why he personally opposed capital punishment: (1) because it destroyed rather than reformed those it punished; (2) because it was irreversible in cases of error; (3) because juries, reluctant to participate in a process leading to death, sometimes would "hold out against a verdict of Guilty, whereby the culprit often escapes any legal punishment at all"; (4) because "the man once hung is of no more use . . while the imprisoned felon is a life-long moral lesson"; and (5) because "judicial killing" tended to promote in "men the idea and feeling of vengeance for injuries and to diminish the natural abhorrence of bloodshed" (*Tribune*, Dec. 31, 1842). Greeley's reasons were nothing new in themselves—each, in fact, was given careful attention in John L. O'Sullivan's influential *Report to the New York Legislature*, first published in book form a year earlier in 1841—but they exposed a rationale for abolition to a broad audience whom it might not otherwise reach.

In the decade following the *Somers* affair, both Greeley and the *Tribune* would become leading voices in the anti-gallows campaign during the years Melville wrote his early fiction. While the *Tribune* continued to publish numerous anti-gallows articles and reports, some of them written by Margaret Fuller (a staff writer for the paper, beginning in 1844), the *Tribune's* "Responsible Editor" joined O'Sullivan in 1844 to found the New York Society of the Abolition of Capital Punishment, and Greeley himself would speak to thousands on the evils of capital punishment in lectures he gave at popular lyceums in rural New York outside the city.[25] Greeley would later refine that argument in "Death by Human Law," an essay that culled material from his lectures and took for its basis his 1842 *Tribune* article on the *Somers* affair. That essay was published in Greeley's *Hints of Reform* (1850), a book owned by Melville and published the same year as *White-Jacket*.[26]

## "SHALL SUFFER DEATH!": WHITE-JACKET'S
## PORTRAIT OF DESPOTISM

In 1843, Greeley's publishing house printed the *Somers Mutiny Affair*, one of three different works that anthologized documents relevant to the *Somers* case in book form for popular consumption.[27] Greeley's edition began with a list, which read like a playbill, of all those directly involved in the affair, with particular attention to MacKenzie—the drama's hero or antihero, depending on one's perspective (25). The opening pages ended with full citations of the three Articles of War relevant to the case: Article 24, "the Mutiny and Sedition Law of 1789"; Article 13, "the Law of 1800"; and Article 14. Each article, in the magisterial tone of military law, broadly defined the crime of mutiny and tersely pronounced its punishment: ". . . *shall suffer death*." Those particular articles, and the Articles of War as a whole, also played a starring role in *White-Jacket*, Melville's encyclopedic naval reform novel.

*White-Jacket*, as I briefly demonstrated in chapter 1, provides a unique perspective on capital punishment. Rather than representing some aspect of the death penalty procedure or directly responding to the administration of lawful death (strategies adopted in the literary works examined elsewhere in this book), it registers an intersubjective response to the death sentence as linguistic act, giving special attention to the Articles of War's operative clause, "*Shall Suffer Death!*" Exclamatory throughout and likened to the intermittent "discharge of the terrible minute guns,"[28] the clause is pronounced eight times over the course of three pages in "Monthly Muster round the Capstan," chapter 70 dramatizing the convocation of the ship's "People" and the formal reading of the navy's penal code, thirteen of which "are punishable by death" (292). To each iteration, Melville's representative seaman White-Jacket responds with ironic commentary that dialogizes the monologic letter of the law, exposing its tyranny and opening it up to criticism and parody in ways we have already seen.

Those articles ending "*shall suffer death, or such a punishment as a court martial shall adjudge*" (293) are held up for particular criticism. White-Jacket takes their ambiguity as implying a punishment "worse than death" (293), an anathema to any republican form of government. Humorously horrified, he apostrophizes, "Your honours of the Spanish Inquisition, Loyola and Torquemada!" and "Jack Ketch," an infamous hangman known for his botched executions, challenging them "to match these Articles of War, if you can" in terms of their cruelty (293). Contrasting the principles of American republicanism to the despotism of Old World Europe and the Near East is one of the primary ways by which Melville attacks military provisions for capital punishment in *White-Jacket*. Elsewhere in the chapter White-Jacket cites particular articles, in part or in full, and then subjects them to ridicule. This strategy is most evident when White-Jacket, as representative citizen turned naval subject, quotes from Articles 13, 14, and 20 and interpolates his responses to them:

Art. XIII. "*If any person in the navy shall make, or attempt to make, any mutinous assembly, he shall, on conviction thereof by a court martial, suffer death.*"

Bless me, White-Jacket, are you a great gun yourself, that you so recoil, to the extremity of your breechings, at that discharge?

But give ear again. Here goes another minute-gun. It indirectly admonishes you to receive the grossest insult, and stand still under it:

Art. XIV. "*No private in the navy shall disobey the lawful orders of his superior officer, or strike him, or draw, or offer to draw, or raise any weapon against him, while in the execution of the duties of his office, on pain of death.*"

Do not hang back there by the bulwarks, White-Jacket; come up to the mark once more; for here goes still another minute-gun, which admonishes you never to be caught napping:

Part of Art. XX. *"If any person in the navy shall sleep upon his watch, he shall suffer death."*

Murderous! But then, in time of peace, they do not enforce these blood-thirsty laws? Do they not, indeed? What happened to those three sailors on board an American armed vessel a few years ago, quite within your memory, White-Jacket; yea, while you yourself were yet serving on board this very frigate, the Neversink? What happened to those three Americans, White-Jacket—those three sailors, even as you, who once were alive, but now are dead? *"Shall suffer death!"* those were the three words that hung those three sailors. (294)

It was on the authority of the first two of these articles that MacKenzie executed Spencer, Small, and Cromwell. It is the last, however, that prompts the first of Melville's pointed allusions to the *Somers* affair itself. Written with humor and wit to unsettle the monologism of military law, that reference is both serious and comic in tone. As part of White-Jacket's interpolated response to the article's tyranny, it is droll and disarming; but in comparison to what had preceded it, the allusion strikes a more serious chord, signaling indignation and disbelief at the enforcement of such "bloodthirsty laws" during times of peace. The example is particularly effective in that it drives home the potential of abusive authority through the historical example of the *Somers* affair—the only instance in which our "own citizens," as the Washington's *Madisonian* had put it, "have been put to death" under such law. While treated with measured solemnity when first broached, Melville's commentary on the prospect of lawful death denigrates into a bit of gallows humor as White-Jacket, extending his internal dialogue on the subject, admonishes himself and others to take care, "lest you come to a sad end, even the end of a rope; lest, with a back-and-blue throat, you turn a dumb diver after pearl-shells" (294).

White-Jacket delves into the history of capital punishment as authorized under naval provisions in "The Genealogy of the Articles of War," the topic and title of chapter 71. Likening the articles to a "Turkish code," another reference to foreign despotism, he points to a fundamental contradiction between the republican principles of U.S. government and the navy's penal laws, which, although "solemnly ratified by a Congress of freeman, the representatives of freemen," nonetheless subject "thousands of Americans . . . to the most despotic usages" (297). The hypocrisy of American democracy begins with the fact that the U.S.

Articles of War originated not in America but in England, "whose laws we Americans hurled off as tyrannical, and yet [we] retained the most tyrannical of all." Further probing their foreign roots, White-Jacket links the creation of the articles to "a period of the history of Britain when the Puritan republic had yielded to a monarch; when a hangman Judge Jeffreys sentenced a world's champion like Algernon Sidney to the block" (298). Known as the "Bloody Assizes," this period marked a time in British history when more than three hundred persons were executed. It is thus no accident that this period, under the rule of James II in England, serves as the historical backdrop for Melville's interrogation of the origins of despotic military authority in *White-Jacket* as well as an important part of a broader context for understanding *Billy Budd*, whose drama unfolds over a century later.

Melville furthers this line of inquiry in the next chapter verbosely titled, *"Herein are the good Ordinances of the Sea, which wise Men, who voyaged round the World, gave to our Ancestors, and which constitute the Books of the Science of good Customs"* (300). That title is taken from the opening lines of *Consulate of the Sea*, a code of maritime law based on the practices of Mediterranean ports in the Middle Ages that, White-Jacket shows us, appears progressive when read against the despotism of the U.S. Articles of War. In this chapter, Melville returns to his strategy of ironic citation, quoting and talking back to the letter of the law. Here, however, he focuses on the discretionary authority granted to captains and officers under the articles, as well as the double standards aboard man-of-wars that permit officers and especially captains to violate laws to which seaman are held accountable. "Who put this great gulf between the American Captain and the American sailor?" White-Jacket wonders. Citing a familiar proverb among man-of-war men, he incredulously responds that *"the law was not made for the Captain! Indeed, he may almost be said to put off the citizen when he touches his quarter-deck; and, almost exempt from the law of the land himself, he comes down upon others with a judicial severity unknown on the national soil"* (301). Calling attention to this unacceptable exceptionality, White-Jacket portrays the captain as a veritable king—a noncitizen outside and above the law. This imagery builds and reaches an apotheosis in the final sentence of the paragraph from which I have been quoting: "With the Articles of War in one hand, and the cat-o'nine-tails in the other, he stands an undignified parody upon Mohammed enforcing Muslimism with the sword and the Koran" (301). Law and its enforcement united by way of the captain, who holds a symbol of each in his hands, this orientalized image provides a despotic figurehead to the U.S naval ship of state.

White-Jacket adds to this depiction of the captain as symbolic autocratic by relating an anecdote told to him by an English seaman. The story involves a sailor who, when accused of drunkenness, invokes his right under English law to appeal "the decision of a captain—even in a comparatively trivial case—to the higher tribunal of a court martial." That appeal results in the sailor spending weeks in irons before, "despairing of being liberated, he offered to compromise at two dozen lashes" (302). The bargain, however, is refused by the captain, and the sailor, "at last tried before the bar of the quarter-deck," is "condemned to two hundred lashes" (302). This story provides one of the many examples of abusive authority in the English and U.S. navies. Whether it be "wholly true or not," the tale is enough to evoke again for White-Jacket the horrors of the Spanish Inquisition: "What can be expected from a court whose deeds are done in the darkness of the recluse courts of the Spanish Inquisition? when that darkness is solemnized by an oath on the Bible? when an oligarchy of epaulets sits upon the bench, and a plebeian top-man, without a jury, stands judicially naked at the bar?" (302–3). Whereas the earlier allusion to the Inquisition registers the terror of the death sentence as expressed in the articles, this one emphasizes the process of judgment itself. In it, we have the power relations spelled out in class and antirepublican terms.

It is through this rhetorical onslaught of (anti)republican images and anecdotes— the hangman Judge Jeffrey and the executed "world's champion" Sidney, the horrors of Jack Ketch during the Bloody Assizes, the captain as noncitizen and an "undignified parody upon Mohammed enforcing Muslimism," the "judicially naked" top-man confronting the "oligarchy of epaulets," and the terror of the Spanish Inquisition—that Melville levies his assault on military law and the discretionary authority invested in a captain. And it is within this context that White-Jacket, musing once more on capital punishment statutes under military law, refers to the *Somers* affair for a second time:

> Some may urge that the severest operations of the code are tacitly made null in time of peace. But though with respect to several of the Articles this holds true, yet at any time any and all of them may be legally enforced. Nor have there been wanting recent instances, illustrating the spirit of this code, even in cases where the letter of the code was not altogether observed. The well-known case of a United States brig furnishes a memorable example, which at any moment may be repeated. Three men, in a time of peace, were then hung at the yard-arm, merely because, in the Captain's judgment, it became necessary to hang them. To this day the question of their complete guilt is socially discussed. (303)

Used earlier as an example of the articles' "Murderous" spirit, the *Somers* allusion here provides an actual instance—an instantiation, if you will—of absolute discretionary authority invested in a captain. More than an anecdote or image, the *Somers* affair itself grounds Melville's critique of military law in a concrete historical example, "which at any moment may be repeated." At a loss about how "to characterize such a deed," White-Jacket quotes from Blackstone on the enforcement of such capital statutes during such times: "If anyone that hath commission of martial authority doth, in time of peace, hang, or otherwise execute any man by colour of martial law, this is murder; for it is against the Magna Carta." (303). Judging MacKenzie's actions in terms of Blackstone's *Commentaries*, itself a product of an earlier age, is only part of the point here. The more significant attack comes through Blackstone's citation of the Magna Charta, a product of the medieval period (like the Consulate of the Sea) that, on the use of lethal force during times of peace, comes off as progressive when compared to the U.S. Articles of War.

I have taken the time to work through the tropes, arguments, and narratives composing Melville's attack of the Articles of War in chapters 70, 71, and 72 to show their importance to our understanding of the novel's politics of reform and aesthetic design. In fact, this sequence of late chapters complements the more famous antiflogging chapters at the novel's structural center, which draw similarly from an ethos of republicanism by exposing the Navy's antirepublican practices. Whereas the later chapters focus on the tyranny of the article's capital statutes and the captain's discretionary authority, thus providing the theoretical grounds for a critique of military authority, the earlier ones attack the practice of military law through the ubiquitous example of corporal punishment, a form of punishment conceptually and historically related to capital punishment. Legal historian Stuart Banner provides a helpful way of thinking about such a relation in his idea of "degrees of death," that capital punishment was "more than just one penal technique among others. It was the base point from which other kinds of punishments deviated."[29] As colonial America became the United States and moved, along with European nations, from a culture of punishment to one of discipline in ways that Michel Foucault has documented, it retained aspects of capital punishment that strove to produce what Banner calls "a *symbolic* death, a penalty that mimicked some aspects of capital punishment without actually killing the defendant."[30] The simulated hanging to which Hester is subjected in Hawthorne's *The Scarlet Letter* (1850) provides a literary example of such a symbolic death, as do the frequent floggings that punctuate Melville's depiction and discussion of abusive authority in much of his work.

In *White-Jacket*, a key example of corporal punishment as symbolic death unfolds in the first of the novel's four consecutive antiflogging chapters. Titled "A Flogging," the chapter offers a dramatic representation of corporal punishment, whereas the next three attack the practice on philosophical, legal, and moral grounds, respectively. "A Flogging" sets the stage for the critique to follow by recounting the punishment of four sailors for fighting, a disciplinary act that takes place "at the captain's pleasure" (134). The "pleasure," however, is not just the captain's but the entire crew's; for the repeated cry, "*All hands witness punishment, ahoy!*" announces a fate to be publicly enacted and witnessed by the ship's "People," a republican term used in *White-Jacket* to distinguish seaman from the captain and officers. "To the sensitive seaman," White-Jacket reflects,

> that summons sounds like a doom. He knows that the same law which impels it—the same law by which the culprits of the day must suffer; that by that very law he also is liable at any time to be judged and condemned. And the inevitableness of his own presence at the scene; the strong arm that drags him in view of the scourge, and holds him there till all is over; forcing upon his loathing eye and soul the sufferings and groans of men who have familiarly consorted with him, eaten with him, battled out watches with him—men of his own type and badge—all this conveys a terrible hint of the omnipotent authority under which he lives. (135)

For readers in the 1850s, this scene of public punishment would have certainly conjured up images of public execution—a legal practice recently abolished in the North but still performed in parts of the South. Melville's depiction draws from the anti-gallows argument by humanizing and sympathizing with the condemned, but it does not feature bloodlust and debauchery, essential elements in the anti-gallows execution scenes dramatized by Simms, Child, Lippard, and Judd examined in earlier chapters of my study. Instead, we have something akin to the Puritan execution scene in which the condemned, an object of compassion, is representative of the people, and the witnesses, through spectatorship enforced by the proverbial "strong arm" of the law, are participants inscribed in the ritual of the punishment. In his respect, Melville's scene of symbolic death is more like the one Hawthorne stages in *The Scarlet Letter* (1850), published the same year as *White-Jacket*. Whereas Hawthorne, as we have seen, sustains an analogy between Hester's simulated hanging and "the anticipated execution of some noted culprit,"[31] Melville links corporal and capital punishment by explaining what the summons to witness punishment "conveys" to the seaman: "a terrible hint of the omnipotent authority under which he lives" (135).

If the frequent call to witness corporal punishment "hint[s]" at the supreme authority over life invested in captains under military law, its dramatic enactment can be read as a lesson in the failure of violent punishment as a deterrent to crime—another mainstay of the anti-gallows campaign but one impossible to prove conclusively since capital, unlike corporal, punishment destroys those subjected to it. In "A Flogging," Melville thus shows how the punishment each man receives inures him to violence and promotes violence in kind (rather than deterring it) by illustrating the responses of the three condemned to the scourge. John, the first of the men flogged, comes off the grating brutalized by the experience. "D——mn me!" he curses as he walks among the crew. "It's nothing when you're used to it! Who wants to fight?" The punishment has a similar effect on Antoine, the second man condemned: "At every blow," White-Jacket tells us, "he surged from side to side, pouring out a torrent of involuntary blasphemies. Never before had he been heard to curse. When cut down, he went among the men, swearing to have the life of the Captain" (137). Peter, the scourge's final victim, is subjected to the punishment for the first time. When released, he becomes as brutal as John, who is well acquainted with the scourge: "I don't care what happens to me now!" Peter exclaims. "I have been flogged once, and they may do it again if they will. Let them look out for me now!" (138)

By highlighting the brutalizing effects of flogging Melville was, of course, making a case against *corporal*, not capital punishment. But in the reform culture of Melville's time, arguments against the two forms of punishment were often interrelated. As Myra C. Glenn has shown, the campaigns against corporal and capital punishments were interlinked as "part of a broad spectrum of transatlantic reform which sought to limit, if not abolish, a range of violent, punitive practices."[32] One influential reformer of Melville's time to write against both practices was Greeley, whose "Flogging in the Navy" was published alongside "Death by Human Law" in *Hints of Reform*. Likely drawing upon the republican argument against capital punishment he knew well, Greeley described corporal punishment in the navy as an abuse of authority and a violation of a citizen's inalienable rights. "*Make the Navy Republican*," he repeatedly declares at the end of his antiflogging essay.[33] In *White-Jacket*, Melville develops a similar argument by directly linking corporal and capital punishments in "Some of the Evil Effects of Flogging," the second of the novel's antiflogging chapters. In it, he associates a captain's discretionary authority to flog under the U.S. Naval laws "with the penal laws that prevailed in England some sixty years ago, when one hundred and sixty different offences were declared by the statute-book to be capital, and the servant-maid who but pilfered a watch was hung besides the murderer of a family" (139). The image of the servant-maid hanged beside the depraved murderer under outmoded British law illustrates the profound injustice and arbitrary use of disciplinary practices under U.S. military law. Thus, in connecting corporal and capital punishment by way of this telling comparison, Melville criticizes both practices as products from a barbarous past antithetical to the most basic principles of republican government.

In "Flogging Not Lawful," the third of the antiflogging chapters, Melville extends this argument by invoking the U.S. Constitution and its protections of civil rights and liberties. "If there are any three things opposed to the genius of the American Constitution," White-Jacket reasons to begin the chapter, "they are these: irresponsibility in a judge, unlimited discretionary authority in an executive, and the union of an irresponsible judge and an unlimited executive in one person" (143). Claiming that the captain violates each of these tenets, White-Jacket attacks the letter of naval law with all the gusto that characterizes his later assault on capital provisions in the Articles of War in chapters 70, 71, and 72. Citing Article 32, for example, he finds in the captain a direct violation of the Constitution's doctrine of the separation of powers: "By this article the captain is made a legislator, as well as a judge and an executive" (143). Reading backward, we can see how this line of argument culminates in what Melville later figures in the orientalized image of the captain as an "undignified parody upon Mohammed enforcing Muslimism with the sword and the Koran." Though MacKenzie and the *Somers* affair are not invoked by name in this earlier instance as they are in the later ones, Melville speaks directly to the question of abusive authority and responsibility invested in the captain by virtue of Article 32: "So far as it goes, [this article] absolutely leaves to his discretion to decide what things shall be considered crimes, and what shall be the penalty; whether an accused person has been guilty of actions by him declared to be crimes; and how, when, and where the penalty shall be inflicted" (143–44). The navy thus creates an "absolute one-man power in the captain" (144), a despotism White-Jacket associates with a "Russian Czar," just as the U.S. Articles of War are later likened to a "Turkish code."

As the critique in "Flogging Not Lawful" develops, Melville exposes another constitutional violation that provides the (un)lawful conditions under which enlisted seamen exist on a man-of-war: "In the American Navy, there is an everlasting suspension of the Habeas Corpus," White-Jacket declares; and the American sailor, in essence a citizen at sea, "shares none of our civil immunities . . . For him our Revolution was in vain; to him our Declaration of Independence is a lie" (144). This barrage of (anti)republican arguments, anecdotes, and imagery adds up in the famous antiflogging chapters, much as it does in their less famous counterparts in the later attack on capital provisions under military law in chapters 70, 71, and 72. If we can read Melville's attack on corporal punishment in

*White-Jacket*, as several critics have, as "evidence of the slavery dilemma,"[34] then certainly we can also read it as evidence of the capital punishment controversy given the intimate connections—both historical and conceptual—between these two modes of punishment. Melville's criticism of corporal and capital punishment in the navy, moreover, has important implications for the death penalty under civil and not just military law, just as debates over the *Somers* affair (as military case) had powerfully affected debates about the death penalty under criminal law in the court of public opinion. What is more, *White-Jacket* itself invites us to make connections between military and civilian realms through its governing trope of the ship of state—the novel's central conceit embedded in its subtitle, *The World in a Man-of-War*.

## SHIPS OF STATE: MACKENZIE/MELVILLE

A leitmotif in much of Melville's sea fiction, the ship-of-state metaphor is put to particular use in *White-Jacket*. "For a ship is a bit of terra firma cut off from the main," White-Jacket informs us in the first of the trope's many explicit uses; "it is a state in itself; and the captain is its king" (23). Extending the comparison, Melville describes this ship of state as decidedly undemocratic: "It is no limited monarchy, where the sturdy Commons have a right to petition, and snarl if they please; but almost a despotism like the Grand Turk's. The captain's word is law; he never speaks but in the imperative mood. When he stands on his Quarterdeck at sea, he absolutely commands as far as eye can reach" (23). Written in seriocomic tones that characterize the novel as a whole, the ship-of-state conceit establishes the terms in which relations of authority are to be understood in the world of a man-of-war, with White-Jacket grouped among the "Commons" (elsewhere referred to as "the People"), over whom the captain as "king" rules with "a despotism like the Grand Turk's"—an image that resonates with the antirepublican tropes I have traced in later chapters of the novel.

As Brook Thomas has demonstrated, the ship-of-state figure attained popular currency in literary and legal politics in the decades leading up to and during the Civil War, with Abraham Lincoln as the president most often associated as with the trope, "the captain of the ship of state."[35] In his elegiac "Oh Captain! My Captain!" (1865), Walt Whitman immortalized Lincoln in these terms, mourning the loss of the slain "Captain" on the ship's "deck" while celebrating Union victory and the preservation of the ship of state.[36] If Whitman's poem is the most famous literary work to use the trope in the immediate aftermath of the war, the figure's most famous antebellum usage appears in Henry Wadsworth Longfellow's "The Building of the Ship" (1849), whose closing stanza begins, "Thou,

too, sail on, O Ship of State! / Sail on, O UNION, strong and great!"[37] First published when Melville was writing *White-Jacket*, Longfellow's poem obviously
concerns the growing crisis over the Union and succession (the poem allegedly
brought Lincoln to tears when he heard it read),[38] but the poet had revised the
final stanza to make an explicit pro-Union statement after having dinner with his
good friend Charles Sumner, the influential lawyer, politician, and orator who
would become a leading Republican during the Civil War and one of Lincoln's
chief spokespersons for the prosecution of the war effort. If Sumner helped shape
the poem's revised conclusion, its inception owed much to the work of MacKenzie, an old friend of Longfellow's from whose "Navy" and "Ship" essays the poet
had drawn in writing "The Building of the Ship."[39] First published in the *North
American Review*, MacKenzie's essays were included in the *Encyclopedia Americana*, edited by Francis Lieber, the Columbia University professor and legal
theorist who in large measure drafted the provisions of war for the Lincoln administration. With important connections to Longfellow, Lincoln, Lieber, and
Sumner, MacKenzie's theory of the ship of state and his later defense of it through
lethal force in the *Somers* case provide a helpful way of understanding shifting
ideas of state authority and "Nation" (to use Sumner's preferred term) from the
antebellum to the war period.[40] We can get a good grasp of this shift by contrasting the republican ethos of Melville's military ship and the civilian world for
which it stands in *White-Jacket* to that of MacKenzie's influential model of the
naval ship of state.

MacKenzie presents his model in "Navy" (1830), the first of his *North American Review* essays later collected by Lieber. Anticipating Melville's use of the
ship-of-state metaphor (if Melville had not read and been directly influenced by
the essay), MacKenzie likens authority in a man-of-war to that of an absolute monarchy. Unlike Melville, however, he draws the comparison to defend the despotism
of naval law and to marvel at the "unnatural" harmony of the "social position[s]"
on a war vessel as well as the "artful wonder" of the ship itself. "Each ship offers in
itself a perfect community, self-existent and self-dependent," MacKenzie claims:

> A Ship with its captain, officers, and seamen, forms no imperfect miniature of
> a monarchy, with its king, nobles, and third estate. If there be any difference,
> it is that the graduations are more decided, the despotism more complete.
> This state of things results less from the subordination necessary and common
> to all military establishments, than from the peculiar difficulties and dangers
> attending naval life, which do not allow each man to remain, even in immate-
> rial things, master of his actions, but, inasmuch as the fate of all depends upon

the conduct of each, requires a harmony of action only to be obtained by the most complete subordination to a single will.[41]

MacKenzie's ship of state presents obvious and important differences to Melville's. For Melville, as we have seen, the despotism of the military code points to a contradiction in American republican principles and their actual practices. For MacKenzie, that despotism is necessitated by the exceptional "state of things" on a ship, circumstances that constituted a state unto itself in which the lives of all depend on cooperation with one another and "complete subordination" of all to a "single will." On such a ship and under such a state, the seaman is no citizen (as Melville would describe him) but rather a military subject under the absolute authority of the captain, a "king." Whereas for Melville seamen (whom he calls "the People") are first and foremost U.S. citizens with basic rights protected by the Constitution, for MacKenzie they compose a "third estate"—a telling allusion to the conditions of monarchical rule before the French Revolution, with the "single will" of the captain or king both calling to mind and canceling out Rousseau's republican notion of "the general will."[42]

The differences between MacKenzie's and Melville's notions of authority and civil rights are easy to see through their opposing uses of the ship-of-state metaphor in a military context. Nonetheless, despite what in the end are crucial differences, there is an important similarity in how each writer imagines the United States' exceptional place among other nations as a government *of* and *for* "The People." In fact, this similarity can be seen most clearly when one compares their accounts of witnessing public executions abroad, a scene of foreign despotism that contrasts with the exceptionalism of the republic of the United States. We can begin to see how by looking first at Melville's brief musings and then working through MacKenzie's more extensive reflections in greater detail.

Melville, as far we know, never witnessed a public execution in the United States, where the practice was banished in his native New York in 1833 and throughout almost all of the North by the mid 1840s. Nonetheless, he did witness one in England when he was there in November 1849 to promote the British publication of *White-Jacket*. The execution Melville attended was a sensational one, attracting somewhere between thirty thousand and fifty thousand spectators.[43] It was the double execution of the Mannings, a husband and wife who had murdered a man they hoped to cheat out of his fortune. One of the mid-nineteenth century's most notorious capital cases, the Manning executions generated in England the kind of interest the *Somers* affair did some seven years earlier in America. For writers like Charles Dickens and William Makepeace

Thackeray, who were also among the crowd of spectators, the executions were a national shame—a relic of the nation's barbaric past that prompted both authors to write against the gallows. For Melville, the event must have served as a prime example of that foreign despotism about which he had written with such verve in the new novel he was then promoting in England. If it had, however, Melville would write nothing to that effect, probably because the Manning execution, unlike the *Somers* affair, was not a U. S. event. Documenting the executions in his travel journal, Melville merely noted how he and a friend "walked over Hungerford Bridge to Horsemonger Lane, Borough, to see the last end of the Mannings," paying "half a crown each for a stand on the roof of a house adjoining."[44] He did, however, marvel at the scene: "An inimitable crowd in all the streets. Police by hundreds. Men & women fainting. –The man & wife were hung side by side—still unreconciled to each other—What a change from the time they stood up to be married, together! The mob was brutish. All in all, a most wonderful, horrible, & unspeakable scene."[45]

For a young MacKenzie, the execution scene was hardly an "unspeakable" event. Two decades before Melville went "to see the last end of the Mannings," the man who would authorize a triple execution at sea had written at length about more than one execution he witnessed while traveling in Europe. In fact, what MacKenzie saw and felt at two different executions account for the dramatic conclusions to the opening volumes of his two popular travel narratives, *A Year in Spain: By a Young American* (1829) and *Spain Revisited* (1836). Whereas Melville in *White-Jacket* finds the specter of Old World despotism (figured in the Spanish Inquisition and elsewhere) in a U.S. man-of-war, MacKenzie emphasizes its literal presence in Spain, where rampant crime and the country's despotic criminal justice system serve as frequent reminders of the superiority of the United States and its truly republican institutions. As one of the only recent critics of MacKenzie's early travel narratives puts it, "The sharp contrast between the state of affairs in Spain and the United States instilled, in essence, a self-gratifying, jingoistic message for which the travel writer became a keen yet subtle agent."[46]

Nowhere is this message more apparent than in the two narratives' climactic execution scenes. Throughout both but especially in the first, MacKenzie highlights his own subjective responses in witnessing lawful death as a representative "Young American" reared on republican values. Thus, he begins the account in *A Year in Spain* by expressing a personal abhorrence toward capital punishment, noting how a recent execution he attended in southern France, by way of "the fatal guillotine," had left him with such a "feeling of oppression and abasement, of utter disgust" that he "form[ed] a tacit resolution never to be present at another." Nonetheless, stifling his "repugnance," MacKenzie decides to attend a scene that "could not fail to elicit the unrestrained feelings of the multitude and to bring the national character [of Spain] into strong relief."[47] Treating the execution in part as a social study in foreign barbarism, MacKenzie attends the hanging but consciously foregrounds his own discomfort at several junctures (much like White-Jacket's subjective response to the hypothetical pronouncements of "*Shall Suffer Death!*"). For instance, surveying the mob in the streets of which he was a part, MacKenzie draws an implicit distinction between himself, a representative "Young American," and the scores of Old World Spaniards around him as anticipation of the imminent hangings builds: "I began at last to look with anxiety for the coming of the criminals. But when I came to compare their condition with my own, I could not but reproach myself for my impatience" (344). MacKenzie's self-reproach in these reflections moves from mild upbraiding to a more thorough remonstrance: "I had before been disgusted only with the scene around me; but now, becoming disgusted with myself, I turned away to beguile my impatience by wandering through the neighboring churches" (344). Those meanderings, however, afford little relief. Inside one neighboring church, MacKenzie's thoughts are drawn to the Spanish Inquisition, a point of reference in *White-Jacket* for the horrors of abusive authority under military law. When viewing the church's art, some of its paintings appear to MacKenzie as "ridiculous"; others he describes simply as "bloody" and "disgusting" (345).

Outside and among the spectators again, MacKenzie depicts the first of the executions in grisly detail:

> The last moment of [the condemned's] life had now arrived. The executioner took two of the cords which dangled from the beam, and having once more convinced himself that they were of equal length, he opened the nooses, and placed them about the neck of the malefactor. This done, he let himself down a single step, and seating himself firmly upon the shoulders of his victim, he grasped him tightly about the neck with his legs. He then drew powerfully upon the cords. The strangling malefactor made a convulsive but ineffectual attempt to reach upward with his pinioned arms, and then writhed his body to escape from the torture. This moment was seized upon by the executioner, who threw himself over the edge of the ladder, when both fell downward together. They had nearly turned over, when the ropes arrested their fall, and, as they tightened, they struck across the face of the executioner, and threw his hat aside among the crowd. But he clung to his prey with a resolute grasp,

recovered his seat, and moved upward and downward upon the shoulders of the malefactor. Nor was he left to his own efforts; his assistants below reached the legs of the victim, and drew them downward with all their might.

When this had continued a few minutes, the executioner stood erect upon the shoulders of his victim, and attempted to climb up by the chords, as he probably had been wont to do; but whether he had been stunned by the stroke of the ropes, or had grown heavier and less active since the last execution, his attempt proved abortive, and the loud cries of the multitude, outraged at the brutality, restrained him from a second effort. He then slid down by the body and legs of the criminal, until his feet rested upon the ground, and having tied a rope about the ankles of the dead man, he was drawn aside so as to make room for his companion (350–51).

A gruesome account of lawful death rivaling anything depicted in the fiction of George Lippard, the execution that MacKenzie details paints a grotesque portrait of foreign despotism that Melville intimates more than describes in *White-Jacket*. MacKenzie's scene, in fact, has elements of what Melville imagines in Jack Ketch (the infamous British hangman known for his botched executions) in the figure of the unfit executioner who makes a second attempt to climb triumphantly up the rope from which his handy work had been carried out. The executioner's exploits elicit the Young American's pronounced disgust: "Dreadful propensity of our nature," MacKenzie exclaims in response, "which often leads us to exult in the vilest deeds, provided they be adroitly executed!" (352)

First published in 1829, a year before Connecticut would become the first state to abolish public executions in the United States, MacKenzie's popular book with its showpiece execution scene, certainly contributed to America's movement to abolish public executions—especially with a favorable review of the book by one of America's most celebrated writers, Washington Irving, who praised MacKenzie for depicting the hangings "with the preservation and fidelity of a Flemish painting."[48] One of the most graphic literary executions of the nineteenth century, MacKenzie's account provides the kind of scene Evert Duyckinck had in mind when, writing a year before the *Somers* affair, he called the death penalty "a remnant of barbarity, one of the last tottering relics of the state handed down to us from the days of feudalism."[49] MacKenzie in his travel narrative, unlike Duyckinck in his "Death by Hanging" (1842), was not making an explicit argument against capital punishment in his account of despotic Spain. Nonetheless, he comes close to doing so in the conclusion he draws from it: "Surely, there can be nothing in such a spectacle to promote morality, nothing to make us either better or happier: a spectacle which serves but to create despondency, and to array man in enmity with his condition" (353).

While the anti-gallows sentiment here is directed toward humanity as a whole rather than the inhumanity of a particular nation, it is important to remember that MacKenzie justified his attendance at the execution (an event that Longfellow, another young American then in Spain, intentionally avoided)[50] as an attempt to bring "into strong relief" the country's "national character." MacKenzie continues this project in *Spain Revisited*, wherein he describes in detail a peculiarly "Spanish" method of execution by the garrote, which induces lawful death, as MacKenzie had succinctly explained in *A Year in Spain*, "by placing the criminal in an iron chair, provided with a collar which fits closely about the neck" (339). The execution scene in *Spain Revisited* differs in several ways from the one in MacKenzie's first travel narrative. For starters, no longer among the people in the streets, MacKenzie views it from a balcony and in the company of a Spanish colonel whose callous and military perspective creates a foil to the more sympathetic view of our representative American. "I was at once absorbed by the painful interest which attracted my attention to the person of the culprit," MacKenzie says. "The colonel, on the contrary, was filled with delight at the spirited manner in which his horsemen kept the way open; beating back the more pressing intruders by frequent and forceful blows with the flat of their long Toledo sabres, and reining their steeds most unceremoniously backward upon them."[51] This explicit contrast in perspective is further developed through MacKenzie's concerned reflections and asides to the American reader. For instance, when the condemned—a political prisoner "sentenced [to death] by military commission," as in the hypothetical scenarios Melville imagines in *White-Jacket*—is ceremoniously led to the execution site, MacKenzie describes the event dramatically unfolding "as if the government had still been that of the Absolute King, and the felon a false-hearted liberal."[52] Such a symbolic scenario dramatizes the conflict between the citizen-subject and sovereign authority in stark terms. Similarly, earlier in the scene when the condemned first emerges in plain view, MacKenzie apostrophizes his fellow citizens, remonstrating them to appreciate the civil liberties and rights they may take for granted: "Oh, Americans!, while you pity the land in which liberty is unknown and unappreciated, learn to value the blessings which you enjoy, and cultivate an ever-increasing admiration and love for that birthright of freedom which has been bequeathed to you."[53]

MacKenzie, in this particular appeal and in his more general use of the execution scene to exemplify foreign despotism, sounds much like Melville in his arguments against the tyranny of military law in *White-Jacket*. Hence, despite obvious differences in their conceptions of the ship of state and its relation to military authority, MacKenzie and Melville share a belief in the exceptional state of the American polis and its exceptional place in world history. To be sure, Melville's critique of military law in terms of the ship of state stems from this assumption, and his peculiar brand of American exceptionalism explicitly manifests in the famous passages concluding White-Jacket's attack of corporal punishment. Waxing typological to end "Flogging Not Necessary," White-Jacket likens the United States to "Israel of old" and declares "we Americans" as "the peculiar, chosen people—the Israel of our time" who "bear the *ark* of the liberties of the world" (*White-Jacket* 151, emphasis added). Mixing biblical metaphor with a rhetoric of the American Revolution, Melville rights the ship of state by imagining a new one (an ark) contra the warship with its principles of arbitrary law, violence, and subordination. Appealing like MacKenzie to the American "birthright of freedom," White-Jacket declares, "Seventy years ago we escaped from thrall; and besides our first birthright—embracing one continent of earth—God has given to us, for a future inheritance, the broad domains of the political pagans, that shall yet come and lie down under the shade of our ark, without bloody hands being lifted" (151). Inspired by the American Revolution and fulfilling biblical prophecy, Melville's exceptional ship of state leads by example, putting "the rest of the nations . . . in our rear" (153). Liberty, freedom, and American empire, in other words, necessarily forsake the despotism of military authority.

MacKenzie, to conclude his own defense of the *Somers* executions in the court of public opinion, invokes a similar patriotic image of America's exceptionalism; however, he uses it toward different ends by comparing his preservation of the ship to safeguarding the American state: "The nominal party sinks into comparative unimportance," MacKenzie writes of himself and his own (heroic) action, "and the American nation rears her august form, entreating that her youngest, her favourite offspring, may be saved from its worst enemy,—that it may be saved from the demoralizing, destructive principle of insubordination."[54] If for MacKenzie subordination to the captain's will under military law and in times of national crisis is necessary to the survival of the ship of state, for Melville the principle of subordination is among the navy's greatest liabilities. Safeguarding America's future, according to Melville, means reforming the navy (making it "republican," to invoke Greeley's refrain) in order to reflect the nation's democratic values it serves to protect. It also means keeping in check the powers of military authority so that the civilian realm would not succumb to military despotism. For MacKenzie, in contrast, that despotism is necessary to protect a republic that was so exceptional. From this perspective, MacKenzie can at once denounce the civilian execution scene as a foreign barbarism while defending the military execution under U.S. authority when in a state of emergency, when preserving the ship *or* state.

What we have, then, is a difference in opinion over the powers in a republic granted to the captain of the ship of state, which in civilian terms is the president as commander in chief. Epitomized in antebellum debates over the *Somers* affair and exemplified in MacKenzie's and Melville's opposing visions of the American ship of state, these competing perspectives reach a climax in Lincoln's administration of the Civil War and can be crudely broken down in terms of party lines with the formation of the Republican Party in the mid 1850s. On the one hand, we have a Democratic perspective that sees the president as primarily a civilian whose duties include protecting citizens from the perils of military despotism. Himself a citizen, the president in this view has special authority as chief executive, but that power needs to be checked by constitutional restraints. On the other hand, we have a Republican perspective that justifies the presence of a strong military force as an exception to the republican nation it serves and protects. Republicans at the time, in fact, went so far as to claim that a strict military code was justified by the Constitution itself. We have a prime (and early) example of this logic in a famous defense of the *Somers* affair written by Charles Sumner, later a friend of Melville's who would become, of course, a famous senator and leading Radical Republican during and after the Civil War. Reading Sumner's defense of MacKenzie and a later speech he delivered before Congress during the Civil War against Melville's Democratic stance in *White-Jacket* will not only clarify the political terms of Melville's and MacKenzie's ships of state but help me expose a Republican justification for capital punishment that, as I shall suggest, informs and complicates Melville's treatment of the military execution around which *Billy Budd* is organized.

## "THE SWORD SUSPENDED . . .": THE REPUBLICAN JUSTIFICATION OF THE DEATH PENALTY

As Brook Thomas has shown, Sumner's "The Mutiny of the *Somers*" (1843), published in the *North American Review* a dozen years after MacKenzie's essays appeared in the journal, represents the "legal reasoning that Melville would have heard in defense of MacKenzie," and "Sumner's defense of MacKenzie's actions has remarkable similarities with Captain Vere's justification of his hanging Billy Budd."[55] Analogous to Vere's justification, Sumner's defense also presents a strong contrast with *White-Jacket*. Whereas for Melville in *White-Jacket* a citizen's civil rights are sacrosanct even on a man-of-war, for Sumner (following MacKenzie) those rights are subordinated to the captain's orders and necessarily curtailed in a state of emergency. Moreover, whereas Melville's White-Jacket goes so far as to justify mutiny when one's basic rights are violated (White-Jacket, in a pivotal scene, plans to commit an act of mutiny himself to avoid corporal punishment before Jack Chase successfully intervenes), Sumner describes mutiny as "the highest crime known to law" because it "unlooses the bands of social order and . . . subverts the authority of law."[56] Equating mutiny to treason, Sumner characterizes this gravest of crimes as "an endeavour to overturn the government of the ship, which is a portion of the floating sovereignty of the country" (196). A far cry from "a floating gallows," as the Somers was dubbed in the popular press and treated as such by Melville in White-Jacket, the Somers Sumner describes is a microcosm of the nation transformed into what he calls "a state of war" (228).

Building on the ship-of-state trope later in the essay, Sumner describes MacKenzie as "invested with a duty not unlike that of the dictator, *to see that the ship received no detriment*" (229). As captain in a state of emergency like Melville's Vere, Sumner's MacKenzie shoulders "extraordinary duties" that entail "coextensive powers, or means for the performance of the duties" (228). Thus, "The character cast upon him was at once judicial and executive. He was to judge and to execute" (230). Such a characterization stands in direct opposition to what White-Jacket identifies as an unconstitutional blending of the separation of powers, but it closely parallels the situation that defines Vere's character in Billy Budd. Rather than defending MacKenzie by the letter of the law, Sumner concedes that he has violated it but finds within the law itself grounds for its own violation: "It is acknowledged that Commander MacKenzie has taken the lives of three men without the customary forms of law," he writes in response to a recent article in the Law Reporter arguing the illegality of MacKenzie's actions. "Does the law contain, within itself, any principle, which, under the circumstances of the case, will justify this apparent violation of it? Our answer is, that it clearly does" (228).[57] Sumner supports his answer by elaborating three main arguments. One of them is based on the exigencies of circumstances and the state of emergency that necessitates a quick and drastic response. Another concerns the doctrine of self-defense, "a right founded in the law of nature," Sumner reasons, and constituting "one of the essential elements bound up in [man's] being" (231).

Curiously, Sumner's argument for the "right of self-defence" in the Somers case flies in the face of his own principled objection to the death penalty. Identifying himself as a longtime opponent of the practice, Sumner offered his "testimony against Capital Punishment" in a letter to the Massachusetts Legislature written a dozen years after the Somers affair. Aligning himself with Edward

Livingston, whose anti-gallows writings he read with conviction when a law student, Sumner reasons:

> Punishment is justly inflicted by human power, with a twofold purpose: first, for the protection of society, and, secondly, for the reformation of the offender. Now it seems to me clear, that, in our age and country, the taking of human life is not necessary to the protection of society, while it reduces the period of reformation to a narrow, fleeting span. If not necessary, it cannot come within the provinces of self-defence, and is unjustifiable.[58]

What, of course, marks the exception to these rules are exceptional circumstances when the security of ship or state is at stake. In such a situation, the right of self-defense applies—"A right so important," Sumner had argued over a decade earlier in his defense of MacKenzie, "which, in its exercise, may override the ordinary municipal law, can only be employed under circumstances of a peculiar character." Recourse to the death penalty, Sumner adds in that defense, is like "the sword, suspended in the temple in ancient times, which could only be taken down on a great emergency" (232). Thus, even some committed opponents of capital punishment like Sumner supported the state's ultimate sanction when the ship of state was in jeopardy. In 1868 Longfellow, another proponent of MacKenzie and longtime opponent of capital punishment, wrote an anti-gallows letter to a similar effect in the aftermath of the Civil War.[59]

Sumner draws implicitly from his defense of the death penalty as an exceptional act in "Rights of Sovereignty and Rights of War," an important speech before Congress on May 19, 1862, delivered about a year into the war. According to Sumner (now a leading Republican in the Senate), the national government could employ the ultimate sanction against its citizens on two lawful grounds: on the one hand, it can punish them by the *"Rights against Criminals*, founded on sovereignty"; on the other, it could punish them according to *"Rights against Enemies*, founded on war, which are absolutely without constitutional limitation."[60] Both of the arguments, especially the rights against enemies, played an important role in Sumner's defense of MacKenzie, and those against enemies could punish with greater latitude and fewer restrictions. "Harsh and repulsive as these rights unquestionably are," Sumner writes of those rights, "they are derived from the overruling, instinctive laws of self-defence, common to nations as to individuals. Every community having the form and character of sovereignty has a right to national life, and in defence of such life may put forth all its energies."[61] Justifying here the nation's use of lethal violence by comparing it to an individual's rights to self-defense, Sumner later appeals to both rights against criminals and enemies to legitimate the state's use of ultimate power: "Regarding the Rebels as criminals, you may so pursue and punish them. Regarding them as enemies, you may blast them with that summary vengeance which is among the dread agencies of war, while, by an act of beneficent justice, you elevate a race, and change this national calamity into a sacred triumph."[62] In important ways, the logic of Sumner's "Rights of Sovereignty and Rights of War" extends the grounds of his defense of the Somers executions. In it, we have the same "overruling, instinctive laws of self-defence," the struggle for "national life" that necessitates "harsh laws" and "dread agencies of war" that legitimate MacKenzie's actions to save the "race" of American citizens.

Brook Thomas, in examining civil liberties in a Civil War context, has recently demonstrated the importance of the Somers case in relation to the political ideology of Lincoln and Sumner during the war.[63] Building on Thomas's discussion of Sumner's "Are We a Nation" speech, I have connected Sumner's antebellum defense of MacKenzie to his justification of lethal violence in "Rights of Sovereignty and Rights of War" to suggest a rationale for state violence and use of the death penalty as a military necessity that emerges during the war. At the time of Sumner's "Rights" speech in May of 1862, only sixteen soldiers had been executed under the U.S. Articles of War, the first of them put to death in Kansas on July 14, 1861. In 1863 seventy-two military executions were carried out. In 1864 there were ninety-nine, and in 1865 there were eighty-one.[64] Just as I have linked the republican argument against the death penalty to the Democratic Party, we can associate the justification of capital punishment under military authority during and after the Civil War with the Republican Party—its logic and rationale clearly anticipated by Sumner's antebellum defense of the Somers executions. Yet what distinguishes this political argument from a more straightforward pro-gallows stance is its emphasis on the death penalty under U.S. authority as a military exception—one accepted by influential figures like Sumner, who explicitly supported abolishing capital punishment in the realm of civil law. Another leader in the Republican Party who went so far as to support the application of the death penalty under military authority for civilians during the war was none other than President Lincoln. In Ex parte Vallandigham (1864) and Ex parte Milligan (1866), two of the most famous Supreme Court cases during the Civil War, Lincoln supported upholding the death sentences of two civilians who openly spoke out against the war. The first of these cases has special relevance to my study given that the condemned, Clement L. Vallandigham, was an influential "Peace" Democrat and member of the Ohio House of Representatives who advocated (unsuccessfully) the abolition of the death penalty in his home state in 1845. During the war, Vallandigham became famous not for his opposition to capital punishment but for sarcastically dubbing the President "King Lincoln" who was "crushing out liberty and erecting a despotism."[65]

Vallandigham—whose death sentence, like Mulligan's, was overturned— clearly echoes Melville's staunch Democratic rebuttal to the emerging Republican justification of capital punishment one finds in Sumner's 1843 defense of MacKenzie. By extolling the citizen-sailor's sacrosanct civil liberties protected by the Constitution and decrying the navy's violation of *habeas corpus*, Melville in *White-Jacket* thus expresses a long-standing Anglo-American fear of military despotism—hence the battery of (anti)republican imagery levied against the military ship of state. But although a Democrat, Melville was also a loyal Unionist. Yet far from Copperheads like Vallandigham, Melville was in many ways close in politics to prowar Democrats like his influential uncle, Peter Gansevoort, and Governor Horatio Seymour of New York, two leading party members in the state who disapproved of the war powers Lincoln exercised but unwaveringly supported the war. Although Melville famously sympathizes with the South in the "Supplement" to *Battle-Pieces*, he clearly shows his support for the Union and the war effort in the poems themselves, which, as Deak Nabers argues, "signal the emergence of a conservative Melville, one, unlike the author of *White-Jacket; or the World in a Man-of-War* (1850) and *The Confidence Man: His Masquerade* (1857), wedded to the law's 'power to endure and command loyalty.' "[66] If a "conservative Melville" emerges with the publication of *Battle-Pieces*, that conservatism develops and reaches full maturity in *Billy Budd*, which offers a different take on state violence and the ship of state. By reading Melville's final novella in the context of post–Civil War debates over capital punishment, we can get a new angle on its conflicts—one that complicates Melville's straightforward Democratic position in *White-Jacket*. But before turning to *Billy Budd*, it is first necessary to get a sense of those debates at large in a post–Civil War context. To do so, we can return to the court of public opinion.

## "THE GALLOWS IN AMERICA": CAPITAL PUNISHMENT IN A POSTBELLUM CONTEXT

As historians of the death penalty have shown, it was primarily the Civil War and to a lesser extent the war with Mexico the previous decade that drew reformers' interests and the public's attention away from the anti-gallows campaign.[67] The Mexican-American War had attracted the attention of key reformer John L. O'Sullivan, who supported the violence associated with U.S. imperialism and the concept of "Manifest Destiny," a term O'Sullivan famously coined in support

of that cause. But the Civil War had a much more dramatic effect, not only because it concentrated the nation's attention around the pressing question of slavery and secession but because the inevitability of bloodshed associated with
the impending war led many supporters of the antislavery and anti-gallows
movements alike to abandon the principle of nonresistance—a key tenet in both
abolitionist campaigns.

The impact the war had on the anti-gallows movement is perhaps best demonstrated by way of historical anecdote. In the late 1850s Marvin H. Bovee, a
Democrat and state senator who was instrumental in the successful bid to abolish the death penalty in Wisconsin in 1853, embarked on a nationwide campaign to
promote, as he put it, "the *Anti-Capital Punishment* Cause."[68] A powerful speaker,
Bovee helped to secure moderate changes in the legislation of capital punishment
in New York, Illinois, Iowa, and Minnesota through public lectures and meetings
with key state officials. Bovee's efforts culminated in plans for a book that would
include statements against the death penalty by famous Americans, including
Benjamin Franklin, Charles Sumner, Wendell Philips, Henry Wadsworth Longfellow, and Elizabeth Cady Stanton, to name a few. That book, *Christ and the
Gallows; or, Reasons for the Abolition of Capital Punishment* (1869), was finished
just as the Civil War began. Originally set to be printed in 1861, Bovee's book was
delayed publication by almost a decade because, the author explained in its 1869
preface, "the unhappy civil war had been inaugurated." "To have presented a
work of this kind during the continuance of such a struggle," Bovee went on,
"would have been 'ill-timed,' to say the least; and thus has the work been permitted to quietly sleep in manuscript until the present time."[69]

While the manuscript of *Christ and the Gallows* lay quietly asleep, the all-but-
moribund movement began to show signs of life in the late 1860s with Bovee and
others working behind the scenes. Those efforts are recounted in "The Gallows
in America" (1869), a feature essay in *Putnam's Magazine*, which had published
Melville's "Benito Cereno" (a story concluding with a gallows scene) the previous
decade. The author of the article was Edmund C. Stedman, a prominent New
York City poet, essayist, and man of letters, who would become one of Melville's
few associates in later years when he wrote *Billy Budd*. Like Bovee's *Christ and the
Gallows*, Stedman's essay is of value in part for its reflection on capital punishment during and since the Civil War—a history it surveys in terms of press coverage and genteel responses to such reports:

During the recent war, newspaper accounts of executions were mostly confined to brief announcements of the official facts. Previous to 1860, however,

no more grave and painful matters demanded the reporter's attention. And since 1866 we are again supplied with old full-length descriptions of hangings,— written in what may be termed an artistic and euphuistic style, but trustworthy in the main,—so that an investigator has pretty correct details within easy reach. The loathly record is set continually before us, sought for with an appetite by the groundlings, and avoided with disgust or read with shrinking curiosity by the more refined. The latter are mainly responsible for the law, and I should like to place certain details of its operation plainly before their faces.[70]

Calling attention to the "artistic and euphuistic style" in post–Civil War execution reports, Stedman reminds readers inured to the recent war's violence of the horrors of capital punishment, especially death by hanging. His target audience is not "the groundlings," with their appetite for blood, but "refined" readers who are "mainly responsible for the law." Like antebellum anti-gallows reformers, he makes readers feel their responsibility by emphasizing the republican process by which local and state officials take the lives of citizens in the people's name.

This strategy is most apparent when Stedman stages a satiric dialogue with state officers who are directly or indirectly involved in the administration of lawful death. Taking a page from Melville's dialogic attack of capital statues in *White-Jacket*, Stedman apostrophizes the infamous hangman Jack Ketch and then opens up a broader attack that indicts not just the executioner but the sheriff, governor, judge, and legislatures in the process of state-sponsored killing:

> "What kind of a fellow are you, Master Ketch, who, for a matter of twenty dollars, hide[s] like a rat in your hole, and cut[s] the last thread which holds Death back from a pinioned fellow-being?" Yes, now, how can you too, Mr. Sheriff, stain your reluctant hands? How can you, Mr. Governor, sign the warrant under which the Sheriff makes bold to slay his prisoner? How can you, Your Honor, pronounce the dreadful sentence? And how, I say, can you, Representatives of humanity, in Legislature assembled, permit the code of blood longer to stand written upon the statute-books of your Commonwealth. For, after all, it is with yourselves, collectively and individually, that the ultimate responsibility rests.[71]

With a sarcastic wit characteristic of Melville's *White-Jacket* but somewhat out of place in his own essay, Stedman stops just short of holding "the People" themselves responsible for executions, although the implication is certainly there.

The essay concludes as it had begun by attempting to resuscitate the cause for abolishing the death penalty in the court of public opinion: "A renewed effort is making, this winter, at Albany, for the total abolition of the Death-Penalty. Let the Empire State put herself by the side of Michigan in this reform, and within ten years thereafter the gallows will be banished from every State in the Union" (234). Stedman's call for reform, we know through historical hindsight, was not answered. In the decade that followed, New York would not join the ranks of the abolition states—although two others did. Iowa abolished capital punishment in 1872, as did Maine in 1887 (although both states would reinstate the death penalty within ten years).

Death penalty debates appear in odd places in the aftermath of the Civil War, and as Stuart Banner has shown, arguments in the 1870s and 1880s shift to questions of cruelty and the unnecessary suffering of victims.[72] Stedman, for instance, adopts this perspective by taking what he calls a "material view of the Death-Penalty,"[73] which includes a detailed examination of what transpires each time a condemned subject is hanged. Drawing upon medical language and terminology, he describes the slow torture rather than the quick death that occurs, he contends, in 60 percent of all executions. Fascination with the materiality of lawful death or death by hanging is registered in articles like Putnam's "Is Death Painful?" (1870), which touches on the death penalty but offers no opinion about the expediency of the practice, and Appleton's "Hanging as One of the Fine Arts" (1870), which curiously had little to say about capital punishment. Instead, the Appleton's article, published the same year as Putnam's, examined hanging as a choice form of suicide and cases in which stage performers, who "played at hanging," sometimes became its victims.[74]

Clearly the period was, as Stedman feared, desensitized to state violence because of the massive bloodshed of the recent war. In 1872, Harper's ran a short article titled "The Guillotine" (1872) that spoke indirectly to this phenomenon. The article, which featured illustrations of beheadings, provided a prehistory of a French physician's invention, discussing earlier decapitation devices used in Germany from the medieval period to the dawn of the nineteenth century. It ended with an anecdote about German doctors who in 1795 took an interest in the sensation of decapitation: "Eminent physicians assiduously attended executions, and by striking at the severed head, shouting in its ear, and divers other ways, endeavored to ascertain whether sensation survived the shock of decapitation."[75] Such a concluding tale said as much about contemporary America as it did about eighteenth-century Germany.

Dead but not forgotten, the anti-gallows movement was again brought back to life in E. S. Nadal's "The Rationale of the Opposition to Capital Punishment" (1873), a feature-length essay advocating the abolitionist cause and published in the *North American Review* the same year a *Galaxy* editorial declared: "The capital punishment question is one which, after a certain length of time, like the female suffrage question, the nonresistance question, or the prohibition question, ceases to be absorbingly interesting."[76] Picking up where Steadman left off, fellow literary critic Nadal (who published works in *Scribner's*, *Century*, and the *Atlantic*) attempted to reinvigorate the anti-gallows campaign by emphasizing the inherent cruelty of hanging. He also sought to move the movement beyond its antebellum commonplaces. For instance, speaking of capital punishment and the case against it, Nadal declares: "We need not call it a 'relic of the dark ages'; it is simply passé." Dismissing such claims but acknowledging "a half dozen facts one may count on one's fingers which go far towards proving its retention unnecessary,"[77] Nadal illustrates a simple but forgotten point—"that hanging is a very extraordinary and terrible thing."[78] By calling attention to the phenomenon of hanging itself, Nadal sought to resensitize a culture desensitized to violence. More than Stedman, Nadal anticipates mid-twentieth-century Eighth-Amendment arguments against the death penalty by showing not only how cruel but "how strange a thing it is to put a man to death."[79]

Nadal's concerns about the cruel and unusual process of capital punishment in the court of public opinion were echoed five years later in a case that reached the nation's highest legal court when Wallace Wilkerson, convicted of first-degree murder in Utah, challenged his sentence to be "publicly shot until . . . dead."[80] The Supreme Court in *Wilkerson v. Utah* (1878) did not rule on the question of the death penalty's constitutionality—that would not occur until *Furman v. Georgia* a century later—but instead asked whether lawful death by firing squad was cruel and unusual. Underscoring Wilkerson's guilt, comparing execution by firing squad to other modes (including hanging), and drawing upon the Articles of War (since Utah at the time was a territory rather than state), the Court unanimously upheld Wilkerson's sentence and the constitutionality of lawful death by gunshot, a mode formally adopted in Utah territory in 1852 and first practiced in 1861. With the Court's citation and analysis of the articles' "shall suffer death" clause in *Wilkerson v. Utah*, readers of *White-Jacket* would have been reminded of Melville's criticism of such provisions under military law, applied here to a case under civilian law since Utah territory was under federal jurisdiction.

The debate over the death penalty returned to the court of public opinion in 1881 when the *North American Review* published three essays from a recent conference on the topic. Two of the three participants were major players in the antebellum debates. Stating the case for abolition, an aged and venerable Wendell Philips rehearsed many of the prominent arguments that animated the antebellum anti-gallows cause some thirty years earlier when he was active in the movement and a founding member of the Massachusetts Society for the Abolition of Capital Punishment. He laid particular emphasis on the republican argument against the death penalty, invoking Cesare Beccaria on the subject and situating him among American heirs, Franklin, Livingston, Charles Burleigh, Robert Rantoul Jr., and O'Sullivan.[81] George B. Cheever, arguing for retention, essentially recapitulated the main points of his two monographs *Punishment by Death* (1842) and *Defence of Capital Punishment* (1846).[82] The third participant was Samuel Hand, a distinguished New York attorney and judge on the state's Court of Appeals. Joining Cheever in arguing for retention, Hand began his essay not with past arguments but with the present moment and in terms of the question of authority: "The dispute as to capital punishment is, at the present time, narrowed down to the point whether it is permissible, justifiable, and expedient for the sovereign power, in any case, to punish the crime of murder by inflicting death upon the murderer."[83] Supporting the case on each of these grounds, Hand's response drew from a notion of state power indebted to the Republican justification of capital punishment during the Civil War. Clearly invoking popular sentiment used to defend the war effort, Hand went so far as to claim that "the sovereign may call even upon the blameless citizen, to sacrifice his life for the common good and in resisting the public enemy."[84]

Framed in this way, Hand's rationale suggests the change in authority behind the law that had come with the Civil War and the rise of the Republican Party. It also anticipates—with its attention to the sacrifice of "the blameless citizen"—the justification for capital punishment that Melville's Vere would make in sacrificing blameless Billy Budd some ten years later in his final novella. Over that decade, debates about the death penalty returned to the national stage. One cause for the resurgence was President Garfield's assassination in 1881 (to which Phillips alludes in his *North American Review* essay), but the debate would get a tremendous surge from the advent of the electric chair in the early 1880s and the controversy over electricity as an alternative mode of execution. Nowhere was the debate more intense than in New York (where Melville had been living since 1863), which in 1890 became the first state to administer lawful death by "electrocution," a neologism of the time for execution by electric current. Papers like the *New York Times* as well as the *Tribune* and *Post*, no longer edited by reformers Horace Greeley and William Cullen Bryant, supported the new technology as a more humane method of execution, thus answering concerns of recent opponents of the death penalty, such as Stedman and Nadal, who focused on the inhumanity of hanging per se. While this debate unfolded in the court of public opinion, Newton Martin Curtis, a celebrated Civil-War hero, took the cause for abolition to the New York state legislature, where he served as a representative in the House. Curtis's campaign began in 1884, the year he assumed office, but it culminated in 1890, when a revised version of one of his abolition bills passed in the House by a vote of 74 to 29.[85] When it reached the Senate, however, the bill failed to pass. Not only did the bill not pass, but the next year the Supreme Court ruled in *In Re Kemmler* (1891) that lawful death by electrocution was not unconstitutional.

It was in this context, as Bruce Franklin has shown in a brilliant essay on "*Billy Budd* and Capital Punishment," that Melville wrote his now-famous final work. It is indeed astonishing, as Franklin notes, that no one in the work's illustrious and exhaustive reception (prior to his 1997 article) had noticed that Melville's novella was in essence about the death penalty and, as I have argued regarding *White-Jacket*, shaped in significant ways by contemporary arguments for its abolition. This critical oversight is all the more surprising given that contemporary readers, as Franklin contends, would have certainly read the work in the context of contemporaneous debates over the death penalty. In Franklin's words, "If *Billy Budd* had been published in 1891, when Melville wrote 'End of Book' on the last leaf of the manuscript, few readers at the time could have failed to understand that the debate then raging about capital punishment was central to the story, and to these readers the story's position in that debate would have appeared unequivocal and unambiguous."[86] Astutely demonstrating Melville's literary engagement with these debates, Franklin is right to claim that "*Billy Budd* derives in part from the American movement against capital punishment."[87] Nonetheless, he overstates the case in assigning the work an "unequivocal" and "unambiguous" position in those debates. Rather than offering a clear argument against the death penalty, *Billy Budd* presents conflicting views that do not mount up to a decisive statement on either side of the issue. After all, it is for this reason that the work has generated such contradictory interpretations epitomized, or rather polarized, in the two camps that have come to dominate *Billy Budd* criticism: the "Testament of Acceptance" and "Testament of Resistance" schools.[88] For while Franklin is the first to examine *Billy Budd* in the specific context and terms of capital punishment, arguments within the opposing "Testament" schools implicitly, and often explicitly, turn on how one reads Captain Vere's justification of Billy Budd's execution or how one sees the hanging scene itself—two of the most overdetermined sites in the study of American literature.

Such conflicting scholarship points to tension not only in the novella's reception but in the work itself. To conclude this chapter, I argue that a primary source of that tension stems from an apparent shift in Melville's understanding of and attitude toward capital punishment, influenced by a changed notion of sovereign authority behind the law that came with the Civil War and the emergence of the Republican Party with its support of a strong federal government. If in *White-Jacket* Melville demonstrably shared in the antebellum Democratic Party view of a limited government and its stance against the death penalty, it is not clear how Lincoln's execution of the Civil War (and the widespread executions he authorized) affected Melville's view of the death penalty. We do know, as I suggested earlier, that Melville was an unflagging supporter of the Union and generally approved of the war effort, which included the suspension of habeas corpus, in the civil realm, and massive use of capital punishment under military law—clear violations of specific civil liberties against which Melville repeatedly and vociferously rails in *White-Jacket*. Franklin has done invaluable work situating *Billy Budd* in the context of contemporaneous debates over the electric chair, but we also need to consider the broader postbellum context, one that brought about a new notion of state power founded on military executions, to gauge *Billy Budd's* complicated response to capital punishment. We can begin to do so by returning to the *Somers* affair, which was reinterpreted in the court of public opinion as Melville was at work on his final novella.

## "HISTORY, AND HERE CITED WITHOUT COMMENT": *BILLY BUDD* AND THE *SOMERS* AFFAIR REVISITED

Once regarded as "the source" for *Billy Budd*, the *Somers* affair has ceased to make waves in Melville studies.[89] To be sure, critics since the 1962 publication of the Hayford-Sealts authoritative edition of the text (based on a genetic study of the manuscript) are more likely to underplay or discredit the significance of the case, emphasizing instead source material from the 1880s.[90] Understanding the work in its contemporary context has appropriately turned critical attention away from *Billy Budd* as an "antebellum" work (to be read alongside Melville's earlier fiction) and toward cultural material from its moment of production. Viewing the novella as a product of the mid-1880s has yielded an impressive body of recent scholarship, including Franklin's groundbreaking essay as well as excellent criticism by Robert K. Wallace, Sanford E. Marowitz, and Larry J. Reynolds connecting *Billy Budd* to the 1886 Haymarket affair, a capital case resulting in multiple executions that captured the nation's attention much like the *Somers* affair had nearly a half century earlier.[91] More recently Stanton Garner, Gregory Jay, and Michael T. Gilmore have in different ways demonstrated the importance of reading *Billy Budd* in the specific contexts of Civil War and (post-)Reconstruction politics.[92]

Albeit an antebellum case, the *Somers* affair is an important part of both these contexts. Not only did it influence changing notions of executive power and "Nation," as I have argued, that emerged during the Civil War, but the affair again entered the court of public opinion with two magazine articles on the executions published when Melville was writing *Billy Budd*. The first was Lieutenant H. D. Smith's "The Mutiny on the *Somers*" (1888). Himself a veteran of the Civil War, Smith retold a tale of "mutiny, piracy, and swift and terrible retribution" that justified a captain's use of lethal force to preserve the ship of state.[93] Scholars have speculated that Melville likely read Smith's article given its subject and his family's involvement in the affair.[94] If he had gotten only three paragraphs into the article, Melville would have been reminded of the role played by his cousin Guert Gansevoort, who, in Lieutenant Smith's words, "impress[ed] upon his executive the terrible nature of the alleged crime, which might involve the question of life or death."[95] With the Civil War in the collective memory of his readers, Smith dramatized the exigent situation that prompted and, in his opinion, justified MacKenzie's executive response: "Mutterings, low and ominous were heard from various quarters," Smith wrote of the circumstances leading to the decision to execute, "while black looks and petty acts of insubordination were not wanting. All this, with the insolent airs and menacing manners assumed by some of the men, had the effect of thoroughly arousing Commander Mackenzie and his officers. They were convinced that their lives were in peril, that they were standing over a volcano, which at any moment might overwhelm them with destruction."[96] The principle of subordination, key to MacKenzie's ship of state and to Smith's reconstruction of the affair, was also a key military issue during the Civil War, one that Union generals raised in terms of capital provisions for insubordination following their defeat in the first battle of Bull Run. At that time, any death sentence issued by court-martial in the field required final review from Washington—a process that, from the generals' perspective, "weakened their authority and destroyed the effect of swift capital punishment following serious offenses."[97] By the Law of December 24, 1861, Union generals got their way with the power over final appeals in capital cases granted to divisional commanders in the field. But the increase of executions that came with this power made civilian officers in Washington uneasy, which led to an amended policy in July 17, 1862. From that point on, any death sentence pronounced in the field required final approval directly from the president.[98]

Like an army in the field during the war, MacKenzie and his men (in Smith's account) were thus beleaguered with insubordination and threatened with insurrection. And like a strong general, Smith's "Commander MacKenzie was not a man to flinch in the hour or danger or emergency. He had carefully studied the situation, and he adopted what appeared to him the best and most politic course."[99] That course, of course, required "the immediate execution of the three mutineers" to ensure "the safety of the vessel."[100] In "The Murder of Philip Spencer" (1889), Gail Hamilton argued precisely the opposite point in a three-part series of essays published the following year in *Cosmopolitan*. Echoing Melville's denouncement of the *Somers* affair as "Murderous" in *White-Jacket*, Hamilton focused on the execution (what she calls "murder") of the alleged ringleader and mocked the idea that MacKenzie "had met the emergency with the most courageous promptness by hanging young Spencer at the yard-arm."[101] Whereas Smith began his article by foregrounding the dire circumstances of the affair and the executive powers invested in the captain, Hamilton started hers with the civilian authority of William H. Seward, then governor of New York, who decried the executions as "appalling" and MacKenzie's actions as "cowardly and murderous."[102] Taking a page from *White-Jacket*, Hamilton repeatedly emphasized the violation of the executed men's civil rights and the "ridiculous" charge of mutiny by which their deaths were justified. "To such logic were the lives of three American citizens sacrificed," she says of the alleged insubordination and mutinous threat. "On such reasoning three American citizens were hanged," she writes a page later, again underscoring the citizenship and concomitant rights of those executed.[103] Wyn Kelley, one of the only recent critics to examine *Billy Budd* in light of the *Somers* affair (and Hamilton's account of it), has with good reason wondered what prompted the public's interest in the *Somers* case some forty years after it occurred.[104] My answer is that it had much to do with renewed interest in death penalty debates that had resurged in the late 1880s.

Certainly the antebellum author of *White-Jacket* would have concurred with Hamilton. But the postbellum narrator of *Billy Budd* adopts a very different attitude toward the *Somers* affair, even though it is similarly alluded to at a crucial moment involving the "Mutiny Act" of the Articles of War and the question of capital punishment. In *White-Jacket*, as we have seen, the affair marks the crowning example of unwarranted military despotism; it illustrates historically and in concrete terms the abusive potential of state authority that undercuts the republican values the military supposedly serves and protects. In *Billy Budd*, by contrast, the *Somers* affair is explicitly "cited" but "without comment," a silence that speaks volumes when read against the sharp criticism it elicits in *White-Jacket*. Its citation in *Billy Budd*, moreover, comes by way of an extended narrative intrusion, thus affording Melville an opportunity to speak his mind, to denounce the case and capital punishment under military law as he had in *White-Jacket*. The intrusion and allusion to the *Somers* case occur just as Captain Vere—like Commander MacKenzie—leaves his officers to determine for themselves the fate of the accused, after he has presented to them a forceful argument for the necessity of an execution:

> Not unlikely they were brought to something more or less akin to that harassed frame of mind which in the year 1842 actuated the Commander of the U.S. brig-of-war *Somers* to resolve, under the so-called Articles of War, Articles modeled upon the English Mutiny Act, to resolve upon the execution at sea of a midshipman and two petty-officers as mutineers designing the seizure of the brig. Which resolution was carried out though in a time of peace and within not many days' of home. An act vindicated by a naval court of inquiry subsequently convened ashore. History, and here cited without comment. True, the circumstances on board the Somers were different from those on board the *Bellipotent*. But the urgency felt, well-warranted or otherwise, was much the same.
>
> Says a writer whom few know, "Forty years after a battle it is easy for a noncombatant to reason about how it ought to have been fought. It is another thing personally and under fire to direct the fighting while involved in the obscuring smoke of it. Much so with respect to other emergencies involving considerations both practical and moral, and when it is imperative promptly to act. The greater the fog the more it imperils the steamer, and speed is put on through at the hazard of running somebody down. Little ween the snug cardplayers in the cabin of the responsibilities of the sleepless man on the bridge."[105]

A loaded reference and dialogized trope for "Murderous" authority in *White-Jacket*, the narrator's allusion to the *Somers* affair here conveys none of White-Jacket's vitriol and little irony, present only (and if at all) in the reference to "the urgency felt, well warranted or otherwise." Instead, the allusion provides a historical analogue and sympathetic frame for understanding "the harassed frame of mind" in which Vere and his men find themselves in deciding this trying case—a point Melville drives home through an analogy likening Vere's duties to his ship and men to "the responsibilities" of a steamer's captain to his ship and passengers.

Vere may, as testament-of-resistance critics argue, initially prejudge Billy's act ("Struck dead by an angel of God! Yet the angel must hang!" he says in the immediate aftermath of the murder [101]), and he may ultimately be wrong in his decision. But Melville certainly intended to present readers with a difficult, undecidable, case—one that each of us, as his narrator puts it, "must determine for himself by such light as this narrative may afford" (102). Perhaps the moment we get closest to Melville's own take on Vere's (and MacKenzie's) dilemma occurs in the citation from "a writer whom few know" in the preceding extract. If, as Hayford and Sealts note, Melville is facetiously quoting himself here,[106] then what we have is a postbellum Melville reassessing a case he had judged quite differently in *White-Jacket*. As if in response to Hamilton, a "non-combatant" like himself writing "forty years after" the fact, Melville reminds an audience of his contemporaries (if the work were to have such a readership) of "the emergencies involving considerations both practical and moral" as well as the "imperative" for prompt action confronting those in positions of authority during moments of crisis. In this respect, *Billy Budd* provides a response to the *Somers* affair closer to Lieutenant Smith's than to Hamilton's and to his own earlier response in *White-Jacket*. Michael Rogin, in his classic psychobiography *Subversive Genealogies*, explains this apparent shift in terms of politics and family dynamics, reading Melville's rereading of the affair in *Billy Budd* as a symbolic reunion with his family. In *White-Jacket*, Rogin argues, Melville "condemned the hangings on the *Somers*" and "stood against his own kin, for Guert Gansevoort was deeply implicated in the executions."[107] Standing "with the executed sailor sons on the *Somers* and against his own family" in *White-Jacket*, Melville evidently reconsidered the purpose of military despotism in *Billy Budd*: "It was as if," in Rogin's words, "Melville was saying to MacKenzie, to his own clan, and to himself, the best defense of the murderous authority under which we live must look as I portray it here."[108]

Writing specifically about *Billy Budd* and capital punishment, Franklin and, more recently, Paul Jones have closely aligned Melville's thinking on abusive authority in *Billy Budd* with *White-Jacket* or the antebellum period to produce readings within the testament-of-resistance school that interpret Vere's justification ironically and thus see the work itself as an unequivocal attack on capital punishment. Jones, for instance, provocatively suggests that *Billy Budd* provides Melville's antebellum argument against the death penalty—a point on which Melville felt compelled to be silent out of respect for his father-in-law, Chief Justice Lemuel Shaw, whose position required him to pronounce death sentences upon those convicted of first-degree murder. In Jones's words, "*Billy Budd* is the statement Melville might have made in the 1850s on the issue of capital punishment if family obligations had not muzzled him."[109] An intriguing "what if" (*had Billy Budd* been written some forty years earlier and before the war), Jones's speculation fails to consider Melville's pointed attacks on the *Somers* executions in *White-Jacket*—an attack on a capital case directly involving his own blood and published when Shaw was presiding over capital trials like John W. Webster's trial, which was examined in the previous chapter.[110] Likewise, Franklin too easily connects Melville's overt diatribe on corporal and capital punishment in White-Jacket—what I have associated with the antebellum Democratic Party view on abusive state power—to the subtle, indirect, and ironic criticism of the death penalty in Billy Budd.[111] That argument is certainly there; but so too is the argument justifying capital punishment as, in Vere's words, "a military necessity" (113). In fact, the justification has equal if not greater weight in the book when we factor in a comparative analysis of Melville's use of the Somers affair in White-Jacket and Billy Budd, which is key to understanding each work's respective position on state authority and the death penalty. Thus, through the novella's sympathetic treatment of Vere, it is possible that Melville has come to "accept" (a loaded term in Billy Budd criticism) the course of action taken by MacKenzie in the Somers case and writ large in the hundreds of military executions executed by way of executive authority during the war. Melville, after all, implicitly accepted such authority through his support of the Union war effort evident in Battle-Pieces.

At the same time, as "resistance" readers would have it, Melville might have presented Vere's point of view only to undercut it. But rather than choosing one side in this long-standing critical debate, what we can say with some certainty is that Melville strove to complicate any position readers might take for or against Vere. For instance, while Vere's authority might be ironically undercut, in the end Melville might still have felt Vere justified in his decision. Why? Because from a legal point of view—which Vere embodies—acts of lethal, extralegal violence like Billy's blow that kills the master-of-arms need to be replaced by rule of law ("forms, measured forms" [128]), even if that law is flawed. Melville, in fact, lends credence to this view by likening Billy's blow to an act of war, describing how Billy's "right arm shot out," his narrator says, "quick as the flame from a discharged cannon at night" and "dropped to the deck" the killed British officer (99). In accord with Melville's narrator, Vere picks up on this simile during the trial by ruling out Billy's intent and the circumstances surrounding his action, focusing his officers' attention only on the consequences of the deed itself.

Thus law, especially under military law during war as Vere presents his case, demands its "justice" despite the moral scruples of its agents—an argument Melville has made famous through Vere's rationale for Billy's execution. That position, as Robert Cover has powerfully shown, has historical antecedents in the legal decisions of antislavery jurists such as Shaw, Lieber, and John McLean (associate justice of the Supreme Court), each of whom upheld the laws of slavery despite their personal objections to the nation's peculiar institution.[112] Judges "look to the law, and to the law only," McLean explains in ruling on one fugitive slave case. "In these matters," he states in another, "the law, and not conscience, constitutes the rule of action." Lieber similarly reasons: "Not I but the law, which is given to me, and which is my master says this."[113] Quoting these figures in the context of Melville's work in relation to the Civil War, Deak Nabers has recently drawn from Cover's classic argument in characterizing the legal crisis between law and justice (or "right," to use Melville's term) that motivates much of the conflict in *Battle-Pieces*.[114]

To get a sense of Melville's attitude toward extralegal violence in a Civil War context we can turn briefly to "The Scout toward Aldie," one of the best-known poems from *Battle-Pieces*. Dramatizing a Union regiment's search for the Confederate guerrillas known as "Mosby Rangers," the poem at one point stages an exchange between a colonel and a major (the poem's two central characters) as they come across the remains of a makeshift gallows:

> "Of course, but what's that dangling there?"
> "Where?" "From the tree—that gallows-bough;"
> "A bit of frayed bark, is it not?"
> "Ay—or a rope; did *we* hang last?—
> "Don't like my neckerchief any how;"
> He loosened it: "O ay, we'll stop
> This Mosby—but that vile jerk and drop![115]

Imbued with a bit of gallows humor reminiscent of *White-Jacket*, this stanza and its central question—"did *we* hang last?"—prompts an explanatory note from Melville: "Certain of Mosby's followers, on the charge of being unlicensed forages or fighters, being hung by order of a Union cavalry commander, the Partisan promptly retaliated in the woods. In turn, this also was retaliated, it is said. To what extent such deplorable proceedings were carried, it is not easy to learn."[116] In providing further context to the scene in the book's "Notes," Melville clearly condemns the cycle of extralegal violence but leaves unanswered the question of the legitimacy of lawful executions, or even if the Union cavalry commander's initial order to hang in this instance was a just one. In *Billy Budd*, that question is not so much unanswered as it is problematized through the competing perspectives on the military execution at the heart of the novella. As violent as the state power to execute is—and Melville exposes us to that violence in *Billy Budd* and "Benito Cereno" (the latter ending with a brutal state-sanctioned execution and decapitation)—it still may be preferable to extralegal violence, whether it be the retaliatory hangings during the Civil War or the lethal blow Billy gives to the master-at-arms. Such a perspective, of course, would be endorsed from a Vere point of view.

It may be impossible to say with certainty whether *Billy Budd* is Melville's statement for or against the death penalty, his final "Testament of Acceptance" or "Resistance." But what we can say is that Melville was not simply restating his views on state authority and capital punishment articulated in *White-Jacket*. Whether one condemns Vere or not, sees the book as pro– or anti–capital punishment, it is clear that the *form* (and not just the tone) of these two works is radically different. In *White-Jacket*, we have a first-person narrator who speaks out directly against the *Somers* affair and capital punishment; in *Billy Budd*, we have a third-person narrator who explicitly reserves judgment. In *White-Jacket*, Melville invokes the ship-of-state metaphor to argue for a republican state contra the despotic one the novel so thoroughly critiques, thereby transforming *The United States* man-of-war on which he actually served into the fictive *Neversink* through which he savages military despotism to champion the unassailable republican ethos on which "The United States" itself was founded. In *Billy Budd*, Melville again employs the ship of state as a leitmotif but quickly shifts focus from *The Rights of Man*, a merchant ship named after Thomas Paine's book defending the French Revolution, to the *Bellipotent*, the man-of-war that preserves the political state in which "The Rights of Man" are possible. What we have in *Billy Budd*, then, is not only a different ship of state but a different state of affairs, one that reimagines the relation of the individual to the authority of the law, whose "forms, measured forms" Captain Vere defends against the well-intentioned but ultimately destructive forces of revolutionary France. In order to do so, the ship of state called the *Bellipotent* has to adopt the "powers of war" (inscribed in its name), just as the United States had to go to civil war to save the Union and preserve the Constitution, the nation's "forms, measured forms."

## "THE FATHER IN THE FACE": FORCE BEHIND (THE) LAW IN *BILLY BUDD*

Writing on *Billy Budd* and capital punishment, it is tempting to focus on Billy before the law, Melville's grand figure of condemned innocence. From this perspective, it is easy to see in Vere a veritable "parody of the usual argument for capital punishment for the sake of deterrence,"[117] as Franklin characterizes the captain's position, specifically in regard to his belief in the MacKenzian principle of "arbitrary discipline" and the death penalty's power to deter insubordination. Vere's stance is stated in its most extreme when, playing prosecuting attorney (and witness) to his officers' jury during the drumhead trial, he opposes "natural justice" to the king's law, declaring the ship's allegiance to the king alone (110). Supposing a guilty verdict and death sentence to follow their proceedings, Vere asks his officers: "Would it be so much we ourselves that would condemn as it would be martial law operating through us? For that law and the rigour of it, we are not responsible. Our avowed responsibility is in this: That however pitilessly that law may operate, we nevertheless adhere to it and administer it" (110–11). There is much to be concerned about when agents of the law abrogate responsibility for acts they authorize. This logic, after all, is dangerously close to the infamous "Nuremberg Defense" in which Nazi war criminals justified their participation in the Holocaust by claiming that they were only following orders, letting the law, as Vere might say, "operate" through them, "however pitilessly." But Vere is too virtuous and venerable, too moral and complex a character, to be reduced to a caricature of the pro–capital punishment position. In fact, shortly before the trial scene Melville's narrator describes him as "exceptional in the moral quality" and a "veritable touch-stone of [humanity's] essential nature" (96), qualities that round off earlier descriptions of Vere's veracity (as in his name) and remarkable intelligence.

Even so, read long after World War II, it is a commonplace today to view Vere as a figure of totalitarianism, a military commander and yes-man of the state. And it is no accident that testament-of-resistance scholarship first emerged and thrived in the wake of the second Great War. It is, however, more important to read *Billy Budd* in the context of the Civil War, the great war through which Melville himself lived, wherein the problematic, Vere-like figure of despotism (at least from a radical Democratic perspective) was none other than President Lincoln, "The Great Emancipator," who invoked emergency measures—including the suspension of habeas corpus—in an effort to save the ship of state. As Lincoln famously put it in justifying the implementation of those measures on the first Fourth of July during the war, "Is there, in all republics, this inherent and fatal weakness? Must a government, of necessity, be too strong for the liberties of its own people, or too weak to maintain its own existence?"[118] The dilemma that President Lincoln poses in this special message to Congress clearly resonates with the one that Captain Vere poses at Billy's trial in acknowledging his officers' and his own desire for clemency but recognizing how a "clement sentence" would be seen by the crew as "pusillanimous," a sign of weakness in the ship of state. Defending his use of wartime powers like Vere, Lincoln would become by the Civil War's end the final authority to authorize not one military execution (as Vere does) but more than two hundred.

According to Stanton Garner, Melville had one particular Civil War execution in mind when dramatizing Billy Budd's trial and execution. It was the summary court-martial and military execution of another young and romantic "Billy," one William E. Ormsby. Melville had first heard the story of Ormsby in April 1864 when visiting the Army of the Potomac—a classified visit enabled by none other than Charles Sumner, who described Melville in a field pass as "a loyal citizen & my friend."[119] As Garner notes, the parallels between the cases of William Budd and William Ormsby are striking, particularly "Ormsby's loyal last words" expressing his support for the Union cause (cf. Billy's famous "God bless Captain Vere!" [123]) and the justification of the death penalty by the commanding officer,[120] Colonel Charles Russell Lowell, nephew of the famous poet James Russell Lowell. Melville likely heard the details of Ormsby's execution from Lowell himself, who issued the death warrant in MacKenzian fashion, declaring that "for such an offense death is the only punishment and the Comdg officer hopes and believes that the Summary execution today will prevent forever the necessity of the repetition in this Command."[121] Colonel Lowell and the condemned Ormsby make for a provocative pair in rethinking *Billy Budd*'s execution scene in light of the Civil War. A literary man and officer of rank and reputation cut down in his prime (the colonel was killed in October 1864 during the Battle of Cedar Creek), Lowell is an intriguing model for what a young Captain Vere might have been like. Ormsby, in turn, is equally compelling as a source for Billy—not so much the "innocent" Billy of the narrative proper but the more mature and likely guilty-as-charged speaker of "Billy in the Darbies," the execution ballad that now concludes the novella but initially served as the book's poetic genesis.[122]

The *"might-have-been* is but boggy ground to build on" (57, emphasis in original), as *Billy Budd*'s speculative narrator observes. But following Franklin's speculations about how Melville's contemporaries *might have* read the novella had it been published in 1891, as well as the recent "speculative reading[s] of *Billy Budd*" in light of the Civil War and Reconstruction by critics such as Garner, Michael T. Gilmore, and Gregory Jay, it is worthwhile to wonder how readers might have interpreted Billy's execution in the 1890s. No doubt, as Franklin conjectures, they would have read the execution in the context of contemporaneous debates over the death penalty. But given its military context, might they have associated Billy's execution with the widespread use of capital punishment during the Civil War? Melville, at least, invites such an association in summing up the verdict following the novella's trial scene: "In brief," we are told, "Billy Budd was formally convicted and sentenced to be hung at the yard-arm in the early morning watch, it being now night . . . In war-time *on the field* or in the fleet, a mortal punishment decreed by a drum-head court—*on the field* sometimes decreed by but a *nod from the General*—follows without delay on the heel of conviction without appeal" (114, emphasis added). If Melville had not been thinking of the Civil War with its epic field battles (some of which he commemorated in *Battle-Pieces*), then why clarify the terms of Billy's summary execution *at sea* with repeated references to those conducted "on the field"? And why provide the example of the sovereign "nod from the General" (as opposed to a ship's captain) that may precede a field execution "without appeal"?

Of the Civil War executions Melville might have known or had in mind when writing *Billy Budd*, Ormsby's would have particularly intrigued him not only for its romance but for the question of authority, for it was one of the few documented executions carried out without due forms of law—namely presidential review and approval. Allegedly seduced by a Virginian woman, Ormsby deserted his picket station and later joined (in what Garner construes as mutiny) Mosby's Rangers, the elusive object of Union pursuit in Melville's poem "The Scout toward Aldie." Young and naive (if not exactly "innocent" like Melville's Billy), Ormsby was captured and returned to his regiment; Colonel Lowell then convened a drumhead court-martial, like the one Vere oversees, that deliberated into the night and sentenced Ormsby to be put to death the next morning. Lowell's decision was controversial to say the least, since he was not authorized to convene a court-martial—let alone execute a death sentence. Given that many "deserters had been pardoned by the President," as Edward W. Emerson, Lowell's early twentieth-century biographer (and son of Ralph Waldo Emerson) speculates, the "President would probably have pardoned [Ormsby], who was young and infatuated of a Southern girl."[123] That Lowell's superiors, General C. C. Augur and Secretary of War Edwin M. Stanton, did not report the incident suggests, as Emerson notes, their tacit approval of Lowell's actions.[124]

The Ormsby case was likely one of the sources from which Melville drew in dramatizing the confrontation between the citizen-subject and sovereign authority represented in Billy Budd and Captain Vere respectively, as was the *Somers* affair to which he explicitly refers in the novella. Again, it is easy (and appropriate) to sympathize with Billy, condemned innocence personified, but Melville also wants us to sympathize with Vere and his dilemma. *Billy Budd* is obviously Billy's book, but it is equally Vere's, whose conflict Melville obsessed over during his final and protracted stages of revision.[125] If the Ormsby and *Somers* cases help us understand particular aspects of the novella's central conflict, it would behoove us to think more generally about Vere's dilemma in terms of the one facing President Lincoln, as I have suggested to conclude this chapter. There are, indeed, striking parallels between Vere and Lincoln. Not only are both scholars and intellectuals, men of principles and conviction, and captains of the ship of state during moments of national crisis, but both are also symbolic father figures: Lincoln to the country as a whole (or at least the North) and to Union soldiers in particular; and Vere to the young men of the *Bellipotent* and to Billy in particular.

Melville, in fact, explicitly characterizes Vere as symbolic father at two crucial junctures in *Billy Budd*. One occurs during the final private meeting between the captain and the condemned, wherein Vere is compared to "Billy's father" and the situation he faces—the sacrifice of the son—is likened to the biblical parable of Abraham and Isaac (115). The other transpires in the interrogation scene immediately before and after the murder of the master-at-arms, first when Vere speaks to Billy (whom he calls "my boy") in "fatherly" tones that ironically trigger Billy's violent blow, and then again as Vere, face covered, rises from the victim's prostrate form: "Slowly he uncovered his face; and the effect was as if the moon emerging from eclipse should reappear with quite another aspect than that which had gone into hiding. The father in him, manifested towards Billy thus far in the scene, was replaced by the military disciplinarian" (99–100). Comparing Vere to a celestial body through the metaphor of a lunar eclipse, Melville elevates Vere's stature as sovereign and registers the profound transformation in him from "father" to "military disciplinarian," the competing identities that highlight and heighten the burden of his executive responsibility. In "The Martyr," a short ballad from *Battle-Pieces*, Melville had used a similar image to describe Lincoln, seeing in the slain president "the father in his face."[126]

"Father Abraham," as Lincoln was popularly known during the Civil War and long after (when Melville was writing *Billy Budd*), was a complex figure like Vere. Known also as "The Great Pardoner" for the death sentences he pardoned or commuted and identified as "The Forgiver" in Melville's "The Martyr" (in which he is the sacrificial figure), Lincoln in fact authorized more military executions than all other U.S. presidents combined. While deifying Lincoln through allusions to Christ and Christianity in "The Martyr," in a note to another poem from *Battle-Pieces* Melville acknowledges a different perspective on the president from biased southerners who regarded "Abraham Lincoln, by nature the most kindly of men . . . as a monster wantonly warring upon liberty. He stood for the personification of tyrannic power."[127] Such descriptions of Lincoln back then could easily stand in for descriptions of Vere today as seen from a testament-of-resistance perspective. At the same time, we cannot say that Melville fully endorsed

Vere's use of the state's absolute power to kill, even though—with Lincoln and the Civil War in mind—he may had grudgingly acknowledged the necessity of this new authority behind the law. What we can say, however, is that *Billy Budd* registers this change of authority brought about by the Civil War, a shift that affected debates about the death penalty. Turning in chapter 6 to 1925, one year after *Billy Budd* was first published, we will see how Theodore Dreiser's *An American Tragedy* registered a different change in the politics and poetics of capital punishment.

# Capital Punishment and the Criminal Justice System in Dreiser's *An American Tragedy*

The city editor was waiting for one of his best reporters, Elmer
Davies by name, a vain and rather self-sufficient youth who was
inclined to be of that turn of mind which sees in life only a fixed
and ordered process of rewards and punishments. If one did not do
exactly right, one did not get along well. On the contrary, if one
did, one did. Only the so-called evil were really punished, only the
good truly rewarded—or Mr. Davies had heard this so long in his
youth that he had come nearly to believe it.

Dreiser, "Nigger Jeff" (1901; 1918)

First written and revised around 1895 and later in 1899 before being published
in *Ainslee's Magazine* in 1901, and then further developed in 1917 for his collection *Free and Other Stories*, Theodore Dreiser's "Nigger Jeff" has a complicated
composition history not unlike Melville's *Billy Budd*.[1] And like *Billy Budd*, "Nigger Jeff" centers around a naive protagonist, Elmer Davies, and culminates in an
execution—albeit an extralegal one. Dreiser's tale, too, is essentially structured
around the hanging of its titular character, although the condemned in "Nigger
Jeff" is no beloved Billy Budd but a veritable cipher standing in for the countless
African Americans illicitly executed from the mid-1880s, when Melville began
writing his tale, to the revised publication of Dreiser's lynching story in 1918.[2]
Organized like *Billy Budd* around an execution, however, "Nigger Jeff" focuses
on neither the executed nor the judge/executioner but on the inner thoughts and
beliefs of one of its spectators.

In earlier parts of this book, particularly in chapter 2 on Simms and Child,
I have looked at literary representations of the criminal subject *before the law*,
whereas in the previous chapter I principally examined relations of power *behind*
it. Dreiser's "Nigger Jeff" adds an important layer to my discussion of subject
formation through its interrogation of the "good" subject *within* the law: Elmer

Davies, a young urban professional and representative citizen. The formative moment in Davies's development as a journalist occurs when he is sent to report on a lynching-in-the-making in Baldwin, a neighboring rural community. The "story" Davies covers culminates later in what Dreiser's narrator calls "mob justice," an act in which "the people" of Baldwin wrest the rape suspect from the sheriff's custody and summarily hang him from a nearby tree.[3] A "hired spectator" (82), Davies does nothing to stop the lynch mob and later watches, "widemouthed and silent" (105), as the hanging takes place. In dramatizing the extralegal execution, Dreiser offers an ironic object lesson in the horrors of lynching that is very much in the tradition of nineteenth-century anti-gallows literature, like the scenes dramatizing or imagining the enactment of lawful capital punishment in John Neal's *Logan,* William Gilmore Simms's *Guy Rivers,* Lydia Maria Child's "Elizabeth Wilson," George Lippard's *The Quaker City,* and Sylvester Judd's *Margaret,* to name but a few. Thus Davies, who at the story's outset "sees in life only a fixed and ordered process of rewards and punishments" (76), in the end comes to experience the profound injustice of lynching but ultimately fails, as we shall see, to note his own complicity in the event he represents for his curious readers.

The unfixing of Davies's ideology of rewards and punishments gradually develops as the tale's lynching plot unfolds. It attains fullest expression just moments before the execution itself: "Why should anyone have to die this way?" Davies asks himself. "Why couldn't the people of Baldwin or elsewhere have bestirred themselves on the side of the law before this, just let it take its course? . . . Still, also, custom seemed to require death in this way for this. It was like some axiomatic, mathematic law—hard but custom" (103). Davies's quandary, which Dreiser expresses through free-indirect discourse, epitomizes the irresolvable tension between popular and legal conceptions of justice in the story. By first posing and then answering the question of justice, Davies opposes the social law of "custom" to juridical law, the positive law to which the people of Baldwin and "elsewhere" are bound as citizens of the state in which the lynching occurs.[4] While at first condemning "the people" for being on the wrong side of the law and failing to let it take its course, he quickly acknowledges the legitimate place of "custom." But custom here overtly flies in the face of legal justice. For it is only members of a racial minority for whom the white "people" (unquestionably an ironic term in the story) "require death in this way for this"; and it is a lynch mob—not the state and its supposedly disinterested wheels of justice—that exacts the penalty of death. In fact, the mob itself is an inanimate agent of popular justice, governed by the "axiomatic, mathematical law" of custom. As Davies goes on to imagine the mob and its *mobilization*, "The silent company, an articulated, mechanical and therefore terrible thing, moved on. It also was axiomatic, mathematic" (103). Albeit an outraged group hell-bent on vengeance, the people paradoxically personify the law of custom by virtue of being *im*personal: a "mechanical and therefore terrible thing" whose actions offer a programmatic response of retributive violence.

An obtuse hero, Davies fails to develop an appropriate response to the savage violence he witnesses. Instead of motivating the actions of a concerned citizen, the lynching serves as artistic inspiration. "The night, the tragedy, the grief, he saw it all," we are told of Davies in the tale's penultimate paragraph. "But also with the cruel instinct of the budding artist that he already was, he was beginning to meditate on the character of the story it would make—the color, the pathos" (111). Precisely because the ultimate lesson of mob justice is lost on "the budding artist," who becomes more interested in "story" and "character," its moral lesson is all the more apparent to Dreiser's implied readers, who are to take from the tale what Davies forgets in the end but at one point feels: "Lynchings, he now saw, were horrible things" (95), we are told from Davies's perspective just moments before the mob's victim is captured. Emphasizing mob violence as a "thing" (a term used several times for the raw phenomena of the lynching experience), Dreiser calls attention to a horrific violence to which decades of callous depictions and justifications had inured readers.[5] In doing so, he adopts a line of reasoning similar to E. S. Nadal, whose "object" in "The Rationale of the Opposition to Capital Punishment" (1873), as we saw in chapter 5, "is to show that hanging is a very extraordinary and terrible thing."[6]

❦

I have begun with "Nigger Jeff"—its naive protagonist, illicit execution, and aesthetic design—because it produces a stark contrast when juxtaposed to the representation of legal justice and the elaborate scene of lawful capital punishment in *An American Tragedy* (1925), Dreiser's classic novel published a quarter century after the short story was first printed. In fact, a sustained comparison of these two works would illustrate that *An American Tragedy* reverses the stakes and consequences that inform the scene of execution, thereby denoting a shift in where Dreiser locates sovereign agency and social responsibility. Whereas the short story, for instance, concerns a virtually anonymous black man whom "the people" of Baldwin execute outside and against the law, Dreiser's elephantine novel deals with a young white male who is executed within and by the law of the state in which he is incarcerated. Moreover, whereas responsibility for the execution in "Nigger Jeff" can be limited to the participants in the lynch mob and does not necessarily extend to spectators such as the journalist and future readers of his article (although they, too, are implicated), responsibility for the execution in *An American Tragedy*, by virtue of being a state-sanctioned act, extends to every citizen of the state in which it occurs. As Philip Gerber puts it in a classic essay tellingly titled "Society Should Ask Forgiveness," in *An American Tragedy*,

> the structure of American society was attacked; the book's readers would find themselves disclosed as participants in a tragic situation of immense proportions; they would soon discover themselves responsible for a hero who was a murderer. Dreiser was calculatedly and openly set on a bold attempt to exonerate the boy, lifting the responsibility off his shoulders and placing it squarely upon the inhabitants of every city and hamlet in the nation.[7]

In short, Dreiser's novel complicates the scene of execution—its participants, protocol, and drama—by redefining the sovereign will of the people and by broadening the pale of responsibility. My purpose in this chapter, however, is not to flesh out a comparative analysis of "Nigger Jeff" and *An American Tragedy*. For one thing, a more provocative comparison could be made by contrasting the relation between state sovereignty and the death penalty in *An American Tragedy* with the appeal to an "inherent sovereignty" of the people and the southern practice (or "custom") of lynching in *The Marrow of Tradition* (1901), Charles W. Chesnutt's novel about post-Reconstruction race relations that was published the year Dreiser first published "Nigger Jeff."[8] Instead, my point in comparing lynching and the death penalty to open this chapter is to unsettle the opposition between mob and legal forms of justice as I turn our attention to Dreiser's treatment of the criminal justice system in *An American Tragedy* and the novel's participation in early twentieth-century debates about the institution of capital punishment. We can begin by looking at the novel's overall structure, its play on tragedy and travesty, on the American dream and its nightmarish reality.

### AN AMERICAN TRAVESTY

Books 1 and 2 of *An American Tragedy* chronicle the rise from pecuniary obscurity to social prominence of Clyde Griffiths, a typical if not representative American subject of the post–World War I era. Each of these books explores the external forces and the internal characteristics that shape Clyde's identity, and book 2 culminates with the death (probable murder) of Roberta Alden, an attractive yet poor "factory girl" who is pregnant with Clyde's child. Book 3, however, marks a major shift in both narrative and dramatic perspective. Adopting a mode of narration that more than one critic has called "documentary,"[9] it detaches readers from their sympathetic involvement with the protagonist as it recounts in pains-taking detail the pursuit, capture, trial, and execution of Clyde for murder in the first degree. Book 3 thus transforms Clyde into a subject of the law. Legal defini-tions of agency and responsibility generate the central conflict of the book, and in it the diffuse body of the criminal justice system displaces Clyde as the novel's privileged center of consciousness. To put it crudely, if books 1 and 2 tell "an American tragedy," the pathetic story of a youth driven to murder, then book 3 dramatizes what we might call an American travesty,[10] an ironic social critique of a judicial system that assumes absolute sovereignty over its condemned citi-zens (like Clyde) while endlessly deferring responsibility for that act of supreme authority.

Dreiser's criticism of capital punishment and the criminal justice system lies primarily in his subversion of the jury system as well as in his attention to the close yet anxious relationship between sovereignty and responsibility as embod-ied in two of the novel's high-ranking state officials: the district attorney of Cataraqui County and the governor of New York. While the judge, jury, district attorney, and governor all contribute to the legal decision that brings about Clyde's death, responsibility for that decision is diffused and deferred through the judicial system and, by extension, the social body it supposedly serves and protects. An American Tragedy thus problematizes the relation between popular sovereignty and social responsibility, the two overarching concepts of my study that presuppose one another but are by no means mutually dependent. For even though popular or state sovereignty implies a collective yet autonomous entity fully respon-sible to itself, the modern state—like the monarchical state out of which it emerges and to which it bears some resemblance—certainly can act irresponsibly. In fact, the vexed relation between sovereignty and responsibility received particu-lar attention from Harold J. Laski, an influential American socialist and legal thinker who argued in the late teens and earlier twenties—shortly before Dreiser began writing An American Tragedy—that popular sovereignty was coextensive with what he called "state-responsibility."[11]

In An American Tragedy, "the State" is not only irresponsible but cruel and malicious to those like Clyde who, without sufficient financial or intellectual re-sources, become cogs in its proverbial wheels. Indeed, through his representa-tion of the modern criminal justice system, Dreiser gives a face and personality to vindictive state authority in Orville Mason, the district attorney who leads the prosecution of Clyde for first-degree murder. Throughout the trial, Mason per-sonifies not only the state's power over Clyde but the avenging will of the people. Whereas law and custom represent two opposing principles of justice in Dreiser's

"Nigger Jeff," they come together in the depiction of Mason as a malicious state prosecutor in the supposedly neutral space of the courtroom. During Clyde's trial, Dreiser's narrator repeatedly undercuts Mason's prosecutorial strategies by calling attention to their theatricality and ulterior motives. When Mason delivers his opening statement, for example, Dreiser provides parenthetical commentary to accentuate the way Mason self-consciously evokes an atmosphere of drama: "'The people of the state of New York *charge*,' (and he hung upon this one word as though he desired to give it the value of rolling thunder), 'that the crime of murder in the first degree has been committed by the prisoner at the bar—Clyde Griffiths.'"[12] Mason's speech here thunders like the avenging voice of the people or the wrathful voice of the Old Testament God, and his emphasis on the word *"charge,"* italicized here and throughout these opening remarks, reverberates with the hateful anticipation of the lethal "charge" of electricity inevitably to fill Clyde's body. For what underwrites Mason's authority is his figurative association with the electric chair.

This association becomes clearer when we consider the anticipation of Mason's "opening charge" (i.e., opening statement) from the perspective of Clyde and his defense attorneys, Belknap and Jephson:

> And Clyde, as well as Belknap and Jephson, now gazing at [the jury] and won-dering what the impression of Mason's opening charge was likely to be. For a more dynamic and electric prosecutor under these particular circumstances was not to be found. This was his opportunity. Were not the eyes of all the citi-zens of the United States upon him? He believed so. It was as if someone had suddenly exclaimed: "Lights! Camera!" (639)

Like the ultimate instrument of state power against its citizens, Mason is figured as an "electric prosecutor." Here and elsewhere in the novel the district attorney exudes electricity, the very force by which death is legally administered in the state of New York. Dreiser sustains this comparison between Mason and the electric chair by repeatedly describing the district attorney as "blazing with this desire to undo [Clyde]" (702, 735). But unlike the cold impersonality of the chair and the lethal violence it inflicts in governmental secrecy, Mason expresses the people's hostility toward Clyde in a personal, vindictive display of power that is publicly performed. By doubling the figures of the district attorney and the elec-tric chair, Dreiser creates an image of Mason as an embodiment of what Austin Sarat calls "the specter of law's own violence," that is, a representation of lawful violence in capital trials that is allegedly different from the physical violence that takes place "beyond law's boundaries."[13]

Moreover, the explicit invocation of cinematography ("Lights! Camera!") and the reference to the trial as Mason's "opportunity" show that he is not a disinterested agent of the state. On the contrary, he turns the courtroom into a melodramatic spectacle to achieve political gain and, consequently, blurs the distinction between mob rule and legal justice. By prosecuting Clyde maliciously, the district attorney will increase his popularity and hence stand a stronger chance of attaining a coveted judgeship in the upcoming elections. To this end, he presents a distorted narrative of the evidence and circumstances surrounding Roberta's death—an interpretation that not only plays to the jury's moral attitude about premarital sex but also points to Clyde as "a murderer of the coldest and blackest type" (735), an unfair and inaccurate depiction of Clyde, as readers know from the intimate and sympathetic portrayal of him in books 1and 2 of the novel. As Sally Day Trigg points out, Mason even goes so far as to submit irrelevant but prejudicial evidence before the judge and jury.[14] For instance, he brings in a trunkful of Roberta's personal belongings for the sole purpose of having her grieving father identify them. The judge strikes this testimony from the record, but, as the narrator informs us, "its pathetic significance by that time was deeply impressed on the minds and hearts of the jurymen" (650). And even before Mason's opening statement, "the jury," we are told, "were all convinced of Clyde's guilt before they even sat down" (738–39).

This insistence on the jury's prejudice subverts the popular notion of a jury as an arbitrator of natural justice and common sense as well as further collapses the distinction between mob and legal forms of justice. "Instead of a group of inspired truth-finders," as Trigg argues, "a jury is just a collection of normal people who reflect the biases and prejudices of the community from which they are drawn, in Clyde's case a rural town of fundamentalist religion."[15] In a capital case such as Clyde's, the duty of the jury is to determine objectively the facts of the crime and decide if these facts fit the statute for the death penalty. More often than not, however, a jury fits a person—rather than a criminal act—to a corresponding punishment. One such example occurs during jury selection for Clyde's trial. When asked if he believes in capital punishment, a prospective jurist responds: "I certainly do—for some people" (634). This statement is revealing not only because it says what the accepted jurists all think but also because it conflates or confuses the person with the crime. And it is precisely this conflation or confusion of person and deed—often two discrete entities—that underlies the logic of personal accountability in criminal law. For what enables the jury to render a guilty verdict and what leads to Clyde's death sentence is the indissociable image of Clyde *and/in* the act of murder.

Legal theorist Meir Dan-Cohen has challenged such an essentialist view of criminal responsibility by drawing a distinction between "a *momentary* and a *total* self": the former consists of a "snapshot," whereas the latter provides a "motion picture" of the self.[16] Applied to *An American Tragedy*, this distinction complicates Mason's depiction of Clyde as a stable, autonomous subject who acts with deliberation and can therefore be held wholly accountable for his actions. In elaborating his theory of legal responsibility, Dan-Cohen rejects the paradigm of free will and the notion of the self as a "fixed entity defined prior to and independent of social relationships."[17] Instead, he posits a "contingent self," an understanding of one's being that is largely shaped by social and environmental factors, as well as contingencies arising at a particular moment.

Articulated in the late twentieth century, Dan-Cohen's theory of a "contingent self" complicates and formalizes operating assumptions of the legal realism movement of the early twentieth century, which put lived experience and social circumstances above both established forms and time-honored traditions in legal thought and practice.[18] Indeed, such principles were at work in the theory of criminal psychology practiced by Clarence Darrow, without question the most famous trial lawyer and death penalty opponent of Dreiser's time. As Darrow put it during a debate on capital punishment, "What was the state of mind when the homicide was committed? The state of mind is one thing when a homicide is committed and another thing weeks or months afterward, when every reason for committing it is gone. There is no comparison between [them]. There never can be any comparison between [them]."[19] Darrow's attention to the discrepancy between these two states of mind unsettles the indissociable image of a defendant/murderer often evoked by prosecutors in capital murder trials, such as the 1830 Francis Knapp and 1850 John W. Webster trials examined in chapter 4 as well as Clyde's in *An American Tragedy*.

Darrow made the preceding point in a well-publicized (and subsequently published) debate in 1924 while Dreiser was at work on *An American Tragedy*. Held in New York City before a large audience, the debate was sponsored by the League for Public Discussion and addressed the question, "Is Capital Punishment a Wise Policy?" Darrow took the negative position and sparred with Alfred J. Talley, a New York City judge outraged by the views on criminology and capital punishment that Darrow had expressed about a month earlier in his defense of Leopold and Loeb, one of the most famous cases of first-degree murder in U.S. history whose press coverage Dreiser closely followed while writing *An American Tragedy*.[20] No doubt the infamous Leopold-and-Loeb case, which much of the nation like Dreiser was following, influenced the composition of *An*

American Tragedy, just as Hawthorne's investigation of evidentiary value in *The House of the Seven Gables* was certainly affected by the 1850 John W. Webster capital trial then unfolding in Massachusetts while Hawthorne was writing his crime romance. And like the widely publicized 1842 O'Sullivan-and-Cheever debate in New York City some eighty years earlier, the Darrow-Talley debate in 1924 did much to promote the capital punishment controversy in Dreiser's day. A closer look at Darrow's position contra Talley, as well as his strategies in defending Leopold and Loeb, will help me highlight important dimensions in a realistic critique of capital punishment—a literary attack on this long-standing political institution in which not only Dreiser but the famous lawyer Darrow, as we shall see in this chapter's conclusion, engages in a legal novel of his own.

## DARROW/DREISER: LEGAL AND LITERARY REALISMS

In his 1924 debates with Darrow, Judge Talley begins his position for the death penalty by rationalizing the right and necessity of the state to impose the maximum penalty through appeals to scripture, historical precedence, and so-called common sense. For instance, he claims that the universal declaration, "Thou shall not kill," is inscribed in the "statute books of every civilized country" and offers fair warning to any would-be killer that the penalty for committing murder shall be death. Such a declaration, Talley explains, is not savage or unusual but based on rational principles that ensure the very existence of the "State" as a sovereign entity. "Is there anything barbaric or unnatural about a sovereign state making that declaration to its citizens?" he asks. "We must have not merely a declaration of a law," he answers, "but we must have a sanction to that law if any State can hope to endure."[21] Talley elaborates this claim about the government's "right" to take life by drawing an analogy between the state and an individual whose life is being threatened: "Now if I, as an individual, have that right to kill in self-defense," Talley asks, "why has not the State, which is nothing more than an aggregation of individuals, the same right to defend itself against unjust aggression and unjust attack?" (21). This comparison between the sovereign state, "an aggregation of individuals," and the sovereign individual, responsible to himself or herself, undergirds Talley's argument and speaks to age-old assumptions of conventional social-contract theories from Hobbes and Locke to Rousseau that justified the death penalty as a building block of traditional governments.

In his rebuttal to Talley, Darrow proceeds from a different set of assumptions, one that places lived experiences over time-honored traditions and sees law as a response to particular social, political, and moral situations rather than repository of universal principles and ideals. Darrow thus concedes Talley's point about the state's "right" to kill but then goes on to collapse the distinction between "right" and "power":

> We might ask why people kill. I don't want to dispute with [Judge Talley] about the right of the State to kill people. Of course, they have got a right to kill them. That is about all we do. The great industry of the world for four long years was killing. They have got a right to kill, of course, that is, they have got the power. And you have got a right to do what you get away with. The words power and right, so far as this is concerned, mean exactly the same thing. So nobody who has any knowledge of philosophy would pretend to say that the State had not the right to kill. (32)

For Darrow, centering an argument on the state's "right" to kill is as silly as asking why people kill in the first place. In this way, he attacks Talley's position by ridiculing the very idea of broaching the topic of legal rights by way of such an analogy. While his ironic allusion to World War I undercuts the moral premise of Talley's position, the pressure that Darrow applies to the concept of "right" plays off the morally relativistic slogan, "Might makes right." For on one hand, Darrow appropriates the pragmatic argument that, since the state has the power, of course it can claim to have the "right"; on the other, he implies that such a right is not morally or ethically "right." To be sure, to say that the state has the "right" to kill does not, for Darrow, make state-sanctioned executions "right" on moral or ethical grounds. From this position, Darrow later directs the debate back to the question of morality by challenging the propriety of Talley's analogy between the state and an individual who kills: "Now, why am I opposed to capital punishment?" he asks. "It is too horrible a thing for a State to undertake. We are told by my friend, 'Oh, the killer does it; why shouldn't the State?' I would hate to live in a State that I didn't think was better than a murderer" (39). By paraphrasing Talley's argument in his own terms, Darrow offers another way of looking at the underlying logic informing the death penalty: should the state abide by the moral code of a murderer? For Darrow, the answer is a resolute no. He argues, instead, that the state ought to be held to a higher standard of ethics and morality.

Six weeks earlier, Darrow had developed this line of argument at length in his highly publicized defense of Leopold and Loeb, two boys from wealthy families who confessed to the crimes of premeditated kidnapping and murder. Whereas D.A. Mason in Dreiser's novel exploits Clyde's trial as a platform to begin his campaign for a coveted judgeship, Darrow used the Leopold and Loeb trial to showcase his views on capital punishment. His basic strategy in arguing the case was twofold: first, to avoid any potential jury that would surely be "poisoned," as he put it, by popular prejudice against his clients;[22] and, second, to prevent the diffusion of responsibility for the decision of his clients' fate by ascribing final authority in the judge presiding over the case. To this end, Darrow pled the young killers guilty so that he could present mitigating evidence and a plea for mercy directly before the judge in a bench trial.

In his closing remarks during the penalty phase of the trial, Darrow begins his argument by foregrounding the difficulty of assigning legal responsibility in this case—a point that he emphasizes repeatedly by examining psychological and environmental factors that had diminished the boys' appreciation for the consequences of their actions. Unlike the "malice aforethought" and the act of "cold-blooded" murder for which District Attorney Mason both holds Clyde fully responsible and demands "exact justice" (*An American Tragedy* 639–40), the principles of social environment and biological predisposition to crime inform Darrow's theory of criminal responsibility. In fact, noting that there are two theories of "man's responsibility," Darrow articulates his progressive theory of criminal behavior against the kind of assumptions held by Mason. He thus rejects "the old theory that if a man does something it is because he willfully, purposely, maliciously, and with a malignant heart sees fit to do it" and subscribes, instead, to a modern understanding of criminology that sees "every human being [as] the product of the endless hereditary back of him and the infinite environment around him." This "old theory," he adds, "goes back to the possession of man by devils."[23] At the same time, Darrow holds the state to a higher level of responsibility. In fact, he wryly inverts the language of intent-to-kill murder and applies it to the presiding judge, calling attention to the sovereign authority as well as the indivisible burden of responsibility invested in his decision: "Your Honor," Darrow tells the judge, "if these boys hang, you must do it. There can be no division of responsibility here. You can never explain that the rest overpowered you. It must be by your deliberate, cool, premeditated act, without a chance to shift responsibility."[24] By reminding the judge of his power and the extraordinary consequences of his decision in this particular case, Darrow conjoins sovereignty and responsibility—two concepts between which there is a demonstrable rift in *An American Tragedy*.

Of course, the concentration of power in a single individual (such as a judge) can be a dangerous thing, and the distribution of authority in the criminal justice system is designed precisely to prevent one agent from acting tyrannically, that is, without responsibility for his or her actions. *An American Tragedy* thus warns against the underside of this system by exposing the severance of sovereignty and responsibility that begins with the jury's verdict of "guilty." But the jury's decision does not in itself bring about Clyde's death. It only recommends the death penalty, thereby authorizing the judge in the case to determine Clyde's fate and to utter, as he does, the juridical performative par excellence: "You are hereby sentenced to the punishment of death . . ." (753). The passive construction of this speech act is telling. Rather than declaring "I hereby sentence you to death"—an explicit performative insofar as it locates the authority of the utterance in the first-person "I," the judge, who names the act he performs or brings into being[25]—the death sentence pronounced by Judge Oberwaltzer in *An American Tragedy* diffuses the agent or sovereign responsible for sanctioning Clyde's death. In other words, there is no "I," no indivisible source of authority, from whom this pronouncement is delivered.

Indeed, a closer look at this death sentence illustrates the diffusion of sovereignty among the agents responsible for authorizing Clyde's death: "Clyde Griffiths," Judge Oberwaltzer declares,

> the judgment of the Court is that you, Clyde Griffiths, for the murder in the first degree of one, Roberta Alden, whereof you are convicted, be, and you are hereby sentenced to the punishment of death; and it is ordered that, within ten days after this day's session of Court, the Sheriff of this county of Cataraqui deliver you, together with the warrant of this Court, to the Agent and Warden of the State Prison of the State of New York at Auburn, . . . and upon some day within the week so appointed, the said Agent and Warden of the State Prison of the State of New York at Auburn is commended to do execution upon you, Clyde Griffiths, in the mode and manner prescribed by the laws of the State of New York." (753)

Hardly the terse performative, "I sentence you to be hanged by the neck until dead," that Sandy Petrey has used to differentiate illocutionary and perlocutionary force in his book on speech-act theory,[26] the death sentence given to Clyde, with its "whereofs," "saids," and repetitious phrases, offers a Dickensian parody of legal language and "HOW NOT TO DO IT."[27] For no individual or single authority authorizes Clyde's death sentence or will later enforce his execution, and a series of passive constructions (e.g., "you are," "it is," "is commended") link one statement to another in this single sentence whose linguistic verbosity mirrors the opaque structure of the judicial system on whose behalf it speaks.

Within this system, decisions, of course, are made by the state, and persons are put to death; but responsibility for those acts is endlessly deferred through a hierarchical chain of command. Although the lack of financial support in Clyde's case precludes elaborate motions and appeals made on his behalf,[28] his case does go to the Court of Appeals and then to the governor, the final authority in this diffuse chain of state sovereignty. As it turns out, however, the governor is merely a figurehead, a nominal chief of state who claims that his hands are tied by the jury's verdict and the subsequent decision to uphold that finding in the Court of Appeals. Dreiser's narrator describes this scenario from the perspective of Governor David Waltham when Clyde's mother, whom the narrator had earlier dubbed an "American witness to the rule of God upon earth" (742), begs for the governor's mercy and a commutation of her son's sentence:

> Like the pardon clerk before him, [Governor Waltham] had read all the evidence submitted to the Court of Appeals, as well as the latest briefs submitted by Belknap and Jephson. But on what grounds could he—David Waltham, and without any new or varying data or any kind—just a re-interpretation of the evidence as already passed upon—venture to change Clyde's death sentence to life imprisonment? Had not a jury, as well as the Court of Appeals, already said he should die? (802)

As the state's chief executive, Governor Waltham certainly has the power to commute Clyde's sentence. He is unable or unwilling to perform that act, however, not because of a conviction in Clyde's guilt or a firm belief in the institution of capital punishment itself, but because of his deference to the two previous decisions—especially the jury's verdict, which bespeaks popular opinion. In addition, since most of the people of New York support the death penalty, and since Waltham's position (like Mason's) depends on the popular vote, the governor feels compelled merely to repeat the decisions already handed down. The fact that Waltham believes that no "re-interpretation" can be made undermines his position as the sovereign of the state of New York. For as the German jurist Carl Schmitt was to argue at the time Dreiser had begun writing *An American Tragedy*, the "Sovereign is he who decides on the exception."[29] So just as Mason had distorted justice to gain popular support for an upcoming election, and just as a prejudiced jury of "the people" had come to a verdict of "guilty" without considering Clyde's defense, Waltham's failure to act decisively in the appeals process marks another instance in which mob rule operates under the guise of state authority.

Thus, the decision to execute Clyde comes to the governor as an already decided event, a death warrant recommended by the district attorney and sanctioned by the jury, to which the governor rubber stamps his signature. The final exchange between Governor Waltham and Clyde's mother clarifies this point: "Oh, my dear Governor," Mrs. Griffiths pleads, "how can the sacrifice of my son's life now . . . repay the state for the loss of that poor, dear girl's life . . . ? Cannot the millions of people of the state of New York be merciful? Cannot you as their representative exercise the mercy that they may feel?" (802). Mrs. Griffiths's argument does not just appeal to the governor's sympathy; it also questions the eye-for-an-eye logic that underlies most theories in support of the death penalty. For her, it makes no sense for the state to demand repayment in kind for murder, for the very reason that human life cannot be situated within such an exchange or economy. Although touched by her emotional plea, the governor fails to address the reasoning behind her argument. Instead, he appeals to a reified notion of the law as a mechanized system that operates apart from his influence or intervention: "I am very sorry," the governor tells Mrs. Griffiths. "But if the law is to be respected its decision can never be altered except for reasons that in themselves are full of legal merit. I wish I could decide differently" (803). According to the governor, the question of mercy is not his to adjudicate. That judgment lies solely in the hands of the law. For him, the law is self-generating; its authority comes from within—despite the fact that the conditions for the possibility of a gubernatorial pardon or commutation necessarily place the governor outside the law when considering such matters. Governor Waltham allows space here for an exception to the rule of law, but only for reasons that are "in themselves" legal. This double bind thus places him in the ironic position of not being able to grant a wish that entirely lies in his power: the "wish," as he puts it, to "decide differently."

Yet the governor's wish to decide differently is not just an infelicitous phrase or malapropism. It significantly foregrounds the moment of the decision, a thematic concept at the heart of any meditation on the death penalty and one that pervades Dreiser's novel at a structural level. Taken together, the words "decide," "decidedly," and "decision" occur more than one hundred times in book 3 alone of *An American Tragedy* (statistically, that is once every three pages). Again and again in book 3, the inexorable question of Clyde's guilt confronts each authority within the criminal justice system as he decides where to locate responsibility for Roberta's death. Whereas the ending of book 2 hinges upon the irresolvable question of guilt from Clyde's point of view—the undecidable question that Shawn St. Jean has used to exemplify the Derridean aporia of "différance"[30]—book 3 culminates with a response to this question from the perspective of legal justice, which, as we have already seen, finally comes before Governor Waltham, himself a former district attorney and judge. "To be just," as Jacques Derrida has argued, "the decision of a judge, for example, must not only follow a rule of law or a general law but must also assume it, approve it, confirm its value, by a reinstituting act of interpretation, as if ultimately nothing previously existed of the law, as if the judge himself invented the law in every case."[31] According to this definition, the governor fails to offer a "just" decision about Clyde's guilt: he neither supports nor rejects the earlier verdicts through what Derrida calls a "re-instituting act of interpretation" or what Waltham himself considers "just a re-interpretation"; instead, Waltham lets these previous decisions stand as immu-table decrees. The governor, then, is not a free and responsible agent but, in Derrida's words, merely a "calculating machine."[32] And he acts precisely in such a mechanical, preprogrammed manner when, just two days before Clyde's exe-cution, he receives a last-minute appeal from Mrs. Griffiths and has his secretary wire her back an evasive reply: "Governor Waltham does not think himself justi-fied in interfering with the decision of the Court of Appeals" (809).

Ironically, the governor's decision not to decide constitutes a decision to evade responsibility for Clyde's death. For by deciding not to decide, Waltham avoids acting as sovereign and assuming the responsibility that necessarily entails a sov-ereign act such as reaffirming or commuting Clyde's death sentence. But what epitomizes the disjunction between sovereignty and responsibility in *An Ameri-can Tragedy* is not any one state representative within the system but the system itself, quite literally the actual structures and facilities processing those who are to be executed. Like the agents composing the chain of sovereignty that autho-rizes Clyde's death sentence but without taking responsibility for it, the build-ings, cells, and interior spaces of the prison compound exert an oppressive, cruel authority "for which," we are told, "no one was primarily responsible." The novel best captures this structure of deferral and deference in the figure of the "death house," the building in which the condemned are housed prior to execution:

> The "death house" in this particular prison was one of those crass erections
> and maintenances of human insensitiveness and stupidity principally for
> which *no one primarily was really responsible.* Indeed, its total plan and proce-
> dure were the results of a series of primary legislative enactments, followed by
> *decisions* and *compulsions* as devised by the temperament and seeming neces-
> sities of various wardens, until at last—by degrees and *without anything worthy
> of the name of thinking on any one's part*—there had been gathered and was
> now being enforced all that could possibly be imagined in the way of *unneces-
> sary and really unauthorized cruelty or stupid and destructive torture.* And to
> the end that a man, once condemned by a jury, would be compelled to suffer
> not alone the death for which his sentence called, but a thousand others before

that. For the very room by its arrangement, as well as the rules governing the lives and actions of the inmates, was sufficient to bring about this torture, willy-nilly. (758–59, emphasis added)

The "death house," ironized by quotation marks, serves as an emblem for the contradictory logic of a modern criminal justice system that asserts absolute authority over the lives of the citizens it executes while abrogating any responsibility for those acts. Like the decision to execute, the process of execution is one for which no one is accountable. The physical environment and the torments of confinement conspire with thoughtless prison wards, guards, politicians, and legislatures to subject condemned subjects to a "willy-nilly" process of psychological torture, with each inmate's cell arranged so that each prisoner can see each other's suffering. This process is brought to a climax each and every time an inmate is taken, with elaborate ceremony, to the electric chair and particularly when the execution itself occurs. For the duration of each electrocution the lights throughout the building flicker and dim, "an idiotic or thoughtless result," Dreiser's narrator tells us, "of having one electric system to supply the death voltage and the incandescence of [each prisoner's cell] and all other rooms" in the death house (773). Insofar as each inmate is made vicariously to experience the electrocution of those whose lawful death precedes his or her own, Dreiser portrays the death house as a modern-day torture chamber as well as a crowning bureaucratic figure of "human insensitiveness and stupidity," a facility that operates independent of human control and exists as much because of "compulsions" as it does because of "decisions," two causes of action that have disparate motivating factors. For while "compulsions" result from irresistible or irrational impulses, "decisions" are supposed to be arrived at after careful consideration.

Dreiser's depiction of capital punishment as psychological torture raises what will become a familiar argument against the death penalty by the mid-twentieth century: that lawful death constitutes a cruel and unusual punishment.[33] In making such an argument, *An American Tragedy* clearly participates in the invigorated campaign against capital punishment then sweeping across the nation. That movement had begun at the turn of the century when scientific and sociological studies, as well as populist views and greater awareness of prison conditions, helped to change social attitudes toward crime and capital punishment. In 1909, Kansas would become the first state to abolish the death penalty in the twentieth century, and nine others would follow by 1917. Dreiser's *An American Tragedy*, which attracted national attention when first published in 1925, can been seen as contributing to this interstate campaign. It did so not only by exposing its wide readership to new views on crime and criminology but by dramatizing how cruel and unusual the administration of lawful death in modern America had become. But as history has shown, such Eighth Amendment arguments in legal and extralegal discourse did not positively affect federal law until the 1972 Supreme Court decision in *Furman v. Georgia*, which ruled the death penalty unconstitutional as it was then administered.[34]

In addition to voicing specific opposition to the cruelty of capital punishment, *An American Tragedy* registers a broader anxiety about the movement toward state-sponsored executions during the first quarter of the twentieth century. For when Dreiser wrote early versions of "Nigger Jeff" in 1895 and 1901, death sentences for capital crimes were most often carried out by local officials rather than state authorities. In fact, the first state-supervised execution in the United States did not take place until 1864, and legal executions continued to be performed at the local level through the early 1920s. Criminologist William J. Bower, writing about "The Movement to State-Imposed Executions," characterizes this shift in the administration of the death penalty: "In the 1900s the balance shifted to state-imposed executions, and locally imposed executions outnumbered those under state authority by more than three to one. In the 1910s executions under state authority became more common than either those under local authority or those outside the law. By the 1920s the majority of all executions were state imposed, and the proportion under state authority continued to increase each decade thereafter"[35] Thus, by the time *An American Tragedy* was published the administration of capital punishment across the nation had come largely under the authority of state officials, and condemned prisoners were executed in state (as opposed to local) prisons. That the publication of Dreiser's novel coincides with the centralization of capital punishment under state control makes the work a curious reflection of the tension surrounding the concept of state sovereignty during this transformative period in the history of the death penalty in America. We can look at one particular reflection by looking particularly at one lawyer's reflections on Dreiser's novel in terms of its representation of capital punishment and the criminal justice system in modern America.

### "A BEAUTIFUL LEGAL PROBLEM"

As a popular and critical success, *An American Tragedy* certainly helped to shape debates about the death penalty after its publication in ways it would be difficult to quantify. Darrow himself favorably reviewed the novel in the *New York Evening Post*, writing how it left him "haunted by the face of a helpless boy, strapped to an iron chair at Sing Sing,"[36] while another of the novel's numerous reviewers, after citing the depiction of the "death house," touted the author's "double indictment" of capital punishment and criminal justice system: "Can the limits of modern ingenuity in the infliction of legal torture be extended farther in the direction of diabolism? Mr. Dreiser has spared no effort to make his double indictment complete."[37] The novel's influence on death penalty debates, however, was perhaps most evident in a national essay contest that Dreiser's publishers sponsored in 1926 on the topic, "Was Clyde Griffiths Guilty of Murder in the First Degree?"[38] The winner of the contest and its prize of five hundred dollars (a considerable sum for its day) was Albert Lévitt, professor of law at Washington and Lee University, who, in a letter one year earlier to Dreiser, had praised the novel as the finest "description of criminal procedure" available in Anglo-American literature. Lévitt, in the letter, also mentioned that he planned to design a final exam question about Clyde's legal responsibility for the classes he was then teaching in criminal law. "It will test their knowledge of the law," the law professor wrote, "as no other question I can think of. It is a beautiful legal problem."[39] One can only imagine how Lévitt's students responded to the question or how grappling with it affected their future work in the profession or outlook on the death penalty.

Lévitt's own response, the award-winning answer published a year later, explores the novel's complexities by examining four competing answers he enumerates: "1. The answer given by the law governing murder in the first degree. 2. An answer based upon a system of Christian ethics. 3. An answer based upon the facts as the jury saw them. 4. An answer based upon the societal conditions under which Clyde Griffiths lived" (222). To articulate answers from each of these perspectives, he divides his essay into four corresponding sections, each with a set of organizing questions. His most extensive analysis takes place in the essay's final section, "The Social Background." He begins that section by asking, "Was the social organization of which Clyde Griffiths was a part to blame for the death of Roberta Alden?" (233). After addressing society's defensive *no* to the question, Lévitt answers in the affirmative: "I believe that the state (the social organization, the groups that are in control of the governmental machinery, the individuals who actually make the laws what they are) in spite of a theory of democratic control of human conduct, is to blame for the death of Roberta and the weakness of Clyde" (233). Lévitt's response clearly draws from recent studies in sociology and criminology propounded by the likes of Darrow and other legal realists; for him, the "weakness" of criminal subjects like Clyde is largely the result of the agents and institutions that make up organized society. Thus, in ascribing primary responsibility to the "state," instead of Clyde, Lévitt rejects nineteenth-century assumptions of free will and intentional murder as they inform many of the criminal statutes of his day and are embodied in District Attorney Mason's misguided prosecution in *An American Tragedy*. Furthermore, by opposing *his* answer to the state's "theory of democratic control of human conduct," Lévitt sets up an explanatory framework for exploring criminal acts such as murder that problematizes the simple ascription of responsibility onto a free, autonomous subject.

Lévitt's critique of social responsibility, as opposed to individual responsibility, continues in this liberal fashion up until the final question his essay poses: "Does capital punishment deserve a place in modern criminology?" (240) His answer to this question swings dramatically to the other side of the political spectrum as he locates total responsibility for the act of murder on the individual who commits it. This shift in the ascription of responsibility reveals an interesting source of tension in Lévitt's argument—one that, as we shall see, perhaps lies at the bottom of *An American Tragedy* as well. To address the question of capital punishment's "place in modern criminology," Lévitt divides his response into two points. The first answers the question in general terms:

> 1. Speaking generally, I think it does. The modern state has no high regard for human life. One need but to recur to the present industrial situation within which thousands of innocent lives are destroyed yearly, by swift or slow means, and to the maintenance of war as a legal institution to prove this. I cannot get excited about the execution of weaklings or evil-doers. There are times when human beings act so that they become unendurable menaces to organized society. There is no reason why they should be conserved. I have no hesitancy about shooting a mad dog or killing a rattlesnake. Some men are as dangerous as both of these. I see no reason why they should be permitted to exist. (240–41)

Rather than identifying the exploitation under industrial capitalism and the recent world war as reprehensible violations of human rights, Lévitt begins by justifying the institution of capital punishment precisely because of these other violations. He invokes World War I, as Darrow does in his debate with Judge Talley, to epitomize the social climate of the times and the modern state's disregard for human life; but, unlike Darrow, he draws upon that example to support the use of the death penalty. Lévitt then dismisses any sense of social responsibility in connection with "the execution of weaklings or evil-doers," a claim that explicitly contradicts his opening premise that the state bears most of the blame for the "weakness of Clyde" (233). Indeed, whereas he had earlier implicated the state in the construction of criminal susceptibilities, Lévitt now falls back on outmoded assumptions about deliberate, premeditated murder as well as individual responsibility and autonomy. Finally, by dehumanizing the criminal subject, Lévitt reduces the complexities that his essay had earlier raised about social complicity in homicidal acts to a simple solution of permanent incapacitation of the murderer: "I have no hesitancy about shooting a mad dog or killing a rattlesnake," he asseverates. "Some men are as dangerous as both of these. I see no reason why they should be permitted to exist." The simplicity of these statements, in contrast to the complications raised in *An American Tragedy*, reduces the scene of capital punishment to a situation in which a single authority, an "I," functions as judge, jury, and executioner.

Lévitt's second point addresses the question concerning capital punishment as it directly pertains to *An American Tragedy*:

> 2. Speaking specifically, I cannot see any reason why Clyde should have been permitted to live. He was a spiritual weakling with criminal susceptibilities . . . So far as I can see Clyde was a noxious weed. I see no reason why he should not be destroyed. Technically he was not guilty of the death of Roberta. Morally, socially, he was guilty of her death and of other offenses against the law. He managed to escape detection for the other offenses, at the time they were committed . . . It is immaterial, to my mind, how the law got him. Once the law had him, it was justified in ridding the world of him, so far as death can rid the world of any species of life. He was a bit of poison ivy. There is no reason, so far as I can see, for letting him continue to grow in the field of human life, or on a prison wall. (241)

Again, whereas Lévitt had spent so much of his argument up to this point demonstrating the large extent to which "the state," as he earlier put it, "is to blame for the death of Roberta and the weakness of Clyde" (233), he suddenly shifts responsibility to Clyde. Previously he saw Clyde as a product of his environment; he now explains away Clyde's criminal activity as a biological outgrowth of his innate being, figuring him as a "noxious weed" and "a bit of poison ivy." Such botanical metaphors, with their genetic explanation of criminal behavior, are antithetical to the broader context of environmental determinism within which Lévitt frames his discussion of Clyde's limited responsibility for Roberta's death. From this essentialist position, Lévitt proceeds to justify the legality of Clyde's execution for reasons that, in themselves, are not legal. For even though he determines that Clyde was *not* "technically" (i.e., legally) guilty of murder, Lévitt has no problem with the law executing him for what he deems are social and moral offenses. As he glibly puts it, "It is immaterial, to my mind, how the law got him. Once the law had him, it was justified in ridding the world of him, so far as death can rid the world of any species of life." The malicious finality with which Lévitt speaks of the law's destruction of Clyde not only echoes District Attorney Mason's contempt for Clyde as a depraved murderer but also belies the air of level-headed objectivity that Lévitt strives to sustain throughout his essay. And yet, after justifying Clyde's legally endorsed execution on moral and social grounds, Lévitt goes on, in the very next and final paragraph of the essay, to conclude: "The state is primarily to blame for the death of Roberta, Clyde and their unborn child" (241).

If the "state is primarily to blame" for this American tragedy, these three deaths around which *An American Tragedy* is organized, then why should Clyde assume absolute responsibility for them and have his life taken by the very agent that Lévitt himself principally holds accountable? This discrepancy in Lévitt's thought helps to foreground the tension in his argument about the status of Clyde's guilt. On one hand, when Lévitt applies a Freudian social theory to Dreiser's realistic portrayal of Clyde's act of murder, he determines that Clyde is not alone responsible for Roberta's death but that her death is the result of a complicated web of events implicating an entire society. On the other, the moral horror of Clyde's crime leads Lévitt to condemn him unequivocally, which means placing complete responsibility on Clyde.

Lévitt's argument is, to say the least, contradictory.[40] But rather than conclusively demonstrating the weakness of arguments for the death penalty, Lévitt's conflicting position actually raises the possibility that some arguments against the death penalty succumb to a similar contradiction. For instance, in having Clyde accept complete responsibility for Roberta's murder and suffer death, Lévitt justifies Clyde's death sentence just as Mrs. Griffiths—from a corresponding yet opposing moral perspective within the novel—places total responsibility for *Clyde's* death on the putative sovereign of New York, Governor Waltham. As she wires the governor two days before Clyde's execution, "Can you say before God that you have no doubt of Clyde's guilt? . . . If you cannot, then his blood will be upon your head" (809). What Mrs. Griffiths's moral response shares with Lévitt's is a desire to stop the deferral of responsibility by holding one individual accountable. But if we apply the same realistic portrayal to the *state* as we applied to Clyde's act of murder, then we are forced to conclude that no *one* authority can ultimately be held responsible. After all, if we want one person (e.g., the judge, district attorney, or governor) wielding state authority to accept responsibility for Clyde's death, then why can't we ask the same of Clyde and hold him responsible for Roberta's death?

In the final analysis, then, the issue is not simply one of locating a (sovereign) agent responsible for an act. Rather, the issue involves the *judgment* of a specific kind of act: the killing of a human being. The question informing that act of judgment, as Darrow had put it, is whether the state should adopt the same moral code as a murderer. Darrow's answer is an emphatic no. Nonetheless, such a response does not absolve the murderer of his guilt. In fact it admits the guilt of the murderer, an admission that raises important questions about the dominant narrative strand of *An American Tragedy*, the "realistic" one that I have been tracing, which endlessly defers responsibility for murder by showing how such an act is caught up in a casual web. But that narrative strand is not the only one within *An American Tragedy*. Dreiser's novel complicates even Darrow's moral stand by refusing to privilege its realistic narrative over what we can call its *moral* one—a refusal that, in turn, makes it even more difficult to judge any one individual wielding state authority. That is, Dreiser gives us not only a realistic account of the process by which the state defers authority in sentencing someone to die (so that no one person can be held individually accountable); he also appeals to the reader to locate a point in that web of responsibility at which one person or agent can be held morally culpable for the act. This double thrust in *An American Tragedy*, this dialectical process by which the novel's moral imperatives confront the dominant structure of realistic narration and description, is similar to the narrative form of Dreiser's *Sister Carrie*, in which, as Sandy Petrey argues, the predominant mode of realistic narration is offset by intrusive passages of authorial moralizing.[41] Whereas these conflicting registers (i.e., realistic and moral) are much less obvious in *An American Tragedy*, they are still there. Perhaps the power of Dreiser's novel is not that it avoids contradictions by adopting a simple anti–death penalty position, one with which good liberals can all agree, but that it dramatizes the conflict between moral and realistic perspectives that one faces when deciding upon this difficult issue.

To get a better idea of how this conflict operates in *An American Tragedy*, we can liken the interplay of moral and realistic perspectives in Dreiser's novel (and Lévitt's essay) to what Robert Cover has called "the moral-formal dilemma" of a judicial decision, the predicament that judges face when ruling on a law with which they personally disagree.[42] As Cover reminds us, a judicial decision in theory should never simply reflect the moral stance of a particular judge. Instead, it ought to take into account formal principles that govern and constrain a judge in terms of precedence, statutes, and Constitution, as well as his or her specific place vis-à-vis other lawmaking bodies and within the hierarchical structure of the judicial system more broadly. Cover's attention to the formal principles that regulate, if not constitute, the judicial decision helps to qualify the Derridean concept of the "just" (and judicial) decision I used earlier to analyze the sovereign authority of Governor Waltham. For what enables the performative force of a judicial decision is precisely the sociojuridical context as well as the conventions and rules of law that authorize this speech act in the first place. Without this supportive context and these governing rules, a judicial decision would always run the risk of becoming judge-made law—a legislative rather than a judicial act that could usurp the authority of the legislative branch of government.[43] Thus, like the moral-formal dilemma that a judge may face when formulating a decision, the reader of *An American Tragedy* is placed before the loaded and perennial question, as stated in the Darrow-Talley debate, "Is Capital Punishment a Wise Policy?" While the answer provided by Dreiser's realism is an immediate "of course not," the moral indignation directed at murder throughout the novel calls into question the integrity of that initial response.

My attention here to the moral undertones of *An American Tragedy* runs counter to the author's expressed intentions in writing the novel. For Dreiser in no way intended to write his novel from a moralistic point of view. As he stated in a letter the same year that Lévitt's essay was published, "My purpose [in writing *An American Tragedy*] was not to moralize—God forbid—but to give, if possible, a background and a psychology of reality which would somehow explain, if not condone, how such murders happen—and they have happened with surprising frequency in America as long as I can remember."[44] It is precisely this "psychology of reality" that "condone[s]" Clyde's murder and holds society largely responsible for it. This psychology, moreover, speaks to what I have described as the novel's dominant realistic thrust that drives the narrative and problematizes questions of criminal agency and social responsibility. At the same time, however, one cannot rule out the voice (and many voices) of morality in the novel that demands someone be held responsible—whether it be Clyde for his act or any of the various state agents for theirs. To put it in more concrete terms, whereas Mrs. Griffiths, District Attorney Mason, and even at times Dreiser's narrator, as well as Lévitt, all presume the existence of a universal morality and pontificate about ethical imperatives, Dreiser's literary realism persistently opens up the moral arguments by which a killer is judged in order to investigate the social and psychic causes of murder and society's responsibility for them.

In this respect, we might conclude that Dreiser's novel offers a critique of the criminal justice system à la legal realism, the progressive movement in American law between the two world wars that strove to discredit and displace the classical legal theory that had constituted the dominant legal ideology of the nineteenth century. One critic to do so is John P. McWilliams Jr., who explicitly links the aims of Dreiser's literary realism to those of legal realism by emphasizing how the plot of Dreiser's novel challenges basic premises of nineteenth-century criminal law:

> First-degree murder, for which Clyde is tried and convicted, assumes both malice aforethought and deliberate intent. Clyde had wished Roberta obliterated but had not been able to bring himself to deliberate commission of the act. The crucial issue at stake here is the very premise of nineteenth-century American criminal justice—the belief in the freedom of the will. The deterministic way in which Clyde's entire life has been recreated convinces us that such concepts as "will," "intent," "malice," and "aforethought," are too crude to be applied to twentieth-century conditioning of human life.[45] (92)

What I hope my reading of An American Tragedy adds to McWilliams's list are the larger rubrics under which these "crude" concepts fall: "sovereignty" and "responsibility," two categories around which it is equally important to place quotation marks in any discussion of criminal law and the problem of murder in this novel. Significantly shaped by his environment and inheriting a weak will from his father (who is virtually a nonentity in the rich psychology of Clyde's inner life), Clyde presents a case study for understanding the making of a modern murderer, one who commits a capital crime without "intent," "malice," or "aforethought," as those concepts are traditionally understood.

Yet, in spite of his realistic portrayal of legal procedures and compelling arguments for abolishing capital punishment, Dreiser fails to confront the moral-formal dilemma of the death penalty in its starkest terms. Rather than representing a clear case of first-degree murder, as was the 1906 case of New York v. Gillette on which he based the novel,[46] Dreiser equivocates the extent to which Clyde bears responsibility for administering the "unconscious" and "unintentional" blow that precipitates Roberta's death (492–93). In this respect, An American Tragedy exemplifies what Amy Kaplan has identified as one of the major reversals in recent debates about the political status of American literary realism: "From a progressive force exposing the conditions of industrial society, realism has turned into a conservative force whose very act of exposure reveals its complicity with structures of power."[47] By centering his novel on a travesty or miscarriage of justice, Dreiser avoids the more difficult question of assessing criminal responsibility and moral demands for the death penalty in a case where the condemned is unquestionably guilty by legal standards of the day. It is, after all, much easier to condemn a system that condemns to death a possibly innocent man than it is to attack the underlying principles according to which that system operates.

If Dreiser shies away from the more difficult question of executing the legally guilty, that is precisely the question that Clarence Darrow addresses in his long-forgotten novel, *An Eye for an Eye* (1905). As a way of ending this chapter and book, as well as preparing for the epilogue to follow, I would like briefly to reflect on lawfully killing the legally guilty as Darrow addresses the issue in his early twentieth-century novel, the first such work entirely focused on the question of capital punishment.

### DEAD MAN TALKING

Published two decades before *An American Tragedy*, Darrow's *An Eye for an Eye* tells the story of Jim Jackson, a representative murderer (like Dreiser's Clyde) who kills his wife with a chimney poker one fateful night. Darrow's novel, like Dreiser's, spends much of its time dramatizing the mental and environmental factors that make a murderer. It, too, is written in the third person, but Darrow's novel is dominated by the voice of the condemned and his breathless confession on the eve of his execution. Jim, the dead man talking, tells his story to Hank Clery, a childhood friend who has come to visit him for the first time since his arrest and incarceration. In telling his tale in these terms, Darrow offers an updated, modern version of the criminal conversation narrative, a subgenre of early gallows literature popular in America since the late seventeenth century.[48] The "conversation" that Darrow stages, however, is more monologue than dialogue, with Jim assuming the role of Puritan ministers of yore, by dictating and controlling almost everything that is said about the causes of crime and the purpose of punishment.

But since Jim, Darrow's representative realistic murderer, is unschooled in modern theories of crime and criminology and thus cannot intelligibly explain why he killed his wife, Darrow writes himself into the novel as a liberal penal reformer who frequently visits the prison and to whom Jim, at various times, refers as "that feller." Through the feller's progressive perspective, coupled with "everything" Jim says in explaining himself, Darrow shows how capital punishment is incommensurate with almost any capital crime. A prime example of this combined talking strategy occurs when the feller is first introduced and Jim first discusses the murder itself:

> There was a feller came over here to the jail to talk to our Moral Improvement
> Club and he had some queer ideas. Most of the prisoners rather liked what he
> said and still they thought he was too radical. I never heard any such talk before

and I don't quite see how they let him do it, but I've thought about what he said a good deal since then and think mebbe there's somethin' in it. He was a good deal different from the other ones that come. Most of 'em tell us about our souls and how we can all make 'em white if we only will. They all tell us that we are a bad lot now; but he kinda claimed that the people inside the jail was just like the people outside, only not so lucky; that we done things because we couldn't help it and had to do 'em, and that it's worse for the people on the outside to punish the people on the inside than to do the things we done. Now, I hain't had anything to do but think about it and what I done, and it don't seem as if I could help it. I never intended to kill anybody but somehow everything just led up to it, and I didn't know I was gettin' in to it until it was done, and now here I am. Of course, when I was out I used to rail about these criminals and think they was awful bad just the same as every one else did, but now I see how they got into it too, and how mebbe they ain't so bad; even them carbarn murderers,—if they'd been taken somewhere out west on a ranch where they could have had lots of air and exercise and not put in school which wa'n't the place for boys like them, I believe they'd 've come out all right and been like most other boys and sobered down after they got older.[49]

Poverty, contingencies, and dumb luck, we learn from Jim and the "too radical" feller in passages like this one, have more to do with Jim's crime than anything he consciously wills or intends. Society's response of murder for murder in kind—"an eye for an eye," as the novel's title ironically puts it—is therefore portrayed as more cold-blooded, premeditated, and deliberate than almost any murder committed outside the law. The feller explicitly develops this argument through Jim's paraphrasing of it; but so too does Jim, albeit indirectly, when he compares his representative domestic murderer to the more extreme killers represented here in the notorious "carbarn murderers," a gang of four young men responsible for killing seven people in Chicago from July 9 to December 4 in 1903. For both the feller and Jim, the point is that the crime of murder—that of Jim's or these "boys"—is almost always a complex product of mental and environmental influences beyond any individual's control.

The liberal feller, through Jim's voicing, lends further support to this argument by way of a curious metaphor: "That feller that I told you about," Jim later tells Hank, "made out that a man was a good deal like a machine, or an engine of some kind, and when the steam was turned on he had to go. He said that if the blood was pumped up in the head, it made us do things; it made some people write poetry, and some make speeches, and some sing, and some fight, and some kill folks, and they couldn't really help it if they was made that way and the blood got pumped up in the head" (78). Likening murder to literary production and other aesthetic acts, Darrow here makes an extreme point about biological determinism—one that anticipates an argument he would make infamous years later in successfully saving from the gallows Leopold and Loeb, two so-called depraved killers not unlike the carbarn murderers. And at the time Darrow later presented these arguments in the courtroom, Dreiser, as we have seen, was developing his own literary version of legal realism through a probing analysis of criminal subject formation in *An American Tragedy*. In fact, Robert Penn Warren, one of Dreiser's famous admirers, would later see such determinism at the heart of Clyde's characterization. Echoing Darrow's feller who likened "man" to a "machine" in order to explain criminal behavior, Warren aptly describes Clyde as "a mechanism with a conscience."[50]

Twenty years before Dreiser animated such a mechanism in Clyde, Darrow first showcased his views on the death penalty and determinism in *An Eye for an Eye*, thereby using literature to address the court of public opinion. In this court, as opposed to a legal one, Darrow's representative murderer could take the witness stand to present crucial evidence in his defense deemed irrelevant and therefore inadmissible at his courtroom trial for murder. Through Jim's uninterrupted testimony—his attempt to tell "everything" related to his crime—Darrow draws from a central tenet of legal realism: that experience, rather than formal logic, should provide the basis for understanding and applying the law.[51] Such lived experience, as least in Jim's case, renders the formality as well as the morality of capital laws utterly obsolete. In fact, making morality beside the point is one of the main points of *An Eye for an Eye*, whose title refers negatively to state vengeance via an outmoded biblical dictate. This amoral "moral" permeates the novel, particularly the narrative frame that envelops Jim's confession. For the novel begins by setting the stage for Jim's monologue and establishing the role to be played by Hank, a silent interlocutor (for the most part) and stand-in for the reader in need of a lesson in the horrors of state-sponsored execution. In this respect Hank is similar to Dreiser's Elmer Davies, the representative subject within the law and silent witness to a lynching who is shown the savage immorality of such violence in "Nigger Jeff." Through the eyes of Hank—a believer, like Davies, in a fixed system of reward and punishment—we see Jim as a "demon" when Hank recalls first reading of the murder in the paper: "Hank did not understand how this could be true," we are told in the novel's opening frame, "but as the evidence seemed plain he made up his mind that Jim had really always been a demon, but that he had managed to keep it hidden from his friends. Hank really did not want to go to the jail to see Jim; somehow it seemed as if it was not the same fellow that he used to know so well, and then he was afraid and nervous about talking with a man who was going to be hanged next day" (5).

By the novel's closing frame, Hank not only comes to see Jim as the "same fellow" he has always known; he also sees in Jim's lethal violence an act that *any* fellow (including Hank himself) might have done under similar circumstances. As Hank says in farewell to Jim, the dead man talking to whom he has been listening all night, "I didn't know how it was—when I come I felt as if you'd been awful bad, and of course I know it wan'n't right, but somehow I know it might have happened to me, or most anybody, almost, and that you ain't so bad." Emphasizing the lesson taught through Jim's talking and the feller's theorizing, Hank continues: "I don't think I'll ever feel the same about the fellers that go to jail and get hung. I don't know's they could help it any more'n any of us help the things we do" (210). In the transformation of Hank's thinking about crime and punishment, Darrow presents a new way of viewing criminal responsibility—one influenced by contemporaneous theories of legal realism then emerging in the writings of Oliver Wendell Holmes Jr. and others. Dreiser, as we have seen, would plumb the logic of legal realism to new depths in his epic inversion of the proverbial American Dream in *An American Tragedy*. But like the amoral realism that drives Dreiser's literary realism and asks us to condone Clyde and condemn society, the amoral "moral" of Darrow's *An Eye for an Eye* succumbs to a similar unintentional moralizing. For in presenting Jim ultimately as a common "feller"—someone subjected to a confluence of mental and environmental influences beyond his control rather than a master of mind and circumstances— Darrow, a professed atheist well before the turn of the twentieth century, offers an interpretation of murder that shares common ground with the Puritan execution sermon, the genre par excellence of early American gallows literature. As Karen Halttunen has thoroughly demonstrated, execution sermons so popular in the late seventeenth and eighteenth centuries taught their audiences to see the executed felon as a "common sinner" like themselves rather than a moral "monster" or "aberration," as the murderer would often come to be constructed in popular fiction and print culture from the early nineteenth century until today.[52] Darrow suggests a similar identification with the criminal, minus the morality.

In considering Hank's enlightened (if not moral) perspective at the end of Darrow's legal novel, we have come full circle to where my study started. We have returned, however, not to the execution sermon, with its attention to sin and morality, but to the object lessons in the Enlightenment critique of capital punishment. In fact, I began chapter 1 with John Neal's point-by-point exegesis on the inexpediencies of capital punishment in *Logan* (1821), the first American novel with an out-and-out anti-gallows scene. In Darrow's *Eye for an Eye*—the first American novel written entirely on the question of capital punishment and expressly for its abolition—the administration of the death penalty and the argument against its practice have changed in obvious and significant ways. Even so, both the bureaucracy of and the argument over lawful death still dealt fundamentally with questions concerning sovereignty and responsibility, umbrella categories that are problematized every time a person is lawfully put to death by "the people" (or public) of a republic. More than Darrow or any novelist since, Dreiser cuts to the quick of debates over the legitimacy of the death penalty in his representation of a criminal justice system that claims sovereignty but abrogates responsibility for the executions it authorizes. While Darrow's dead-man-talking trope is a crude convention when compared to the cacophony of competing perspectives brilliantly brought to life in *An American Tragedy*, it nonetheless illustrates perhaps more forcefully an arresting peculiarity of capital punishment: that the death penalty is virtually the only means of death (the one universal human experience) in which the subject knows beforehand exactly how, by what means, and precisely when his or her life will end.

In *An Eye for an Eye*, the phenomenal fact of such a fate is behind every word Jim utters but nowhere more strangely than when his incessant talking is interrupted by the construction of the gallows on which he is to die:

Just then the noise of pounding and driving nails and low voices was heard over in the court yard.

"What's that?" Hank asked.

"Don't you know! That's the fellers buildin' the scaffold; they always do it the night before. Strange, ain't it; somehow it don't seem to me as if it was really me that was goin' to be hung on it; but I s'pose it is. Now, isn't it strange about the governor; just one word from him could save my life. I'd think he'd do it, wouldn't you?" (64)

It is indeed "strange" that the state, comprised of other "fellers," is conspiring to kill Jim, a vibrant fellow in perfect health, as he tells a tale that at least in part diminishes his responsibility for his wife's death. "Strange," too, is it that at any moment in his narration Jim could cease to be a dead man talking, that "just one word" from the governor could bring the entire execution procedure (now in full swing, so to speak) to a sudden halt. The phenomenon of a gubernatorial pardon, in other words, is equally peculiar in that the elaborate process that had brought Jim to his imminent death could be undone, obliterated, by a word, telegraph, or phone call from a single executive agent representing the state. The power to decide in such situations marks the specter of sovereignty like nothing else in a democratic republic such as the United States. For under no other circumstances does one individual lawfully hold a power over another's life or death. But with that authority, as I have argued in this book, comes a commensurate responsibility. Curiously, that responsibility is structurally imbalanced—a point Dreiser pointedly illustrates in Governor Waltham's decision *"not to decide"* when confronted with Clyde's appeal for a pardon or commutation of his death sentence. As Dreiser makes clear, if Waltham grants clemency, he will keenly feel the burden of that responsibility in the form of public reaction—a "response" to Waltham's *respons*ible decision that could make him seem irresponsible and cost him his office in the next gubernatorial election. In contrast, by deciding not to decide (which amounts to upholding Clyde's verdict and death sentence) the weight of Waltham's public—or rather, *republican*—responsibility is negligible by comparison. It is precisely this structural imbalance between sovereignty and responsibility that accounts for much of the tension and contradictions at play in the history of the debate over the death penalty in the United States.

# "The Death Penalty in Literature"

Next time you read in the papers that an execution is about to take place I invite you to try to picture exactly what is going on behind the walls of that prison. To put yourself in the place of the man who, after weeks of the mental strain of appeals, petitions, and farewell visits, is now assured that there is no hope; then put yourself in the place of the warders who have to take out the man who has been their constant companion for weeks and see him killed in cold blood; of the governor who has to tell the prisoner that a reprieve has been refused; of the chaplain and the doctor whose functions are degraded by having to assist at this barbarous ceremony; of the man who is paid by the State to do the very thing for which his victim is hanged and to devote the latest applications of science to make death as certain and swift as it can be made; of the Home Secretary who has had the duty of deciding whether a fellow creature is fit to live; having done all this ask yourselves if you are surprised that a coroner should have denounced the proceedings as a relic of barbarism.

J. W. Hall, Common Sense and Capital Punishment (1924)

Published across the Atlantic and almost a century after *The Record of Crimes in the United States* (1834), whose prefatory "Observations on the Curiosity of Those Who Go to Witness Public Executions" I began this book by discussing, J. W. Hall's *Common Sense and Capital Punishment* was first presented as a speech in 1924 before England's Joint Parliamentary Advisory Council. Hall's speech, like Humanity's "Observations" in *The Record of Crimes*, forced its audience to confront the spectacle of law's sovereign violence and to acknowledge its complicity in a public process (however "private") carried out in the people's name and through republican government. It, too, was part of a larger national movement to abolish the death penalty; but whereas Humanity's "Observations" is indicative of a popular extralegal discourse for the abolition of capital punishment that had only recently established a national presence in antebellum America, Hall's *Common Sense and Capital Punishment* constituted legal discourse itself and contributed to one national campaign among many then well underway in Europe. England, in fact, had come late to this international movement. "I come to express the views of those who are working *at the present time* for the Abolition of Capital Punishment," Hall tells his audience of legislators and politicians at the outset of his speech, emphasizing that this campaign is "no new movement, and that far from being pioneers of a new, untried and revolutionary idea we are really in this country limping painfully in the wake of our more progressive neighbours."[1]

At that time, Britain's "more progressive neighbours" included a host of nations that had abolished the death penalty either de jure or de facto. Among the former were Holland, Italy, Norway, and Austria, which had banned the practice in 1870, 1889, 1902, and 1921 respectively; the latter included Belgium, Denmark, Finland, Sweden, and Switzerland, in each of which no execution had occurred for at least the past three decades—in over ninety years in Finland's case. Hall, in his speech, also identified Portugal, Romania, Estonia, Latvia, and Lithuania as "countries with no capital punishment by law."[2] With the exception of a brief reference to the state of Maine near the end of his pamphlet, however, Hall failed to look to the other side of the Atlantic, where three U.S. states had abolished the death penalty two decades before Holland became the first European nation to do so. Between 1907 and 1917, nine more U.S. states would do the same.[3]

In reflecting on the history of the abolition of capital punishment in an international context, it is important to note the example first set by the United States. "In 1846," as William A. Schabas writes in the opening of his magisterial *The Abolition of the Death Penalty in International Law*, "Michigan became the first jurisdiction to abolish capital punishment permanently."[4] That movement in international law, Schabas explains, is largely a post–World War II phenomenon, beginning with the *Universal Declaration of Human Rights* adopted by the United Nations in 1948 and culminating in the ratification of Protocol No. 6 to the *European Convention of Human Rights* in 1985 that effectively banned the death penalty in almost all of Europe. But it has substantial roots, I would argue, earlier in the twentieth century and in speeches and pamphlets like Hall's *Common Sense and Capital Punishment*. Some of those roots, in fact, extend well into the nineteenth century and can be found not only in American literature, as I have shown in this book, but in British and European literature as well.

Literary critic J. A. T. Lloyd makes a point along these lines in "The Death Penalty in Literature," two essays published in the mid-1920s in the *Fortnightly Review*, a distinguished literary journal printed in both London and New York.[5] An early instance of law-*in*-literature criticism, Lloyd's essays connect important nineteenth-century British, French, and Russian authors to the anti–capital punishment movement and emerging discourses of criminology developing at the present moment. In fact, Lloyd quotes at length from Hall's *Common Sense and Capital Punishment* in the second of these essays, which was published in 1927. He does so in the midst of analyzing works by William Makepeace Thackeray and Victor Hugo, citing Hall "because quietly and unpretentiously, almost in the manner of Thackeray, without rhetoric, without overemphasis, he asks the casual reader to follow for himself imaginatively, as Victor Hugo followed it, *le dernier jour d'un condamné.*"[6] Updating the experience of witnessing the death penalty from when it was publicly preformed, Hall "invite[s]" fellow citizens to put themselves not only in the shoes of the condemned but in those of various state agents—the prison wards, the governor, chaplains, doctors, executioners, and coroners—directly involved in the modern execution process. Appealing to a collective "you," Hall reminds *us* of our participation in capital punishment when carried out under a republican form of government, thus turning the constative events one reads in newspapers into performative acts—invitations "to picture exactly what is going on behind the walls of that prison."[7] And nothing on either side of the Atlantic imagined exactly what went on behind those walls as vividly as Theodore Dreiser's *An American Tragedy* (1925), published the same year as the first of Lloyd's "The Death Penalty in Literature" essays but mentioned in neither of them.

The second essay was occasioned by some oversights in the first: "A correspondent," Lloyd explains to begin the article, "has brought it home to me that a recent article in these pages on the death penalty in literature was woefully incomplete; that no such article, in fact, should see daylight without a reference to Hugo, to Dickens, and to Browning."[8] Examining these authors in the second, the first essay surveys the subject in works by Thackeray, Anatole France, Fyodor Dostoevsky, and Leo Tolstoy. It begins with Thackeray's 1840 sketch, "Going to See a Man Hanged" (first published in *Fraser's* magazine and later included in Thackeray's *The Book of Snobs* [1846–47]), which was based on the infamous execution of Benjamin Courvoisier that Thackeray (along with Dickens) had witnessed in person earlier that year.[9] To give a sense of both the novelist's and critic's anti-gallows arguments, I here cite at length Lloyd citing and analyzing Thackeray, whose intrigue and disgust are expressed through the fictive Mr. Titmarch and an anonymous sensitive man in the crowd:

The author of *Vanity Fair*, however, could not sleep much before that significant morning, "could not help thinking, as each clock sounded, what is *he* doing now? Has he heard it in his little room in Newgate younder?" So it was after a practically sleepless night that Mr. Titmarch drove with his friend X. to witness the end of the murderer. In the dispersing grayness of the morning many people were already astir with the same fixed intention: "The ginshop keepers have many of them taken their shutters down, and many persons are issuing from them pipe in hand. Down they go along the broad, bright street, their blue shadows marching *after* them; for they are all bound the same way and are bent, like us, upon seeing the hanging." The shop windows were crowded for the occasion with sightseers of all kinds: "Many young dandies are there with moustaches and cigars; some quiet fat family parties of simple honest tradesman and their wives, as we fancy, who are looking on with the greatest imaginable calmness and sipping their tea."

There seems to have been on that twentieth of July, 1840, a curious absence of any sense of horror: "We were all, as far as I could judge, in just such a frame of mind as men are in when they are squeezing at the pit-door of a play, or pushing for a review or a Lord Mayor's show." Interrogated as to why she had come so early to such a place, a little girl answered with breathless eagerness, "We've koom to see the man hanged!" But one person, at all events, in that vast crowd was sensitive to the infectious degradation of the scene: "It seems to me that I have been abetting an act of frightful wickedness and violence, performed by a set of men against one of their fellows, and I pray God that it may be soon out of the power of any man in England to witness such a hideous and degrading sight." Obviously, this verdict of William Makepeace Thackeray applies not only to the public spectacle of an execution, but the death penalty itself, and it is curious how identically authors, utterly different as their views may be in other respects, have regarded this particular phase of human justice.[10]

Quoting and analyzing details from Thackeray's execution sketch, Lloyd calls attention to an anti-gallows literary attack of the spectacle of lawful violence similar to the critique I have traced in execution scenes in works by John Neal, William Gilmore Simms, Lydia Maria Child, George Lippard, Sylvester Judd, and others. In Thackeray's case, that critique reaches its fullest expression in the sensitive man's pronounced disgust in the spectacle around him, a pronouncement Lloyd takes as Thackeray's "verdict" against not only public execution but capital punishment itself. Lloyd's remarks here do double duty, not only serving as his specific conclusion regarding Thackeray's literary execution scene but providing his thesis and a model analysis for what follows in the rest of the article, which reads similar anti-gallows statements by characters as expressing their authors' anti-gallows politics.

It is indeed "curious," as Lloyd states in his thesis, "how identically [these] authors, utterly different as their views may be in other respects," have universally condemned capital punishment. But as I hope to have shown in my book, the death penalty in literature is more than just a curiosity. To be sure, its negative depiction in important literary works certainly impacted the anti–capital punishment cause as well as progressive attitudes toward criminals in Lloyd's day as well as those of the influential writers he discusses. Lloyd, in fact, suggests as much to conclude his first "The Death Penalty in Literature" essay. Beginning with Thackeray and the spectacle of lawful violence, he ends with Dostoevsky and the criminal mind to indicate how the famous novelist's work, particularly *Crime and Punishment* (1866), has influenced criminal law and jurisprudence in France: "In his book *Les Passions Criminelles*," Lloyd writes in his essay's penultimate paragraph, "M. Berard des Glajeux, President of the Paris Assize Court of Appeal, cites a French judge's reference to *Crime and Punishment* as the book which had most helped him in his study of criminology. 'I should say emphatically to young magistrates,' M. des Glajeux adds, 'Read Dostoievsky.'"[11]

～

No doubt American literature over the long nineteenth century, as I have construed the period, similarly affected judges, legislators, politicians, and influential citizens in the United States, thus making the period's poets and novelists, as Percy Bysshe Shelley famously declared, "the unacknowledged legislators of the world."[12] There is, however, no hard evidence—at least none that I have found— explicitly linking literary works from the period to legal debates that directly led to the ratification of anti-gallows bills or the repeal of capital statutes. Gregg D. Crane and Robert A. Ferguson have recently argued for the importance of such hard evidence in law-and-literature studies, thus advocating a *literature*-in-law approach that inverts the *law*-in-literature paradigm within which my book has primarily operated.[13] Crane, for instance, has brilliantly shown how Harriet Beecher Stowe's *Uncle Tom's Cabin* (1852) directly influenced Charles Sumner's impassioned arguments against slavery and the Fugitive Slave Act on the Senate floor. Ferguson, likewise, has illustrated the powerful role literature and literary figures played in shaping legal views in the capital trial of John Brown, what he calls "the first modern courtroom event."[14] As important as such evidence is, however, it would be a mistake to underestimate the role imaginative literature played in shaping debate and legislation pertaining to the death penalty. Literature, after all, often impacts politics without leaving a demonstrable trace, affecting hearts and minds in ways that other discourses, such as the law, often cannot, thus making *Uncle Tom's Cabin's* explicit participation in legislative debates idiosyncratic rather than exemplary.

Writing on "The Death Penalty in Literature" more than eighty years after Lloyd first took up the topic, I am tempted to remind him—as his contemporary "correspondent" did of Hugo, Dickens, and Browning—of glaring omissions in his inaugural foray into the field. There was, indeed, a whole century's worth of writers from across the Atlantic who took up the subject in significant ways, as my study has shown.[15] Given America's considerable role in the campaign to end capital punishment during the first half of the nineteenth century, it is painfully ironic that today the United States stands virtually alone among Western democratic republics in sustaining the practice. This peculiar example of "American exceptionalism" is especially striking when one considers it in light of the current situation abroad, where almost every European country has now abolished the death penalty and abolition itself is a prerequisite for any nation to join the Council of Europe.[16] With this contemporary climate in mind, I would like to end my study by returning to its beginnings. My example involves two figures, one from law and the other from literature, crucial to my earlier chapters. The first is Edward Livingston, whose writings against the death penalty influenced Victor Hugo and other French authors who took up the anti–capital punishment cause in their country in the 1830s. The second is James Fenimore Cooper, without question the foremost American novelist of his day. Drawing from a transatlantic perspective on the death penalty in literature afforded by their writing and, as we shall see, a near exchange of ideas on the subject will enable me to underscore three central interrelated aims explored in this book: how literature could and did influence death-penalty reform; how legal forms *in*formed literary forms; and how the figure of capital punishment was configured into a broader metaphor for the confrontation between the citizen-subject and sovereign authority.

⁓

In June 1829, Livingston, the distinguished politician and legislator, wrote to Cooper asking for his help in promoting the campaign to end capital punishment. By the time of Livingston's letter, Cooper was at the height of his fame and had written some of his most popular and critically acclaimed works, including *The Pioneers* (1823), *The Pilot* (1824), *The Last of the Mohicans* (1826), and *The Prairie* (1827). Interestingly enough, the last of these novels turns on a curious enactment of capital punishment: the extralegal execution of Abiram White for the murder of his nephew, Asa Bush. A fascinating case of fratricide, the scene evokes the biblical parable of Cain and Abel (in which Cain is *not* killed for his brother's murder) and places the gruff Ishmael Bush in the ironic position of judge and executioner. Because the scofflaw Bush in the past had shot a sheriff and is presently implicated in a kidnapping, some critics have taken his action as a symbol for injustice in Cooper's work.[17] And because the extralegal hanging over which Bush presides closely imitates the procedures for lawful hanging, one could also see the scene as criticism of a similar practice conducted from within the law.[18] But if Livingston had in mind the literary execution of Abiram White, he did not mention it in the letter. Nor did he mention the near executions in *The Spy* or the grisly hanging of the Skinner, which unquestionably casts a negative light on capital punishment in the novel. Instead, Livingston appealed to Cooper's literary celebrity and "the obligation which that celebrity has created," he told him, "of using your talents in such a way as to promote the greatest good." Without "further preface," Livingston got to his point: "I know not whether you have ever turned your attention to the state of our penal law, or have formed an opinion on the great question whether death ought ever to be inflicted as a punishment—I have, and have come to the conclusion that as society is now formed neither justice nor necessity nor expediency require or permit this punishment."[19]

Enclosed with the letter, Livingston included his two seminal penal reports that were first presented to the Louisiana state legislature in 1821 and 1822 and had widely circulated since then in book and pamphlet form in both the United States and abroad (again, their influence on Hugo is especially noteworthy). Referring to his own work, Livingston went on to appeal to Cooper's duty as a citizen of both the United States and the world, asking him "to cooperate in the abolition of a practice supported only by prejudice and the fear of innovation which outrages humanity, and disgraces the legislation of the civilized world" (174). In his defense of an "outrage[d] humanity," Livingston thus seeks redress from the domain of literature, since reform through legal and extralegal means had not yielded the desired results. The famous novelist, the famous lawyer reasoned, was in a unique position to effect that change:

> You are one of the very, very few, whose work are not only read in all civilized nations, but by all the reading part of every nation. The department of literature which you have for the most part adopted is one that enables you to impress most forcibly on the mind the truths you may wish to inculcate. The skill with which you embody the passions and exemplify their operation and effects, the genius which enables you to give to fiction all the interest of reality, the knowledge of human nature by which you detect and expose the most se-

cret workings of the mind, and the command of language and descriptive powers you possess, to throw into the most interesting form the incidents your fancy creates, all these fit you in the most eminent degree for the task I propose. (175)

More than mere flattery, Livingston's remarks call attention to the important cultural work that popular fiction—and especially the novel—could perform in the arenas of law and politics. Two decades later Stowe's *Uncle Tom's Cabin* would demonstrate the full potential of such a claim by becoming, as Lincoln famously put it, "the book that started this great [civil] war."[20] None of Cooper's novels had the political impact of Stowe's international best seller (few literary works ever have), but they did engage seriously with legal issues and influenced contemporary political issues, as important law-and-literature scholarship by Brook Thomas, John P. McWilliams, Wai-Chee Dimock, and Charles Hansford Adams has shown.[21]

Valued today for his nuanced analyses of jurisprudential themes and issues, Cooper was potentially of great use to reformers in his own day because of his reputation and readership. In Livingston's terms, he could "impress most forcibly on the mind the truths [he] may wish to inculcate." Such a statement suggests the ideological use to which a Cooper novel on capital punishment could be put, making such a work, as we might say today, a sort of polyvocal laboratory in which various positions both for and against capital punishment could be imagined and experimented with, precisely because no one would literally swing if the law in literature got it wrong.[22] In fact, getting it *wrong* in literature could ironically help the law in reality to get it right by dramatizing fictive scenarios in which death sentences were enacted that relied on erroneous judgments and mistaken or manufactured evidence, thereby producing the kind of tragedy or travesty of justice later depicted in fiction by Hawthorne, Child, William Starbuck Mayo, Dreiser, and others.

Livingston was clearly thinking along these lines when proposing the specific "task" he hoped Cooper would undertake:

It is that of exemplifying (in a work written expressly with that view) the evils of capital punishment. One of the most prominent among them (its irremediable nature) seems to me to offer the finest field for a display of your powers in describing the effects of an erroneous judgment founded on false or mistaken testimony—the unavailing efforts of conscious innocence; its uncredited association, its despair; the remorse of the mistaken jurors and judge when the falsity of the charge is discovered too late for redress; the chain of circumstances by which guilt was presumed or the motives for the perjury by which it was asserted, in your hand, might be worked up into a picture that would cause the hardiest advocate for capital punishment to pause in his desire to inflict it, and I will answer for it, would not disgrace the master hand that drew it. (175)

Livingston, in his proposal, outlines a veritable formula for a politicolegal thriller, a commonplace of today's ever-so-popular crime and mystery genre (recent novels by John Grisham, Scott Turow, Barry Siegel, and Earnest J. Gaines, to name a few, come to mind).[23] A conventional model for the contemporary novel, the formula first emerged, as we saw in chapter 2, in the mid-nineteenth century when a number of works were structured in some way around a capital trial or involved two or more of the elements Livingston enumerates. Cooper's first popular novel *The Spy* (1821) is an early example of such a work, particularly in its climax dramatizing the race against the clock to prevent the execution of an innocent man. A later example is Cooper's *The Ways of the Hour* (1850), examined along with *The Spy* in chapter 3, which reads as though it were a belated response to Livingston's letter, given that there is no evidence of Cooper directly replying to it. Indeed, with its depiction of misleading circumstances and mistaken testimony, and the conviction and near execution of a women for a crime she did not commit, *The Ways of the Hour* gives form to the formula Livingston suggested for a novel "exemplifying . . . the evils of capital punishment." Cooper's final novel, as we have seen, even reaches its climax in the conviction and sentencing of the innocent Mary Monson; the verdict and death sentence are overturned only when one of Monson's supposed victims (she was convicted of arson and a double murder) is identified among the courtroom crowd in the immediate aftermath of her sentencing.

In this respect, the novel's premise of Monson's "conscious innocence" and its reliance on "erroneous judgment" (to apply Livingston's terms) go a long way in executing the kind of plot Livingston had envisioned—although not so far as to dramatize the horrors of an irremediable punishment "too late for redress." Yet if Cooper *did* have Livingston's letter in mind when writing his final novel, he did *not* "work up" the kind of anti-gallows "picture" that Livingston had desired. For Cooper's *Ways* goes out of its way to make an *anti*-anti-gallows statement in two scenes involving the novel's putative spokesperson, Tom Dunscomb, a gentleman-lawyer of the old school who is in many ways Livingston's opposite number. In one of those scenes (as we have seen) Dunscomb silences a reform-minded Mrs. Horton by asserting that the gallows is an institution necessary for society's "protection" and the prevention of "others from committing murder."[24] Nonetheless, Dunscomb's argument for capital punishment should not be mistaken for Cooper's—an argument I make contra Lloyd's thesis regarding famous European authors in "The Death Penalty in Literature," in which he takes the statements of characters for those of the author. For one thing, Dunscomb's pro-gallows stance is more symptomatic of Cooper's late conservatism than it is a definitive statement of the author's literary politics on the administration of lawful death. It is, in other words, more of a corrective aimed at the faddish "ways of the hour" of which the movement to abolish the death penalty—like women's rights and the campaign to end slavery—was a primary symptom for Cooper in the 1840s, as death penalty and similar reform was for Hawthorne's conservative "thoughtful observer" in "Earth's Holocaust" (1844) published in the middle of the decade.[25] For another, Dunscomb's position flies in the face of much of Cooper's earlier writing in which capital punishment serves not only as a *leitmotif* for political tyranny and the barbarism of Europe's past but also as an organizing principle in the architecture of his fiction.[26]

The gallows, after all, accounts for much of *The Spy*'s narrative scaffolding (as it does in Hawthorne's *The Scarlet Letter* and *The House of the Seven Gables*), while the novel propounds a general argument against capital punishment through the Lawton-Sitgreaves exchange analyzed in chapter 3. Similarly, whereas *The Spy, The Ways of the Hour,* and *The Prairie* all involve or revolve around (near) executions, the dramaturgy of the death penalty plays an important structural role in *The Wing-and-Wing* (1842), at the center of which unfolds an elaborately staged military execution eerily anticipatory of the 1842 USS *Somers* hangings that elicited Cooper's pronounced ire. Set during the Napoleonic Wars like Melville's *Billy Budd, The Wing-and-Wing* dramatizes the enactment of lawful death in decidedly negative terms to conclude chapter 14: "There was a horrible minute, of the struggles between life and death," we are told of the historical Admiral Francesco Caraccioli's execution for treason, "when the body, so late the tenement of an immortal spirit, hung, like one of the jewel-blocks of the ship, dangling passively at the end of the spar, as insensible as the wood which sustained it."[27] Far from demonstrating "the prompt, unerring, and almost terrific majesty of punishment," as one character characterizes the death penalty in Cooper's *The Chainbearer* (1845),[28] the central execution in *The Wing-and-Wing*—described from the perspective of a third-person, omniscient narrator—elicits disgust among those who witness it: "A LONG summer's evening did the body of Francesco Caraccioli hang suspended at the yard-arm of the Minerva,"

Cooper writes to begin chapter 15, "a revolting spectacle to his countrymen, and to most of the strangers who had been the witnesses of his end."[29]

If, as Harrison Hayford and Merton Sealts suggest, the military execution in *The Wing-and-Wing* was possibly a source from which Melville drew in writing *Billy Budd*, it is interesting to note that Cooper was virtually the only writer of consequence to condemn the *Somers* executions in their immediate aftermath—although Melville would denounce them some seven years later in *White-Jacket*. Yet regardless of Cooper's intention in dramatizing *The Wing-and-Wing*'s central execution, the scene could be and probably was read in the context of anti-gallows activism, perhaps not in its original context but when the chapter dramatizing it was cited in full as part of a review of "Cooper's new novel" in the November 26, 1842, edition of Greeley's *New York Tribune*—a widely circulating paper known for its anti-gallows politics. It is, in other words, no accident that—of all the novel's chapters—the execution chapter was excerpted by the *Tribune*'s reviewer.

Yet there is more to complicate a discussion of Cooper and capital punishment. The death penalty in his work, as it is in much of the fiction and nonfiction examined in the preceding chapters, not only provides a drama or spectacle but is an object of interest in its own right. In "The Eclipse," a personal essay likely written in 1831 not long after Livingston had written him, Cooper reflected with deep sympathy on the plight of a condemned man whose execution in his native Lake Otsego he was to witness in 1806. In dramatic fashion, however, that execution was stopped at the last minute through a stay issued by the governor. Perhaps the memory of that experience informed one or more of the many literary executions Cooper would later plot in his fiction. A year after writing "The Eclipse," Cooper gave literary form to this anti-gallows sentiment in *The Headsman* (1832), the final novel in his European trilogy, which explored the hateful institution of capital punishment from the inside out. Taking the prejudice faced by a family born into the role of state executioner as its ostensible subject, the novel elicited Cooper's pronounced distaste for a savage practice on which Europe's glorious "Republics" depended to maintain social order and class relations. Like *The Bravo* (1830), the inaugural novel in the trilogy, *The Headsman* drew upon the thematic of the death penalty to attack so-called European Republics that were, in actuality, despotic oligarchies committed to protecting the interests of those in power.

In *The Headsman*, this point is most clearly illustrated in the contrast developed between Balthazar, the hereditary headsman of Berne and the novel's namesake, and Peter Hoffmeister, the hereditary bailiff of Vévey and a petty tyrant. Balthazar, on the one hand, is a virtuous, gentle man who gives voice to republican principles and who detests the profession to which tradition has condemned him. Peterchen (as the bailiff is called), on the other, is a snobbish elitist and minion of the state who relishes his authority and envies that of Balthazar, "the last avenger of law"—a title that Balthazar bears with self-loathing and that Peterchen pronounces, when we first meet him, with awe and admiration. Introduced as a parody of what Cooper's narrator criticizes as "the conservative principle,"[30] Peterchen later extols the virtues of authoritarian government and arbitrary rule in a lengthy speech he has occasion to deliver before the people: "The object of all authority is to find the means of its own support," he begins. "Thus, government is established in order that it may protect itself," he goes on. Near the end of the speech, he concludes by calling upon "Fellow citizens" to support a "government that likes itself, and whose first duty it is to protect itself and its officers at all hazards, even though it might by accident commit some seeming injustice."[31]

The Bravo, what many Cooper scholars consider his most overtly political novel, takes such a government and its mealy-mouthed rhetoric of legitimation as its principle object of analysis. Cooper, in fact, explicitly announces this purpose in the book's preface. He begins it by distinguishing monarchies from republics: "In the latter," he explains, "we find aristocracies and democracies blended in the same appellation."[32] Endeavoring "to give his countrymen, in this book, a picture of the social system of one of the *soi-disant* republics of the other hemisphere" (17), Cooper strives to disabuse fellow Americans of the high regard they may have for European nations through a political critique of the despotic regimes that support their cultures. Assuming, moreover, that a "history of the progress of political liberty, written purely in the interests of humanity, is still a desideratum in literature" (17), Cooper introduces his critique as an examination of the "false commencement" on which so-called European republics have been founded, noting that within them "it would be found that the *citizen*, or rather the *subject*, has extorted immunity after immunity, as his growing intelligence and importance have both instructed and required him to defend those particular rights which were necessary to his well-being" (17, emphasis added). Echoing Bailiff Peterchen in *The Headsman* but without the irony, Cooper highlights in *The Bravo*'s preface the curtailment of the citizen-subject's rights under oligarchies masquerading as republics. Although the novel takes form as an historical romance of the Republic of Venice in the early eighteenth century, its critique of European polity is not meant merely for philosophical contemplation but for immediate and practical action. "The mildest and justest governments in Europe are, at this moment," Cooper baldly declares in the preface, "theoretically despotisms" (18).

At that moment Cooper himself had been living for several years in Europe, where he had taken a keen interest in the political revolutions then unfolding in Poland, Czechoslovakia, and especially France, whose July Monarchy of 1830 had brought into power Louis Philippe, the self-professed "citizen-king." Initially supported by Marquis de Lafayette, France's arch-republican with whom Cooper had developed a close friendship while in Europe, Philippe soon renounced the republican platform on which he was elected in order to reestablish an oligarchy. It was to oppose this particular regime and to expose more generally the hypocrisy of European "Republics" that Cooper wrote *The Bravo*, what many critics rank among his best work despite its frequent reliance on authorial intrusions in which Cooper, as James Grossman puts it, "sometimes lectures for several pages on the nature of true republican institutions."[33] It is, in fact, through such intrusions that Cooper defines and develops his ideal of republican government; this definition, however, comes through a negative example exemplified, so to speak, through his detailed depiction of the historic Republic of Venice. Fundamental to his republican ideal is the overarching concept of "responsibility," a key term for Cooper and one that *The Bravo*'s narrator, at a crucial moment in the novel, identifies as "the essence of a free government" (417). More often, however, Cooper speaks to this ideal in the novel through its negative manifestation: the systemic deployment of "irresponsible power" (173, 174, 276, 282, 418), a term Cooper repeatedly uses to characterize the base principles by which the Venetian government operates. While the action of the novel illustrates this point through the bad example of a false republic, Cooper points toward a positive definition, one revolving around the concept of sovereign responsibility, in the concluding paragraph of the novel's preface: "Were we to characterize a republic," Cooper declares, "we should say it was a state in which power, both theoretically and practically, is derived from the nation, with constant responsibility of the agents of the republic to the people: a responsibility that is neither to be evaded nor denied" (18).

It is precisely this "constant responsibility" that underlies the vexed relation between sovereignty and responsibility, "of the agents of the republic to the people," that I have examined in terms of the death penalty in literature. Implicit throughout my study, this relation constituted the primary focus of my concluding chapter, which demonstrates the evasion of responsibility for the sovereign authority to put to death a citizen in a democratic republic. Such an act dramatizes what we might think of as a republican cognitive dissonance, a state in which the political state assumes absolute authority over the citizens it executes while end-lessly deferring responsibility for that supreme act of judgment. Such a scenario is, as I have argued, precisely what Dreiser describes in his critique of capital punishment and the criminal justice system in *An American Tragedy*. Yet nearly a century before Dreiser, Cooper demonstrated the point by way of a literary ex-ecution in *The Bravo*, a work in which "the government of Venice," as Cooper himself said, "became the hero of the tale."[34] More antihero than hero, the gov-ernment is pitted against the people, and the novel itself is structured around two executions. The first concludes volume 1 with the republic's covert assassina-tion of the poor, virtuous, old republican Antonio Vecchio in a scene that Coo-per's narrator, reflecting on it to begin volume 2, calls "the fearful execution of the fisherman" (207). The second dramatically unfolds in the novel's conclusion, which is built around the capture, condemnation, and public beheading of Ja-copi Frontoni, a reputed Bravo (and scapegoat of the state) who is framed by members of Venice's congress for Antonio's murder. The drama is heightened by the revelation of Jacopi's innocence of all past crimes attributed to him and by the impression the novel gives that Jacopi will be pardoned before the death sentence is carried out.

Cooper's critics have admired *The Bravo* in part because its climactic literary execution—the lawful beheading of the reputed Bravo—comes by way of Coo-per's literary execution, that is, his careful management of plot, character, spec-tacle, and other formal properties of narrative. Whereas Cooper concludes both *The Spy* and *The Ways of the Hour* by preventing the lawful executions toward which each novel's plot precipitously builds, "Cooper has in *The Bravo*," Donald A. Ringe argues, "the artistic integrity to end his narrative unhappily by allowing Jacopi to be killed unjustly as both the meaning and artistry of the book de-mand."[35] Robert Emmet Long similarly finds *The Bravo*, despite some minor flaws, to be "tonally perfect and unusually attentive to composition and form,"[36] while Grossman, in a classic biography on Cooper, finds in Jacopi's beheading "a brilliant reversal" in our readerly expectations that "stuns us into enlighten-ment."[37] Like Jacopi's beheading, many of the literary executions in *Literary Ex-ecutions* strive to stun readers into enlightenment.

૮ᵕ

Jacques Derrida, in his seminars on the death penalty shortly before his death (and in a posthumously published interview with Elizabeth Roudinesco)[38] re-peatedly insisted that literature—*not* philosophy—has historically provided an intellectual space for political resistance to capital punishment. Indeed, with the notable exception of Cesare Beccaria, Enlightenment and romantic philosophers generally assumed the necessity of the death penalty in articulating their theories of enlightened government. John Locke, whose political theory inspired both the United States' Declaration of Independence and Constitution, began the *Second Treatise of Government* (1690) by rationalizing capital punishment as the origin or foundation of law: "*Political Power* then I take to be *a Right* of making Laws with Penalties of Death," Locke wrote to begin the third and final point that concludes chapter 1 of the *Second Treatise*.[39] Jean-Jacques Rousseau similarly legitimated the death penalty in *The Social Contract* (1762), arguing in "On the Right of Life or Death" (book 2, chapter 5) that the citizen who breaks the law of the state "wages war with it," and "when the guilty party is put to death, it is less as a citizen than as an enemy."[40] Some thirty-five years later Immanuel Kant, in *The Philosophy of Law* (1796), defended capital punishment on the grounds of equality, contending that it was the only penalty commensurate with the crime of murder: "There is no *Likeness* or proportion between Life, however painful, and Death; and there is no Equality between the crime of Murder and the retaliation of it but what is judicially accomplished by the execution of the Criminal . . . The Equalization of Punishment with Crime is therefore only possible by the cognition of the Judge extending even to the penalty of Death."[41]

Four years before Kant rationalized the death penalty for murder, Benjamin Rush, as we saw in chapter 1, argued against such logic in *Considerations on the Injustice and Impolicy of Punishing Murder by Death* (1792). Twenty years after that, Livingston would write the first of his seminal penal reports that would command a transatlantic audience. In writing Cooper in 1829, Livingston hoped he could inspire a fellow citizen to make the American movement for abolition an international one. Such a campaign, however, would have to wait another hundred years for its international inauguration. When Cooper did take up the death penalty in literature after receiving Livingston's letter, even if not in direct response to it, he used the occasion to look across the Atlantic at the misuses of authority and the abrogation of responsibility in contemporary European "republics." Close to two centuries later, European republics today are now looking back across the Atlantic to the United States, once a worldwide leader in the campaign to end capital punishment, wondering when it will abandon by federal mandate what has become, in the twenty-first century, America's peculiar institution.

# Notes

### INTRODUCTION. The Cultural Rhetoric of Capital Punishment

1. For accounts of Hawthorne's interest in *The Record of Crimes*, see David S. Reynolds's *Beneath the American Renaissance* (New York: Random House, 1988), 23, and his *Waking Giant: America in the Age of Jackson* (New York: HarperCollins, 2009), 260. See also Harold Schechter's *True Crime: An American Anthology* (New York: Library of America, 2008), 69. Among the twenty-three criminal biographies included in *The Record of Crimes* was that of Francis Knapp, whose 1830 Salem trial and execution fascinated a young Hawthorne.

2. *The Record of Crimes in the United States* (Buffalo: H. Faxon & Company, 1834), v. Hereafter cited in text parenthetically.

3. *The Collected Writings of Walt Whitman: The Journalism*, vol. 1, 1834–1846, ed. Herbert Bergman, Douglas A. Noverr, and Edward J. Recchia (New York: Peter Lang, 1998), 160. Whitman's "Capital Punishment and Social Responsibility" was originally published in *The Sun*, Nov. 2, 1842.

4. Quinby, *The Gallows, the Prison, and the Poor-House: A Plea for Humanity; Showing the Demands of Christianity in Behalf of the Criminal and Perishing Classes* (Cincinnati: G. W. Quinby, 1856), 56–57, emphasis in original.

5. For an excellent analysis of the Tucker case, see Kristin Boudreau, "The Sweetheart of Death Row: Karla Faye Tucker and the Problem of Public Sentiment," in *The Spectacle of Death: Populist Literary Responses to American Capital Punishment* (Amherst: Prometheus Books, 2006), 187–202. Austin Sarat provides a superb analysis of *Last Dance*, alongside other recent films featuring the death penalty, in "State Killing in Popular Culture: Responsibility and Representation in *Dead Man Walking*, *Last Dance*, and *The Green Mile*," in *When the State Kills* (Princeton: Princeton UP, 2002), 209–46.

6. Written while the present study was near completion, Jones's book, *Against the Gallows: Antebellum American Writers and the Movement to Abolish Capital Punishment* (Iowa City: Iowa UP, 2011), is valuable (among other reasons) for its rich survey of popular-but-forgotten antebellum literary works in relation to death penalty reform. My work also addresses questions of literature in relation to this reform. In fact, I published two essays on the topic prior to Jones's work in the area (including a long overview article, "The Anti-gallows Movement in Antebellum America" in *Liberty Ltd.: Civil Rights, Civil Liberties, and Literature*, ed. Brook Thomas [Tübingen: Gunter Narr Verlag, 2006], 145–78), as well as a dissertation "Literary Executions" (University of California,

Irvine, 2005) that concerned the subject in relation to lynching as an illicit form of capital punishment. While sharing a similar focus and some authors with Jones, my approach differs considerably by engaging a law-and-literature perspective and by attending to questions of literary form over the long nineteenth century (not just the antebellum period). I also analyze figures Jones does not mention or only briefly discusses. Ultimately, however, *Literary Executions* and *Against the Gallows* complement each other and, read together, illustrate the importance of reassessing American literature before 1925 in terms of the controversies surrounding capital punishment.

7. More than anything else, Reynolds's landmark *Beneath the American Renaissance* has illustrated the importance of reading major American writers of the nineteenth century in relation to popular contemporaries and in terms of social movements of the day. The list is indeed long, but other influential works that focus on popular (as opposed to canonical) literature in this area include Jane Tompkins, *Sensational Designs: The Cultural Work of American Fiction, 1790–1860* (Oxford: Oxford UP, 1986); Michael Denning, *Mechanic Accents: Dime Novels and Working Class Culture in America* (New York: Verso, 1987); and Shelley Streeby, *American Sensations: Class, Empire, and the Production of Popular Culture* (Berkeley and Los Angeles: U of California P, 2002). Of these authors, Reynolds is the only one to note anti-gallows reform which he briefly mentions among other "important movements," including "naval reform, peace reform, prison reform, opposition to capital punishment, agrarianism, antidueling, education reform" (85).

8. Historian David Brion Davis first broke ground on the subject in a 1957 essay, "The Movement to Abolish Capital Punishment, 1787–1861," *American Historical Review* 63:1 (1957): 23–46, and in his study *Homicide in American Fiction: A Study of Social Values* (Ithaca: Cornell UP, 1957), a pioneering interdisciplinary study that, as one recent critic of murder in twentieth-century American culture puts it, "allows us a first glimpse at the discursive characteristics of murder narrative: the psychiatrization of the murderer; sexuality and gender as pathology; confession, secrecy, and truth; metaphysical speculation and the mystification of mortality." See Sara L. Knox, *Murder: A Tale of Modern American Life* (Durham: Duke UP, 1998), 5. Since then, however, relatively little work has been done on American literature and the death penalty, as Bruce H. Franklin notes in his important essay on the subject, "*Billy Budd* and Capital Punishment: A Tale of Three Centuries," *American Literature* 69:2 (1997): 337–59. For more recent work linking specific literary works to death penalty debates, see John Cyril Barton, "An American Travesty: Capital Punishment & the Criminal Justice System in Dreiser's *An American Tragedy*," *REAL (Research in English and American Literature)*, vol. 18, *Law and Literature*, ed. Brook Thomas (Tübingen: Gunter Narr Verlag, 2002), 357–84; John Cyril Barton, "The Anti-gallows Movement in Antebellum America," also in *REAL* (2006); Paul Christian Jones, "The Politics of Poetry: *The Democratic Review* and the Gallows Verse of William Wordsworth and John Greenleaf Whittier," *American Periodicals* 17 (2007): 1–25; Paul Christian Jones, "'I put my fingers around my throat and squeezed it, to know how it feels': Anti-gallows Sentimentalism and E. D. E. N. Southworth's *The Hidden Hand*," *Legacy* 25:1 (2008): 41–61; Paul Christian Jones, "'That I could look . . . on my own crucifixion and bloody crowning': Walt Whitman's Anti-gallows Writing and the Appeal to Christian Sympathy," *Walt Whitman Quarterly Review*

27 (Fall 2009): 1–27; and John Cyril Barton, "William Gilmore Simms & the Literary Aesthetics of Crime and Capital Punishment," *Law & Literature* 22:2 (2010): 220–43.

9. My use of *citizen-subject* owes much to Etienne Balibar's philosophical investigation of these terms in his essay "Citizen Subject," in *Who Comes after the Subject?*, ed. Eduardo Cadava, Peter Conner, and Jean-Luc Nancy (New York: Routledge, 1991), 33–57. My understanding of the *subject* and *subjectification* here are influenced by Louis Althusser's classic account of subject formation in "Ideology and Ideological State Apparatuses (Notes towards an Investigation)," in *Lenin and Philosophy, and Other Essays*, trans. Ben Brewster (New York: Monthly Review P, 1971), 127–86. I am not, however, suggesting an oppositional relationship between citizen and subject, as many recent critics have. As Brook Thomas reminds us in *Civic Myths*: "The fact that all citizens are subjects is important to stress, because a number of literary critics assume that advocates of citizenship deny it" (9). For an excellent overview of theoretical approaches toward studies of citizenship, see "Introduction: Working on/with Civic Myths," in Brook Thomas's *Civic Myths: A Law-and-Literature Approach to Citizenship* (Chapel Hill: U of North Carolina P, 2008), 1–26.

10. Cooper, *An American Democrat; or, Hints on the Social and Civic Relations of the United States of America* (Cooperstown: H. & E. Phinney, 1838), 9–10. Hereafter cited in text parenthetically.

11. This point, of course, almost goes without saying. I cite here only a few representative authorities. See Ian Watt, *The Rise of The Novel: Studies in Defoe, Richardson, and Fielding* (Berkeley and Los Angeles: U of California P, 1957); Georg Lukács, *The Historical Novel*, trans. Hannah Mitchell and Stanley Mitchell (Lincoln: U of Lincoln P, [1962] 1983); Frederic Jameson, *The Political Unconscious: Narrative as a Socially Symbolic Act* (Ithaca: Cornell UP, 1981); and Michael McKeon, *The Origins of the English Novel, 1640–1740* (Baltimore: Johns Hopkins UP, 1987).

12. Kristin Boudreau, *The Spectacle of Death: Populist Literary Responses to American Capital Punishment* (Amherst: Prometheus Books, 2006), 23, 21.

13. Rodensky, *The Crime in Mind* (New York: Oxford UP, 2003), 6.

14. Ibid., 5.

15. Mailloux, *Disciplinary Identities: Rhetorical Paths of English, Speech, and Composition* (New York: Modern Language Association, 2006), 2.

16. Mailloux, *Rhetorical Power* (Ithaca: Cornell UP, 1989), xii. For further discussions of rhetorical hermeneutics, see *Rhetorical Power*, ix–x, 57, 15–18, 133–35, and "Interpretation and Rhetorical Hermeneutics," in Mailloux's *Reception Histories: Rhetoric, Pragmatism, and American Cultural Politics* (Ithaca: Cornell UP, 1998), 43–71.

17. "As an exercise in cultural history," Masur writes in his introduction to *Rites of Execution: Capital Punishment and the Transformation of American Culture, 1776–1865* (New York: Oxford UP, 1989), "this book takes beliefs seriously. Ideas cannot be separated artificially from the so-called reality of society. Beliefs are themselves tangible and meaningful; thoughts are actions. Rituals, as cultural performances and dramatic representations, constitute a text that provides another window onto ideological assumptions, social relations, and collective fictions" (7).

18. See Halttunen, *Murder Most Foul: The Killer and the American Gothic Imagination* (Cambridge, MA: Harvard UP, 1998), 37–48.

19. Cohen, *Pillars of Salt, Monuments of Grace: New England Crime Literature and the Origins of American Popular Culture, 1674–1860* (Oxford: Oxford UP, 1993), 34.

20. See, especially, Thomas's *Cross-Examinations of Law and Literature* (Cambridge: Cambridge UP, 1989), as well as his *The Failed Promise of Contract and American Literature Realism* (U of California P, 1997) and *Civic Myths: A Law-and-Literature Approach to Citizenship.* A prime example of the New Historicism, Thomas's law-and-literature studies help to expose what Walter Benn Michaels, in *The Gold Standard and the Logic of Naturalism* (Berkeley: U of California P, 1987), famously describes as a unifying logic of a given age. In his most recent book, however, Thomas clarifies a misunderstanding of his work as attempting "to uncover a hidden 'logic' of an age." Rather, Thomas sees his work as "provid[ing] a perspective on literary and legal history as well as aspects of U.S. culture and society that is not available when these relatively autonomous disciplines are studied alone" (*Civic Myths*, preface).

21. Philip English Mackey, "Historical Introduction," in *Voices against Death: American Opposition to Capital Punishment, 1787–1977* (New York: Burt Franklin, 1977), xix.

22. Ibid., *Voices*, xxxix.

23. Qtd. in Stuart Banner, *The Death Penalty: An American History* (Cambridge, MA: Harvard UP, 2002), 213.

24. Ibid., 215.

25. Hayne, "Shall the Jury System Be Abolished?," *North American Review* 139:335 (1884): 354.

26. Qtd. in Banner 189. My discussion of the shift from the gallows to lethal electricity and gas in the administration of the death penalty draws from Banner's excellent account. See chap. 7, "Technological Cures," ibid., 168–207.

27. Qtd. in ibid., 198.

28. As Raymond Paternoster notes in *Capital Punishment in America* (New York: Lexington Books, 1991): "The first execution to take place under state authority occurred in Vermont, and not until January 20, 1864" (7).

29. Ibid., 7.

30. Masur 61.

31. Masur cites Garrison's use of the term *anti-republican* in reference to the death penalty (112). The material on Garrison and the *Liberator* that unfolds elsewhere in my argument is drawn from my own primary-source research.

32. See chap. 6, "The Two Abolitions," in Canuel's *The Shadow of Death: Literature, Romanticism, and the Subject of Punishment* (Princeton: Princeton UP, 2007), 142–67.

33. As Banner notes, "Lydia Child proposed circulating anti-capital punishment petitions along with anti-slavery petitions, because she knew that the same people would be willing to sign both" (136–37).

34. Parker, "Crime and Its Punishment," in *Sins and Safeguards of Society*, ed. Samuel B. Stewart (Boston: American Unitarian Association, 1907), 326.

35. Bovee, *Christ and the Gallows; or, Reasons for the Abolition of Capital Punishment* (New York: Masonic Publishing Company, 1869), 286–87.

36. Longfellow, "The Rope Walk," lines 18, 36–38, in *The Complete Poetic Works of Longfellow*, vol. 2 (Boston: Houghton Mifflin, 1893), 285.

37. Qtd. in S. D. Carpenter, *Logic of History: Five Hundred Political Texts; Being Concentrated Extracts of Abolitionism; Also, Results of Slavery Agitation and Emancipation*, 2nd ed. (Madison: S. D. Carpenter, 1864), 69. See 66–73 of Carpenter for a collection of contemporaneous responses to Brown's execution, including one by Horace Greeley that echoed Emerson's famous remarks: "John Brown, dead," Greeley asserted (and Carpenter quoted), "will live in millions of hearts. It will be easier to die in a good cause even on the gallows, since John Brown has hallowed that mode of exit from the troubles and temptations of this mortal existence" (qtd. in Carpenter 63).

38. *Liberator*, May 17, 1844. This edition of the *Liberator* also included extensive coverage and protest concerning the case of John L. Brown (not to be confused with the later John Brown of Harpers Ferry). Like his famous namesake, this Brown was also a white abolitionist; he was under sentence of death in South Carolina for aiding the escape of a fugitive female slave. One of the articles on this Brown case, titled "Man to be Hanged in America for Aiding the Escape of a Female Slave," mixed a particular statement against Brown's execution with a more general statement against capital punishment for any crime: "That the punishment of a human being by death, for any offence, is at all times most revolting,—that, while there are many, and they seem to be rapidly increasing, who deny the right to take away life by judicial sentence for any crime, there are others who deem it to be at least a questionable measure; but it is the opinion of this meeting [of the Glasgow Emancipation Society], that there will be few, if any, found, even under the most despotic governments, who will attempt to justify the punishing with death of John L. Brown" (*Liberator*, May 17). Many later reports in the *Liberator* chronicled or took up the anti-gallows cause more directly. For instance, an article published January 3, 1845 noted: "A meeting held at which Garrison and others resolve to petition the legislature to abolish capital punishment in this Commonwealth." A year later, the magazine published a "notice" to commemorate "the FIRST ANNIVERSARY OF THE MASSACHUSETTS SOCIETY FOR THE ABOLITION OF CAPTIAL PUNISHMENT" (*Liberator*, Jan. 9, 1846). For other representative anti-gallows reports or arguments in the *Liberator*, see articles published in the following editions: Feb. 7, 1845; June 1, 1845; Apr. 27, 1855; and Apr. 12, 1850.

39. For a recent history of the capital punishment in the state, see Alan Rogers's *Murder and the Death Penalty in Massachusetts* (Amherst: U of Massachusetts P, 2008).

40. See "Capital Punishment—an Exciting Scene in the Legislature," *New York Tribune*, Feb. 28, 1843.

41. My list of New York papers that supported the anti-gallows movement is culled from Philip English Mackey's *Hanging in the Balance: The Anti–Capital Punishment Movement in New York State, 1776–1861* (New York: Garland, 1982).

42. *The Hangman/The Prisoner's Friend* remained for some time the only periodical solely devoted to the cause. Four years after its first publication, its founder Charles Spear noted that it "is a remarkable fact that [*The Prisoners' Friend*] is the only journal known in the world that is wholly devoted to the Abolition of Capital Punishment and the Reformation of the Criminal" (June 3, 1849).

43. See *New York Tribune*, May 17, 1845.

44. Masur 136–37.

45. Duyckinck, "Death by Hanging," *Arcturus: A Journal of Books and Opinion* 3 (Jan. 1842): 98–103, 99.

46. For a discussion of the anti-gallows movement in relation to O'Sullivan and the Young America movement in literature, see Edward L. Widmer's *Young America: The Flowering of Democracy in New York City* (Oxford: Oxford UP, 2000), esp. 66–83.

47. Simms in a letter of Feb. 9, 1846, to Evert Duyckinck. See Simms, *The Letters of William Gilmore Simms*, ed. Mary C. Simms Oliphant, Alfred Taylor Odell, and T. C. Duncan Eaves (Columbia: U of South Carolina P, 1953), 142.

48. For an account of these circumstances, see Margaret B. Moore, *The Salem World of Nathaniel Hawthorne* (Columbia: U of Missouri P, 1998), 111–13.

49. For a brilliant analysis of higher-law arguments concerning slavery and race relations in the nineteenth century, see Gregg D. Crane's *Race, Citizenship, and Law in American Literature* (Cambridge: Cambridge UP, 2002). I adopt a similar line of argument in various moments in this book but look at higher-law appeals in terms of debate over capital punishment.

50. Saidiya V. Hartman, *Scenes of Subjection: Terror, Slavery, and Self-Making in Nineteenth-Century America* (New York: Oxford UP, 1997).

51. Spear, *Essays on the Punishment of Death* (Boston: C. Spear, 1845), 224. I am indebted to Bruce Franklin, who cites Spear on this double standard in his essay "*Billy Budd* and Capital Punishment."

52. Masur 157.

53. Among other articles, in the March 4, 1846, edition of the *Tribune*, Fuller attacked Cheever's stance in favor of capital punishment in a review of Cheever's book, *A Defence of the Punishment of Death* (New York: Wiley and Putnam, 1846). For a brief discussion of other articles in the *Tribune*, see Margaret Fuller, *Critic: Writings from the New-York Tribune, 1844–1846*, ed. Judith Mattson Bean and Joel Myerson (New York: Columbia UP, 2000).

54. Stanton, letter to Marvin H. Bovee, in *Christ and the Gallows*, 175.

55. Ibid., 173–74.

56. Stanton calls capital punishment a "relic of barbarism" in her letter written for Bovee's *Christ and the Gallows*. See Sumner's and Whittier's letters in Bovee's book for their uses of the term (56, 286). Others who denounce the death penalty in these terms in *Christ and the Gallows* include C. C. Washburne, Robert Laird Collier, and Theodore Tilton. In "Death by Hanging," Duyckinck says that "hanging is a remnant of barbarity" (99).

57. Qtd. in Bovee 174.

58. Jones makes this line of argument a focal point in *Against the Gallows*. In particular, see his chapters on Whitman and E. D. E. N. Southworth.

59. Spear, *The Hangman* (Boston: Charles Spear, 1845), 69. I am indebted to Jarrod Roark for pointing me to this material from *The Hangman* and *The Prisoner's Friend* and helping me integrate it into my argument.

60. Spear, *The Prisoner's Friend* (Boston: Charles Spear, 1845), 169.

61. Reynolds 70.

62. Poe, *Edgar Allan Poe: Selected Stories* (Oxford: Oxford UP, 1998), 231; Whitman, "Revenge and Requital: A Tale of a Murderer Escape," *United States Magazine and the Democratic Review* 17 (July–Aug. 1845): 106; Southworth, "Thunderbolt to the Hearth,"

in *Old Neighborhoods and New Settlements; or, Christmas Evening Legends* (Philadelphia: Hart and Carey, 1858), 88; Darrow, *An Eye for an Eye*, ed. R. Baird Shuman (Durham: Moore, 1969).

63. For additional discussions concerning temperance and temperance reform in nineteenth-century American literature, see in particular the collection of essays edited by David S. Reynolds and Debra J. Rosenthal, *The Serpent in the Cup: Temperance in American Literature* (Amherst: U of Massachusetts P, 1997). Other recent work on temperance and temperance reform in nineteenth-century American literature includes Ryan C. Cordell, "'Enslaving You, Body and Soul': The Uses of Temperance in *Uncle Tom's Cabin* and 'Anti-Tom' Fiction," *Studies in American Fiction* 36:1 (2008): 3–26; John Crowley, *The White Logic: Alcoholism and Gender in American Modernist Fiction* (Amherst: U of Massachusetts P, 1994); Eric Gardner, "Forgotten Manuscripts: William Jay Greenly's Antebellum Temperance Drama," *African American Review* 42:3–4 (2008): 389–406; Glenn Hendler, *Public Sentiments: Structures of Feeling in Nineteenth-Century American Literature* (Chapel Hill: U of North Carolina P, 2001); Robert S. Levine, "Disturbing Boundaries: Temperance, Black Elevation, and Violence in Frank J. Webb's *The Garies and Their Friends*," *Prospects: An Annual Journal of American Cultural Studies* 19 (1994): 349–73; George Monteiro, *Stephen Crane's Blue Badge of Courage* (Baton Rouge: Louisiana State UP, 2000); Gretchen Murphy, "Enslaved Bodies: Figurative Slavery in the Temperance Fiction of Harriet Beecher Stowe and Walt Whitman," *Genre: Forms of Discourse and Culture* 28 (Spring–Summer 1995): 95–118; Elaine Frantz Parsons, *Manhood Lost: Fallen Drunkards, and Redeeming Women in the Nineteenth-Century United States* (Baltimore: Johns Hopkins UP, 2003); Reynolds, *Beneath the American Renaissance*; Michael Warner, "Whitman Drunk," in *Publics and Counterpublics* (New York: Zone Books, 2002); Nicholas Warner, *Spirits of America: Intoxication in Nineteenth-Century American Literature* (Norman: U of Oklahoma P, 1997); Susan Marjorie Zieger, *Inventing the Addict: Drugs, Race, and Sexuality in Nineteenth-Century British and American Literature* (Amherst: U of Massachusetts P, 2008). I am grateful to Jarrod Roark for help with this bibliography.

64. For additional discussions concerning race and slavery in nineteenth-century American literature, see in particular Eric J. Sundquist, *To Wake the Nation: Race in the Making of American Literature* (Cambridge, MA: Belknap-Harvard UP, 1993). See also the following works in the Cambridge Studies in American Literature and Culture Series: Gregg D. Crane, *Race, Citizenship, and Law in American Literature* (Cambridge: Cambridge UP, 2002); John D. Kerkering, *The Poetics of National and Racial Identity in Nineteenth-Century American Literature* (New York: Cambridge UP, 2009); Maurice S. Lee, *Slavery, Philosophy, and American Literature, 1830–1860* (New York: Cambridge UP, 2005); Arthur Riss, *Race, Slavery, and Liberalism in Nineteenth-Century American Literature* (New York: Cambridge UP, 2006). Other recent work on race and slavery in nineteenth-century American literature includes Katherine Clay Bassard, "Private Interpretations: The Defense of Slavery, Nineteenth-Century Hermeneutics, and the Poetry of Frances E. W. Harper," in *There before Us: Religion and American Literature, from Emerson to Wendell Berry*, ed. Roger Lundin (Grand Rapids, MI: Eerdmans, 2007); Diane N. Capitani, *Truthful Pictures: Slavery Ordained by God in the Domestic, Sentimental Novel of the Nineteenth Century South* (Lanham, MD: Lexington Books, 2009); Kathleen Diffley, "The Roil of Contemporary Debate: Uncovering

Literature and Culture in Nineteenth-Century America," *Journal of the Midwest Modern Language Association* 35:1 (2002): 88–95; Michael T. Gilmore, *Slavery, Race, and Free Speech in American Literature* (Chicago: U of Chicago P, 2010); John C. Inscoe, "Slavery and African Americans in the Nineteenth Century," in *High Mountains Rising: Appalachia in Time and Place*, ed. Richard A. Straw and H. Tyler Blethen (Urbana: U of Illinois P, 2004); Agnieszka Soltysik Monnet, *The Poetics and Politics of the American Gothic: Gender and Slavery in Nineteenth-Century American Literature* (Surrey: Ashgate, 2010); and two recent dissertations: Andrea Stone, "Healthy: Medicine, Law, Literature and a Nineteenth-Century Black Rhetorics of Physicality" (Ph.D. diss., U of Toronto, 2009), and Mark F. Wood, "Crises of Authority: Honor Violence in Nineteenth-Century American Literature" (Ph.D. diss., U of Kentucky, 2006). I am grateful to Jarrod Roark for help with this bibliography.

65. See, for instance, Robert Weisberg's discussion of "law *in* literature" in his seminal essay, "The Law and Literature Enterprise," *Yale Journal of Law and the Humanities* 1:1 (1989): 1–67, and Robert Cover's discussion of the legal process, especially in criminal law, as "inherently dramatic" in his essay, "The Bonds of Constitutional Interpretation: Of the Word, the Deed, and the Role," *Georgia Law Review* 20 (1986): 815–33. It is also important to note that critics not working directly in law and literature have called attention to the way a legal form, particularly that of a criminal trial, helps to structure, resolve, or bring to a climax the central drama of a literary work. For instance, in his analysis of *Bleak House* in *The Novel and the Police* (Berkeley and Los Angeles: U of California P, 1988), D. A. Miller argues that Dickens's use of the criminal trial simplifies and resolves the more complicated issues the novel raises through the civil suit of *Jarndyce vs. Jarndyce*.

66. Attending in these ways to questions of form, the present work contributes to what Marjorie Levinson and others have termed the "New Formalism": a movement rather than a coherent methodology positioned, as its name suggests, against the New Historicism and positing, in a variety of ways, a return to aesthetic form and its importance in cultural studies. See Levinson, "What Is New Formalism?," *PMLA* 122:2 (2007): 558–69. At the same time, however, my work squarely works within the New Historicist paradigm exemplified in law-and-literature studies by Brook Thomas, Wai Chee Dimock, Gregg D. Crane, and Deak Nabers.

67. Morrow, "Capital Punishment," in *American Literature through History*, vol. 1, ed. Tom Quirk and Gary Scharnhorst (New York: Scribner's, 2006), 202.

68. Guest, *Sentenced to Death: The American Novel and Capital Punishment* (Jackson: UP of Mississippi, 1998), xv–xvi. See also Anne Algeo, *The Courtroom as Forum* (New York: P. Lang, 1996). Technically, Guest starts with *McTeague* (1899), an odd beginning by Guest's own admission since this novel, unlike the others he examines, does not include an execution scene or deal with the criminal justice system or the death penalty. Concentrating on Frank Norris's *McTeague*, Dreiser's *An American Tragedy*, Richard Wright's *Native Son*, Truman Capote's *In Cold Blood*, and Norman Mailer's *Executioner's Song*, Guest sees the twentieth-century execution novel as a successor to the nineteenth-century "diagnostic biography," his term for popular criminal biographies, confession narratives, and court transcripts that are exemplified, one might say, in *The Record of Crimes in the United States*, best-selling anthology of notorious criminals. Algeo, in *The Courtroom as Forum*, treats the same novels as Guest, save for

*McTeague.* She claims that since the publication of An American Tragedy, a major American novel engaging the death penalty has been published roughly every fifteen years. While sharing some of Guest's and Algeo's concerns, my study of American literature and capital punishment over the long nineteenth century goes beyond telling "the story of a life that leads to the gallows" in order to get at how those stories contributed to an interstate campaign to abolish capital punishment.

CHAPTER 1.  Anti-gallows Activism in Antebellum American Law and Literature

1. For a comprehensive history of New York's engagement with anti-gallows activism, see Philip English Mackey's *Hanging in the Balance: The Anti–Capital Punishment Movement in New York State, 1776–1861* (New York: Garland, 1982). Mackey's study also provides a detailed account of the anti-gallows movement in eighteenth- and early nineteenth-century Pennsylvania.

2. David Brion Davis, *Homicide in American Fiction* (Ithaca: Cornell UP, 1957), 296.

3. Philip English Mackey, "Historical Introduction," in *Voices against Death: American Opposition to Capital Punishment, 1787–1977* (New York: Burt Franklin, 1977), xxii.

4. Davis 299.

5. John Neal, *Logan: A Family History,* 2 vols. (Philadelphia: H. C. Carey and I. Lea, 1822), 8. Hereafter cited in text parenthetically.

6. Edward Livingston, *The Complete Works of Edward Livingston on Criminal Jurisprudence,* vol. 1, Series in Criminology, Law Enforcement, and Social Problems (repr., Montclair, NJ: Patterson Smith, 1968), 43.

7. Ibid., 44.

8. Neal and Livingston, here, are making an argument about the spectacle of sovereign violence inflicted upon the body of the condemned long before Michel Foucault developed that argument in the opening chapters of *Discipline and Punish: The Birth of the Prison,* trans. Alan Sheridan (New York: Pantheon Books, 1977). It should also be noted that Livingston's writings against the death penalty were extremely influential in France when that country experienced its own movement to abolish capital punishment, from roughly 1826 to 1831. Indeed, Livingston's work, which was widely reviewed and discussed in French newspapers (most notably *Le Globe*), helped initiate the debate in that country. For a discussion of Livingston's impact on the abolition movement in France, see Sonja Hamilton's "La plume et le couperet: enjeux politiques et litteraires de la peine de mort autour de 1830" (Ph.D. diss., Johns Hopkins U, 2003), 71–73.

9. Livingston 45.

10. Qtd. in Louis P. Masur, *Rites of Execution: Capital Punishment and the Transformation of American Culture* (New York: Oxford UP, 1989), 117.

11. Ibid.

12. Neal, *Wandering Recollections of a Somewhat Busy Life: An Autobiography* (Boston: Roberts Brothers, 1869), 390.

13. Ibid.

14. Ibid.

15. In his "Historical Introduction," Mackey provides a description of public executions and legislative responses to them that resonates with Neal's account in *Logan*

and is therefore worth quoting at length: "To many Americans in the 1820s and 1830s, the most obvious flaw in the institution of capital punishment was public executions, which, intended as a sobering and edifying ceremony, had too often turned into a disgraceful scene of commercialism, riot, and bloodlust. A scheduled hanging could be expected to draw thousands, sometimes tens of thousands, of eager viewers. Exploited by local merchants, plied with drink and excited by the prospect of a bloodcurdling event, witnesses often become unruly. Pushing and fighting were not uncommon as the victim was led to the scaffold or as the crowds surged to view the corpse. Cursing onlookers might revile the widow or tear at the scaffold and rope for souvenirs. Drunkenness and violence at times ruled the town far into the night after such a display of public justice" (xx). Following this description, Mackey writes: "Appalled by such scenes, legislators in northern states, beginning with Rhode Island in 1833, Pennsylvania in 1834, and New York, Massachusetts, and New Jersey in 1835, enacted laws calling for private hangings" (xx). In his more recent *The Death Penalty: An American History* (Cambridge, MA: Harvard UP, 2002), legal historian Stuart Banner notes that Connecticut, which is not mentioned by Mackey, was the first state to abolish public executions in 1830, eight years after the publication of *Logan*. For an excellent discussion of the movement toward private executions, see "Into the Jail Yard," chapter 6 of Banner's book.

16. Masur 54. For a reception history of Beccaria's *On Crimes and Punishment* in eighteenth-century America, see also Paul Spurlin, "Beccaria's Essay on Crimes and Punishments in Eighteenth-Century America," *Studies on Voltaire and the Eighteenth Century* 27 (1963): 1489–1504.

17. Beccaria found the death penalty justifiable only in times of war when the imprisonment, rather than execution, of a condemned political figure jeopardized the security of the state or when the execution of a condemned citizen was "the one and only deterrent to dissuade others from committing crimes." See Cesare Beccaria, *On Crimes and Punishments*, ed. David Young (Indianapolis: Hackett, 1986), 48. Hereafter cited in text parenthetically.

18. Montesquieu takes up the general question of sovereign authority in relation to civil and criminal laws in volume 1, book 6 of *The Spirit of Laws* (1748; English ed., 1750) He writes specifically about tyranny in book 19, in the course of which he coins the influential phrase: "All punishment which is not derived from necessity is tyrannical." See Baron de Montesquieu, *The Spirit of Laws* (New York: Prometheus Books, 2002), 299. Beccaria makes this broad point the specific focus of *On Crimes and Punishments*. For instance, he begins chapter 2, "The Right to Punish," with the following claim: "Every punishment which does not derive from absolute necessity, says the great Montesquieu, is tyrannical. The proposition may be made general thus: every act of authority between one man and another that does not derive from absolute necessity is tyrannical. Here, then, is the foundation of the sovereign's right to punish crimes: the necessity of defending the depository of the public welfare against the usurpations of private individuals" (8).

19. Masur 53.

20. Ibid.

21. Benjamin Rush, *Considerations on the Injustice and Impolicy of Punishing Murder by Death* (Philadelphia: Carey, 1792), 18–19, emphasis in original.

22. Ibid., 19.

23. Robert Rantoul Jr. *Memoirs, Speeches and Writings of Robert Rantoul, Jr.*, ed. Luther Hamilton (Boston: J. P. Jewett, 1854), 428. Hereafter cited in text parenthetically.

24. Rantoul's Christian argument was popularized by Charles Spear in *Essays on the Punishment of Death* (Boston: Spear, 1844), a study that, by May 1845, had sold more than five thousand copies and by 1846 had gone through seven editions (Masur 136–37).

25. Hugo Adam Bedau, preface to *Voices against Death: American Opposition to Capital Punishment, 1787–1977*, ed. Philip English Mackey (New York: Burt Franklin, 1977), v.

26. O'Sullivan, *Report in Favor of the Abolition of the Punishment of Death by Law* (New York: Arno Press, 1974), 5. Hereafter cited in text parenthetically.

27. Robert D. Sampson, *John L. O'Sullivan and His Times* (Kent: Kent State UP, 2003), 101.

28. Livingston 201.

29. Ibid., 201–2.

30. The society soon changed its name to the New York State Society for the Abolition of Capital Punishment. The *Anti-Draco*, edited by O'Sullivan, was not published beyond its maiden issue of March 1844.

31. O'Sullivan, "The Gallows and the Gospel," *United States Magazine and Democratic Review* 12:57 (1843): 227–36, 227. Hereafter cited in text parenthetically.

32. Mackey, "Historical Introduction," xxiii–xxiv.

33. For Cheever's reference to Genesis 9:6 as "the Divine Statute," see *Punishment by Death: Its Authority and Expediency* (New York: John Wiley, 1849), 120. Cheever identifies the verse as the "citadel of the argument" on the first night of his debate with O'Sullivan at the Tabernacle. See "Argument in Reply to J. L. O'Sullivan, Esq." appended to *Punishment by Death*, 236.

34. Cheever, *The Punishment of Death*, 162.

35. Cheever, *A Defence of Capital Punishment* (New York: Wiley and Putnam, 1846), 49.

36. See Cheever, *Capital Punishment: The Argument of Rev. George B. Cheever, in Reply to J. L. O'Sullivan* (New York: Saxton and Miles, 1843), 39. In the introduction to the second part of his first book, *Punishment by Death: Its Authority and Expedience*, Cheever directly attacked the interpretation O'Sullivan had popularized of Genesis 9:6 as *prediction* rather than command: "It is argued by our opponents that the statute in Genesis is simply and merely permissive, but not an injunction. But it follows, according to this construction, that God gives to any and every man the permission to kill the murderer" (120). For discussions of the O'Sullivan–Cheever debate, see Masur (147–52), Sampson (101–4), and Mackey (*Hanging*, 181–83).

37. Between October 1837 and April 1845, Hawthorne contributed twenty-three works to the *Democratic Review* (Hawthorne, *Selected Letters of Nathaniel Hawthorne*, ed. Joel Myerson [Columbus: Ohio UP, 2002], 139). In addition to "Egotism, or the Bosom Serpent," Hawthorne's "The Artist of the Beautiful" was published along with "Capital Punishment: The Proceeding of the Recent Convention of the Friends of the Abolition of the Punishment of Death" in the *Democratic Review*'s June 1844 issue. In August 1846, moreover, an article Hawthorne edited, "Papers of an Old Dartmoor Prisoner," was

published alongside "An Essay on the Ground and Reason of Punishment," a featured work that attacked the death penalty and advocated for its abolition.

38. Hawthorne, "Earth's Holocaust," *Mosses From an Old Manse* (Columbus: Ohio State UP, 1974), 381. Hereafter cited in text parenthetically.

39. Hawthorne, "The New Adam and Eve," *Mosses From an Old Manse* (Columbus: Ohio State UP, 1974), 247. Hereafter cited in text parenthetically.

40. Whittier, "Lines, Written on Reading Several Pamphlets Published by Clergymen against the Abolition of the Gallows," *United States Magazine and Democratic Review* 11:52 (1842): 374–375, 375.

41. Whittier, "Human Sacrifice," *Democratic Review* 12:59 (1843): 475–78. The poem was reprinted in Whittier's collection, *Songs of Labor and Reform*. Further citations appear in text parenthetically by line number.

42. See Masur 141–50, for a discussion of a conservative Protestant response to anti-gallows reformers. For representative works by Waterbury, see *The Brighten Age: A Poem* (Boston: Crocker and Brewster, 1830); *Advice to a Young Christian, on the Importance of Aiming at an Elevated Standard of Piety* (New York: American Tract Society, 1843); and *Sketches of Eloquent Preachers* (New York: American Tract Society, 1864).

43. W, "Correspondence of the N. Y. Evangelist," *New York Evangelist* 13:49 (Dec. 8, 1842): 192.

44. "Abolition of the Death Penalty in Massachusetts," *Liberator*, March 1854, 52.

45. Ibid.

46. For Cheever's praise of Wordsworth or use of the poet to support his work, see *Punishment by Death*, 157, 184, 221–22. Cheever claims, for instance, that Wordsworth "communicate[s] a power and majesty to the whole theory and practice of a just human law, of which it were a fearful thing if the state should be shorn" (157). If in *Punishment by Death* Cheever holds up Wordsworth as a positive literary example, in *A Defense of Capital Punishment* Cheever points to Dickens as a bad example, at one point lamenting how the great novelist sentimentalizes the execution scene rather than seeing it as a solemn warning: "We cannot avoid being struck with this shameful inconsistency in one who, perhaps, ranks yet as the most popular novelist of the age. No man indulges in more of this mischievous sentimentalism than Dickens" (51).

47. O'Sullivan, "Wordsworth's Sonnets on the Punishment of Death," *United States Magazine and Democratic Review* 10:45 (1842): 272–88, 272.

48. Ibid., 273.

49. Ibid., 279, emphasis in original.

50. For Whitman's many anti-gallows writings, see *The Collected Writings of Walt Whitman: The Journalism*, vol. 1, *1834–1846*, ed. Herbert Bergman, Douglas A. Noverr, and Edward J. Recchia (New York: Peter Lang, 1998). For an excellent discussion of Whitman's work in this context, see Paul Christian Jones, "'That I could look . . . on my own crucifixion and bloody crowning': Walt Whitman's Anti-gallows Writing and the Appeal to Christian Sympathy," *Walt Whitman Quarterly Review* 27 (Fall 2009): 1–27.

51. Walt Whitman, "A Dialogue," *United States Magazine and Democratic Review* 17:89 (1845): 360–64, 360. Hereafter cited in text parenthetically.

52. In light of the convict's argument, it is interesting to note that, for a short time later in the nineteenth century, the state of New York *did* make it illegal for the press to represent or provide the details of an execution. As legal scholar Michael Madow ex-

plains: "In 1888, the New York legislature, having grown impatient with what it believed were sensationalistic news reports, made it a crime for any newspaper to publish the details of an execution. The New York press defied the ban and waged a vigorous and successful campaign for its repeal on behalf of 'the people's right to know'" (467). See Madow, "Forbidden Spectacle: Executions, the Public and the Press in Nineteenth Century New York," *Buffalo Law Review* 43 (Fall 1995): 462–562.

53. Whitman, "Hurrah for Hanging!," in *The Uncollected Poetry and Prose of Walt Whitman*, ed. Emory Holloway, vol. 1 (New York: Peter Smith, 1932), 108–9.

54. Lippard, *The Quaker City*, ed. David S. Reynolds (Amherst: U of Massachusetts P, 1995). See book 5, chapter 3 of Lippard's novel, "Hurrah for the Gallows!," 503–11.

55. Hawthorne, *The Scarlet Letter*, eds. William Charvat, Roy Harvey Pearce, Claude M. Simpson, Fredson Bowers, and Matthew J. Bruccoli (Columbus: Ohio UP, 1962).

56. Ibid., 37.

57. Ibid., 38.

58. Ibid., 39.

59. In *Hawthorne's Mad Scientists: Pseudoscience and Social Science in Nineteenth-Century Life and Letters* (Hamden: Archon Books, 1978), Taylor Stoehr argues that Hawthorne likely drew from Charles Spear in creating Hollingsworth's character: "Some readers have thought that [noted activist and early transcendentalist] Orestes Brownson was Hawthorne's model," but Stoehr sees Spear as a "likelier candidate" (227). Stoehr explores other possible models for Hollingsworth, such as "Judge John W. Edmonds, President of the Board of Inspectors at Sing Sing and founder in 1844 of the New York Prison Association" and "Reverend William Henry Channing, one of the Prison Association's most active members," but "only Charles Spear was as unswervingly devoted to his one career as Hollingsworth" (227–28).

60. In "P.'s Correspondence," *Mosses from an Old Manse*, vol. 2 of *Hawthorne's Works* (Boston: Houghton, Mifflin, 1882), Hawthorne pays odd homage to Neal: "How slowly our literature grows up! Most of our writers of promise have come to untimely ends. There was that wild fellow, John Neal, who almost turned my boyish brain with his romances; he surely has long been dead, else he never could keep himself so quiet" (*Mosses* 426). For accounts of Neal's influence on Hawthorne, see Benjamin Lease, *That Wild Fellow John Neal and the American Literary Revolution* (Chicago: U of Chicago P, 1972). See also Reynolds's "Hawthorne's Cultural Demons," chapter 9 in *Beneath the American Renaissance* (Cambridge, MA: Harvard UP, 1988) for an account of Hawthorne's interest in gallows and crime literature.

61. Melville, *White Jacket; or, the World in a Man-of-War* (Evanston: Northwestern UP, 2000), 292. Hereafter cited in text parenthetically.

62. Thoreau, "A Plea for John Brown," *Political Writings*, ed. Nancy L. Rosenblum (Cambridge: Cambridge UP, 1996), 156.

63. Qtd. in Jones, *Against the Gallows* (Iowa City: U of Iowa P, 2011), 27.

64. Ibid.

65. Qtd. in Louis Ruchames, ed., *A John Brown Reader* (London: Abelard-Schuman, 1959), 296.

66. For a discussion of this unsent letter, see Edward Waldo Emerson and Waldo Emerson Forbes, eds., *Journals of Ralph Waldo Emerson, 1856–1863* (Boston: Houghton Mifflin, 1913), 239–41.

67. Alexis de Tocqueville provides an international perspective on the anti-gallows reform movement in the second volume of *Democracy in America*, trans. Harvey C. Mansfield and Delba Winthrop (Chicago: U of Chicago P, 2000): "There is no country where criminal justice is administered with more kindness than in the United States. Whereas the English seem to want to preserve carefully the bloody traces of the Middle Ages in their penal legislation, the Americans have almost made the death penalty disappear from their codes. North America is, I think, the sole region on earth where for fifty years the life of not a single citizen has been taken for political offenses" (538).

### CHAPTER 2. Simms, Child, and the Aesthetics of Crime and Punishment

1. Simms, *Beauchampe; or, the Kentucky Tragedy; A Sequel to Charlemont* (Chicago: S. A. Maxwell, 1888), 335.

2. For representative accounts of how print technology in the 1830s and 1840s led to a proliferation of crime literature, see David Ray Papke, *Framing the Criminal: Crime, Cultural Work, and the Loss of Critical Perspective, 1830–1900* (Hamden: Archon Books, 1987); Daniel A. Cohen, *Pillars of Salt, Monuments of Grace: New England Crime Literature and the Origins of American Popular Culture, 1674–1860* (Oxford: Oxford UP, 1994); Karen Halttunen, *Murder Most Foul: The Killer and the American Gothic Imagination* (Cambridge, MA: Harvard UP, 1998); and Stuart Banner, *The Death Penalty: An American History* (Cambridge, MA: Harvard UP, 2002).

3. As W. B. Gates notes, Simms's revisions mainly consisted in dividing the 1842 two-volume edition of *Beauchampe* into two separate novels and adding descriptive chapter headings to each. Volume 1 was retitled *Charlemont; or, the Pride of the Village*; volume 2 was retitled *Beauchampe; or, The Kentucky Tragedy; A Sequel to Charlemont*. See Gates, "William Gilmore Simms and the Kentucky Tragedy," *American Literature* 32 (May 1960): 158–66.

4. In this chapter, I examine the arguments of Leonard Bacon and, especially, George Barrell Cheever as representative of a pro-gallows ministry. Other prominent work by such figures include John McLeod, *The Capital Punishment of the Murderer: An Unrepealed Ordinance of God* (New York: Robert Carter, 1842), and William Patton, *Capital Punishment Sustained by Reason of the Word of God* (New York: Dayton and Newman, 1842), both published the same year as Simms's first edition of *Beauchampe*.

5. See Cohen, particularly the introductory overview and part 1 of his study.

6. A recent edition of Cooper's *The Ways of the Hour* (Amsterdam: Fredonia Books, 2002) makes this point on the book's back cover: "*The Ways of the Hour* should be considered a classic in the history of the mystery novel—as it is perhaps the first novel to revolve almost entirely about a courtroom murder trial." Other well-known novels—such as Brown's *Wieland*, Scott's *The Heart of the Midlothean*, and Dickens's *Bleak House*—involve significant courtroom and trial scenes as a component of their plots, but Cooper's final novel is the first (that I have found) to revolve around a capital trial from start to finish. Beginning with the investigation of an arson and double murder, *The Ways of the Hour* documents the behind-the-scenes lawyering and development of legal strategies, the interviewing of witnesses, and the unfolding of legal procedures, such as the process of jury selection. Moreover, the novel culminates with the drama of a courtroom trial and concludes with a verdict and the formal act of sentencing. Today,

of course, this formula is often employed by writers of popular crime novels and legal thrillers, but Cooper is likely the first novelist to use it to structure an entire work.

7. A study of criminal propensity within a single family, McConnel's novel attends to the circumstances that help to create a criminal but focuses on hereditary traits passed on from one generation to another. "The outline of the following story," McConnel writes in the preface, "was designed to illustrate certain mental and moral laws by which characteristics are transmitted from parent to offspring—and thus to show how 'the sins of the father are visited upon the children, even from the third and fourth generation'" (iii). Published the same year as *The House of the Seven Gables*, McConnel's Hawthornian tale of "the sins of the father" centers around the villainous James Glenn, who murders his rival and frames his cousin Henry Glenn for the crime. See *The Glenns: A Family History* (New York: Scribner's, 1851).

8. Ibid, 152.

9. Thompson, *The Rangers; or, The Tory's Daughter*, vol. 1 (Boston: Benjamin B. Mussey and Company, 1851), 66.

10. My notion of the aesthetics of crime and capital punishment owes much to Joel Black's concept of "the aesthetics of murder" and what Austin Sarat calls "the cultural life of capital punishment." See Black, *The Aesthetics of Murder: A Study in Romantic Literature and Contemporary Culture* (Baltimore: Johns Hopkins UP, 1991), and Sarat, *When the State Kills: Capital Punishment and the American Condition* (Princeton: Princeton UP, 2001). For an inquiry into the aesthetics of capital punishment that complements mine, see the essays in "Symposium: The Art of Execution," published in the summer issue of *Law and Literature* 15:2 (2003), especially Ed Morgan's "On Art and the Death Penalty: 'Invitation to a Beheading'," 279–91. For an analysis of recent scholarship treating crime and crime fiction, see Gregg Crane's "Reasonable Doubts: Crime and Punishment," *American Literary History* 18:4 (2006): 797–813.

11. See John Caldwell Guilds's *Simms: A Literary Life* (Fayetteville: U of Arkansas P, 1992) for the most recent and thorough literary biography of Simms's life. According to Guilds, Simms published eighty-two books (112). The influential southern journals Simms edited were *Magnolia; or, Southern Appalachian* (1842–43), the *Southern and Western Monthly Magazine and Review* (1849–54), and the *Southern Quarterly Review* (1849–54). He was also a founding editor of *The Album* and the *Southern Literary Gazette*. For other biographical accounts of Simms, see J. V. Ridgley's *William Gilmore Simms* (New York: Twayne Publishers, 1962); Jon L. Wakelyn's *The Politics of a Literary Man: William Gilmore Simms* (Westport: Greenwood Press, 1973); and Charles S. Watson's *From Nationalism to Secessionism: The Changing Fiction of William Gilmore Simms* (Westport: Greenwood Press, 1993). My discussion of Simms's life draws from these sources, especially Guilds's *Simms*.

12. Review by Edgar Allan Poe in *Broadway Journal*, Sept. 20, 1845.

13. See Guilds, *Simms*, 123–24. Simms, in a letter to James Lawson, claims to have lost the "Lt. Gov. by one vote, & this with 9/10ths of the Legislature in my favor." See *The Letters of William Gilmore Simms*, vol. 2, ed. Mary C. Simms Oliphant, Alfred Taylor Odell, and T. C. Duncan Eaves (Columbia: U of South Carolina P, 1953), 251.

14. Modern biographies of Child—including Helene G. Baer's *The Heart Is Like Heaven: The Life of Lydia Maria Child* (Philadelphia: U of Pennsylvania P, 1964); Milton

Meltzer's *Tongue of Flame: The Life of Lydia Maria Child* (New York: Crowell, 1965); William S. Osborne's *Lydia Maria Child* (Boston: Twayne Publishing, 1980); Deborah Pickman Clifford's *Crusader for Freedom: A Life of Lydia Maria Child* (Boston: Beacon Press, 1992); and Carolyn L. Karcher's *The First Woman in the Republic: A Cultural Biography of Lydia Maria Child* (Durham: Duke UP, 1994)—each include a brief reference or a few sporadic ones to Child's interest in the abolition of capital punishment. Osborne (with three separate references) and especially Karcher (with eight) have the most to say on the subject, but none of these biographers treat Child in the context of death penalty reform or examine her fiction in terms of anti-gallows thematics and activism. Karcher is the only one to comment on the fiction in this regard, noting in an endnote that "'The Juryman' is especially remarkable for its insights into the violent impulses that the partisans of capital punishment share with the criminals they would chastise" (709). I am grateful to Carolyn Karcher for pointing me to other Child stories ("Elizabeth Wilson," "Hilda Silfverling," and "Rosenglory") that engage questions about crime and criminal injustice. Very little has been published on the Child stories I consider in this chapter, and nothing that discusses them (save for "The Juryman") in relation to the anti-gallows movement in which Child participated by attacking capital punishment in her popular New York letters.

15. Spear frequently cites Child, along with Rantoul and O'Sullivan, in grounding his arguments against capital punishment. For Spear's references to Child, see *Essays on the Punishment of Death*, 10th ed. (Boston: published by the author, 1845), 114, 200, 208–10.

16. Louis P. Masur, *Rites of Execution: Capital Punishment and the Transformation of American Culture, 1776–1865* (New York: Oxford UP,1989), 122.

17. For *Woodcraft* as Simms's response to Stowe, see Joseph V. Ridgley, "*Woodcraft*: Simms's First Answer to *Uncle Tom's Cabin*," *American Literature* 31:4 (1960): 421–33, and Charles S. Watson, "Simms's Answer to *Uncle Tom's Cabin*: Criticism of the South in *Woodcraft*," *Southern Literary Journal* 9:1 (1976): 365–68.

18. Simms refers to *Guy Rivers* as "the first of my regular novels" in the "Dedicatory Epistle to Charles R Carroll, Esq. of South Carolina," dated November 15, 1854, and published in the Redfield edition of the novel (New York, 1855). Technically, his novella *Martin Faber* (1833) can be seen as his first novel, since it was published in book form. *Martin Faber*, however, is significantly shorter than the works composing Simms's Border Romances.

19. See, for instance, John Caldwell Guild's afterword to Simms, *Guy Rivers: A Tale of Georgia* (Fayetteville: U of Arkansas P, 1993), 449–70, and Alexander Cowie's "Contemporaries and Immediate Followers of Cooper, II," in *The Rise of the American Novel* (New York: American Book Company, 1948), 228–46. In *William Gilmore Simms*, Ridgely makes the opposite point. For him, "Guy remains a literary paste-up: he is the Elizabethan avenger of the tragedy of blood, the villain hero of Bulwer, and Byron's Cain" (47). In contrast, Ridgley claims that with "Ralph Colleton, Simms manages to be somewhat more original. He is Simms's first portrait of a young Southern aristocrat, the prototype of a long line" (48).

20. Simms, *Guy Rivers*, 46. Hereafter cited in text parenthetically.

21. Burke, *A Philosophical Enquiry into the Origins of Our Ideas of the Sublime and Beautiful*, ed. J. T. Boulton (London: Routledge & Kegan Paul, 1958), 47. For a dis-

cussion of Burke's example in terms of a broader cultural theory of the aesthetics of murder, see the introduction to Joel Black's *The Aesthetics of Murder*.

22. Guilds, afterword to *Guy Rivers*, 449. In *Simms*, Guilds discusses Murrell as a model for the criminal gang leader in *Richard Hurdis*, as does Mary Ann Wimsatt in *The Major Fiction of William Gilmore Simms: Cultural Traditions and Literary Form* (Baton Rouge: Louisiana State UP, 1989), 97–101. In fact, Wimsatt claims that Murrell serves as model of all the villains in Simms's Border Romances, *except* for Guy Rivers (121). For a detailed study of Murrell as a source for Simms, see Dianne C. Luce, "John A. Murrell and the Imaginations of Simms and Faulkner," in *William Gilmore Simms and the American Frontier*, ed. John Caldwell Guilds and Caroline Collins (Athens: U of Georgia P, 1997): 237–57.

23. Those five states were Pennsylvania, New Jersey, New York, Massachusetts, and New Hampshire. See Banner 343–44, for a complete list of the dates when northern and southern states abolished public executions.

24. For a discussion of the themes and conventions of British Newgate literature, see Keith Hollingsworth, *The Newgate Novel, 1830–1847: Bulver, Ainsworth, Dickens, and Thackeray* (Detroit: Wayne State UP, 1963).

25. Execution sermons, trial reports, and criminal biographies often concluded with a narrative of the final days or hours of a condemned's life, as did the Newgate novel, such as Henry Fielding's classic in the genre, *The Life and Death of Jonathan Wild, the Great* (1743). See Cohen, particularly "An Overview," 3–38, and "Saints and Sinners," 41–80, part I of his study, for a discussion of the conventions of early American gallows literature.

26. As Rodensky puts it, "It need not be by inference from external evidence that third person narrators offer the thoughts of their characters; they can hold themselves out as representing thoughts directly. Novels invite readers to imagine that they are in the mind of the criminal. This access to the mind distinguishes fiction—and the novel in particular—from law, from history, from psychology, and even from other literary genres, like biography and drama." See *The Crime in Mind: Criminal Responsibility and the Victorian Novel* (Oxford: Oxford UP, 2003), 6.

27. "Around mid-century, the popular literature of murder in America began a major reconstruction of the murderer, from common sinner [in the execution sermon] into moral alien, in response to the new understanding of human nature provoked by the Enlightenment." Halttunen, *Murder Most Foul*, 35.

28. Guilds, *Simms*, 49. See also Kevin W. Jett, "A Seductive Plea from the Gallows: Reconsidering William Gilmore Simms's *Martin Faber*," *Mississippi Quarterly* 52 (1999): 559–66.

29. Simms, *Martin Faber: The Story of a Criminal* (Whitefish, MT: Kessinger Publishing, 2006), 2–3. Hereafter cited in text parenthetically.

30. Guilds, in the "Historical and Textual Commentary" to *Martin Faber*, can be seen as speaking for most critics when he notes that Simms made two significant changes to the text when revising it for the 1837 edition. The first was "the seemingly unaccountable shift in point of view—from first person to third person—which marred the final chapter of the 1833 version was corrected in the revised edition, giving the book a consistent first-person narrator throughout" (68).

31. Simms, *Confession; or, The Blind Heart* (New York: AMS Press, 1970), 196. Hereafter cited in text parenthetically.

32. For instance, both O'Sullivan and Cheever take up the story of Cain and Abel in their respective arguments against and for capital punishment. See O'Sullivan, *Report in Favor of the Abolition of the Punishment of Death by Law* (New York: Arno Press, 1974), 28–30; George Barrell Cheever, *Punishment by Death: Its Authority and Expediency* (New York : J. Wiley, 1849), 166–69.

33. Cheever, *A Defence of Capital Punishment* (New York: Wiley and Putnam, 1846), 16.

34. Ibid., 70.

35. Ibid., 166, 168.

36. Cheever, *Punishment by Death*, 221.

37. Ibid., 226.

38. For a discussion of Simms's use of Shakespeare, see Edward P. Vandiver Jr., "Simms's Border Romances and Shakespeare," *Shakespeare Quarterly* 5:2 (1954): 129–39.

39. For other literary works that retell or were inspired by "The Kentucky Tragedy," see Thomas Holley Chivers's *Conrad and Eudora* (Delmare, NY: Scholar's Facsimiles and Reprints, 1978; originally published 1834); Charles Fenno Hoffman's *Greyslaer: A Romance of the Mohawk* (Gross Pointe, MI: Scholarly Press, 1868; originally published 1840); Edgar Allan Poe's *Politian*, in *Collected Works of Edgar Allan Poe* (Cambridge, MA: Harvard UP, 1969); and Robert Penn Warren's *World Enough and Time* (New York: Random House, 1950).

40. Qtd. in Davis, *Homicide in American Fiction* (Ithaca: Cornell UP, 1957), 230. That Poe refers to the historical Colonel Solomon Sharp as "Sharpe" (Simms added a final "e" to his characters, Sharpe and Beauchampe) suggests that he had Simms's romance in mind when writing these remarks about the actual Beauchamp-Sharp murder case.

41. Simms, *Beauchampe*, 66. Hereafter cited in text parenthetically.

42. Cheever, *A Defence of Capital Punishment*, 29.

43. Ibid., 30.

44. For an analysis of O'Sullivan's role in the Young America movement, see Edward L. Widmer's *Young America: The Flowering of Democracy in New York City* (Oxford: Oxford UP, 1999), particularly chap. 1, "The Politics of Culture: O'Sullivan and *The Democratic Review*."

45. *Letters of William Gilmore Simms*, vol. 2, ed. Mary Simms Oliphant, Alfred Taylor Odell, and T. C. Duncan Eaves (Columbia: U of South Carolina P, 1953), 142.

46. Simms, *The Cassique of Kiawah* (Fayetteville: U of Arkansas P, 2003), 69.

47. Ibid., 69–70.

48. Voltaire, *Candide* (Harmondsworth: Penguin, 1947), 111. For a gloss on Voltaire's satiric use of this phrase in *Candide*, see Clive Emsley's *Hard Men: The English Novel and Violence since 1750* (London: Habelond and London, 2005), 150.

49. Simms, *The Cassique of Kiawah*, 424–25.

50. See John Caldwell Guilds's introduction and Kevin Collins's afterword to *The Cassique of Kiawah* (2003) for arguments about *The Cassique of Kiawah* as Simms's greatest achievement. See also Guilds's *Simms*, 229–33.

51. Child, *Letters from New-York*, ed. Bruce Mills (Athens: U of Georgia P, 1998), 60. Hereafter cited in text parenthetically.

52. Simms's *Beauchampe* concludes similarly with a suicide pact between husband and wife. Beauchampe's wife succeeds in killing herself, but a drugged and wounded Beauchampe is dragged to the gallows. In Simms's novel, the criminal-hero dies before he ascends the scaffold, thus cheating the state of its victim. In the historical case, Beauchamp (note that Simms adds a final "e" to his fictionalized "Beauchampe," as he does to "Sharpe," to romanticize his characters and to distinguish them from their real-world counterparts) does attempt suicide in the manner Simms describes. However, the actual Beauchamp does in fact die on the gallows and not from the drug overdose and self-inflicted knife wounds that take the life of Simms's Beauchampe, thus sparing him an ignominious death by lawful hanging.

53. In thinking of Bartleby at one point, Melville's lawyer-narrator reflects on the circumstances of the Colt case: "I remembered the tragedy of the unfortunate Adams and the still more unfortunate Colt in the solitary office of the latter; and how poor Colt, being dreadfully incensed by Adams, and imprudently permitting himself to get wildly excited, was at unawares hurried into his fatal act—an act which certainly no man could possibly deplore more than the actor himself. Often it had occurred to me in my ponderings upon the subject, that had that altercation taken place in the public street, or at a private residence, it would not have terminated as it did. It was the circumstance of being alone in a solitary office, up stairs, of a building entirely unhallowed by humanizing domestic associations—an uncarpeted office, doubtless, of a dusty, haggard sort of appearance; —this it must have been, which greatly helped to enhance the irritable desperation of the hapless Colt." "Bartleby," in *The Piazza Tales and Other Prose Pieces, 1839–1860*, ed. Harrison Hayford, Hershel Parker, and G. Thomas Tanwelle (Evanston, IL: Northwestern UP, 1987), 36.

54. See Halttunen, "The Murderer as Common Sinner" and "The Birth of Horror," in *Murder Most Foul*, 7–32, 33–59.

55. Child, *Fact and Fiction: A Collection of Stories* (Boston: C. S. Francis & Co., 1846), 126. Hereafter cited in text parenthetically.

56. Leonard Woolsey Bacon, "Shall Punishment Be Abolished?," *New Englander and Yale Review* 4:16 (1846): 563–88, 564.

57. Ibid.

58. Ibid., 565.

59. Ibid.

60. The historical Elizabeth Wilson was executed in Pennsylvania on January 3, 1876, reportedly twenty-three minutes after her pardon arrived (although it was not delivered by her brother). As Child remarks in the story's introductory notes, the execution was still alive in the community's memory, in part because of a popular broadside poem commemorating her death. I thank Sharon Hunter for bringing this poem to my attention.

61. Child, *Autumnal Leaves: Tales and Sketches* (New York: C. S. Francis & Co, 1857), 47. Hereafter cited in text parenthetically.

CHAPTER 3. Literary Executions in Cooper, Lippard, and Judd

1. George Lippard, *Legends of the American Revolution, "1776"; or, Washington and His Generals* (1847; rpt., Philadelphia: Leary, Stuart & Co. 1876), 221.

2. See Sarat, "To See or Not to See: On Televising Executions," in *When the State Kills* (Princeton: Princeton UP, 2002), 187–208. Sarat's argument is positioned as a

response to Wendy Lessor, who also opposes capital punishment but argues against televised executions in "KQED v. Daniel Vasquez," in *Pictures at an Execution* (Cambridge, MA: Harvard UP, 1993), 24–46. Both Sarat and Lessor, in their exploration of murder and the capital punishment in contemporary American culture, speak to the complexities of artistic representations of violence both within and outside the law.

3. For a recent historical study of the infamous "Kentucky Tragedy," see Dixon D. Bruce, *The Kentucky Tragedy: A Story of Conflict and Change in Antebellum America* (Baton Rouge: Lousiana State UP, 2006).

4. Cheever, *A Defence of Capital Punishment* (New York: Wiley and Putnam, 1846), 51.

5. As Lazar Ziff writes in *Literary Democracy: The Declaration of Cultural Independence in America* (New York: Viking Press, 1981): "In the period 1844–1854, which saw the publication of *The Scarlet Letter* and *Moby-Dick*, George Lippard was, in all probability, American's most widely read novelist" (94). Ziff bases this claim on sales figures and compares Lippard to Cooper, "whose books were more durably printed and bound" and who thus "may have reached a wider audience, in the home and through circulation in rental libraries, than is indicated by the sales figures alone" (94). Still, the sales of Lippard's works, especially *The Quaker City* (which went through twenty-seven editions in five years), were staggering—a point that Ziff emphasizes through citing sales figures for Lippard's best-selling novel. For accounts of Lippard's popularity, see also David S. Reynolds's introduction to *The Quaker City; or, The Monks of Monk Hall* (Amherst: U of Massachusetts P, 1995) as well as Reynolds's edited collection of Lippard's work, *George Lippard, Prophet of Protest: Writings of an American Radical, 1822–1854* (New York: P. Lang, 1986).

6. H. Bruce Franklin makes a compelling case for *Billy Budd* as an anti–death penalty book in his landmark essay, "*Billy Budd* and Capital punishment: A Tale of Three Centuries," *American Literature* 69:2 (1997): 337–59. I take up *Billy Budd* and Franklin's essay in chapter 5 of this study.

7. Cooper, *The Spy: A Tale of the Neutral Ground* (New York: AMS, 2002), 221. Hereafter cited in text parenthetically.

8. Charles Hansford Adams, *The Guardian of the Law: Authority and Identity in James Fenimore Cooper* (University Park: Pennsylvania State UP 1990), 28–29. As Adams later writes, "throughout *The Spy* the legitimacy of civil authority is examined in terms of law. Indeed, the novel is very much about the relationship between justice and law, between principles and mere rules. The plot, of course, turns largely on legal matters. Much of the action concerns the various American efforts to bring Harvey Birch to justice, while the 'trials' organized by Lawton and the Cow-Boys are important elements in the novel's structure. Similarly, Wharton's trial is one of the pivotal events in the story. More generally, justice, both legal and extralegal, is the central issue raised in *The Spy*" (30).

9. See Dieter Schulz, "Revolution and the Language of Feeling in Early American Literature: James Fenimore Cooper's *The Spy*," *Anglistentag 1991 Düsseldorf: Proceedings* (Tübingen; Niemeyer, 1992): 160–73.

10. Ibid., 161–64.

11. For an extended discussion of the play's influence on the novel, see Maurice Hunt, "James Fenimore Cooper's *The Spy* and Shakespeare's *Measure for Measure*," *Conference of College Teachers of English Studies* 72 (2007): 71–79.

12. Not only does Dixon's *The Clansman* employ a body swap, but it concludes with the race against the clock to prevent an execution dramatized in the novel's penultimate chapter, "A Ride for a Life." See *The Clansman: An Historical Romance of the Ku Klux Klan* (New York: A. Wessels Company, 1907).

13. Cesare Beccaria, *On Crimes and Punishments*, ed. David Young (Indianapolis: Hackett, 1986), 48.

14. In addition to the figures named in the text, Louis P. Masur identifies William Bradford, the Federalist attorney general under Washington, and Founding Fathers John Jay and James Madison as "opponents of capital punishment." Like Rush, Franklin, and Jefferson, each of these influential figures "considered the death penalty morally and politically repugnant." See Masur, *Rites of Execution: Capital Punishment and the Transformation of American Culture, 1776–1865* (New York: Oxford UP), 61–62.

15. Benjamin Rush, *Considerations on the Injustice and Impolicy of Punishing Murder by Death* (Philadelphia: Carey, 1792), 19.

16. Wayne Franklin uses this term in his introduction to *The Spy* (New York: Penguin, 1997), xxiv. In addition to Franklin's useful discussion of André in Cooper's novel and its historical context, for a superb cultural history of the André case in works other than Cooper's *The Spy* from the Revolutionary War through the late nineteenth century, see Larry J. Reynolds's "Patriot and Criminals, Criminal and Patriots: Representations of the Case of Major André," *South Central Review* 9:1 (1992): 57–84. For historical treatments of André, see Andy Trees, "Benedict Arnold, John André, and His Three Yeoman Captors: A Sentimental Journey or American Virtue Defined," *Early American Literature* 35:3 (2000): 246–73, and Robert E. Cray Jr., "Major John André and the Three Captors: Class Dynamics and Revolutionary Memory Wars in the Early Republic, 1780–1831," *Journal of the Early Republic* 17:3 (1997): 371–97.

17. Bruce A. Rosenberg. "Cooper's *The Spy* and the Popular Spy Novel," *American Transcendental Quarterly* 7:2 (1993): 115–25, 118.

18. Cooper, *Notions of the Americans: Picked Up by a Travelling Bachelor* (Albany: State U of New York P, 1991), 187.

19. Ibid., 189.

20. Ibid., 437.

21. Qtd. in Jon Yorke, "The Evolving Human Rights Discourse of the Council of Europe: Renouncing the Sovereign Right of the Death Penalty," in *Against the Death Penalty: International Initiatives and Implications*, ed. Jon Yorke (London: Ashgate Press, 2008), 51.

22. As Susan Manning, in a review of new scholarly editions of *Notions* and *Red Rover*, writes: "For the student of Cooper, and of American literature, the *Notions of the Americans* carries greater interest than the novel, despite a reception which was initially tainted by the *Rover*'s shortcomings. A review of September 1828 conceded that the *Notions* might have value as a political document, but declared acerbically that 'as a work of amusement, it is almost as destitute of interest as the Red Rover.' The reviewer had a point [Manning adds]. A hugely long and earnest work, the *Notions* labours under a minimally fictional framework in which an enlightened—and titled—European visits American in the company of an American alter ego (Cadwallader), and reports back in letters to a range of correspondents in Europe." See Manning in *Review of English Studies*, n.s., 44:175 (1993): 450–52, 450.

23. Walter Benjamin, "Critique of Violence," in *Reflections: Essays, Aphorisms, Autobiographical Writings*, trans. Edmund Jephcott (New York: Schocken Books, 1972), 286.

24. Ibid. This, of course, is one of the central points in Jacques Derrida's well-known critique of Benjamin's "Critique of Violence." See Derrida, "Force of Law: The Mystical Foundation of Authority," *Cardozo Law Review* 11:5–6 (1990): 920–1045.

25. Cooper, *Notions*, 187.

26. Grossman, *James Fenimore Cooper* (Stanford: Stanford UP, 1967), 28.

27. Ringe, *James Fenimore Cooper*, rev. ed. (Boston: Twayne, 1988), 14.

28. Grossman 28.

29. Lippard, *Legends of the American Revolution*, 223.

30. *The Quaker City; or, The Monks of Monk Hall*, ed. David S. Reynolds (Amherst: U of Massachusetts P, 1995), 375. Hereafter cited in text parenthetically.

31. As noted in chapter 1, Michigan abolished the death penalty in 1848, followed by Rhode Island in 1851, and Wisconsin in 1853.

32. In particular, see Rantoul's "Letters on the Death Penalty," written to the governor of Massachusetts, in *Memoirs, Speeches and Writings of Robert Rantoul, Jr.*, ed. Luther Hamilton (Boston: J. P. Jewett, 1854), 495–515. Rantoul's "Letters" provide extensive analysis of murder and execution rates as well as the crimes for which individuals were condemned to death in Massachusetts and in regions, such as Tuscany, Belgium, and Russia, that had experimented with abolition. For the use of such statistics, see also Spear, *Essays on the Punishment of Death* (Boston: Spear, 1844), 76–87; Quinby, *The Gallows, the Prison, and the Poor-House: A Plea for Humanity; Showing the Demands of Christianity in Behalf of the Criminal and Perishing Classes* (Cincinnati: G. W. Quinby, 1856), 31; and O'Sullivan, *Report in Favor of the Abolition of the Punishment of Death by Law* (1842; New York: Arno Press, 1974), 107–10; and Charles C. Burleigh, *Thoughts on the Death Penalty* (Philadelphia: Merrihew and Thompson ,1845), 94–98.

33. For representative essays in early American penal reform in Pennsylvania, see the work collected in *Reform of Criminal Law in Pennsylvania: Selected Enquires, 1787–1819* (New York: Arno Press, 1972). Essays include William Bradford's "An Enquiry How Far the Punishment of Death Is Necessary in Pennsylvania" (1793), William Roscoe's "Observations on Penal Jurisprudence, and the Reformation of Criminals" (1819), Benjamin Rush's "Considerations on the Injustice and Impolicy of Punishing Murder by Death" (1792), and Benjamin Rush's "An Enquiry into the Effects of Public Punishments upon Criminals, and upon Society" (1787).

34. Neal, *Logan: A Family History*, vol. 2 (Philadelphia: H. C. Carey and I. Lea, 1822), 11–12.

35. In his introduction to *The Quaker City*, David S. Reynolds speculates that the poor Charley story influenced Melville's *Billy Budd* (xxix). Melville may have been influenced by Lippard's account of Poor Charley, but I would like to suggest, in turn, that Lippard, in making Charley a nineteen-year-old embroiled in some kind of murder plot at sea, was likely influenced by the 1842 *Somers* affair, which involved nineteen-year-old Philip Spenser who allegedly was planning a mutiny that led to his execution. I look closely at that the *Somers* affair in the context of Melville's work and death penalty debates in chapter 5.

36. Helen Prejean, *Dead Man Walking: An Eyewitness Account of the Death Penalty in the United States* (New York: Random House, 1993); *Dead Man Walking*, Polygram Filmed Entertainment, Tim Robins, director, 1996.

37. I am indebted to Peter Caster's insight into the peculiarity of the death sentence as a speech act in his paper, "Literary Execution in *Light in August* and *Go Down, Moses*," presented at NEMLA, Hartford, Connecticut, March 2001.

38. For Reynolds's use of the term *shock-gothic* in reference to Lippard's work, see "Radical Sensationalism: George Lippard in His Transatlantic Contexts," in *Transatlantic Sensations*, ed. Jennifer Phegley, John Cyril Barton, and Kristin Huston (Surrey: Ashgate, 2012), 77–96.

39. My discussion of the *Quaker City Weekly* draws from and is indebted to Shelly Streeby's *American Sensations: Class, Empire, and the Production of Popular Culture* (Berkeley and Los Angeles: U of California P, 2002).

40. Qtd. in ibid., 44.

41. Ibid.

42. Lippard, *The White Banner*, vol. 1 (Philadelphia: George Lippard, 1851), 151. Hereafter cited in text parenthetically.

43. Given Lippard's characterization of Hughes as a pro-gallows zealot, one would expect to find abundant evidence of Hughes's participation in death penalty debates. However, careful examination of the *Complete Works of the Most Rev. John Hughes, D.D., Archbishop of New York*, ed. Lawrence Kehoe, vol. 1 (New York: American News, 1864), does not support such a strong characterization on Lippard's part. The best evidence I have found for Hughes's endorsement of capital punishment occurs in his "Sermon on Jubilee," wherein he discusses the righteousness of "death as a punishment" for King David's first son because "David sinned" (508), and in his "Sermon before Congress," in which he speaks of humanity's "disobedience" and "the accumulations of guilt and familiarity with depravity in the progress of time" that justify the "penalties, as marked in the book of revelation—in the book of Genesis" (546). Such references and appeals to Genesis were commonplace among Cheever and other outspoken ministers in their defense of capital punishment. In "Relation between the Civil and Religious Duties of the Catholic Citizen," from the *Complete Works of the Most Rev. John Hughes, D. D. Archbishop of New York*, vol. 2, ed. Lawrence Kehoe (New York: Catholic Publication House, 1864), Hughes similarly connects positive and divine law, arguing that "to protect society, the human law must repose on the eternal basis of spiritual law, whose witness is the eye of One who penetrates into the deepest recesses of the soul. Were it not for this influence, human law would be weak and inefficient to restrain crime" (146). Of course, Lippard's sardonic treatment of Hughes in *The White Banner* could have been based on public speeches or debates (planned or impromptu) for which there is no print record today. I thank Desiree Long for help with this research.

44. Masur 7.

45. One of his most popular shorter works, "Jesus and the Poor," creates what David S. Reynolds calls "a kind of urban 'Young Goodman Brown,' by using supernaturalism and dream imagery to mock the pious pretensions of respectable Philadelphians." See Lippard, *George Lippard, Prophet of Protest: Writings of an American Radical, 1822–1854*, ed. David S. Reynolds (New York: P. Lang, 1986), 69.

46. In chapter 3 of *A Defence of Capital Punishment*, Cheever complained of "the miserable slang about the gallows and the Gospel" (49). See also Masur 151–52.

47. Qtd. in Lippard, *George Lippard, Prophet of Protest*, 101. For Denning's use of the term, *labor aesthetic*, see his chapter "Mysteries and Mechanics of the City," in *Mechanic Accents: Dime Novels and Working-Class Culture in America* (New York: Verso, 1987), especially 100–102.

48. Pierson, *Jamie Parker, the Fugitive* (Hartford: Brocket, Fuller, and Co., 1851), 174, emphasis in original.

49. Smith, *The Newsboy* (New York: J. C. Derby, 1854), 93–94. A decade earlier, Smith also published an anti-gallows sonnet, "Capital Punishment" (1846), collected in *The Poetical Writings of Elizabeth Oakes Smith* (New York: Redfield, 1846), 121.

50. Smith, *Newsboy*, 362–63.

51. Lee, *Merrimack; or, Life at the Loom* (New York: Redfield, 1854), 22.

52. Ibid., 94.

53. Ibid., 54, emphasis in original.

54. Judd, *Margaret: A Tale of the Real and Ideal, Blight and Bloom*, rev. ed. (Upper Saddle River, NJ: Gregg Press, 1968), 264.

55. Ibid.

56. Judd, *Margaret: A Tale of the Real and Ideal, Bright and Bloom* (Boston: Mordan and Wily, 1845), 346–47. References to this (the first) edition of *Margaret* are hereafter cited in text parenthetically.

57. As a rule, execution sermons created sympathy for the condemned as a "common sinner," to use Karen Halttunen's phrase, but they did not use that sympathy (as Judd and other novelists of the 1840s and 1850s did) to criticize capital punishment. On the contrary, the execution sermon as a genre accepted the social function of the death penalty and instead focused attention on sin and the condemned's penance and afterlife. See chapter 1, "The Murderer as Common Sinner," in Halttunen's *Murder Most Foul: The Killer and the American Gothic Imagination* (Cambridge, MA: Harvard UP, 1998), and part I of Daniel A. Cohen's *Pillars of Salt, Monuments of Grace: New England Crime Literature and the Origins of American Popular Culture* (Oxford: Oxford UP, 1993), for detailed analyses of the execution sermon as a popular literary genre.

58. *Vulgar* was the term contemporary critics of *Margaret* used to denigrate parts of the novel. For a helpful summary of *Margaret's* critical reception, see "The Critics," in Francis B. Dedmond's biography *Sylvester Judd* (Boston: Twayne, 1980), 75–86.

59. [B. O. Peabody], Review of *Margaret*, *North American Review* 62 (Jan. 1846): 102–41, 137.

60. For a valuable historical account of the anti-gallows movement in Maine and Judd's role in it, see Edward Schriver, "The Reluctant Hangman: The State of Maine and Capital Punishment," *New England Quarterly* 63:2 (1990): 271–87.

61. Judd, *Margaret*, rev. ed., 307.

62. Ibid.

63. See Evelev's "Picturesque Reform in the New England Village Novel, 1845–1867," *ESQ: A Journal of the American Renaissance* 53:2 (2007): 148–83.

64. For a brief discussion of these Cooper novels as pro-gallows works, see Paul Jones, *Against the Gallows* (Iowa City: U of Iowa P, 2011), 29–30.

65. As Cooper puts it in the preface to *The Ways of the Hour* (New York: Putnam's, 1850), "The object of this book is to draw the attention of the reader to some of the social evils that beset us; more particularly in connection with the administration of criminal justice" (iii).

66. Ibid., 192.

67. Ibid., 193.

68. Ibid.

69. Ibid, 321–22.

CHAPTER 4. **Hawthorne and the Evidentiary Value of Literature**

1. Hawthorne, "Hall of Fantasy," in *Pioneer: A Literary and Political Magazine*, ed. J. R. Lowell and R. Carter, 1 (Feb. 1843): 53. The tale was first published in Lowell and Carter's *Pioneer*, but when Hawthorne later included it in *Mosses from the Old Manse*, he omitted the reference to O'Sullivan.

2. As Gavin Jones (among others) explains: "In 1854, English writer and politician R. Monckton Milnes asked Nathaniel Hawthorne to select a few books he considered most characteristically American. Along with Henry David Thoreau's *Walden* (1854), Hawthorne sent his friend Sylvester Judd's *Margaret* . . . , even though he doubted that Milnes would be able to appreciate the novel precisely because it was so 'intensely' American" (449). See Jones, "The Paradise of Aesthetics: Sylvester Judd's *Margaret* and Antebellum American Literature," *New England Quarterly* 71:3 (1998): 449–47.

3. For a discussion of Hawthorne in relation to Cheever, see Margaret B. Moore, "Hawthorne and the Lord's Anointed," *Studies in the American Renaissance* (1988): 27–36. See also Margaret B. Moore, *The Salem World of Nathaniel Hawthorne* (Columbia: U of Missouri P, 2001), 111–13, and David S. Reynolds, *Beneath the American Renaissance* (New York: Knopf, 1988), 38, 66.

4. Hawthorne, *Mosses from an Old Manse* (Columbus: Ohio State UP, 1974), 393. Hereafter cited in text parenthetically.

5. Hawthorne, *The American Notebooks* (Columbus: Ohio State UP, 1972), 237.

6. Qtd. in Edward B. Hungerford's "Hawthorne Gossips about Salem," *New England Quarterly* 6 (Sept. 1933): 445–69. Incidentally, the victim Hawthorne refers to did not die from his wounds.

7. Qtd. in ibid., 455.

8. Welsh, *Strong Representations: Narrative and Circumstantial Evidence in England* (Baltimore: Johns Hopkins UP, 1992), 17.

9. Ibid., 17, 24.

10. Hawthorne, *The House of the Seven Gables* (Columbus: Ohio State UP, 1965), 8. Hereafter cited in text parenthetically.

11. For a helpful discussion of the metaphor of the "chain" in law and literature, see Brook Thomas's *American Literary Realism and the Failed Promise of Contract* (Berkeley and Los Angeles: U of California P, 1997), 147–48. See also Thomas, *New Historicism and Other Old Fashion Topics* (Princeton: Princeton UP, 1991), 93–94; and Thomas, "Ineluctable though Even: On Experimental Historical Narratives," *Common Knowledge* 5:3 (1996): 163–88.

12. My discussion of the White murder and its relation to Hawthorne draws from Brook Thomas's "*The House of the Seven Gables*: Hawthorne's Legal Story," in *Cross-Examinations*

*of Law and Literature* (Cambridge: Cambridge UP, 1987), 45–70. However, whereas Thomas addresses parallels of structure or "plot" in the White murder case and Hawthorne's novel, I offer a comparative analysis of *The House of the Seven Gables* and Daniel Webster's summation in the Frank Knapp murder trial. For literary critics who briefly discuss the White murder in relation to Hawthorne, see F. O. Matthiessen, *The American Renaissance: Art and Expression in the Age of Emerson and Whitman* (London: Oxford UP, 1941), 214–15, and Reynolds, *Beneath the American Renaissance*, 250–52. Reynolds also suggests that the White murder case serves as a source for Poe's "Tell-Tale Heart" (231). For a discussion of the White murder case in the context of popular crime literature, see Karen Halttunen, *Murder Most Foul: The Killer and the American Gothic Imagination* (Cambridge, MA: Harvard UP, 1998), 60–62, 120–23.

13. Qtd. in Howard A. Bradley and James A. Winans, *Daniel Webster and the Salem Murder* (Columbia: Artcraft Press, 1956), 8.

14. Webster's summation, for instance, is anthologized in Ephraim London's *The World of Law and Literature; A Treasury of Great Writing about and in the Law, Short Stories, Plays, Essays, Accounts, Letters, Opinions, Pleas, Transcripts of Testimony; from Biblical Times to the Present* (New York: Simon and Schuster, 1960), 406–39.

15. Noted lawyer and statesmen, Samuel McCall, qtd. in Bradley and Winans 219. See "Summation in the Trial of John Francis Knapp for the Murder of Joseph White," in London, 406–39.

16. Near the end of Hawthorne's "Mr. Higginbotham's Catastrophe," written shortly after the Knapp trial, a young niece of the supposedly murdered Mr. Higginbotham defends Dominicus Pike, the young man who started rumors of her uncle's death. Young Miss Higginbotham's plea for mercy quells an outraged community determined to teach Dominicus a painful lesson for the mischief caused by his gossip. At the end of her speech, the tale's narrator comments, "Daniel Webster never spoke nor looked so like an angel as Miss Higginbotham, while defending [Dominicus] from the wrathful populace at Parker's Falls." See "Mr. Higginbotham's Catastrophe," in *Twice Told Tales* (Columbus: Ohio State UP, 1974), 116. Based on this (ironic) allusion to Webster's skills in forensic oratory, Hungerford has speculated that Hawthorne drew the image from Webster's closing argument in the Knapp trial, an event Hawthorne likely attended (460–61).

17. Hawthorne, "Mr. Higginbotham's Catastrophe," 116.

18. Daniel Webster, "Summation in the Trial of John Francis Knapp for the Murder of Joseph White," in London 410. References to Webster hereafter cited in text parenthetically.

19. Qtd. in Bradley and Winans, 70.

20. Ibid.

21. Qtd. in James R. Mellow, *Nathaniel Hawthorne in His Times* (Boston: Houghton Mifflin, 1980), 25.

22. The narrator of Lee's *Merrimack; or, Life at the Loom* (New York: Redfield, 1854) identifies herself as a reader of Hawthorne: "I have read Hawthorne's 'Tales' more times than he had 'told' them" (147).

23. Hawthorne, *The American Notebooks*, 310. The journal entry I cite is undated but included just after one dated October 13, 1851, and just before another dated October 22, 1851.

24. Robert Sullivan, *The Disappearance of Dr. Parkman* (Boston: Little, Brown, 1971), 63. My account of the Webster murder case draws from Sullivan's study as well as Brook Thomas's *Cross-Examinations of Law and Literature*, 202–6. For accounts of the Webster case in the context of popular print culture, see also Halttunen 126–132, 272–276. See Simon Schama, "Death of a Harvard Man," in *Dead Certainties: Unwarranted Speculations* (New York: Vintage, 1992), for an historical account in novel form of the Parkman murder case.

25. Qtd. in *Classics in Murder: True Stories of Infamous Crime as Told by Famous Crime Writers*, ed. Robert Meadley (New York: Ungar, 1986), 284.

26. The defense challenged this evidence through the expert testimony of Dr. William Morton, a physician renowned for discovering anesthesia, who said it would be impossible to identify for whom these teeth were made because of the extensive fire damage they withstood while in the furnace. Despite Morton's testimony, the preponderance of circumstantial evidence against Webster was bolstered through statements by prominent witnesses for the state, such as Oliver Wendell Holmes, who testified: "I am familiar with the appearance of Dr. Parkman's form, and I saw nothing dissimilar" in the discovered remains (qtd. in Sullivan 89). In terms of probative value, Holmes's testimony was not particularly compelling, but it shows how evidence gains authority because of the stature of expert witnesses.

27. Sullivan 144.

28. Ibid., 172.

29. Member of the Legal Profession, *A Statement of Reasons Showing the Illegality of That Verdict upon Which Sentence Has Been Pronounced against John W. Webster for the Alleged Murder of George Parkman* (New York: Stringer & Townsend, 1850), 22.

30. Qtd. in Sullivan 169.

31. For witness testimony that Parkman was seen walking the streets of Boston after he was allegedly murdered, see Stone 158–63.

32. In his *Report* (New York: Arno Press, 1974), O'Sullivan claims: "There have been cases in which men have been hung on the most positive testimony to identity, (aided by many suspicious circumstances,) by persons familiar with their appearance, which have afterward proved grievous mistakes, growing out of remarkable personal resemblances" (188–89).

33. Ibid., 116–17, emphasis in original.

34. Spear, *Essays on the Punishment of Death* (Boston: C. Spear, 1845), 107–21.

35. Quinby, *The Gallows, the Prison, and the Poor-House: A Plea for Humanity; Showing the Demands of Christianity in Behalf of the Criminal and Perishing Classes* (Cincinnati: G. W. Quinby, 1856), 58–59, emphasis in original.

36. Ibid., 59.

37. Quod, "Harry Black, a Story of Circumstantial Evidence, Founded on Fact," *Democratic Review* 11:53 (1842): 508–28.

38. Ibid., 527.

39. See both Mayo, "The Captain's Story," *Democratic Review* 18:94 (1846): 305–11, and Mayo's collection, *Romance Dust from the Historic Placer* (New York: Putnam, 1851), 34–54.

40. Mayo, "The Captain's Story," in *Romance Dust from the Historic Placer*, 34. Hereafter cited in text parenthetically.

41. Alice Gray [pseud. Julia A. Matthews], "The Red Cloak; or, Murder at the Road-side Inn," *Lily Huson; or, Early Struggles 'Midst Continual Hope: A Tale of Humble Life* (New York: H. Long and Brother, 1851), 286–301.

42. Ibid., 286.

43. Qtd. in James W. Stone, *Report of the Trial of Prof. John W. Webster Indicted for the Murder of Dr. George Parkman* (Boston: Phillips & Sampson, 1850), 277. Hereafter cited in text parenthetically.

44. Welsh 17, 24.

45. For a discussion of photography and its legal uses in nineteenth-century American courtrooms, see Jennifer L. Mnookin, "The Image of Truth: Photographic Evidence and the Power of Analogy," *Yale Journal of the Humanities* 10:1 (1998): 1–74. Photography and the daguerreotype have long interested critics of *The House of the Seven Gables*. For two excellent recent discussions, see Alan Trachtenberg, "Seeing and Believing: Hawthorne's Reflections on the Daguerreotype in *The House of the Seven Gables*," *American Literary History* 9:3 (1997): 460–81, and Susan S. Williams, "The Aspiring Purpose of an Ambitious Demagogue: Portraiture and *The House of the Seven Gables*," *Nineteenth-Century Literature* 49:2 (1994): 221–44.

46. The first critic to treat Jaffrey Pyncheon's death as a murder was Alfred H. Marks in his 1956 essay, "Who Killed Judge Pyncheon? The Role of the Imagination in *The House of the Seven Gables*," *PMLA* 17 (1956): 355–69. According to Marks, the evidence suggests that Clifford is responsible for the judge's death insofar as his ghostly apparition startled the judge and induced the heart attack that killed him. More recently, Clara B. Cox has made a case for Holgrave as the judge's murderer in "'Who Killed Judge Pyncheon?' The Scene of the Crime Revisited," *Studies in American Fiction* 16:1 (1988): 99–103. Challenging Marks's theory, she fingers Holgrave for the crime for several reasons. To begin with, not only was Holgrave in the house at the time of the judge's death but, as a descendant of Matthew Maule, he had good reason to see dead the present-day Pyncheon, who most resembles the Puritan forebear who led the crusade against his forefather. Moreover, whereas Clifford and Hepzibah, like Holgrave, had the opportunity to commit the crime as well as their own motive for seeing Judge Pyncheon dead, only Holgrave, Cox argues, possessed the means of precipitating the judge's death as it occurred. He knew of the Pyncheons' predisposition to apoplexy, and this fact, along with his own skills in mesmerism, could enable him to place the judge in a hypnotic state conducive to producing a heart attack.

Cox's argument is even more compelling if we consider evidence that she does not: namely, Holgrave's curious explanation to Phoebe about why he had taken the photograph of the dead judge: "As a point of evidence that may be useful to Clifford," Holgrave explains, "and also as a memorial valuable to myself,—for, Phoebe, there are hereditary reasons that connect me strangely with that man's fate,—I used the means at my disposal to preserve this pictorial record of Judge Pyncheon's death" (*Seven Gables* 303). Holgrave never makes it clear how this evidence "may be useful to Clifford," but as a "memorial valuable" to himself, coupled with a cryptic admission that his own past is "strangely" connected with the dead man's "fate," his statement suggests his own ill will toward the judge—evidence that could be used against him. Moreover, as material evidence, the picture not only places Holgrave at a potential crime scene but could be interpreted as Holgrave's self-conscious effort to *create* evidence—a manipulation of circumstances similar to the act with which Holgrave charges the judge in the death of old Jaffrey.

In addition to Marks and Cox, Paul J. Emmett has entertained the question, "Who Killed Judge Pyncheon?" For Emmett, the most likely suspect is neither Clifford nor Holgrave but rather Hepzibah. See Emmett, "The Murder of Judge Pyncheon: Confusion and Suggestion in *The House of the Seven Gables*," *Journal of Evolutionary Psychology* 24 (2003): 189–95.

47. Arendt, *The Human Condition* (Chicago: U of Chicago P, 1958), 183.

48. Ibid., 237.

49. Ibid.

50. In his excellent study, *Devils and Rebels: The Making of Hawthorne's Damned Politics* (Ann Arbor: U of Michigan P, 2008), Larry J. Reynolds "posits that a Christian pacifism, not unlike that of the Quakers, serves as the foundation of [Hawthorne's] politics . . ." (xvi). If Reynolds is correct (as I believe he is), then the vindictive violence of *The House of the Seven Gables'* "Governor Pyncheon" chapter is all the more conspicuous. Drawing from Jacques Derrida's analysis of "that dangerous supplement" in *Of Grammatology*, trans. Gayatri Chakravorty Spivak (Baltimore: Johns Hopkins UP, 1974), I argue here that the violence expressed through Judge Pyncheon's death supplements or undercuts the novel's principle message of reconciliation and forgiveness.

51. That the judge's death takes shape *as if* it were an execution has been suggested by more than one critic. Walter Benn Michaels, in his monumental *The Gold Standard and the Logic of Naturalism: American Literature at the Turn of the Century* (Berkeley and Los Angeles: U of California P, 1987), has characterized the mean-spirited joy with which Hawthorne celebrates the judge's sudden demise as an "execution," whereas Marks, in his seminal essay, "Who Killed Judge Pyncheon?" charges Hawthorne with killing the judge and argues: "No murder was ever planned so calculatedly as was Judge Pyncheon's demise in this novel" (355). Michaels, in *The Gold Standard*, characterizes the judge's death more directly as an "execution," using that term himself: "Celebrating the death—one might better call it the *execution*—of Judge Pyncheon, the romance joins the witch hunt, the attempt to imagine an escape from capitalism, defending the self against possession, property against appropriation, and choosing death over life (101, emphasis added).

52. Hawthorne, *The Scarlet Letter* (Columbus: Ohio UP, 1962), 43.

53. For the most comprehensive account of Hawthorne's firing and Upham's involvement in it, see Stephen Nissenbaum, "The Firing of Nathaniel Hawthorne," *Essex Institute Historical Collections* 144 (April 1978): 57–86. For a representative account, see also Moore, *The Salem World of Nathaniel Hawthorne*, 185–97.

54. Hawthorne, *The Scarlet Letter*, 48.

55. Banner, *The Death Penalty: An American History* (Cambridge, MA: Harvard UP, 2002), 65.

56. Hawthorne, *The Blithedale Romance* (Columbus: Ohio State UP, 1962), 214.

57. Ibid.

58. Hawthorne, *The Marble Faun* (Columbus: Ohio State UP, 1968), 168.

59. Ibid., 170.

60. Ferguson, *Law and Letters in American Culture* (Cambridge, MA: Harvard UP, 1984), 240.

61. Noting the chapter's fame today and popularity during its own time, biographer James Mellow calls it "a high point in the book and a great set piece in nineteenth-century American writing" (361).

62. Hawthorne, *The Blithedale Romance*, 241.

63. Stewart, *Death Sentences: Styles of Dying in British Fiction* (Cambridge, MA: Harvard UP, 1984), 15.

64. See Edward L. Widmer, *Young America: The Flowering of Democracy in New York City* (Oxford: Oxford UP, 2000), esp. 66–83.

65. David Brion Davis articulates this argument in his classic study, *Homicide in American Fiction, 1798–1860: A Study in Social Values* (Ithaca: Cornell UP, 1957): "Although advocates of capital punishment usually began their argument by citing Old Testament authority and by denying historical progress, the legal profession found a more persuasive doctrine in a new philosophy of justice. In 1843, George Barrell Cheever spoke of 'intrinsic justice' and of 'moral necessity,' which required that murderers be punished invariably with death" (296–97).

66. Hawthorne, "Chiefly about War Matters," *Atlantic Monthly*, July 1862, 54.

67. Ibid.

68. Ibid.

## CHAPTER 5. Melville, MacKenzie, and Military Executions

1. Melville, *Battle-Pieces and Aspects of War*, ed. Hennig Cohen (New York: Thomas Yoseloff, 1963), 35.

2. Despite Christological references (e.g., "*the cut on the crown*" and "*the streaming beard*"), Melville's Brown is more of a trope ("meteor of the war") than the eulogized or sentimental figure variously depicted by Thoreau, Whittier, and Emerson in the depictions of Brown I discussed to end chapter 4. For a discussion of Melville's representation of Brown alongside those of Thoreau and Whitman, see Kent Ljungquist, "Meteor of the War: Melville, Thoreau, and Whitman Respond to John Brown," *American Literature* 61:4 (1998): 674–80.

3. Robert I. Alotta, *Civil War Justice: Union Army Executions under Lincoln* (Shippensburg, PA: White Mane, 1989), x. For a list of the 167 known soldiers known to be executed during the war, see the appendix to Alotta's study.

4. Melville, *Typee: A Peep at Polynesian Life* (Evanston, IL: Northwestern UP, 1968), 125.

5. Ibid.

6. Ibid.

7. Ibid.

8. My understanding of MacKenzie's life and career is indebted to Philip James McFarland, *Sea Dangers: The Affair of the Somers* (New York: Schocken, 1985), which presents the most thorough biographical treatment of MacKenzie. See also Barbara Ryan's "Alexander Slidell Mackenzie," in *American Travel Writers, 1776–1864*, ed. James J. Schramer and Donald Ross (Detroit: Gale, 1997), 224–30.

9. The *Somers* affair, especially in Melville scholarship of the 1940s and 50s, is a recognized source for *White-Jacket* and especially *Billy Budd*. It has also served (often briefly) as a point of reference for numerous critics. Brook Thomas is virtually the only literary critic to examine MacKenzie's actual writings in relation to Melville's work.

However, whereas Thomas looks at MacKenzie's *North American Review* "Ship" essay as well as his "Defence in the Case of the *Somers'* Mutiny," I examine Melville in relation to MacKenzie's two travel narratives, *A Year in Spain: By a Young American* (Boston: Hilliard, Gray, Little and Wilkins) and *Spain Revisited* (London: Richard Bentley, 1836), in addition to MacKenzie's essay, "The Navy," *North American Review* 30:67 (1830): 360–89.

10. Philip English Mackey, *Hanging in the Balance: The Anti–Capital Punishment Movement in New York State, 1776–1861* (New York: Garland, 1982), 172.

11. Stuart Banner's otherwise superb and comprehensive *The Death Penalty: An American History* (Cambridge, MA: Harvard UP, 2002) largely overlooks the significance of capital punishment in a Civil War context, noting "the movement to abolish the death penalty tailed off in the late 1850s, as sectional controversy and slavery crowded out other issues, and the movement virtually ceased during the Civil War" (134). Similarly, Louis Masur's excellent intellectual history *Rites of Execution: Capital Punishment and the Transformation of American Culture, 1776–1865* (Oxford: Oxford UP, 1991) says nothing about the widespread military executions during the war, whereas Daniel A. Cohen's *Pillars of Salt, Monuments of Grace: New England Crime Literature and the Origins of American Popular Culture, 1674–1860* (Oxford: Oxford UP, 1994) and Karen Halttunen's *Murder Most Foul: The Killer and the American Gothic Imagination* (Cambridge, MA: Harvard UP, 1998) end before the Civil War begins. Paul Jones's *Against the Gallows* (Iowa City: U of Iowa P, 2011) follows this pattern by examining literature in relation to death penalty reform before the Civil War.

12. My understanding of civil liberties in the context of the Civil War owes much to Brook Thomas's *Civic Myths: A Law-and-Literature Approach to Citizenship* (Chapel Hill: U of North Carolina P, 2008), although Thomas's work does not focus on Melville. My treatment of Melville's work in this context draws from Stanton Garner, *The Civil War World of Herman Melville* (Lawrence: UP of Kansas, 1993), Deak Nabers, *Victory of Law: the Fourteenth Amendment, the Civil War, and American Literature, 1852–1867* (Baltimore: Johns Hopkins UP, 2006), Michael T. Gilmore, *The War on Words: Slavery, Race, and Free Speech in American Literature* (Chicago: U of Chicago P, 2010), and Gregory Jay, "Douglass, Melville, and the Lynching of Billy Budd," in *Frederick Douglass and Herman Melville: Essays in Relation*, ed. Robert S. Levine and Samuel Otter (Chapel Hill: U of North Carolina P, 2008), 369–95.

13. Michael Paul Rogin connects Melville's participation in a mutiny on the *Lucy Ann*, an act for which he was imprisoned in Tahiti in 1842, with news of the *Somers* affair. See Rogin, *Subversive Genealogy: The Politics and Art of Herman Melville* (Berkeley and Los Angeles: U of California P), 84. See also Hershel Parker, *Herman Melville: A Biography, 1819–1851* (Baltimore: Johns Hopkins UP, 2005), 264.

14. MacKenzie, "The Navy," 361.

15. "The Brig *Somers,*" *Scientific American* 2:16 (1847): 125.

16. Qtd. in Hayford, ed., *The Somers Mutiny Affair* (Englewood Cliffs: Prentice Hall, 1959), 75. Further references to sources from this text hereafter cited in text parenthetically.

17. *New York Tribune*, Dec. 22, 1842.

18. For representative accounts of how print technology in the 1830s and 1840s led to a proliferation of crime literature, see David Ray Papke, *Framing the Criminal: Crime,*

*Cultural Work, and the Loss of Critical Perspective, 1830–1900* (Hamden: Archon Books, 1987); Cohen; Halttunen; and Banner.

19. *Liberator,* Jan. 27, 1843.

20. Mackey, *Hanging in the Balance,* 173.

21. See chapter 2, note 40, for Melville's reference in "Bartleby" to the Colt murder.

22. For an account of the *Tribune's* anti-gallows activism, see Mackey, *Hanging in the Balance,* 152–53, 173–76, 191–94.

23. *New York Tribune,* Dec. 22, 1842.

24. *New York Tribune,* Dec. 31, 1842.

25. Philip English Mackey, *Voices against Death: American Opposition to Capital Punishment, 1787–1977* (New York: Burt Franklin, 1977), 111.

26. Merton M. Sealts has identified Greeley's *Hints of Reform* as a source in his "Check List" (Nos. 81, 234) in *Melville's Reading* (Columbia: U of South Carolina P, 1988), 61.

27. In addition to Greeley's *Proceedings of the Court of Inquiry Appointed to Inquire into the Intended Mutiny on Board the United States Brig of War Somers . . . , Reported for "The New-York Tribune"* (New York: Greeley & McElrath, 1843), see *Proceedings of the Naval Court Martial in the Case of Alexander Slidell MacKenzie . . . , to Which Is Annexed an Elaborate Review, by James Fennimore [sic] Cooper* (New York: Henry G. Langley, 1844), and MacKenzie's own *Case of the Somers' Mutiny* (New York: Tribune Office, 1843).

28. Melville, *White Jacket; or, The World in a Man-of-War* (Evanston, IL: Northwestern UP, 1990), 293. Hereafter cited in text parenthetically.

29. Banner 54.

30. Ibid.

31. Hawthorne, *The Scarlet Letter* (Columbus: Ohio State UP, 1962), 49.

32. Glenn, "The Naval Reform Campaign against Flogging: A Case Study in Changing Attitudes toward Corporal Punishment, 1830–1850," *American Quarterly* 35 (1983): 408–25, 409. See also H. Edward Stessel, "Melville's *White-Jacket*: A Case against the 'Cat,'" *Clio* 13 (1983): 37–55.

33. Greeley, *Hints toward Reforms in Lectures, Addresses, and Other Writings* (New York: Harper and Brothers, 1850), 334, 335, emphasis in original.

34. For representative accounts of Melville's criticism of slavery in *White-Jacket,* see Priscilla Allen Zirker, "Evidence of the Slavery Dilemma in *White-Jacket,*" *American Quarterly* 18 (1966): 477–92; Keith Huntress, "'Guinea' of *White-Jacket* and Chief Justice Shaw," *American Literature: A Journal of Literary History, Criticism, and Bibliography* 43:4 (1972): 639–41; Carolyn Karcher, *Shadow over the Promised Land: Slavery, Race, and Violence in Melville's America* (Baton Rouge: Louisiana State UP, 1980); Thomas, *Cross Examinations in Law and Literature* (Cambridge: Cambridge UP, 1987), 149, 161; and Samuel Otter, "'Race' in *Typee* and *White-Jacket,*" in *The Cambridge Companion to Herman Melville,* ed. Robert S. Levine (Cambridge: Cambridge UP, 1998), 12–36.

35. Thomas, *Civic Myths,* 92. My discussion in what follows owes much to Thomas's analysis of the ship-of-state trope in both *Cross-Examinations* and *Civic Myths.* Whereas Thomas in *Cross-Examinations* examines the trope in Melville's work (particularly *White-Jacket*) and antebellum culture at large, in *Civic Myths* he traces it from

the *Somers* case through Lincoln's and Sumner's writings during the Civil War. Drawing from both these works, I link Melville's and MacKenzie's use of the trope to a Civil War context that informed theories of military authority under the Lincoln administration.

36. Whitman, *Complete Poetry and Collected Prose* (New York: New York UP, 1963), 467.

37. Longfellow, "The Building of the Ship," in *Works*, vol. 1, ed. Samuel Longfellow (Boston: Houghton Mifflin, 1886), 225.

38. Thomas, *Civic Myths*, 92.

39. In addition to both Thomas's *Cross-Examinations* (151–55) and *Civic Myths* (92–95), for a discussion of the importance of MacKenzie's work in the shaping of Longfellow's poem, see Hans-Joachim Lang and Fritz Fleischman, "'All This Beauty, All This Grace': Longfellow's 'The Building of the Ship' and Alexander MacKenzie's 'Ship,'" *New England Quarterly* 54 (1981): 104–18.

40. Thomas, *Civic Myths*, 103–17.

41. MacKenzie, "The Navy," 361.

42. See Jean-Jacques Rousseau, *On The Social Contract*, in *The Basic Political Writings*, trans. Donald A. Cress (Indianapolis: Hackett, 1987), esp. 147–48, for Rousseau's political theory of the "general will."

43. For a detailed account of Melville's attendance at the Mannings' execution, see Charlotte H. Lindgren's "The Trial and Execution of the Mannings," *Melville Society Extracts* 123 (July 2002): 5–9. The Mannings' execution is also briefly discussed by Jay Leyda, *The Melville Long: A Documentary Life of Herman Melville, 1819–1891* (New York: Harcourt & Brace, 1951), 330–31.

44. Qtd. in Lindgren 7.

45. Ibid.

46. Pere Gifra-Adroher, *Between History and Romance: Travel Writing on Spain in the Early Nineteenth-Century United States* (London: Farleigh Dickinson UP, 2000), 96.

47. MacKenzie, *A Year in Spain: By a Young American*, vol. 1 (London: John Murray, 1830), 337. Hereafter cited in text parenthetically.

48. Qtd. in McFarland 7. Irving's review of *A Year in Spain* was published in the *Quarterly Review* 44 (Feb. 1831): 319–42.

49. Duyckinck, "Death by Hanging," *Arcturus: A Journal of Books and Opinion* 3 (Jan. 1842): 98–103, 99–100. Six months earlier, Duyckinck had published another article on the subject: "The City Article: Capital Punishment," *Arcturus* 8 (July 1841): 115–22. See Mackey, *Hanging in the Balance*, 152–53, for Duyckinck's promotion of the anti-gallows cause.

50. As McFarland, quoting from a letter Longfellow had written to MacKenzie, characterizes Longfellow's decision *not* to attend the execution: "The young scholar was quarrelling with himself every day, so he said, 'for not having seen more bullfights—and sometimes fret myself into a fever for not having been hard-hearted enough to see the tragedies of the Plaza de Cebaba': those hangings of two robbers that [MacKenzie] had witnessed in Madrid and described so vividly" (23).

51. Mackenzie, *Spain Revisited*, vol. 1 (New York: Harper & Brothers, 1836), 364.

52. Ibid., 359.

53. Ibid., 357.

54. MacKenzie, *Case of the Somers' Mutiny: Defense of Alexander MacKenzie, Commander of the U.S. Brig Somers, before the Court Martial Held at the Navy Yard, Brooklyn* (New York: Tribune Office, 1843), 30.

55. Thomas, *Cross-Examinations*, 208.

56. Sumner, "The Mutiny on the *Somers*," *North American Review* 57:120 (1843): 195. Hereafter cited in text parenthetically.

57. For the article to which Sumner alludes here, see "The Case of the *Somers*," *Law Reporter* 6, ed. Peleg W. Chandler (Boston: Bradbury, Soden, and Co., 1844): 1–13.

58. Sumner, "Against Capital Punishment," Letter to a Committee of the Massachusetts Legislature, Feb. 12, 1855, in *The Works of Charles Sumner*, vol. 3 (Boston: Lee and Sheard, 1871), 526.

59. In a letter dated May 22, 1868, published in Marvin H. Bovee's *Christ and the Gallows; or, Reasons for the Abolition of Capital Punishment* (New York: Masonic Publishing Company, 1869), Longfellow provided a brief statement in support of abolishing capital punishment, noting "I am, and have been for many years, an opponent of capital punishment." Longfellow concluded the letter by "[w]ishing [Bovee] complete success in effacing the death penalty from all the statute books of our country" (287).

60. Sumner, "Rights of Sovereignty and Rights of War: Two Sources of Power against the Rebellion," in *The Works of Charles Sumner*, vol. 7 (Boston: Lee and Sheard, 1872), 24.

61. Ibid., 34.

62. Ibid., 52.

63. Thomas, *Civic Myths*, 92–94.

64. "Appendix Two: Descriptive List of Soldiers Executed," in Alotta's *Civil War Justice*, 202–9. Unless otherwise noted, my reference to Civil War executions draws from the data provided in Alotta's appendix.

65. Qtd. in Brian McGinty, *Lincoln and the Court* (Cambridge, MA: Harvard UP, 2009), 186.

66. Nabers 21.

67. Banner, for instance, notes that "the movement to abolish the death penalty tailed off in the late 1850s, as sectional controversy and slavery crowded out other issues, and then the movement virtually ceased during the Civil War" (134). See also David Brion Davis, "The Movement to Abolish Capital Punishment in America, 1787–1861," *American Historical Review* 63:1 (1957): 44–46. Historian Mackey also notes that the Mexican-American War attributed to the demise of the anti-gallows movement: "The reasons were many," Mackey writes in reference to the movement's loss of momentum, "but the paramount problem was the Mexican War and the factionalism and sectionalism it fostered" (*Voices* xxvii). Haines in *Against Capital Punishment: The Anti–Death Penalty Movement in America, 1972–1994* (Oxford: Oxford UP, 1996), similarly argues that the "anti–death penalty movement began to lose its momentum during the late 1840s, due largely to the distracting effects of the Mexican War and to growing North-South tensions over slavery" (9).

68. Bovee v.

69. Ibid., vii–viii.

70. Stedman, "The Gallows in America," *Putnam's Magazine* 13 (Feb. 1869): 225–35, 227. H. Bruce Franklin has connected Stedman to Melville and the writing of *Billy*

*Budd*: "Stedman met Melville in 1888. On October 20, 1888, Melville returned books lent to him by Stedman with a letter in which he wrote, 'And your own book in many of its views has proved either corroborative or suggestive to me.' In 1890 Stedman arranged a dinner for Melville at the Author's Club, one of the few recognitions of the author in his later years. Stedman's son Arthur became a good friend of Melville in the last two years of the writer's life and after Melville's death worked with Elizabeth Melville in reissuing four of his books" (358). See Franklin, "*Billy Budd* and Capital Punishment: A Tale of Three Centuries," *American Literature* 69:2 (1997): 337–59.

71. Stedman 232.

72. Banner 169–76.

73. Stedman 227.

74. "Is Death Painful?," *Putnam's Magazine* 15 (Mar. 1870): 311–18; "Hanging as One of the Fine Arts," *Appleton's Journal of Literature, Science and Art*, Dec. 3, 1870, 670–71, 670. I draw upon this example from *Appleton's*, and the one following from *Harper's*, in the introduction I coauthored to *Transatlantic Sensations*. See John Cyril Barton and Jennifer Phegley, "Introduction: An Age of Sensation . . . Across the Atlantic," in *Transatlantic Sensations* (Surrey: Ashgate Press, 2012), 1–22.

75. "The Guillotine," *Harper's New Monthly Magazine*, July 1872, 186–87, 187.

76. "Nebulae," *Galaxy* 15:5 (1873): 721–24, 721.

77. Nadal, "The Rationale of the Opposition to Capital Punishment," *North American Review* 116:283 (1873): 140–50, 140.

78. Ibid.

79. Ibid., 145. Prescient in this regard, Nadal's argument here prefigures Jacques Derrida's influential deconstruction of law/justice and the undecidability of the "just" decision. Derrida, in an oft-cited example, speaks of a judge merely enforcing the law as a "calculating machine" that does not "ensure justice but mere conformity to the law"; see Derrida, "Force of Law: 'The Mystical Foundation of Authority,'" *Cardozo Law Review* 11:5–6 (1990): 920–1045, 961. Nadal a century earlier criticizes the role of a governor in a capital case who acts as a "mere executive machine." In Nadal's words: "It will not do to say that the governor is a mere executive machine, that his function is not a judicial one, and that his only business is to see the sentence of the law properly carried out." This aspect of judicial review is one of the disturbing "things" Nadal finds wrong in the "absent-minded, mechanical manner" in which "we go on hanging people" (Nadal 140, 143).

80. *Wilkerson v. Utah*, 99 U.S. 130 (1873).

81. Philips, "The Death Penalty," *North American Review* 133:301 (1881): 550–60.

82. Cheever, "The Death Penalty," *North American Review* 133:301 (1881): 534–41, 535.

83. Hand, "The Death Penalty," *North American Review* 133:301 (1881): 541–50, 541.

84. Ibid., 542.

85. Mackey, *Voices*, 141.

86. Franklin 338. Franklin also discusses Curtis's campaign in the context of *Billy Budd* and offers an excellent analysis of "the battle of the currents" over electrocution as a proposed method of lawful death as Melville was writing *Billy Budd*. In addition to Banner's *The Death Penalty*, see also Elizabeth Barnes, "Communicable Violence and the Problem of Capital Punishment in New England, 1830–1890," *Modern Language*

*Studies* 30:1 (2000): 7–26, for an insightful discussion of the emergence of the electric chair in late nineteenth-century American culture.

87. Franklin 338.

88. These two competing schools of thought emerged, first, with E. L. Grant Watson's seminal essay "Melville's Testament of Acceptance," *New England Quarterly* 6:2 (1933): 319–37, and Phil Withim's influential response, "*Billy Budd*: Testament of Resistance," *Modern Language Quarterly* 20:2 (1959): 115–27. Also known respectively as "straight" and "ironic" readings, these approaches have directly influenced dozens of essays and books—too numerous to cite here—and indirectly affected many more dealing with *Billy Budd* and how one interprets Vere's argument for Billy's execution as well as the hanging scene itself.

89. Charles Roberts Anderson first argued for the importance of the *Somers* affair as a source in "The Genesis of *Billy Budd*," *American Literature* 12 (Nov. 1940): 328–46. Additional evidence is discussed in Arvin Newton, "A Note on the Background of *Billy Budd*," *American Literature* 20 (Mar. 1948): 51–55. Other early essays in which the *Somers* plays a prominent role include Edward H. Rosenberry, "The Problem of *Billy Budd*," *PLMA* 80:5 (1965): 489–98; Norman Holmes Pearson, "*Billy Budd*: The King's Yarn," *American Quarterly* 3:2 (1951): 99–114; David Ketterer, "Some Co-ordinates in *Billy Budd*," *Journal of American Studies* 3:2 (1969): 221–37; Richard Harter Fogle, "*Billy Budd*: The Order of the Fall," *Nineteenth-Century Fiction* 15:3 (1960): 189–205; Roland A. Duerksen, "The Deep Quandary in *Billy Budd*," *New England Quarterly* 41:1 (Mar. 1968): 51–66; C. B. Ives, "*Billy Budd* and the Articles of War," *American Literature* 34:1 (1962): 31–39. Since the mid-1960s, only a handful of critics have worked closely with the *Somers* as a source for *Billy Budd*. For instance, see Rogin 288–316; Thomas, *Cross-Examinations*, 152–55, 206–14; Caleb Crain, *American Sympathy: Men, Friendship, and Literature in the New Nation* (New Haven: Yale UP, 2001), 258–62; and Wyn Kelly, "Tender Kinswoman: Gail Hamilton and Gendered Justice in *Billy Budd*," in *Melville & Women*, ed. Elizabeth A. Schultz and Heskill Springer (Kent, Ohio: Kent State UP, 2006), 98–117.

90. In their introduction to the authoritative edition of *Billy Budd* (Chicago: U of Chicago P, 1962), Harrison Hayford and Merton M. Sealts Jr. argue: "The commonly accepted view that the *Somers* mutiny case was in effect the 'source' of *Billy Budd* must be modified. The assumption has been, in general, that when Melville set out to write the story he adapted his central characters and situations from those involved in the events aboard the American brig-of-war." Summarizing the case and its influence on *Billy Budd*'s trial scene and "Tom Tight" from *John Marr and Other Sailors*, Hayford and Sealts acknowledge "obvious similarities in the two cases" but also point to "obvious differences," emphasizing the latter (28). "Freed from what has seemed a sufficient 'source' in the *Somers* mutiny case," they conclude, "scholars may now reassess the importance of the case relative to that of such literary parallels as those pointed out by McElderry and by Richard Gollin in Douglass Jerrold's *Black-Ey'd Susan* and *The Mutiny at the Nore* and Marryat's *The King's Own*—parallels far closer to Billy himself as a character and to this original situation than anything in the *Somers* case. Scholars may also be encouraged to look for new parallels and sources. In literature, for example, the naval novels of Cooper offer a surprising number of affinities, in characters, situations, and themes, as well as in particulars of style and phrasing. His *Two Admirals* and *Wing-*

*and-Wing* are especially suggestive, the former having a naval officer not unlike Captain Vere, the latter having a setting in Nelson's fleet in the Mediterranean waters and containing navel trial scenes and a hanging at the yardarm" (30). These works (and others) may have influenced Melville's writing of *Billy Budd*, but it is important to keep in mind that the *Somers* affair, unlike these other (possible) sources, is explicitly invoked.

91. See Robert K. Wallace, "*Billy Budd* and the Haymarket Hangings," *American Literature* 47:1 (1975): 108–13; Sanford E. Marovitz, "Melville among the Realists: W. D. Howells and the Writing of *Billy Budd*," *American Literary Realism* 34:1 (2001): 29–46; and Larry J. Reynolds, "*Billy Budd* and American Labour Unrest: The Case for Striking Back," in *New Essays on Billy Budd*, ed. Donald Yannella (Cambridge: Cambridge UP, 2002), 21–47.

92. "Speculative" is Michael T. Gilmore's term for his provocative reading of *Billy Budd* in the context of Civil War and (post-)Reconstruction politics in "Speak, Man! *Billy Budd* in the Crucible of Reconstruction," *American Literary History* 21:3 (2009): 492–517. As Gilmore describes his approach: "What follows is a speculative reading of *Billy Budd* in light of the historical currents shaping the culture after Reconstruction. The interpretation can only be speculative because Melville goes to great lengths to efface his own context, and because assertions of certainty would violate the tale's investment in the unsaid and the provisional. Caution is further enjoined by the absence of hard evidence about Melville's politics in this period. About this thinking on post-Reconstruction concordat, there are hints but nothing definitive" (499). Gregory Jay, whose work Gilmore admiringly cites (492, 513–14), offers an equally rich and suggestive reading of *Billy Budd* in terms of lynching and post-Reconstruction race relations. See Jay, "Douglass, Melville, and the Lynching of Billy Budd," in *Frederick Douglass and Herman Melville: Essays in Relation*, ed. Robert S. Levine and Samuel Otter (Chapel Hill: U of North Carolina P, 2008), 369–95. Jay begins his essay by posing what at first seems a preposterous question: "Was Billy Budd lynched?" (369). Stantan Garner, on whose work my understanding of Melville and the Civil War most heavily draws, has produced a masterwork in such speculative criticism through his well-documented *The Civil War World of Herman Melville*.

93. Lieutenant H. D. Smith, "The Mutiny on the *Somers*," *American Magazine* 8 (June 1888): 109–14, 109.

94. Anderson was the first to claim that Melville had read and was influenced by Smith and Hamilton in his 1940 *American Literature* essay, "The Genesis of *Billy Budd*." Other earlier critics, such as Leon Howard in *Herman Melville: A Biography* (Berkeley and Los Angeles: U of California P, 1951), 352, and Robert Penn Warren, ed., in *Selected Poetry of Herman Melville* (New York: Random House, 1967), 82–83, speculate about Melville's use of these two sources. In *Melville's Sources* (Evanston: Northwestern UP, 1987), Mary Bercaw Edwards identifies both Smith and Hamilton as sources for *Billy Budd* (54, 86, 120).

95. Smith 109.

96. Ibid., 112.

97. Alotta 4.

98. Ibid.

99. Smith 112.

100. Ibid., 113.

101. Hamilton, "The Murder of Philip Spencer," *Cosmopolitan* 7 (June–Aug. 1889): 133–40, 248–55, 345–54, 133.

102. Ibid., 134.

103. Ibid., 249, 250.

104. Kelly 102.

105. Melville, *Billy Budd*, ed. Hayford and Sealts, 114. Hereafter cited in text parenthetically.

106. See the editors' note for leaf 282 of *Billy Budd*, 183.

107. Rogin 7.

108. Ibid., 297.

109. Jones, *Against the Gallows: Antebellum Writers and the Movement to Abolish Capital Punishment* (Iowa City: U of Iowa P, 2011), 23.

110. Moreover, Shaw's own dilemma may have been very different from how Jones imagines it. Shaw could have easily been personally against the death penalty but felt compelled to comply with capital laws, just as he personally was against slavery but felt obliged to uphold the Fugitive Slave Act in his rulings. In fact, the dilemma Shaw faced when ruling on fugitive slave cases is a central point of what Robert Cover calls the "moral-formal dilemma" in his classic study, *Justice Accused* (New Haven: Yale UP, 1975).

111. In particular, see the conclusion to Franklin's essay, 353–54.

112. See the discussion of "The Judicial 'Can't,'" in Cover 119–23.

113. Qtd. in ibid., 119–20.

114. See Nabers 30–32.

115. Melville, *Battle-Pieces*, 169–70.

116. Ibid., 254.

117. Franklin 350.

118. Lincoln, *Lincoln Speeches and Writings, 1859–65*, ed. Don E. Fehrenbacher, vol. 2 (New York: Library of America, 1989), 250.

119. Garner 301.

120. Ibid., 308.

121. Ibid.

122. See Hayford and Sealts's "Editor's Introduction: Growth of the Manuscript" to *Billy Budd* for a discussion of the relationship between "Billy in the Darbies" and what would become *Billy Budd*; see also their introduction for a discussion of the older "apparently guilty as charged" speaker of the ballad and the younger, "innocent" protagonist of the narrative (2).

123. Emerson, *Life and Letters of Charles Russell Lowell* (Boston: Houghton Mifflin, 1907), 451.

124. Emerson explains the circumstances and tacit approval of Lowell's unlawful act: "It not being warranted by the Army Regulations for a subordinate officer to call a 'Drumhead Court-martial' and execute its sentence, except in case of emergency, when too far away to communicate with his superiors, and Colonel Lowell being in daily communication with headquarters at Washington, he expected, on reporting the matter that afternoon, to receive at least a severe reprimand. On the contrary, no mention was made of it at all. The fact probably was that General Augur, and Mr. Stanton, who

would naturally be consulted in such a case, were both pleased at Colonel Lowell's action, for if the case had been referred to Washington, the President would probably have pardoned the man, who was young and infatuated of a Southern girl; but they could not commend Colonel Lowell for going beyond the authority of the regulations, therefore deemed silence the best means of expressing their approval" (451).

125. See Hayford and Sealts's "Editor's Introduction: Growth of the Manuscript," 1–12, for a discussion of the various stages in Melville's composition of Billy Budd and Melville's preoccupation with Vere's character in later stages of revision.

126. Melville, "The Martyr," in Battle-Pieces, 130. In an editorial note to this line, Hennig Cohen explains: "Lincoln's office and his personality caused him to be affectionately known as 'Father Abraham' (e.g., in the Union recruiting song, 'We Are Coming Father Abr'am' by James Sloan Gibbons), echoing the phrase used by Christ in speaking of the Old Testament patriarch (Luke 16:30)," 266. For an extended discussion of Lincoln as national father figure, see William C. Davis's Lincoln's Men: How President Lincoln Became Father to an Army and a Nation (New York: Free Press, 1999), esp. chap. 9, "Where Are You Now, Father Abraham?" For a fascinating discussion of Lincoln as a figure in collective memory following the Civil War, see Barry Schwartz's Lincoln and the Forge of National Memory (Chicago: U of Chicago P, 2000), especially part 1 of his study, "Nineteenth Century: Symbolizing Nationhood."

127. Melville's note to "The Frenzy in the Wake," in Battle-Pieces, 260.

## CHAPTER 6. Capital Punishment and the Criminal Justice System in Dreiser's An American Tragedy

1. "Nigger Jeff," of course, is no Billy Budd in terms of the complexity of its composition and reception history. But as Donald Pizer notes, Dreiser did produce "three major versions" of the story from the time he covered an 1893 Missouri lynching as a young reporter for the St. Louis Republic to the story's publication in Free and Other Stories (1918). See Pizer, "Theodore Dreiser's 'Nigger Jeff': The Development of an Aesthetic," American Literature 41:3 (1969): 332. Dreiser's "Nigger Jeff" was first published in Ainslee's Magazine in 1901 and later revised for inclusion in his collection Free and Other Stories. "A Victim of Justice," Dreiser's first version of the story, was written in the 1890s, whereas a later version, "The Lynching of Nigger Jeff," served as a basis for the Ainslee publication. My references are to the 1918 version of "Nigger Jeff" published in Free and Other Stories (New York: Modern Library, 1918). See Pizer's "Theodore Dreiser's 'Nigger Jeff': The Development of an Aesthetic" for a discussion of the complex genesis of Dreiser's lynching story.

2. For a provocative exploration of Billy Budd in the context of racial lynching, see Gregory Jay, "Douglass, Melville, and the Lynching of Billy Budd," in Frederick Douglass and Herman Melville: Essays in Relation, ed. Robert S. Levine and Samuel Otter (Chapel Hill: U of North Carolina P, 2008), 369–95.

3. Dreiser, "Nigger Jeff," 85. Hereafter cited in text parenthetically.

4. See Richard Lingeman, Theodore Dreiser: At the Gates of the City, 1871–1907 (New York: Putnam, 1986), 218.

5. The texts making up Ida B. Wells's antilynching campaign provide the most comprehensive attack of lynching reports and apologies in the popular press. See Wells, Southern Horrors and Other Writing: The Anti-lynching Campaign of Ida B. Wells, 1892–1900,

ed. Jacqueline Jones Royster (Boston: Bedford Books, 1997). By the time Dreiser began writing early versions of his lynching story in 1893, Wells had already published the first of her antilynching pamphlets, *Southern Horrors: Lynch Law in All Its Phases* (1892), which was followed by *A Red Record: Tabulated Statistics and Alleged Causes of Lynchings in the United States* (1895). A chief strategy in Wells's campaign, as in Dreiser's story, was to dramatize accounts of lethal mob violence as a form of antilynching protest.

6. Nadal, "The Rationale of the Opposition to Capital Punishment," *North American Review* 116:283 (1873):138–50, 140, 145.

7. Gerber, "Society Should Ask Forgiveness," in *Theodore Dreiser* (New York: Twayne, 1964), 148.

8. "If an outraged people, justly infuriated, and impatient of the slow processes of the courts, should assert their inherent sovereignty, which the law after all was merely intended to embody, and should choose, in obedience to the higher law, to set aside, temporarily, the ordinary judicial procedure, it would serve as a warning and an example to the vicious elements of the community, of the swift and terrible punishment which would fall, like the judgment of God, upon any one who laid sacrilegious hands upon white womanhood." This proposition in support of lynching, although situated (and ironized) within the free-indirect discourse of Chesnutt's narrative, comes from the perspective of Major Carteret and his entourage of "White Supremacists" at the *Morning Chronicle*. While Carteret uses his newspaper to disseminate racist propaganda throughout the novel, the preceding proposition is especially insidious in that it is later published in the paper as a means to incite the "people" of Wellington to form a lynch mob. In addition, references to the "people" here and elsewhere are particularly ironic given that two-thirds of the community of Wellington is black. See Chestnutt, *The Marrow of Tradition*, ed. Eric J. Sundquist (New York: Penguin, 1993), 186. For an analysis of Chesnutt's novel in these terms, see John Cyril Barton, "The Necessity of an Example: Chesnutt's *The Marrow of Tradition* and the Ohio Anti-lynching Campaign," *Arizona Quarterly* 67:4 (2011): 27–58.

9. F. O. Matthiessen literally refers to *An American Tragedy* as a "documentary novel," while Robert Penn Warren claims that "*An American Tragedy* can be taken as a document, both personal and historical." See Matthiessen, "Of Crime and Punishment" [1950], in *Theodore Dreiser* (Connecticut: Greenwood P, 1973), 191, and Warren, *Homage to Theodore Dreiser* (New York: Random House, 1971), 141. For more recent discussions of *An American Tragedy* as "documentary" or as a social document, see Donald Pizer, *The Novels of Theodore Dreiser* (Minneapolis: U of Minnesota P, 1976), and Shelley Fisher Fishkin, *From Fact to Fiction: Journalism & Imaginative Writing in America* (Baltimore: Johns Hopkins UP, 1985).

10. My play on *tragedy* and *travesty* owes much to Sally Day Trigg, who writes about *An American Tragedy* as a "travesty" of justice. "The trial [Dreiser] describes," she concludes, "is a travesty. The men who direct the proceedings are adversaries focused more on victory and political prizes than on truth. The jury, primed by sensational press accounts, is the epitome of partiality, basing their judgments on biases, emotions, and public opinion. And the defendant is a mechanism, construed by the forces of society and by his own nature and lacking the free will assumed by the law." See Trigg,

"Theodore Dreiser and the Criminal Justice System in *An American Tragedy*," *Studies in the Novel* 22:4 (1990): 429–40, 438.

11. See Laski's trilogy on this subject: *Studies in the Problem of Sovereignty* (New Haven: Yale UP, 1917), *Authority in the Modern State* (New Haven: Yale UP, 1919), and *Foundations of Sovereignty and Other Essays* (New York: Harcourt, Brace, 1921). In particular, see "Responsibility of the State in England," in *Foundations*, which elaborates the concept of "state-responsibility." This article first appeared in the *Harvard Law Review* 32:5 (1919): 447–72. In the context of international politics, it is interesting to note that the Brookings Institute in Washington, D.C., has drawn an explicit link between sovereignty and responsibility in its study, *Sovereignty as Responsibility: Crises Management in Africa* (Washington, DC: Brookings Institution, 1996).

12. Dreiser, *An American Tragedy* (New York: New American Library, 1964), 640. Hereafter cited in text parenthetically.

13. Sarat, "Narratives of Violence in Capital Trials," *Law & Society Review* 27:1 (1993): 23. My point here differs slightly from the discussion of legal violence in Sarat's essay. Sarat "focuses on the representation of violence in capital trials and the ways lawyers use linguistic structures to represent different kinds of violence." In particular, he argues that legal violence, like violence outside the law, "must be put into language, and it must be put into language in a way that reassures us that law's violence is different from and preferable to the violence it is used to punish and deter" (23).

14. Trigg 433.

15. Ibid.

16. Dan-Cohen, "Responsibility and the Boundaries of the Self," *Harvard Law Review* 105 (1992): 950–1003, 966. My use of these terms is suggestive rather than restrictive. Dan-Cohen himself acknowledges that these "analogies are imprecise," especially the comparison of a "total self" to a "motion picture." He writes: "If the analogy between the total self and a motion picture were accurate, a total self would be simply the series of momentary selves put together sequentially. This is not quite what I have in mind, however. Instead, think of the total self as a single composite picture that incorporates all the momentary selves" (966).

17. Ibid., 961.

18. The famous opening paragraph to Oliver Wendell Holmes's *The Common Law* (1881; Cambridge, MA: Harvard UP, 2009) nicely sums up key principles of American legal realism: "The life of the law has not been logic: it has been experience. The felt necessities of the time, the prevalent moral and political theories, intuitions of public policy, avowed or unconscious, even the prejudices which judges share with their fellow-men, have had a good deal more to do than the syllogism in determining the rules by which men should be governed. The law embodies the story of a nation's development through many centuries, and it cannot be dealt with as if it contained only the axioms and corollaries of a book of mathematics" (3). For helpful studies of American legal realism, see Wilfrid E. Rumble, *American Legal Realism: Skepticism, Reform, and the Judicial Process* (Ithaca: Cornell UP, 1968), and Wouter de Been, *Legal Realism Regained: Saving Realism from Critical Acclaim* (Stanford: Stanford Law Books, 2008).

19. Darrow, *Debate Resolved: That Capital Punishment Is a Wise Public Policy* (New York: League for Public Discussion, 1924), 32.

20. As one of Dreiser's recent biographers notes: "Dreiser had followed the Leopold-Loeb trial closely in 1924 while he was writing the *Tragedy*, though he was more interested in the psychology of the murderers than in Darrow's tactics" (Lingeman 288). For a discussion that examines the extent to which Dreiser was influenced by Darrow's rhetorical strategies in arguing the Leopold and Loeb case, see David Guest, "Theodore Dreiser's *An American Tragedy*: Resistance, Normalization, and Deterrence," in *Sentenced to Death: The American Novel and Capital Punishment* (Jackson: UP of Mississippi, 1998), 45–74.

21. Darrow, *Debate Resolved*, 19. Hereafter cited in text parenthetically.

22. Darrow, *Attorney for the Damned*, ed. Arthur Weinberg (New York: Simon and Schuster, 1957), 25.

23. Ibid., 56.

24. Ibid., 24.

25. See Lecture III in J. L. Austin, *How to Do Things with Words*, ed. J. O. Urmson and Marina Sbisà (Cambridge, MA: Harvard UP, 1962), 25–38.

26. "Death," Petrey writes, "the ultimate non-conventional event, eradicates all possibility of participation in collective procedures. Again, however, it isn't obvious that we should demarcate certain deaths from a jury's classically performative 'We find the defendant guilty' and a judge's equally classic 'I sentence you to be hanged by the neck until dead.' Such utterances possess their illocutionary force solely through the conventions codified in Rule A. 1 [of Austin's *How to Do Things with Words*], but it's still silly to cut them off from the non-conventional death that follows them. Like war, death is such an overpowering physical reality that it seems obscene to compare it to the conventional reality underlying speech-act theory. Yet like a declaration of war, a condemnation to death is a speech act that can't be convincingly separated from the events it authorizes. Illocutionary force, a purely conventional creation, is not a reality if we oppose that real and the conventional. Yet illocutionary force is eminently a *force*; the conventional creations of collective interaction dominate the lived experience of every one of the interaction's participants." See Petrey, *Speech Acts and Literary Theory* (New York: Routledge, 1990), 18–19.

27. "HOW NOT TO DO IT" refers, of course, to Dickens's famous parody of the Circumlocution Office in *Little Dorrit* (Oxford: Oxford UP, 1982), 145–65. That Dickens initially planned to title the novel *Nobody's Fault* suggests an affinity with Dreiser's deferral of responsibility in the institutional structures of society. And as J. Hillis Miller has argued regarding the novel's working title, to say that something is nobody's fault "is another way of saying it is everybody's fault, that the sad state of the world is the result of a collective human crime or selfishness, hypocrisy, weakness of will or sham." See J. Hillis Miller, "Dickens's Darkest Novel," in *Dickens: Dombey and Son and Little Dorrit*, ed. Alan Shelston (London: Macmillan Publishers, 1985), 160. My comparison of Dreiser to Dickens in this regard, however, is merely suggestive. For unlike Dickens's satire, Dreiser's parody does not so much exaggerate legal language as it appropriates its official voice and style by situating it within the (ironizing) discourse of the novel. Compare, for instance, the passive construction of the death sentence pronounced upon Clyde to the one given to Nicola Sacco and Bartolomeo Vanzetti in the famous capital trial of 1927: "Nicola Sacco . . . Bartolomeo Vanzetti, it is ordered by the court that you suffer the punishment of death by the passage of a current of electricity

through your body within the week beginning on Sunday, the tenth day of July, in the year of Our Lord, one thousand nine hundred and twenty-seven. This is the sentence of the law." Qtd. in Howard Florence, "Shall the State Take Human Life?," *American Review of Reviews* 75 (June 1927): 613–16, 613.

28. While Clyde's affluent relatives ultimately refuse to provide financial assistance beyond the defense at the trial, the narrator alludes to the influential role money plays—or *would* have played, in Clyde's case—from the perspective of Samuel and Gilbert Griffiths, Clyde's wealthy uncle and cousin: "For as Mr. Griffiths and his son well knew . . . there were criminal lawyers deeply versed in the abstrusities and tricks of the criminal law. And any of them—no doubt—for a sufficient retainer, and irrespective of the primary look of a situation of this kind, might be induced to undertake such a defense. And, no doubt, via change of venue, motions, appeals, etc., they might and no doubt would be able to delay and eventually effect an ultimate verdict of something less than death, if such were the wishes of the head of this very important family" (588–89). For a discussion that focuses on the influential role of money in Clyde's trial, see Guest's "Theodore Dreiser's *An American Tragedy*: Resistance, Normalization, and Deterrence."

29. Schmitt, *Political Theology: Four Chapters on the Concept of Sovereignty*, trans. George Schwab (Cambridge, MA: MIT Press, [1922] 1985), 5.

30. As St. Jean, quoting Dreiser, argues, "Clyde himself doubts whether he is responsible: 'And the thought that, after all, he had not really killed her. No, no. Thank God for that. He had not. And yet (stepping up on the near-by bank and shaking the water from his clothes) had he? Or had he not?' (*AT*, 494). Clyde's own wonder is a linguistic expression of irresolvable tension, of *différance*, and yet the overwhelming question obtrudes itself: is he guilty? This is precisely the question that book 3 concerns itself with: a massive search for the 'truth' which leads to the trial and the jury's verdict" (13). See Shawn St. Jean, "Social Deconstruction and *An American Tragedy*," *Dreiser Studies* 28 (Spring 1997): 3–24, 13.

31. Derrida, "Force of Law: The Mystical Foundation of Authority," *Cardozo Law Review* 11:5–6 (1990): 920–1045, 961.

32. Ibid.

33. What Dreiser's representation adds to this familiar argument is a systemic image of the "death house" as a veritable torture chamber, a structure whose overall design—its arrangement of cells so that they all face one another—ensures that each inmate vicariously experiences the deaths of those executed before him. "Presumably an improvement over an older and worse death house," the narrator tells us, "[this one] was divided lengthwise by a broad passage, along which, on the ground floor, were twelve cells, six on a side and eight by ten each and facing each other" (*American Tragedy* 759). The parallel arrangement of the cells so that each one faces others inverts the model of the Panopticon that Michel Foucault employs as the crowning example of his theory of power relations in modern society. That is, instead of preventing prisoners from seeing one another in order to force them to internalize the gaze of authority, the structure of the "death house" enables each prisoner to see, hear, and witness the suffering of others, as well as a condemned man's final procession toward the door at the center of the structure which leads directly to the execution room. And even the hidden or invisible moment of execution is made *visible* to others on death row by the dimming of the prison lights (773).

34. A full list of articles and books invoking Eighth Amendment arguments against capital punishment during the early twentieth century well exceeds the scope of a brief endnote. I list here only three examples that echo quite closely Dreiser's point about the "thousand" deaths the condemned is to endure before suffering his own. In "State Manslaughter," *Harper's Weekly* 48 (Feb. 6, 1904): 196–98, William Dean Howells argued: "State homicide seems more barbarous and abominable than any but that most exceptional private murder, since it adds the anguish of foreknowledge to the victims doom" and that those condemned die "a thousand deaths in view of the death they are doomed to" (qtd. in Mackey 154–55). In a 1921 article ironically titled "Making Death Easy," a journalist for *Overland* claimed: "The ante-mortem fears of the condemned will prove to be as bad as a thousand deaths before the final and physical termination" (31). And in her 1927 article, "Our Jungle Passions," *Collier's* 80 (Oct. 8, 1927), popular novelist Kathleen Norris suggested that "often the condemned man fluctuates between the decrees of life and death for years. His hopes are raised and dashed, and raised and dashed with a measure of cruelty that sickens even the most casual reader" (qtd. in Mackey 185). For Howells's and Norris's articles, see *Voices against Death: American Opposition to Capital Punishment, 1789–1975*, ed. Philip English Mackey (New York: Burt Franklin, 1976): 150–55, 180–89. For "Making Death Easy," see Laurentine Figura, *Overland* 77 (April 1921): 30–33. For a comprehensive discussion of the Eighth Amendment in legal discourse on the death penalty, see Barry Latzer, *Death Penalty Cases: Leading U.S. Supreme Court Cases on Capital Punishment* (Boston: Butterworth-Heinemann, 1998).

35. Bower, *Legal Homicide: Death as Punishment in America, 1864–1982* (Boston: Northeastern UP, 1984), 57. See also my discussion of Raymond Paternoster's analysis of the shift from local to state-sanctioned executions in the introduction.

36. Qtd. in Jack Salzman, *Theodore Dreiser: The Critical Reception* (New York: David Lewis, 1972), 456. Darrow's review, "Touching a Terrible Tragedy," was published in the *New York Evening Post Literary Review*, Jan. 16, 1926, 1–2.

37. V. L. O. Chittick, "The Work of Ten Years," *Sunday Oregonian*, Jan. 24, 1926. Qtd. in Salzman, 61. In total, Salzman's book contains thirty-one reviews of *An American Tragedy*.

38. See "'American Tragedy' Essay Contest," *Publishers' Weekly* 3 (1926): 1338.

39. Qtd. in Philip Gerber, "'A Beautiful Legal Problem': Albert Lévitt on *An American Tragedy*," *Papers on Language and Literature* 27:2 (1991): 214–42, 218. Hereafter cited in text parenthetically. Gerber's essay contextualizes Lévitt's essay and the publisher's context, printing the essay in full.

40. My point, however, is not simply to criticize the contradictory logic of Lévitt's position. Instead, I want to suggest that the conflicting perspectives embedded in his argument, if not in Dreiser's novel as well, are indicative of the competing theories of social complicity and criminal responsibility that preoccupied late nineteenth- and early twentieth-century American writers. "The Blue Hotel" (1898), Stephen Crane's tale of frontier violence and murder, perhaps best illustrates such competing attitudes in the dialogue with which the story concludes. Several months after the "Swede," the immigrant traveler from New York, is killed in a bar-room altercation by a local gambler of the Nebraskan community in which the Swede as well as the Easterner and cowboy are lodging, the narrative closes with the following exchange about their collective re-

sponsibility in the Swede's death: "We are all in it!" the Easterner exclaims to the cowboy, and passage thus ensues:

"This poor gambler isn't even a noun. He is a kind of adverb. Every sin is the result of a collaboration. We, five of us, have collaborated in the murder of this Swede. Usually there are from a dozen to forty women really involved in every murder, but in this case it seems to be only five men—you, I, Johnie, old Scully; and that fool of an unfortunate gambler came merely as a culmination, the apex of human movement, and gets all the punishment."

The cowboy, injured and rebellious, cried out blindly into this fog of mysterious theory: "Well, I didn't do anythin', did I?"

By ending the story on this note, Crane plays the Easterner's progressive notion of social complicity off the cowboy's uncertain denial of his own involvement in the events that led to the Swede's murder. See Crane, *Great Short Works of Stephen Crane* (New York: Harper & Row, 1968), 354.

41. "*Sister Carrie*," Petrey argues, "juxtaposes two irreconcilable styles, intersperses a series of oleaginous moral meditations among passages of straightforward prose narration with no perceptible moral content. Analyzing the stylistic qualities which distinguish the two forms from each other consistently reveals the same hierarchy. Narration's unpretentious dignity exposes philosophizing as the verbiage of nullity. The basic hypothesis of this essay is that the text of *Sister Carrie* is so structured that its moral passages stand as formal parodies of the language of sentimentality" (102). See "The Language of Realism, the Language of False Consciousness: A Reading of *Sister Carrie*," *Novel* 10:2 (1977): 101–13.

42. See Cover, *Justice Accused* (New Haven: Yale UP, 1975).

43. My juxtaposition of Cover and Derrida perhaps requires further qualification. While acknowledging the legal constraints governing a judicial decision, Derrida in "Force of Law" is more concerned with a concept of "justice," which for him is above or outside human law. For this reason, Derrida speaks of the situation of a judge who, in order to decide justly, must not simply apply the law mechanically (which may be lawful but not just), but must determine just what the law means (i.e., "reinterpret" it) and then decide whether the unique case in question can justly be judged according to the letter of the law, which necessarily is expressed in generalities (e.g., "one should never cross through a red light" or "murder is always a capital offense"). For Derrida, rendering such a judgment can be a difficult and perhaps interminable task. Whereas Derrida focuses on the incommensurability between the generality of the law and the singularity of an individual case, Cover concentrates on the moral-formal dilemma a judge may encounter when ruling on a law with which he or she personally (i.e., morally) disagrees.

44. Qtd. in Robert E. Elias, *Letters of Theodore Dreiser*, vol. 2 (Philadelphia: U of Pennsylvania P, 1959), 458.

45. McWilliams, "Innocent Criminal or Criminal Innocence: The Trial in American Fiction," in *Law and American Literature: A Collection of Essays*, ed. Carl S. Smith, John P. McWilliams Jr., and Maxwell Bloomfield (New York: Knopf, 1982), 45–124.

46. Although Dreiser based *An American Tragedy* on several actual murder cases, his central reliance on *New York vs. Gillette* is well documented. For instance, see Pizer,

*The Novels of Theodore Dreiser*, and Algeo, *The Courtroom as Forum*. Unlike *An American Tragedy*, in which Roberta's drowning is precipitated when Clyde "accidentally" and "unconsciously" strikes Roberta with a camera, Chester Gillette repeatedly (and supposedly intentionally) struck Billie Brown, an eighteen-year-old secretary whom he had impregnated, with a tennis racket before she fell unconsciously into the water. By emphasizing Clyde's state of mind and substituting a camera (a likely object to have on the boating excursion) for a tennis racket as the murder weapon, Dreiser equivocates Clyde's moral responsibility.

47. Kaplan, *The Social Construction of American Realism* (Chicago: U of Chicago P, 1988), 1.

48. For a useful discussion of the criminal conversation narrative in the context of popular gallows literature, see Daniel A. Cohen, *Pillars of Salt, Monuments of Grace: New England Crime Literature and the Origins of American Popular Culture, 1674–1860* (Oxford: Oxford UP, 1993), 3–34.

49. Darrow, *An Eye for an Eye*, ed. R. Baird Shuman (Durham: Moore, 1969), 58–59. Hereafter cited in text parenthetically.

50. Warren, *Homage to Theodore Dreiser* (New York: Random House, 1971), 138.

51. Oliver Wendell Holmes Jr., for example, begins *The Common Law* (1881) by articulating such a principle: "The life of the law has not been logic. It has been experience." See Holmes, *The Common Law* (Boston: Little, Brown, 1881), 1.

52. See Halttunen, *Murder Most Foul: The Killer and the American Gothic Imagination* (Cambridge, MA: Harvard UP, 1998), 7–59.

## EPILOGUE. "The Death Penalty in Literature"

1. Hall, *Common Sense and Capital Punishment* (London: Howard League for Penal Reform, 1924), 2, emphasis in original.

2. Ibid., 9.

3. Iowa abolished the death penalty in 1872, before Italy, Norway, and Austria did and just two years after Holland, the first modern European nation to do so. Maine followed suit in 1876, and Colorado would become the sixth U.S. state to abolish capital punishment before the turn of the twentieth century. The nine U.S. states to outlaw the practice between 1907 and 1917 were Kansas in 1907; Minnesota in 1911; Washington in 1913; North Dakota, South Dakota, Oregon, and Tennessee in 1915; Arizona in 1916; and Missouri in 1917. Of those states, all but Maine, Minnesota, and North Dakota have since reinstated the death penalty. See Banner, "Legislative Abolition," in *The Death Penalty: An American History* (Cambridge, MA: Harvard UP, 2002). 219–23.

4. Schabas, *The Abolition of the Death Penalty in International Law* (Cambridge: Cambridge UP, 2002), 5–6.

5. Founded by Anthony Trollope and printed in both London and New York, the *Fortnightly Review* was among the most influential transatlantic literary journals in the early twentieth century, having published the poetry of Algernon Charles Swinburne, Dante Gabriel Rossetti, and William Morris in the late nineteenth century and the work of major twentieth-century figures, including James Joyce, William Butler Yeats, and Ezra Pound.

6. Lloyd, "The Death Penalty in Literature," *Fortnightly Review* 121 (New York: Leonard Scott Publication Co., 1927): 259, emphasis in original.

7. Qtd. in ibid., 259–60.

8. Ibid., 256.

9. See Thackeray, *The Book of Snobs; and, Sketches and Travels in London* (London: Smith, Elder & Co, 1869), 374–89. Courvoisier, a valet, who murdered his employer Lord William Russell, was put to death in what was one of the most sensational executions in the nineteenth century. In addition to Thackeray, the Courvoisier execution inspired the anti-gallows writing of Dickens, who criticized the mob in the first of four famous letters he would write in opposition to capital punishment. "I did not see one token in the immense crowd; at the windows, in the streets, on the house-tops, anywhere; of any one emotion suitable to the occasion. No sorrow, no salutary terror, no abhorrence, no seriousness; nothing but ribaldry, debauchery, levity, drunkenness, and flaunting vice in fifty other shapes." Writing of those in the crowd of "a perfectly different class" (such as himself and Thackeray), Dickens went on to comment: "I can speak with no less confidence. There were, with me, some gentlemen of education and distinction in imaginative pursuits, who had, as I had, a particular detestation of that murderer; not only for the cruel deed he had done, but for his slow and subtle treachery, and for his wicked defence. And yet, if any one among us could have saved the man (we said so, afterwards, with one accord), he would have done it. It was so loathsome, pitiful, and vile a sight, that the law appeared to be as bad as he, or worse; being very much the stronger, and shedding around it a far more dismal contagion." Qtd. in Philip Collins, *Dickens and Crime* (London: Palgrave Macmillan, 1994), 226. As Collins notes, Dickens's criticism of the Courvoisier execution, first published in London's *Daily News*, concluded by advocating "the total abolition of the Punishment of Death, as a general principle, for the advantage of society, for the prevention of crime, and without the least reference to, or tenderness for any individual malefactor whatever" (qtd. in Collins 226).

10. Lloyd, "The Death Penalty in Literature," *Fortnightly Review* 118 (New York: Leonard Scott Publication Co., 1925): 709–10, emphasis in original.

11. Ibid., 716.

12. Percy Bysshe Shelley, *A Defense of Poetry*, ed. Albert S. Cook (Boston: Ginn, 1891), 46.

13. See Gregg D. Crane's *Race, Citizenship, and Law in American Literature* (Cambridge: Cambridge UP, 2002) and Robert A. Ferguson's *The Trial in American Life* (Chicago: U of Chicago P, 2007).

14. Ferguson 117.

15. In addition to my work in the present volume and elsewhere, see Paul Jones's *Against the Gallows* (Iowa City: U of Iowa P, 2011). Jones's work is particularly valuable for unearthing capital punishment as a subject of debate and interest in popular antebellum literature and for his superb readings of Whitman and E. D. E. N. Southworth in light of the period's anti-gallows movement.

16. For an argument about the exceptionalism of capital punishment in the contemporary United States, see Franklin E. Zimring, "The Peculiar Present in American Capital Punishment," in *The Contradictions of American Capital Punishment* (Oxford: Oxford UP, 2003), 3–15.

17. See for instance Chad T. May, "The Romance of America: Trauma, National Identity, and the Leather-Stocking Tales," *Early American Studies: An Interdisciplinary Journal* 9:1 (2011): 167–86; Donald A. Ringe, *James Fenimore Cooper* (Boston: Twayne,

1988), 29–30; Emily Miller Budick, *Fictional and Historical Consciousness: The American Romance Tradition* (New Haven: Yale UP, 1989); and Kay Seymour House, *Cooper's Americans* (Columbus: Ohio State UP, 1966), 46. John P. McWilliams offers a different interpretation, seeing Bush's illicit act as just; but he also notes the problematic nature of the hanging scene which obviously casts Bush and his deed in a negative light. See McWilliams, *Political Justice in a Republic: James Fenimore Cooper's America* (Berkeley and Los Angeles: U of California P, 1972), 169–74.

18. The extralegal execution of Abiram White unfolds in chapter 32. See Cooper, *The Prairie: A Tale*, ed. James P. Elliot (Albany: State U of New York P, 1985), 357–64.

19. Livingston to Cooper, June 20, 1829, in *Correspondence of James Fenimore Cooper*, vol. 1, ed. James Fenimore Cooper (New Haven: Yale UP, 1922), 174. Hereafter cited in text parenthetically.

20. Qtd. in Harriet Beecher Stowe, *The Annotated Uncle Tom's Cabin*, ed. Henry Louis Gates Jr. and Hollis Robbins (New York: W. W. Norton, 2007), xliii.

21. For representative studies that examine legal themes in Cooper or his work from a law-and-literature perspective, see, Thomas's *Cross-Examinations of Law and Literature* (Cambridge: Cambridge UP, 1989); Dimock's *Residues of Justice: Literature, Law, Philosophy* (Berkeley and Lose Angeles: U of California P, 1997); McWilliams's *Political Justice in a Republic*; and Charles Hansford Adams's *The Guardian of the Law: Authority and Identity in James Fenimore Cooper* (University Park: Pennsylvania State UP, 1990).

22. I thank Gregg D. Crane for suggesting this metaphor.

23. In addition to many legal novels by Grisham—including *The Chamber* (New York: Random House, 1994), which entirely revolves around the appeals process of a capital case—see Turow, *Presumed Innocent* (New York: Time Warner, 1987); Siegel, *Actual Innocence* (New York: Random House, 1999); and Gaines, *A Lesson before Dying* (New York: Knopf, 1993). Of course, dozens of novels and works in the "true crime" genre published over the past twenty years fit within this genre. Two earlier and now canonical novels from the twentieth century that engage the model are Truman Capote's *In Cold Blood* (New York: Random House, 1965) and Norman Mailer's *The Executioner's Song* (New York: Time Warner, 1979).

24. Cooper, *The Ways of the Hour* (New York: Putnam's, 1850), 321–22.

25. Hawthorne, *Mosses from an Old Manse* (Columbus: Ohio State UP, 1974), 393.

26. For a different take on Cooper and capital punishment, see chapter 1 of Paul Jones's *Against the Gallows*, which also examines the near exchange between Livingston and Cooper. I first published on that exchange a year before Jones in my article "Cooper, Livingston, and Death-Penalty Reform," in *James Fenimore Cooper Society: Miscellaneous Papers* 27 (2010): 1–6, which my analysis in this epilogue extends and develops in the broader context of a potential international anti-gallows campaign in the nineteenth century. The primary difference between Jones's and my own argument concerns Cooper's stance on capital punishment. Whereas Jones chiefly uses Cooper as an example of a major writer who supported the death penalty and its retention through his fiction, I argue that Cooper's position on and in relation to capital punishment is more complicated, as evinced in my discussion of *The Spy* and *Notions of the Americans* in chapter 3 and the additional works discussed here in this epilogue. Jones and I also differ in how we treat characters in Cooper's work. Jones assumes, for the most

part, that characters who speak out for the death penalty or against the gallows are speaking for Cooper himself. In contrast, I do not take such characters as rhetorical mouthpieces or transparent reflections of the author's politics. Instead, I assume that each character represents a perspective that needs to be negotiated in relation to other characters, none of whom can be singled out as endorsing Cooper's authorial position. Rather, we must weigh those positions and exchanges to appreciate the competing perspectives Cooper's fiction puts in play, so as not to reduce the complexity of Cooper's work or introduce errors into our own assessments. For example, in making his case for Cooper's anti-gallows politics, Jones succumbs to such an error by misquoting from Cooper's *The Ways of the Hour*, attributing remarks made by Tom Dunscomb, an aristocratic and gentlemanly lawyer of the old school, to Squire Timms, a crass upstart who serves as Dunscomb's foil and all-around opposite number. It is *not* "the lawyer Timms," as Jones claims, who "rejects the 'very common blunder of superficial philanthropists' in asserting that society 'punish[es] for the purposes of reformation' and instead views punishment as a safeguard for the citizenry as it 'keep[s] others from committing murder'" (Jones 30). Those remarks are actually made by Dunscomb. Likewise, it is again not "the lawyer Timms" who "laments that juries are easily swayed against conviction in death penalty cases" but rather Dunscomb who bemoans this phenomenon (Jones 31). On the contrary, Timms relishes in and exploits this supposed fact about juries— and this difference marks one of many that distinguish the two characters' ideological positions in the novel. Thus, Timms and Dunscomb represent two perspectives that need to be played off each other, along with those of other characters and in relation to the dramatic action of *The Ways of the Hour*—which, as Jones himself acknowledges, can be read as an "anti-gallows plot" about the irreversible consequences of capital punishment in the case of error (Jones 32). After all, the novel's plot hinges on a capital trial in which an innocent woman is found guilty of murder and almost put to death for a crime she did not commit. For an extended discussion of the position on negotiating character I advocate here (but in terms of a different author), see John Cyril Barton, "Howells's Rhetoric of Realism: The Economy of Pain(t) and Social Complicity in *The Rise of Silas Lapham* and *The Minister's Charge*," *Studies in American Fiction* 29:2 (2001): 159–87.

27. Cooper, *The Wing-and-Wing; or, Le Feu-follet: A Tale* (New York: Putnam, 1851), 244.

28. Cooper, *The Chainbearer; or, The Littlepage Manuscripts* (New York: W. A. Townsend, 1860), 272.

29. Ibid., 245.

30. Cooper, *The Headsman; or, The Abbaye des Vignerons* (New York: D. Appleton, 1892), 230–31.

31. Ibid., 275–76.

32. Cooper, *The Bravo*, ed. Donald A. Ringe (New York: Twayne, 1963), 17. Hereafter cited in text parenthetically.

33. Grossman, *James Fenimore Cooper* (Stanford: Stanford UP, 1967), 78.

34. Cooper, *A Letter to His Countrymen* (New York: J. Wiley, 1834), 13.

35. Ringe 43.

36. Long, *James Fenimore Cooper* (New York: Continuum, 1990), 98.

37. Grossman 79.

38. Astonishingly, as Derrida notes in "Death Penalties," in *For What, Tomorrow . . . A Dialogue*, trans. Jeff Fort (Stanford: Stanford UP, 2004), no major philosopher has systematically critiqued the death penalty. For Derrida, this oversight is one of "the most significant and the most stupefying—also the most stupefied—facts about the history of Western philosophy: never, *to my knowledge*, has any philosopher as a philosopher, *in his or her own strictly and systematically philosophical discourse*, never has any philosophy *as such* contested the legitimacy of the death penalty. From Plato to Hegel, from Rousseau to Kant (who was undoubtedly the most rigorous of them all), they expressly, each in his own way, and sometimes not without much hand-wringing (Rousseau), took a stand *for* the death penalty." See Derrida and Elisabeth Roudinesco, *For What, Tomorrow*, 146, emphasis in original.

39. Locke, *The Second Treatise on Government*, ed. C. B. Macpherson (Indianapolis: Hackett, 1980), 8.

40. Rousseau, *On the Social Contract; Discourse on the Origin of Inequality; Discourse on Political Economy*, ed. Donald A. Cress (Indianapolis: Hackett, 1983), 35.

41. Kant, *The Philosophy of Law: An Exposition of the Fundamental Principles of Jurisprudence as the Science of Right*, trans. W. Hastie (Edinburgh: T. & T. Clark, 1887), 198.

# Index